Second Edition
A SURVIVAL GUIDE
to
AUSTRALIA
and
AUSTRALIAN-ENGLISH
DICTIONARY

*Formerly AMERICANS' SURVIVAL GUIDE
To AUSTRALIA*

By
Rusty Geller

Cover photo of Bondi Beach by Johnny Bhalla on Unsplash.

"A Survival Guide to Australia and Australian-English Dictionary – Second Edition," by Rusty Geller ISBN 978-1-951985-59-2.

Manufactured in the United States of America.

Dedication

To Chauncey Johnson, who showed me what Australia was about, and to John Edward 'Woodsie' Wood, who showed me how to get along here. *Good onya, mates, I miss you both.*

Acknowledgements for the 2nd edition

I must apologize to my family and friends. In the name of research, I subverted many a social gathering into a cultural-linguistics lesson—with me as the pupil. I'd arrive with a list of a dozen Australianisms that required explanation, and emerge a few hours later with five times that many—the quantity seemed to increase in direct proportion to the amount of beer and wine consumed. I ended up with reams of information about Australian subjects I hadn't known existed. I soon realized that a mere list of Australianisms and their definitions wasn't going to be enough. Originally this was going to be a thin book to sell to tourists, a 500-word Australian-American dictionary with a brief introduction. Once I got going I realized there was a rich treasure-trove of information on culture and history to be revealed. The dictionary of Australian words and phrases increased to almost 1800 words and the brief introduction grew to 300-pages.

I'd like to thank my Australian Brain Trust from the first edition: the Johnson family, John Wood, Billy Hobbs, Ian Sargeant, along with my second edition cultural advisor Isla Cath. Thanks for putting up with the constant questions about things that must have seemed perfectly obvious to you.

A very special thanks to my daughter Molly Geller for the cover design.

Thanks to my publisher, Bobby Bernshausen.

And a very special thanks to the people of Australia for giving me such a ripe subject to write about and for allowing me to become a citizen of your country.

<u>Author's Note:</u> In the text, Aussie words, terms and spellings are printed in italics. The Australian/English dictionary is in the back. If you're looking up a specific word or term, you might want to start with the dictionary. If you need more depth, check the Index or the Table of Contents to see if it's covered in the text section—or you can read the whole darn thing.

Table of Contents

A SURVIVAL GUIDE to AUSTRALIA
and
AUSTRALIAN-ENGLISH DICTIONARY

"Welcome to Australia. Everything you know is wrong."

Introduction to the Second edition (2020)

It's been said that migrating to another country, based on the amount of research required to fit-in and be successful, is like doing a PhD. If so, this book is my thesis.

That premise meshes with something our migration lawyer told us, that moving to Australia is like a 1000-day sentence: it takes three years to acclimatize. Seventeen years later, I'm still not fully over it.

If you're over fifty and you have a choice, I wouldn't recommend changing countries, it can blow your mind. You may go into the whole 'circle-of-grief' cycle mourning your previous life, like I did. By the time I realized this I was too deeply committed with family and finances to go back. Ultimately, despite the bother and stress, I'm glad I made the change. I'm surviving nicely, thank you.

I'm a refugee from America. I moved to Australia from the U.S. when I was fifty-three years old. The transition looked like it was going to be simple, I'd visited a half-dozen times for month-long trips, I'd lived in our Aussie family's home as a local, I knew my way around and besides, the Aussies speak English, how hard could it be? I figured it was going to be like living in America except I'd be driving on the other side of the road and the Queen would be on the money. Boy, was I wrong: on the surface Australia looked similar but I soon discovered, under the sunny façade, there was a completely different culture than I'd expected, that my assumptions were incorrect and, worse, I was irrelevant. To say the least, I was surprised. What had I gotten myself into?

If I'd moved to Japan or India I would have expected obvious differences. In Australia the differences were subtle. I was constantly being faked-out, the similarities seduced me

1

into thinking I knew what was going on, but I soon learned I'd been wrong. Eventually, through trial and error or faux pas resulting in embarrassment, I learned the differences.

Some differences were simple, some were profound. I quickly learned there's a big difference between being a tourist in a country and having to make a serious go of it as a permanent resident. As a tourist you know you'll soon leave so you can ignore the things that annoy you and don't have to worry about things you don't understand. But once you make the commitment and become a permanent resident, all that changes. You soon realize you're going to have to deal with those differences. You can fight it for a while, but that will make you frustrated and unhappy. Eventually you'll have to accept the differences and learn to make them work. Australia isn't going to change for you, you're going to have to change for Australia. And if you don't, you're going to be miserable, like I was for several years. You can always call it quits and move back home. I had no choice, I was one-quarter of a family of four, and we'd made a substantial emotional and financial commitment to move here. Luckily, we had the support of our extended Australian family and we stuck it out. This book covers what we had to learn about Australia in order to survive and thrive. Hopefully my sharing this with you will be of some help. You are not alone, 30% of the people living in Australia were born somewhere else.

The first edition of the book was written in 2007, just four years after we migrated. Emotionally on the 'circle of grief' I was past shock, denial and bargaining but not quite into acceptance: that first edition was a way of venting my anger and frustration. At least I got a book out of it. I took most of that petty angst out of this edition, I guess I'm finally over it. But I digress...

Back then, the facts I was learning to merely function: work, raising kids in a foreign culture, business issues, legal issues, financial issues, taxation, real estate, etc, were piling up. I found I was forgetting what I'd learned and having to ask a second time. I started keeping notes, and they became the basis for the first edition of this book.

Now, thirteen years after the first edition, a lot of water has passed under my bridge. The person I was when I arrived has moved on, and so has Australia. We've both grown, I'm more Australian and Australia is more American. I've found my place and have pretty much fitted in, though my friends will say I'm still a *Yank*.

This book is intended to inform you on two levels. First, we'll cover the factual things that you need to function, like driving on the left side of the road, Aussie phone numbers, banking, healthcare, education, etc. The second level is Aussie attitudes and behaviours, the things you need to understand to get along. Some are obvious, some are subtle, things are not always as they seem.

In the first edition I used American spellings, in this edition I've put it all into Australian, enumerating intentional spellings and words in *italics*. This way you can start getting used to them.

Just because Americans and Australians use a language based on English doesn't mean they speak the same language. In the back of this book is a dictionary of more than 1,800 Australian words, terms, and phrases, translated into North American English. It's probably the most complete list of Australianisms ever assembled.

Welcome to Australia. Keep your mind open as, like Alice, you step through the looking glass. Things are not as they seem...

"You're on your own, mate."

Australians are very independent people. They don't like to meddle in other people's business and they expect no one to meddle in theirs. This is part of the *Fair Go* attitude that is deeply ingrained in the Australian psyche: everyone deserves a chance, a *'fair go'*. A *fair go* is an opportunity to succeed or fail on your own. It's yours, a gift from the Australian people. Use it well.

The down-side of this is, don't expect people to offer you help or advice—*you're on your own, mate*. If you do ask for help, people will generally be glad to assist—in a reserved way—but part of your problem as a new arrival is that you won't know which questions to ask, or even that there was a question. Keep this book handy. It's the Operator's Manual for Australia.

"Are you from Canada?"

When Aussies pick up on a *North American* accent, they will likely ask if you're from Canada, not if you're from the U.S. This is partly because they run into more Canadians than Americans, but mostly it's because they know Canadians are sensitive to being mistaken for Americans, while Americans don't care.

There aren't many Americans in Australia. Most Americans seem to stay in America.

As for the Americans that are here: when asked that 'are you Canadian' question, don't be offended, it's a great opportunity to strike up a conversation. Outside of tourist areas, Americans are a novelty.

Australian overview

The name *Australia* comes from the Latin term *'Terra Australis'* or 'Southern Land'. Australia is a continent surrounded by water, a giant island almost the size of the U.S., situated between Southeast Asia and Antarctica, halfway between Africa and South America. The Pacific Ocean is on its east, the Southern Ocean is on its south, the Indian Ocean is on its west, the Timor Sea, the Arafura Sea, and the Torres Strait are on its north.

It's south of the equator, so all the seasons are reversed: winter is June, July, and August; summer is December, January, and February.

The country is 80% the size of the continental United States, but with just the population of Southern California. As of May, 2019, Australia had 25 million people while the U.S. had 327 million. Most Australians live along the coasts, with three-quarters of them living in the southeast corner. Forty percent of the population lives in Sydney and Melbourne, another twenty percent live in Brisbane, Adelaide, and Perth. Perth is the only major city on the west coast.

I've found there's two Australia's: City Australia and Country Australia. The cities are sophisticated, liberal, modern and busy. The rural regions have an entirely different culture: slower, more conservative and traditional. There are different political parties that represent them, and different TV networks that entertain and inform them.

As you might expect, being a large island almost the size of the U.S., the climate varies. The northern regions of Australia share the same relative latitude (same distance from the equator) as the southern Caribbean. The south coast of Australia shares the same relative latitude as central California, while Tasmania (the island state off the southeast corner) is at the same relative latitude as Oregon or Massachusetts. Climates vary: the tropics are very humid and wet, with rain forests and mangrove swamps, the center of the continent is a dry desert, like Nevada on a bad day, the Australian Alps (between Canberra and Melbourne), have 7,000-foot mountains that are snowed-in every winter. The central east coast, the southeast and southwest corners are temperate, and that's where most of the people live.

The Australian continent is surrounded by water which buffers and moderates the coastal climate. The exception is the northern coast (the *Top End*), where *tropical cyclones* (southern hemisphere hurricanes) periodically strike during the summer months of December through April. This season in the *Top End* is called *The Wet*.

Australia consists of six states and one territory. They are, in clockwise order: Queensland (capital Brisbane), New South Wales (capital Sydney), Victoria (capital Melbourne, [pronounced *Mel-bun*]), Tasmania (capital Hobart), South Australia (capital Adelaide), Western Australia (capital Perth), and the Northern Territory (capital Darwin). There's also the national capital, Canberra, located in the *ACT* (*Australian Capital Territory*), between Sydney and Melbourne.

Those are the facts. Here are the feelings: it's a small country in a big land. With less than the population of Southern California, Australia is really one community spread out over a continent. If a murder occurs in Brisbane, you hear about it 3,000 miles away in Perth. A bus crash in Tasmania is common knowledge in Darwin, and an election in New South Wales is covered in Western Australia. It's quaint yet modern, provincial and cosmopolitan, inbred and worldly: a microcosm of western life on a manageable level.

Immigration

The first immigrants came to what is now known as Australia between 65,000 and 50,000 years ago, depending on which anthropologist you read. They migrated across a land bridge from what is now southeast Asia, and lived a peaceful, subsistence-led life for tens of thousands of years. They later became known as the *Aboriginal People.* They had no immigration policy. Their successors, the British colonials and later the Australian government, invented one.

British settlement was a well-planned 150-year immigration process. The first migrants were 160,000 involuntary convicts who were *transported* between 1793 and 1868, along with their guards. Once they had settled-in and built infrastructure, the colonial government recruited another 200,000 free immigrants from the United Kingdom, mostly agricultural workers from England, Scotland, Ireland and northern Europe.

In the 1850's gold was discovered and people came from all over Europe and North America. Chinese migrated as labourers. In the 1870's South Seas islanders came to work on the Queensland sugarcane plantations. Afghan camel drivers were recruited along with their animals to transport supplies into the desert interior. In the 1890's Japanese pearl divers arrived.

White Australia Policy   After Federation in 1901, the new Australian Parliament passed the *Immigration Restriction Act*, which aimed to stop Chinese and South Sea Islanders from coming to Australia. Section 51 of the Constitution gave the Parliament the power to make laws for *"the people of any race for whom it is deemed necessary to make special laws."* These laws were known as the *White Australia Policy* and were the basis of immigration for the next 50 years.

By the 1930's, the population of Australia was only about 7 million. During World War Two, the far north of Australia was bombed by the Japanese and came under the threat of invasion. Australians realized they didn't have enough population to occupy their own country let alone to defend it. Luckily the Americans came to the rescue. After the war, facing pressure from crowded Asian nations to her north, Australia developed a *Populate or Perish* policy. The goal was to quickly boost Australia's population in the interests of economic and military security.

The first move was to recruit immigrants from the *Mother Country*. Citizens of the UK could migrate to Australia for ten pounds each (about US$50 in today's money), boat passage or airfare included. Thousands took advantage of this, entire families. They were called *Ten-Pound Poms* (*pom*, or *pommy*, is a semi-derogatory term for someone from Britain (see **dictionary**).

Another push for *Populate or Perish* brought a wave of migration came from war-torn southern Europe, mainly Italy and Greece. The government at that time rationalized that though these immigrants weren't British, at least they weren't Asian. Despite *Populate or Perish*, the *White Australia Policy* persisted.

At first there was friction between the Australians and these darker, non-English speaking European immigrants, but eventually everyone found their place. By the second generation, all had assimilated, and Australia started to become multi-cultural. In a café you now had an option, instead of tea and a scone, you could get a cappuccino and a baklava.

Australia was an ideal place for refugees who were willing to work hard. Jobs were plentiful, the opportunities were vast and it was one of the safest countries in the world.

By the mid-60's pressure was on to eliminate the *White Australia* policy. Attitudes on racial questions were changing, and Asia's strategic and economic importance to Australia was growing. Cars and electronics were coming from Japan, oil was coming from Singapore, raw materials were being sold to Indonesia and China. International criticism of Australia's discriminatory immigration policies had intensified and a generational shift was under way in parliament. The policy was eliminated by law in 1973. A requirement to learn to speak English took its place.

In the mid 1970's, after the fall of South Vietnam, a wave

of boat people arrived. Migration began from China, India and the Philippines, and later refugees came from the Middle East and Africa. In the 1990's there was an influx of English-ancestry immigrants from Zimbabwe (the former English colony of Rhodesia) and post-apartheid South Africa. When the British lease ended and Hong Kong went back to Chinese, there was another influx. So, Australia has finally, sometimes painfully, become truly multi-cultural. It still has growing pains but generally differences get worked out on their own.

You meet few American residents, but you're more likely to meet Canadians living in Australia than folks from the U.S. Most U.S. citizens living in Australia are either married to an Australian or are there on work contracts. Given a choice, Americans tend to stay in America.

Modern Australia   When you consider that the country began as a colony of convicts enslaving an indigenous population, it's amazing to see the enlightened social-democracy she has developed into. Her modern cities are spires of glass and steel standing alongside scenic rivers and bays, surrounded by bucolic suburbs. There's an abundance of parks, public sports facilities, walkways, bikeways, and patrolled beaches.

Innovation and invention are common. Arts are celebrated and public funds are set aside to nurture them. There's housing for the poor, not in ghettos but in mainstream neighbourhoods. Universal health care is available to all, as is public education, relatively inexpensive public universities, and career training. Government subsidies help the lower-middle class afford a decent standard of living.

What is lacking as of this writing is a commitment to lessening the industrial effects of climate change. Coal is still being exported to India and China, and burned domestically for electricity. The uptake of renewable energy sources is significant, but much slower than would be expected in a modern, sophisticated country with so much sun and wind. A lot more could be done, but coal mining and gas extraction are significant sources of export revenue and field a formidable political lobby.

British vs American influences
Because of its colonial history, Australia is heavily influenced by its British heritage and culture.

In 1872 the telegraph connected Australia to the rest of the world, but it was expensive and messages were short. Prior to WWII, Australia was still in isolation, sea voyages were lengthy and transoceanic phone calls were expensive. Australians still considered themselves British, Australian homes commonly had pictures of the King hanging on the wall.

After the fall of the British fortress of Singapore to Imperial Japan in 1942, Australians realized the Brits couldn't protect them anymore. Luckily, the Americans came to the rescue, not out of altruism but of necessity: they needed a secure base from which to regroup and fight the war. During the war, thousands of American soldiers and sailors were stationed in Australia and a great deal of fraternization occurred. The popular complaint was *"the Yanks are over-paid, over-sexed and over here."* And, so, the American influence began.

In the 1950's airplane travel gradually shrunk distances. Movies were imported from the UK or Hollywood. When television began broadcasting in 1959 there were some Australian TV shows, but most of the imported shows were from Britain. In the 1970's satellite communication opened up and American media began to dominate, though there's still a considerable amount of game and chat shows from the UK.

Aussies identify with the UK, aspire for America, but want to maintain their identity. One could say there's a melding, Australia looks American, sounds British, but is entirely of itself.

Australians do not want to be the 51st state, nor do they wish to be a puppet of the UK. They love to poke fun at the *Yanks* (Americans), the *Poms* (British) and the *Kiwis* (New Zealanders, whom they consider lesser siblings). Just as Americans have their own brand of English, so do the Aussies, along with their own culture including sports, automobiles, foods, and media.

Australians get a large dose of American media, so they're aware of many American cultural references. On the other hand, most Americans have a limited knowledge of Australia, they imagine the stereotypes: kangaroos, koalas and Crocodile Dundee. There's a lot more to Australia than that. Most Australians would love to travel to the U.S., and many have. Most are dazzled by the diverse geography and the variety of regional cultures in America but are bewildered by the crowds and aggressive lifestyle. Many of Australia's best and brightest have moved to the U.S. because the larger American marketplace allows for greater personal achievement. Hugh Jackman, Nicole Kidman and Rupert Murdoch are prime examples.

Australia is still quite British, though becoming more American every year. I've had to edit-out many differences from the first edition of this book that are no longer different.

As Barry Humphries, known to the world as his alter-ego, '*Dame Edna*', once said, "Whatever American affectations we may maintain here in Australia, we are really provincial English society."

What is the British attitude toward Australia? '*Once a colony, always a colony*'. The Brits condescendingly think of Australians as '*the colonials*.' Aussies will reluctantly acknowledge this, and that's one reason why they like Americans, because the Yanks kicked the Brits out long ago.

On the other hand, the links with Great Britain are much deeper than just being the ancestral homeland for much of the population. It's more about being part of the former British Empire, even though that Empire died in 1942. The Royal family might be an anachronism, but they're our anachronism.

Attitudes about Americans

"I love the States. It represents the best
of everything… and the worst of everything."
Sharryn Jackson, Federal MP for Hasluck

Australians generally like Americans. They watch the movies and TV shows, listen to the music, and read the books, but they don't quite get why Americans work so hard and are so *over the top*: hyperactive, aggressive and determined to boss the world around. They don't quite know what to make of Donald Trump, but hope the American ship of state rights itself before it sinks. They like knowing America is there, Aussies love to travel to the U.S. and many have migrated there.

After living abroad for seventeen years, what strikes me is how inwardly fixated the American people are. Like Narcissus staring at himself in the mirrored pool, Americans see international realities as something out of focus floating in the background of their own reflection.

Aussies are more relaxed. The prevailing attitude is "*she'll be right*" and the answer to any question is usually "*no worries.*" Personal freedom is the most important issue, and anything that compromises that is a hard sell.

The Australian identity
"*The Australian identity was forged by the struggles of the pioneer settlers, by the dauntlessness of the often ill-fated explorers, and by the courage of the ANZAC soldiers who sacrificed their lives at Gallipoli.*"
Inscription on the wall of the National Gallery of Australian Art, Melbourne.

"*Australians have a cautious optimism in a tranquil sea of complacency.*"
Rampaging Roy Slaven, Australian humourist.

Culture
For a country with a small population, Australia has provided more than her share of world class contributions. Culture doesn't begin and end at the Sydney Opera House. Each of the capital cities and dozens of regional areas, have symphonies, opera and ballet companies, jazz and rock concerts, performing in government-built performing arts centres, universities and private venues. Australia has her own writers, actors, painters, and composers, many of whose works have been exported, while others are only known at home.

Australian culture developed far from the influences of America and Europe. Australia has its own music, movies, TV and radio shows, along with its own musicians, actors, stars, and celebrities, so be prepared to 'not get' many cultural references.

Some Australian music stars and groups you probably haven't heard of: Percy Grainger, Delta Goodrem, John Butler Trio, Eskimo Joe, The Waifs, James Morrison (the jazz musician, not the British blues-rock singer), Kate Ceberano, Jane Rutter, and Slim Dusty to list a few.

Some Australian writers: Tim Winton (*Dirt Music, Cloud Street, The Riders*), Thomas Keneally (*Shindler's Ark, The Chant of Jimmy Blacksmith*), Christina Stead (*The Man Who Loved Children*), Miles Franklin (*My Brilliant Career*), and Morris West (*The Shoes of the Fisherman*).

Sad fact is, once someone has made it big, they tend to go to the U.S. or the UK. Famous Aussie movie star exports: Nicole Kidman, Hugh Jackman, Heath Ledger, Mel Gibson, Cate Blanchett, Russell Crowe, Geoffrey Rush, Naomi Watts, Paul Hogan, Toni Collette, Helen Reddy, Olivia Newton-John, Errol Flynn and Rod Taylor.

Here are a few movies to watch to get a feel for the culture: *The Castle, Muriel's Wedding, Strictly Ballroom, Rabbit-Proof Fence, Lantana, The Dish, Bran Nue Dae* and *A Town Like Alice*.

Country music is popular, especially in rural areas. Australia has its own artists and industry. For some reason, most of the singers, like Keith Urban, adopt an American southern accent for their songs.

Basic economics

The Australian dollar is written A$ or AUD, and is sometimes referred to as the *Aussie*. U.S. dollars can be shown as US$ or $US. Exchange rates between the two currencies fluctuate daily.

The value of the Australian dollar is not directly connected to the American dollar, European Euro, Japanese Yen Indonesian Rupiah, Chinese Renminbi, etc. Since the U.S. dollar is the international standard the Aussie's value is often shown related to it. Historically, it has varied. In 1974, the AUD was way up and one Australian dollar was worth $1.43 U.S. By 2001, it had dropped to barely 50 cents. It was a good time to visit Australia, since everything in the country was half-price if you based your thinking in U.S. dollars. In 1996 I bought a vintage Norton motorcycle for A$6000 which was US$3,400 and had enough cash left over to put it in a crate and fly it home in the belly of a Qantas 747.

The *Aussie* has slowly risen since then. In the 2000's construction of iron mines in Australia by Chinese companies followed by large sales of iron ore to China drove it up. In 2004-6 it was around 75 cents to the U.S. dollar, rising toward 90 cents in 2007. It dropped to 70 cents during the GFC but came back up above parity around 2010 and stayed there for a few years, worth the same or a little more than the U.S. dollar.

At that point imported products were becoming too expensive for Australians to buy, and Australian exports were becoming too expensive to sell.

The Reserve Bank of Australia forced the *Aussie* down by lowering interest rates to better align with the rest of the world. At the time of this writing, May 2020, the A$ is hovering around 65 US cents, which means if you wired over US$1000 it would land in Australia at over A$1,540, minus the banks fees, which can go over 2%. [More in the section on **money**.]

One of the reasons the Aussie had gone so high in the mid-2000's was interest rates in the US and Europe were, near zero, while interest rates in Australia were high, over 8%. If you're a global trader and you're getting 1% in the US, why wouldn't you deposit big in Australia and get 8%? In 2003, the year I moved *Downunda* (*Down Under*), when the U.S. prime interest rate was 1 percent and you were lucky to get 1.5% on a passbook account in an American bank, you could get 5% in an Australian account. In financial year 2005/6, the Aussie *share* (stock) market went up more than 20 percent while the U.S. experienced a short spurt and ended where it had begun. In 2007, as the U.S. stock market hit record highs, the Aussie dollar was also up—meaning U.S. dollars had lost value and the U.S. stock market boom was an illusion in actual international monetary value.

Those heady days are over, China cooled things off by stopping buying iron ore and drove the price down from

US$192 per *tonne* (metric ton) in 2011 to US$37/tonne in 2015, and in May 2020 it was US$91/tonne.

The Australian mining boom of the 2000's inflated housing prices due to an influx of international workers, but much of it was due to construction of new mines, and this higher price hasn't had a long-lasting effect on most people's wallets. It did create international real estate speculation which drove up property values, to the detriment of new buyers who have been frozen out of the home market. Interest rates have remained low, *term deposit, or TD's* (CD's) are about 1.5% (May 2020).

Things are expensive in Australia. Except for food, most things are imported. Almost anything imported from North America and Europe will have the double whammy of customs duty and shipping costs. A pair of Levi's can cost A$90. A Bosch cordless drill can be A$200. A new Mustang will cost you A$80,000, a new Toyota Landcruiser with basic equipment is over A$86,000, and a new Dodge Ram 2500 4X4 Laramie diesel will set you back A$165,000.

Conversely, Australia is in Asia so there are lots of cheap imports. A basic Mitsubishi Mirage automobile cost A$15,000, a pair of jeans made in Sri Lanka sells at K-Mart for A$25 and a Chinese cordless drill goes for A$39. Remember, the Aussie dollar is 2/3 an American dollar. So that drill is actually US$25. Of course, the old saying 'you get what you pay for' applies, so keep your receipts.

Because of the high cost of new things, Aussies tend to make those things last longer. There are many well cared-for older vehicles on the road. People tend to fix things rather than discard them. *Op shops*, (opportunity shops), like the *Salvos* (Salvation Army) or *Vinnies* (St. Vincent de Paul Society) are popular places to shop for clothes and housewares. Things get re-used. A paperback book can cost A$20–25 new, but there are *book exchanges* (used book stores) where you can buy books at a third that price and then return them for a credit against the next purchase. *DIY*, (do-it-yourself) is a national tradition.

Lifestyle

Lifestyle is a term that's used a lot in Aussie advertising and in everyday language. It means 'quality of life.' At first I thought it was overused, but the more I see of how Australians live and what they value, the more I realize that it's appropriate.

The normal Aussie work-week is thirty-eight hours (7.6 hours per day), anything more than that is overtime, paid at time-and-a-half. Aussies get four weeks paid *holiday* (vacation) per year, plus there are several *long weekends* (three and four-day weekends) throughout the year. If they have to work those they get *penalty rates*.

Aussies enjoy a great deal of recreation: early morning walks with their dogs, afternoons at the beach, surfing, kite-sailing, boating, pony club, playing in netball or soccer leagues, or weekend cricket games. Most activities end up around the *barbie*, a *stubby* of beer or a glass of wine in hand, enjoying the company of mates. Not a bad *lifestyle*.

"She'll be right" attitude

This is an interesting attitude and it seems to prevail across the culture, though less in the bigger cities of the east. Simply, it's the belief that everything will turn out OK. Australians are great optimists. *Truckies* assume their old crate will hold together, farmers assume the rain will come, pensioners assume their checks will arrive, drivers assume pedestrians will get out of the way (beware when on foot). In other words, that things will turn out OK: *'she'll be right.'*

In practicality, problems arise, whether on a huge project or a backyard task. Those involved will work the problem and then at some point someone will say *"she'll be right,"* and everybody will nod in agreement, and move on. The rationale is not to make too much over something that might not be a problem. This is generally true, but obviously, if done too often, can be a formula for failure. Hopefully Qantas won't adopt this attitude.

The *she'll be right* attitude is often criticized by outsiders as being too laid-back, while insiders say it eliminates unnecessary fuss. You can't buck it—so when you run into it, just do what you have to do, but do it quietly.

"*Ned Kelly*" attitude

It's been said that you can tell a well-balanced Australian by the chip on each shoulder. This was personified by Ned Kelly.

Ned Kelly was the Australian Everyman, the struggling noble underdog, in the Australian vernacular: the *battler*.

Ned Kelly was an Irish-Australian who became the iconic Jesse James/Robin Hood of Australia, glorifying the individual's battle against authority. In the 1880s, he achieved the dubious status as the most notorious *bush ranger* (outlaw) in Australian history. His family—discriminated against because they were Irish and poor—was hounded and abused by the local authorities until Ned, his brother, and some mates decided they'd had enough. They started robbing banks and killing police, but were eventually hunted down. The last epic gun battle saw Kelly wearing boiler-plate armour including a full-head bucket helmet, shooting it out against a small army of constables (the *traps*). The police shot his legs out from under him and he was eventually tried and hanged. The image of the gunman in the iron helmet is still seen on the back of cars, on T-shirts, used as letterboxes and in sculptures throughout the country.

What makes Kelly significant is that—to the ordinary Australian—he was a hero, standing up and fighting for his rights against a cold and corrupt government. This attitude underlies an important mindset of most Australians: a distrust of authority and a thirst for independence from government interference. Aussies routinely disobey laws they disagree with whether it's behind the wheel or behind a desk. *Rorting* (defrauding) the authorities can be sport. They hate politicians with a passion. They'll back their candidate, then as soon as he or she is in office, turn on them as being just another *pollie*. Perhaps this is why it seems Australians work better independently or in small groups.

This feeds into the *never dob* attitude. To *dob* is to inform the authorities about someone, to tell on someone, to *dob them in.* Australians don't like to do this. It's partly the attitude of the *fair go* and partly the idea of *'the battler vs the powers of authority'*. In other words, no matter how bad a person is, turning them in to the police is worse. With a rural population this could be workable, but with a modern urban social environment it's a formula for anarchy. With a small police presence generally unable to back up an individual interfering with someone else's' affairs, it's sometimes best to look the other way, unless it's a life-threatening problem. Before you call the cops about a troublesome neighbour, remember, the cops will come and go and the neighbour will still be there.

This distrust for authority is deeply ingrained. For example, all moves for a *National ID* card have been defeated. This was first proposed in the 1980s. There are government Tax File Numbers and Medicare numbers, but neither of these is asked for outside of their specific uses, like a U.S. Social Security number. Every time the *National ID* card comes up, it's shouted down by public opinion, driven by the deeply ingrained distrust of authority.

Much of this disdain for authority can be traced back to the convict heritage, personified by old Ned Kelly, with his iron helmet and a chip on each shoulder.

Kids' freedom

The Ned Kelly attitude extends to the way kids are dealt with. When I first moved to Australia, I noticed that parents didn't control their kids as much as parents do in the U.S. We'd be in the audience at a school performance and a baby would start crying or someone's toddler would start talking loudly. I expected the parent to try to quiet the child, and if that didn't work, take the kid out of the room. I was surprised to see that the parents would do nothing, and nobody seemed to be bothered by this. I thought it odd at first, but noticed it happening again and again.

I eventually came around to thinking this might be cultural. It's as if restricting the kids' freedom was worse than having them interrupt the proceedings. It's common to be in a public place like a shopping centre, school, waiting room, etc., and see and hear small children throwing tantrums or behaving badly, and the parents doing little or nothing to stop it. You get used to it, but you wonder if this indulgence leads to the sociopathic *hoon* behaviour of young adults [see section on **hoons**].

Mateship

Mateship is a strong friendship between *blokes* (men). An Australian man has a wife and a mate, and rarely are the two the same person.

Day-to-day, the term *mate* (*"How ya goin', mate?"*) is used loosely, just as an American male of a certain age might use 'man' or 'buddy'.

But to be one's *Mate* is to be someone special.

Egalitarianism

Egalitarianism is a belief that all people are equal. This is an underlying attitude in Australia and the basis of the *fair go*. A white Australian might complain about the *aboriginal problem* or about the influx of migrants from the third world, but then include several of each as friends. This is because the Aussie tends to take each person on his or her own merits and character. It's said that it doesn't matter how much money a man makes, what counts is whether he's a good mate and can spin an entertaining *yarn* at a party.

This egalitarianism is most evident along the *foreshores*. Australians love the water, and everybody wants to live next to it—be it a brook, river, bay, or the ocean. Now this might be a bit of a *shocker*, but with few exceptions, in an Australian city you cannot live <u>on</u> a beach, bay, or river.

You can live across the street from the water, but there will always be a road in front of you. There are a few exceptions: some very old *blocks* (lots) established before the zoning laws changed, manmade canals in waterside developments, and properties far from a city—but in ninety-nine percent of Australian urbanized areas, you can't build directly next to the water, there will always be a road in between.

Why? Water features are considered public property, and institutional egalitarianism mandates access for all. The government has eliminated the possibility of having a wall of rich people's houses blocking ordinary folks from the water, as has happened in California and Florida.

This makes for an odd juxtaposition. You can buy an ocean-view *block* along the coast, build your multi-million-dollar dream-house on it, and as you sit on your veranda watching the sunset sipping your chilled chardonnay and nibbling brie, some poor *battler* without a pot to piss in can drive up in his rusted old Ford Falcon, park across the street blocking your view, stumble barefoot down to the beach, beer in hand, and enjoy the same sunset. That's Aussie egalitarianism.

Australian humour

Aussies have a unique take on humour. It's British-based, which means it class-based. Remember, Australia was founded as a penal colony, there were lots of guards to make fun of. Wealthy people didn't make their way down here until there was something worth owning. Once here, the wealthy took advantage of those less well-off who had little alternative other than to make fun of them, too.

Aussies are irreverent but well-meaning, with a lack of pretension, which is reflected in their humour. They love to make fun of anyone who *is full of themselves.*

Show up to work with an odd haircut and you might hear "...did ya' sleep with a lawnmower?" or wear a strange coloured shirt and your workmates might say "...did ya' get dressed in the dark?" It's all in good fun so don't take offense, just laugh it off and maybe have something ready to come back with. Being self-deprecating is a good angle.

Some of the TV humour can be low-brow, Ocker-style. An *ocker* is a stereotyped rough, uncivilized person: a bloke in a *singlet* (tank top), *board shorts* and thongs with a *tinnie* of beer in one hand, leaning on a bar with the other, speaking in Aussie-accented slang.

Paul Hogan (Crocodile Dundee), made his early career portraying the stereo-typical Ocker. *Hoges* had been a labourer on the Sydney Harbour Bridge who parlayed a talent for making people laugh in the pub into winning a TV talent show. He ended up with his own TV program, *The Paul Hogan Show*, in which he played various stereotypical Aussie Ockers in silly, embarrassing situations. He later developed a straighter, humorous-heroic persona as the iconic *Mick Dundee* in the *Crocodile Dundee* movies which he co-wrote and produced.

For 35 years, the comedy team of *Roy and HG* have used the unique vehicle of faux sportscasts to lampoon sports broadcasting norms. In their personas as the intense, retired-jock colour-man *Rampaging Roy Slaven* (John Doyle), and the earnest play-by-play game-caller *HG Nelson* (Greig Pickhaver), they create a zany, often surrealistic alternative view of sport, using the format to slyly satirize Australian culture, politics and history. ABC radio broadcast their alternative play-by-play calling of rugby premiership games, causing thousands of sports fans to turn down the TV sound and turn up Roy and HG's biting, hilarious version.

They reached their height during the 2000 Sydney Olympics when the ABC, desperate to fill a 2-hour late night time slot after the competitions had ended, put them on the air *live*. Being live they could pretty much do anything, because by the time the joke had landed, appropriate or not, it had already been broadcast. Their irreverent take on the staid Olympics caught the nation's imagination, and the show not only became a hit, but developed into the hot-spot for Aussie athletes to drop-in after the events. The show even caught on in the US, though a lot of nuance and inside jokes were lost on an American audience.

One night on their post-Olympics broadcast they improvised their own dry commentary of a replay of the Aussie women's' synchronized swimming competition, elaborating on it as a metaphor for the building of the Sydney Harbour Bridge, describing the performance in historically detailed, accurate, culturally-appropriate, academic context. They also created a mascot, *Fatso the Fat-Arsed Wombat*, who overshadowed the games official mascots (whom Roy and HG disparaged as *"Olly, Millie and Dickhead")*. Fatso ended up being featured by Aussie athletes on the medal podium, much to the organizing committee's chagrin.

Aussies love drag, as the success of *Priscilla Queen of the Desert* can attest to. *Dame Edna Everage* is the creation of comedian Barry Humphries, who for 60 years has been a transformational, genre-jumping drag act. Humphries, in formal gown, purple hair and sequined cat-eye glasses becomes the over-the-top *Dame Edna*. Dame Edna is the queen of the sexual inuendo and in true Aussie tradition slyly attacks politicians, stars and royalty—often to their face. She is capable of saying anything to anyone, addressing her minions in her trademark falsetto with *"hello possums"*, and then tearing into her pretentious and vain targets.

Both *Roy and HG* and *Dame Edna* are typically Australian: using a low-brow initial approach to achieve a high-brow eventual result. Don't underestimate those convict genes.

Not all Australian humour is low-brow. Hannah Gadsby is the antithesis of Dame Edna. Gadsby's one-woman show *Nanette* reflected on her experiences coming out as a gay woman. Her evocative speech, social commentary and emotive narration is a fierce expose' of trauma and homophobic abuse.

Tall poppy syndrome

Australians tend to resent anyone who is successful. That person is considered a *tall poppy*: someone standing above the rest, needing to be cut down to size. This was stronger in previous generations but is still subtly in practice. The problem with this attitude is obvious: if success and achievement are resented, how can there be progress? Luckily, not everyone accepts this, but it's a common trait to be aware of. You might not be aware it's going on, but it's there. Be careful of being perceived as too flashy, especially in business: tone it down, don't *big note yourself,* let your deeds speak for you.

Culture shock

Enough about them, what about you? How do you deal with all this?

The differences from North America to Australia are subtle and can lull you into thinking you know what's going on and then Australian reality rears-up and bites you on the *bum* (ass).

Like the time just after I'd arrived, I was building shelving units for my garage and I went to *Bunnings* (like Home Depot) and loaded my *trolley* (cart) with *timber* (lumber) and *fixings* (screws), all the while checking the prices which seemed reasonable. I went to check out and was shocked, it was triple what I'd estimated, *because the timber was priced by the meter* (39 inches), *not the length.*

Culture shock is real. Tourists and business travellers won't be in the country long enough to get more than an inkling of it. For them the differences will seem amusing, even charming. But for permanent migrants or those on long-term work contracts, the day-to-day differences from American culture can get on your nerves. It's easier for Brits as the thinking is more what they're used to

Sometimes a recent migrant will go into what amounts to a state of mourning, longing for the familiar world they left behind. Some people, especially older migrants, may never recover from this. This can lead to **Depression**, recognize it for what it is and don't deny it. Keep an eye on it and seek help if you feel it's overwhelming. Some people either wither or return to their homeland. The answer to this effect of culture shock is to have a good support system consisting of understanding people who can help you maintain your sense of humour.

There comes a time for every migrant when it strikes them, deeply and emotionally, that they're not going home, that this is it. It finally sinks in that they're going to have to deal with the cultural differences. I'm not just talking about complex concepts like business or legal issues, but about day-to-day living.

This adaptation won't take place overnight. Our migration agent called it *The Thousand-Day Sentence*, because that's how long it takes to adapt: three years. It's not just the big differences, it's the small subtle ones that sneak up and gnaw at you.

This culture shock will come to you after butting your head up against some Australian way of doing things, trying to accomplish something that would be so easy to do in America or Canada, yet is difficult in Australia because you don't understand the terms, don't know where to look, who to call, or what to ask for. Take heart. You're not alone. Others have suffered through the same frustration. That's what this book is about.

Sometimes Australia feels surrealistic, as if you've landed in a science fiction movie—or maybe the Twilight Zone. The Bizarro World from the old Superman comics of my youth comes to mind: a parallel universe where everything is recognizable but backwards from what you'd expect.

The cities look quite similar to the U.S., with wide boulevards, neat suburbs, freeways and downtowns, but everyone is driving on the wrong side of the road! Many things have different names than you're used to, the Australian accent can be hard to understand, shops are closed at unexpected times and businesses and government agencies seem to be run on a Monty Python management model. The longer you stay, the more differences you notice, and it starts to get to you.

Some examples:

You go into a restaurant and take a seat, and the waitress never comes. This is because you're supposed to know to go up to the counter to order your meal. You finally figure that part out and go the counter and wait in line to order a hamburger. The guy behind the counter asks you a question, but because of the accent and the different terms, you don't get what he's saying. Finally, you realize he's asking you if you want *the lot*. You guess that means 'everything on it', and say yes. He hands you a numbered sign and you realize they're going to bring it to your table. Ten minutes later the burger arrives and it's huge. You lift off the top bun and see, besides the patty, there's lettuce, shredded carrots, a slab of bacon, a fried egg, and a thick, round slice of something red and juicy on top. But strangely, there's no cheese.

You ask the counterman what the red thing is and he looks at you like you're from another planet and says, "It's *beet root*, mate". You ask where the cheese is and he says, "You didn't order it, mate". You go back to your table and try to figure how you're going to take a bite of that huge thing. And you look at that slice of beet almost as big as the meat patty. And your thoughts explode: beets! They put beets on a hamburger with *the lot*—but no cheese! Welcome to Oz, mate.

Or you go to breakfast—which almost everyone refers to as *brekkie*—and ask for jelly for your toast. After a funny look from the counterman and after a delay of fifteen minutes, he delivers a bowl to your table—full of Jell-O. And you realize *jelly* is Jell-O—you were supposed to know to ask for *jam*.

Or you get tickets to a play and see printed on them: *Supper will be served after the performance.* You skip dinner looking forward to a nice après theatre buffet, but after the play all they serve is tea, instant coffee, and a few cookies which, they call *bickies* (short for *biscuits*). You eat the *bickies* and have a cup of instant and realize you've learned something new: *supper* means refreshments or an evening snack.

Or you're asked to *tea* at someone's house at *half-six*. You figure out that means six-thirty—you're starting to get the hang of the place—so you think you'd better have dinner first so you won't be hungry, since all they're going to serve is tea (and maybe crumpets?). When you arrive, you discover they're serving a full meal. You've learned that *tea* means dinner—but don't get too smug with your new knowledge, since *tea* can also mean a coffee break, though these are usually referred to as *morning tea* or *afternoon tea,* or a *smoko*.

In the first year, these kinds of discoveries will happen to you a few dozen times a day. Hopefully, you'll have someone to share them with, because a good laugh is therapeutic. Nevertheless, it starts to get to you. One day you'll find yourself on the Internet, listening to a radio station from your old hometown, just to reassure yourself that it's still there and you haven't gone completely mad.

Sometimes you'll feel like you've awakened in a parallel universe but you're the only person that knows it. You look around, and everyone is going about their business as if everything was normal. It's not the Twilight Zone—it's culture shock.

I used to grin, shrug and say to myself, "Australia...what a concept..."

Now, forget about all that. Leave what you knew behind; it no longer counts. Embrace the differences and make peace with them. Forget the cheese and take the beets. If you'd have asked, they would have held the beets and put cheese on your burger, no questions asked—it's Australia; anything goes. Learn to smile and say what the Aussies say: *"No worries...she'll be right."*

History

Pre-History Australia is the oldest continent. In the hills above Perth, near where I live, are exposed granite rock formations that were formed a billion years ago.

The continent that would eventually be known as Australia separated from the other continents about 100 million years ago. Animals and plants evolved in isolation which explains why they're so unique. Most of the land mammals are marsupials, most of the trees are eucalypts. Modern humans arrived about 60,000 years ago, 15,000 years before they arrived in Europe.

The Australian continent was a wetter, greener place at that time. Besides the present-day mix of marsupials, reptiles, and birds, there were *mega-fauna*: huge wombats the size of hippopotami, kangaroos ten-feet tall weighing 500 pounds, and koalas the size of small bears. Fossil remains indicate the mega-fauna was killed-off by climate change as the continent dried and could no longer support such large creatures. Of the mega-fauna, only the saltwater crocodile, the red kangaroo and emu remain.

Humans first settled the Australian continent by migrating south from Asia during the end of the last major ice age, using a land bridge created by shrinking seas. They came in several waves over tens of thousands of years and spread out over the continent.

These original people, *the First Australians*, were all but wiped-out by European invaders. By definition the *First Australians* were also invaders, but they blended into the flora and fauna and learned to subsist on what was there. They had impact, they managed the forests with controlled burning, they hunted and lived off *bush tucker* (native foods). They introduced the dingo, a dog that still exists in the wild today, much like a coyote. Over 60,000 years they became one with the land, and the land became one with them.

These *First Peoples* were members of individual tribes,

with separate cultures and languages, but as Europeans settled the continent they were lumped together as *Aborigines*, a Latin term meaning *'of the beginning'*. They represent the oldest surviving culture in the world. While other world cultures developed and changed, the *First Australians* remained isolated on their island continent until the mid-sixteenth century AD. More on this after we take a look at European settlement.

European exploration   The first recorded landing by a European was Dutch navigator Willem Janszoon on the *Duyfken* in 1606. The Dutch were in the process of colonizing what became known as the Dutch East Indies, present-day Indonesia. Janszoon landed on the Cape York Peninsula in the north east corner closest to New Guinea, and named the continent *New Holland*. But most of the Dutch activity inadvertently was on the west coast.

Before the English invented accurate timepieces, maritime navigation was crude. The Dutch would sail around the southern tip of Africa then turn east and sail for a few months until they thought they were near New Holland (now the west coast of Australia). Then they'd turn north until they reached Batavia in the East Indies. Some ships captains misjudged when to make the northerly turn and wrecked on the New Holland coast. The first permanent European residents were likely the 150 survivors of the *Zuytdorp*, who were shipwrecked in 1712 and stranded between what is now Kalbarri and Shark Bay. They either died or were adopted into local Aboriginal groups. Blue-eyed, blond-haired aborigines were reported 100 years later by the early British explorers.

The Europeans found the land populated with sparse groups of indigenous people who, to them, appeared too primitive to be 'civilised'. These Europeans never took the time to discover that these people had developed a complex culture over 60,000 years.

The Dutch never settled in Australia, finding the spices and natural resources in the Indies more lucrative. The French briefly explored in the late 18th century but never established any outposts.

Enter the British. In 1768, naturalist Dr. Joseph Banks and astronomer Charles Green accompanied Lt. James Cook sailing the *HMS Endeavor* on a three-year voyage to the south Pacific to witness the Transit of Venus, which could verify important astronomical theories. The secondary goal was to explore and chart the coast of what was theorized as a great southern continent. The Dutch had briefly explored the west coast, but no Europeans had been to the east coast, and there was no certainty they were even the same land mass.

In 1770 the expedition found the east coast of *New Holland* and sailed along it, creating navigation charts, all the way to the northern Barrier Reef. Near what is now called *Cooktown*, they crashed into the reef putting a hole in *Endeavor*, and had to put the ship on the beach for repairs which took a month and a half. In those 48 days Cook and the crew met the *Guugu Yimithirr* people and recorded mostly positive interactions with them.

The crew began replenishing provisions and took a dozen turtles from the river, not realizing it violated a custom, and when they refused to share them with the locals, a fight broke out. The British had guns but the natives were excellent spearmen, and it could have gone *pear-shaped* (very badly). A *Guugu Yimithirr* elder intervened, presenting Cook with a broken-tipped spear as a peace offering. It was the first act of reconciliation between the Brits and the First Australians.

During this time the crew had a good relationship with the *Guugu Yimithirr,* recording hundreds of words of their language, including *gangurru* (kangaroo). Despite this interaction, Cook declared the entire continent *'Terra Nullius'*, which is Latin for *'empty land'*, implying that it was uninhabited and therefore up for grabs. When *Endeavor* returned to England in 1771, Cook and Banks presented the government with maps and recommendations for colonies. These were put aside, Britain had other matters to deal with, trouble was brewing in the American colonies.

In 1776 the American Revolution began. The British Empire fought a seven-year war and lost most of its North American colonies. Not only had they lost a source of income but they now needed a new place exile troublemakers. Australia could become the English version of Devil's Island, but with a bonus: not only could they could export their criminals, they could use them to settle the continent at the same time.

British settlement   On 26 January, 1788, the *First Fleet* sailed into Sydney Cove with 11 ships and 1140 convicts and guards. The new colonial governor, Arthur Phillip, named it *New South Wales*. Working under the principle of *Terra Nullius*, Phillip was oblivious to the fact that there were already about 750,000 native peoples with 400-600 separate languages and cultures already living there. [More on this in the next section].

The entire continent was referred to as *New South Wales*. The first mention of the name *Australia* was in 1803 by English explorer Matthew Flinders, when he made the first circumnavigation of the continent and wrote it on his map.

New South Wales was founded as a penal colony to remove Britain's criminals and isolate them on the far side of the world, in those days a six-month journey by wooden sail ship.

Australia's British origins are fundamental to understanding the modern country.

Eighteenth century England had a substantial criminal population. The Industrial Revolution was transforming British society from rural-agrarian to urban. It brought prosperity, productivity, technical innovation and employment for skilled laborers. But with it came urban crowding, poverty, unemployment, pollution and crime. There were serious crimes like highway robbery, and petty crimes like stealing food to feed one's family. In addition, England had conquered Ireland two-hundred years before but the Irish had never stopped rebelling, so there were lots of Irish criminals and political dissidents in English jails. There were so many prisoners they had to be housed in old ships' hulks anchored in the Thames River.

Since the Brits could no longer exile these unfortunates to the American colonies, they decided to ship them to New South Wales, a land so far away that most could never return. The system was antiseptically called *Transportation*. Between 1788 and 1868, about 162,000 convicts, both men and women, were *transported*. It was a convenient source of free labor to develop a tough, dangerous land on the far side of the Earth.

This began an odd relationship between the Australian colony and the mother country, a love-hate relationship that continues to this day. Australia is Britain's naughty step-child.

The white settlers, convicts and freemen, had an uneasy relationship with the *blackfellas* (Aboriginals). Under the principle of Terra Nullius, the Brits had occupied the land, which prevented the blackfellas from pursuing their annual migrations. For thousands of years they had migrated seasonally from food source to food source, as proscribed in their songs, but this had abruptly ended as the British settlers forcibly drove them off with guns. The Aboriginals saw the *whitefellas* shooting their major food source, kangaroo, and figured it would be OK spear a few sheep. Ownership, especially of the land, was not a concept the Aboriginals understood, to them, everything belonged to everybody. The settlers didn't see it that way, they'd hunt down the sheep killers and deal with them harshly.

This schism grew. Occasionally, during the early years of English settlement, small bands of pissed-off Aboriginals would raid a farm, but these were local skirmishes and were treated by the white authorities as police actions. The Aboriginals were formidable warriors skilled in spear-throwing and boomerang, but they were few in number and not organized outside of their individual clans. They had evolved away from war-like behaviour, they didn't make war on each other, they had no such skills so there was no resistance approaching the scale of the U.S.-Indian wars.

The British got on with the business of settlement. They'd had great success in North America and expected the same in Australia. But North America was forested, had rich soil and plenty of rivers. In Australia they found few rivers, the interior was mostly barren desert, only the coastal areas were inhabitable. The Brits eventually settled the continent, but on a more modest scale. It was a hard land to pioneer and farm, but the strong survived and the tradition of the Aussie *battler* was born: tough, tenacious, resourceful, and usually successful.

In the early 19th century Britain became involved in the Napoleonic Wars and did little to develop Australia. Wealthy men acquired land and became '*squatters*', and with little government presence, ran their own fiefdoms. Convicts, though second-class citizens, eventually gained their freedom and worked for the squatters. Those that could save enough to buy land became *squatters:* farmers and *pastoralists or sheep graziers.* High quality Australian wool became the major export back to the mother country.

As the population grew, the colony of *New South Wales* was eventually broken up into six colonies and one large territory. In 1803 the large island south of the continent, first explored by the Dutchman Abel Tasman, was called *Tasmania,* and it was settled with convicts. *Western Australia* was founded as a free colony in 1829, but in 1850 requested convicts to fill a manpower shortage. *South Australia* was settled in 1836 as a free colony, and received no convicts. *Victoria* was spun off New South Wales in 1851 after gold was discovered. *Queensland* became a convict colony in 1859. The *Northern Territory* was established in 1869 with the founding of Darwin. *Transportation* (the convict system) ended in 1868.

In 1851 gold had been discovered in what is now northern Victoria, and a gold rush started. This began a long history of mining in Australia. The miners were poor, many were ex-convicts who saw this as the only way to be able to buy land to farm, land they could never otherwise dream of owning.

Great Britain relied on Australian gold to maintain the British Gold Standard and the diggings developed under strict government restrictions. The Victorian colonial government dominated the gold diggings with a license system that denied miners the profits of their finds. By 1854 the miners had had enough, they organized, ran the government agents out and built a stockade to defend themselves. The government sent in troops. There were minor skirmishes for a few weeks, then late one night the troops did a sneak-attack. Twenty-seven miners and family members were killed. This became known as the *Eureka Rebellion.* The troops won, but the government's move backfired: the people of the colony were shocked that their government would turn so viciously against its own people. The Governor had to back down and eventually allow local governance. The rebels were acquitted in court and some later became members of the reformed Victorian parliament. It was the closest thing Australians had to a revolutionary war. This incident was the beginning of the ideal of the *fair go*, and became a cornerstone of what was to become the Australian nation.

Australia developed along the east and southeast coasts, and in the southwest corner, and the vast interior remained unexplored by non-Indigenous people. Through the nineteenth century various expeditions set out to fill in the blanks in the map. Typical was the 1860-61 *Burkes and Wills Expedition* organized by the Royal Society of Victoria. They set out from Melbourne on the Southern Ocean, bound to the Gulf of Carpentaria in the far north 3250 kms distant, with 19 men and supplies. They made it there but didn't make it back, only one man survived. Accepting the defeat, Burke and Wills became part of the Aussie tradition of celebrating those who endured defeats, along with the WWI Gallipoli campaign and the sufferings of Aussie POW's at the hands of the Japanese after the fall of Singapore. Australians commemorate defeats more than victories, but I'm getting ahead of myself.

By the 1870's, Australia's six separate colonies and one territory were governed independently, but still obedient to Queen Victoria. Its main purpose was as a money-making enterprise. Australia had become the world's largest producer of wool. Major financing came from London. Manufacturing began, but imported English goods provided whatever couldn't be made in Australian workshops. Ties with the mother country remained strong.

Agriculture drove the economy in the last half of the nineteenth and the first half of the twentieth centuries. It's said that Australia rode to prosperity on the sheep's back. Wool and wheat created wealth that enabled the cities to grow.

Post-Colonial Times   Nineteenth-century Australian culture evolved with English provincialism as a base, combining an inward reverence for the bush and an outward need to be accepted in the eyes of the world.

For years, being a descendant of convict stock was a stigma in Australian society, but in the twenty-first century it has become a point of pride, like Americans claiming lineage from the Mayflower.

When convict *transportation* ended in 1868, many free immigrants—mostly British—came looking for opportunity. Though isolated at the far end of the world, Australia prospered. The colonies had self-governance with their own parliaments and courts, though still within the British Empire. Most Australians considered themselves Englishmen.

In the 19th century it took two or three months for a letter to go from Sydney to London via clipper ship, making doing business difficult. In 1872 a telegraph cable was laid from Darwin across to Java and on to London. Australia was now connected to the world.

On January 1, 1901, Australia was declared an independent nation, with the blessings of Queen Victoria and the government of Great Britain. Despite this, Australia remains a constitutional monarchy with the Royal Family of England officially the head of state [more on this in the section on **Government**]. The six Australian colonies became states and were federated with the Northern Territory, into the *Commonwealth of Australia*. Unlike the U.S., there was no Revolutionary War, no Civil War, and there were no competing countries on common borders. Violent rebellion at the birth of the nation and wars of territorial expansion are outside the Australian experience which is why feelings of patriotism aren't as strong as they are in the U.S.

Tucked away on the far side of the world, Australia developed in quiet isolation through the first half of the twentieth century, evolving her own culture and language, the latter a colloquial version of English. She participated in the English wars against the Boers in South Africa (1899–1902) and against the Germans and Turks in World War I. Both were far-off adventures, performed under British Imperial command. At the start of World War II, she contributed troops to the British North African campaign against the Germans and helped bolster the defence of the British fortress of Singapore. And then the Japanese joined the war, and everything changed.

On December 7th 1941 the Japanese attacked the United States Naval Base at Pearl Harbor. The next day they invaded the northern Malay Peninsula with 10,000 troops and advanced through the jungle toward the fortress of Singapore, which was situated on the southern tip of the peninsula.

The British had built the fortress at tremendous expense as a cornerstone of their scheme to protect their Southeast Asian Empire. The plan had been to defend the approaches to Singapore with their great navy, backed up by defensive positions and massive gun batteries in the fortress to repulse a frontal sea attack. But with the Nazi's threatening an invasion of Britain, the Brits had pulled much of their fleet back to the Atlantic.

In early 1942 the Japanese attacked and sank the remaining British fleet using carrier-launched aircraft. Meanwhile, the invasion force had advanced down the undefended Malay Peninsula (by bicycle, would you believe), and attacked the fortress from its undefended rear. Singapore fell in February 1942 and over 20,000 Australian troops were captured. At this time the total population of Australia was just seven million. Australia had lost much of her army and lay exposed to whatever was coming next.

When Singapore fell the British Empire unofficially died with it, and Australia was left on her own. The Japanese invaded New Guinea in January, and Papua in July, Australian territories a hundred miles off the north coast of Queensland.

Against British wishes, Australia hastily withdrew her troops from North Africa where they'd been fighting the German Afrika Corps, returned them to Australian and retrained them as jungle fighters, then deployed them against the Japanese in New Guinea. Australia was no longer an isolated country; she was on the frontlines. Japanese forces repeatedly bombed Darwin, Broome and several smaller towns along the northwest coast.

Meanwhile, the Japanese had forced the United States out of the Philippines, and the Yanks needed another base of operations in the South Pacific, so they could regroup and begin a counter-attack. Knowing a citadel was harder to defeat than an outpost, Australia welcomed the huge amount of men and material the Yanks sent. The Americans soon discovered that they had as much in common with Australia as they had with Great Britain. During the war years, the U.S. and Australia became close allies politically, socially, and economically, ties that remain strong to this day.

By the end of the war, one in seven Australians had served in the military: one-million out of a population of seven-million. 39,000 had been killed, 65,000 had been wounded. With the war finally over, she enjoyed the post-war recovery.

By the early 1950's, improvements in communication and air travel allowed Australia to emerge from isolation and to join the world community. Economically, things had also changed. Synthetics were replacing wool as the *fibre* of choice and the wool industry suffered a depression. About that same time, demand increased for minerals, which Australia had in abundance: iron ore, alumina, and precious metals. By the 1960s, Australia's ride to prosperity had shifted from the sheep's back to the ore train. New fortunes were made and Australia led the world in mining and mineral resource technology.

To the rest of the world, Australia merely changed from being a farm to being a quarry, with a few kangaroos and koalas thrown in for charm.

Populate or Perish   After the war Australia took a hard look at herself and realized she had to increase her population. Having only seven million people on a continent 80% the size of the U.S. wasn't going to be enough to hang onto it.

Much of this has been already covered in the chapter on Immigration. First the Australian government recruited people from the UK: families, single people, orphans and children of unwed mothers (controversial to this day). Then they turned to Europeans: Dutch, Germans, Italians, Greeks. In the 1970's boat people fleeing the communists in Viet Nam, in the 1980's white South Africans and Rhodesians (now Zimbabwe), Hong Kong Chinese after China took the colony back, then Indians and mainland Chinese. In the twenty-first century it's been refugees from war-torn Somalia and Sudan, Lebanon and Iran.

In 2018, 29% of Australia's population was foreign-born, that's almost one-in-three. Foreign accents are everywhere and they're mixed on top of the Aussie accent. Twenty-first century Australia has become a multi-cultural society. There's a blend of the old and the new: the old is hanging on but the new will eventually win out.

Fibre optic phone lines, the Internet and satellite TV have brought Australia closer to the rest of the world in a virtual sense, but physically it is still a far-off destination—an expensive fourteen-hour flight from the west coast of the U.S. to Sydney, or seventeen hours from London to Perth—and this has been a detriment to development. This is alluded to as the *Tyranny of Distance*. But the fact often missed is that being isolated from the rest of the world can be an advantage, both in terms of safety and the need to develop self-reliance. Australia has had to develop her own industries and has been able to manage disease, terrorism, and illegal immigration. The standard of living is among the highest in the world. Though things are expensive to import, the food is good, health care is available to everyone and the beer is cold.

Australia's level of contribution to the world far outweighs her small population. Blessed with sunshine, clean air, abundant natural resources, an optimistic outlook and distance from most of the world's problems is why Australia is called *'The Lucky Country'*...

...but Australia isn't always the shiny, liberal, multi-cultural society it wants the world to see.

Indigenous Australians   *AKA: Aborigines, First Australians, Traditional Land Owners.*   [Author's note: unless you have a strong stomach and/or an attitude of righteous indignation, you may want to skip to the next chapter.]

The original inhabitants who'd lived on the island-continent for 50-60,000 years before the Europeans arrived were almost totally exterminated by what they consider was a European invasion.

Pre-European arrival, food was abundant, bush medicine was there for the taking, and everything was shared. The Aboriginal people had laws that enshrined ethics and a religious mythology governed by the *Dreamtime* that explained the natural environment through journeys into their subconscious. Their oral history had *songs* that proscribed the annual seasonal migrations through the country that provided food and medicine, and elaborate skin group laws that prevented inbreeding. They owned the land as much as the land owned them.

They carried just what they needed, practiced hygiene, cooperated with their families and with the other clans they would meet in their migrations. Their social structure intertwined them with everyone they knew, Aunties and Uncles were honorifics awarded to the elders that guided the younger members of their clan and gave them *the Law*. They lived in harmony with their environment. At times there was abundance, other times there was scarcity, but they only took what they needed, what they could carry with them on their annual migration following food sources through the land. They gathered seeds, flowers, and roots, hunted kangaroo, *bush turkey*, *goannas* (monitor lizards) and insects. Some found time to create elaborate rock art that still graces caves and rock formations in remote areas. They had songs and rituals that celebrated life, but more importantly, guided them on their annual migrations. Most interesting is that they had evolved away from war. They were not war-like, the clans negotiated and worked with each other, they had elaborate rituals for conflict resolution.

In the early 17th century the Europeans arrived. They had not evolved away from war, to them life was war, and to them the world was theirs to conquer. The first arrivals were explorers working for the *VOC*, the *Dutch East India Trading Company*, who were sailing to their colony in Batavia (now Indonesia) for spices, tea, sugarcane and silk. As they passed along the Australian west coast, landing occasionally, some being shipwrecked, they found little they could exploit, and so moved on. They paid little heed to the *'naked black inhabitants'* who mostly avoided them. The Dutch never settled in Australia.

The 1770 expedition led by James Cook on the HMS Endeavor resulted in him declaring it *Terra Nullius*, or *uninhabited land,* despite the fact that it was already inhabited. This established the fallacy that the land belonged to no-one and was therefore up for grabs. The Brits arrived in force to take charge in 1788.

This is an Aboriginal point of view of the British arrival, by the late Aunty Beryl Timbery Beller, an Elder of the Dharawal people, whose ancestors witnessed it, and was recorded in the oral history tradition:

> *"... they were so ignorant they thought there was only one race on the earth and that was the white race. So, when Captain Cook first set foot on Wangal land over at Kundul which is now called Kurnell, he said 'oh let's put a flag up somewhere, because these people are illiterate, they've got no fences'. They didn't understand that we didn't need fences ... that we stayed here for six to eight weeks, then moved somewhere else where there was plenty of tucker (food) and bush medicine and we kept moving and then come back in twelve months' time when the food was all refreshed."*

Oral histories from the Gweagal people say they first saw the white sails approaching and interpreted them as clouds. When the ship came into view below the clouds it probably would have looked to them like a travelling island inhabited by pale-skinned men covered in strange clothing. The Gweagal thought they were spirits of the dead.

Sydney Parkinson, a young artist on the *Endeavor*, wrote in his journal that the natives made threatening gestures with spears and yelled, "Warra warra wai", which the sailors thought meant "Go away". But in the Dharawal language this translates to "You're all dead", which indicates they were warning their own people of invading ghosts and spirits.

Journal entries from the HMS Endeavor describe the Aboriginal men threatening the crew until the sailors shot guns over their heads. A native tree bark shield called the *Gweagal Shield* was captured on the day and is now in the British Museum. It has a bullet hole through it, showing that at least one Gweagal warrior was probably hit.

The Gweagal would have thought the invading 'spirits' very strange. They saw pale-skinned men draped in layers of body coverings who required lots of heavy gear to survive and acted oddly. And worse of all, they carried nasty spears that made a loud noise and could harm you from far away. The Aboriginal people had had no warning, no point of reference, it was unexplainable.

From an Englishman's point of view the Aboriginal people would have appeared equally strange, but Europeans had been encountering natives for centuries as they explored and conquered, and were less amazed and more condescending. The 'natives' looked primitive, naked, very black, with non-European facial features. And these natives were not engaged in what Europeans would recognize as productive activity: they didn't cut down trees, build houses and barns, fence-off land, plant crops or herd animals. These the natives appeared to come and go randomly, lingering, watching, then disappearing.

What the Brits didn't grasp was that they were being studied, as hunters would study an animal they hadn't encountered before to try to figure it out, what it ate, how it behaved, how it moved, how smart it was. As for the Aboriginal people moving about randomly, it was far from that. They were on an annual migratory route following their food sources, as proscribed in their ancient oral history songs. Cook and his men didn't take the time to try to understand them and dismissed them as primitive savages.

Cook didn't ask permission to come ashore, he and his men just walked onto the beach and took charge, the inhabitants could only watch until they were chased away. Cook spent several months exploring and mapping the east coast of Australia. Joseph Banks and his team of scientists collected and described 29,000 plants that Europeans had never seen. On their return to Britain it was Joseph Banks who advocated for colonization of the continent, providing the British government with detailed plans.

Eighteen years later, in 1788, the British *First Fleet* arrived to establish a permanent convict colony. Eleven ships loaded with convicts, guards, livestock, provision and tools, were unloaded in Sydney Cove. Without asking permission of the native inhabitants, an outpost was built and colonisation of the entire continent began.

At that time, the continent was already inhabited by about three-quarters-of-a-million people in over 400 different nations, each with its own language and culture. These people didn't 'own' the land in a European sense with a title-deed, they were *part of the land*, and *the land was part of them*. They always had been and always would be. Or so they thought. When the *First Fleet* arrived in Sydney Cove it is recorded that the new colonial governor, Captain Arthur Philip, was astounded with the fallacy of Cook's *Terra Nullius* theory, saying *"Sailing up into Sydney cove we could see natives lining the shore shaking spears and yelling."*

These would have been the Cadigal people. The Brits went ashore, built houses and stores, protective walls and pasture fences and began their various enterprises: establishing crops, grazing animals and supporting those industries. Governor Phillip ordered that the Aboriginal people should be well treated, but it was not long before conflict began. The colonists did not sign treaties with the original inhabitants of the land.

The colonisers had taken some of the best land without asking and the local tribes didn't like it. The colonists routinely shot kangaroo for meat on the Aboriginals' hunting grounds, but when the Aboriginals speared a sheep for meat they were hunted-down and shot. Aboriginal man Pemulwuy, of the Bidjigal clan, led the local people in a series of attacks against the British colonisers. The Brits tried to frighten the natives off, but soon found that the natives were deadly accurate spear-throwers, their strange elbow-shaped throwing knives (*boomerangs*) could break a man's neck, and if they missed, returned to the thrower for another go. For close-in fighting they had stone-headed clubs. The colonists had weapons that were more deadly: guns, bayonets and swords. But what proved to be the most deadly weapons of all, silent weapons, were the European diseases they had brought.

The Aboriginal people had been isolated for thousands of years from the diseases that had raged through Europe and Asia and had no resistance to the deadly viruses carried by the sailors and convicts. In less than a year, over half the indigenous population living in the Sydney Basin had died from smallpox. The region, once alive with a vibrant mix of Aboriginal clans, now fell silent.
    ---the Aboriginal Heritage Office, Sydney

As the colonists expanded their farms and settlements the

indigenous Australians retreated. More and more settlers and convicts arrived, expanding further inland and up and down the coast. To the Aboriginal people this was unprecedented, they didn't know what to do.

The Brits saw the Aboriginals as unorganized savages. They were in fact well-ordered, with deeply ingrained traditions and laws. The lands they inhabited were divided by verbal agreements developed over thousands of generations, adjusted as climate and population changes required. It was a working, fluid, self-governing society, and had been for millennia.

The British expansion sent the remaining Aborigines who'd been lucky enough to survive the white man's diseases, into exile onto other groups' traditional lands. In a short time, tens of thousands of years of traditional land-use agreements were shattered. They became exiles from their own *Country*.

The white Australians built their colonies, turning the well-watered temperate lands along the coasts into farms and grazing stations. They cut down forests and turned them into pastures. There was no place for the displaced Aboriginal people to go, they didn't know the interior country or it's songs that would guide their annual migration following the *bush tucker* (natural food sources), and those *Countries* were already occupied by other clans.

They retreated until they ran out of places to retreat to, turned into paupers, cut off from what had once been abundance. They became second-class citizens in their own land, workers on settler's farms and in cities. In the vast interior the remnants of indigenous clans survived in the old ways into the early twentieth century, but eventually even the *Red Centre* of the continent fell prey to cattle-grazing and the mining industry.

With their foraging lands taken from them and their numbers decimated by disease, the surviving indigenous people gathered near the colonists' farms, sheep and cattle stations and lived off the discards. The settlers, seeing providential opportunity, put them to work. The Indigenous people became slaves: the men tending the flocks and herds, the women performing household duties. There was no formal ownership as in the American South. The pay was food, tobacco and cast-off clothing. If they ran away state laws authorized police to hunt them down and return them to their stations in neck chains so as to not give their kinsmen any ideas. Repeat offenders were sent to distant prisons. This continued for generations until after the Second World War. Rottnest Island, now a major tourist resort 10 kms off Perth, was used for almost a hundred years as an Aboriginal prison for repeat offenders. Under what was once a campground is a mass grave containing 373 bodies of Aboriginal men, now marked as a memorial. The most common offense was attempting to live free and resisting arrest.

Some station managers took good care of their indigenous charges, but others were abusive. Many white settlers routinely took Aboriginal women for sex. The resulting *half-caste* (mixed blood) children became a moral problem for the strait-laced God-fearing colonialists, who passed cruel and insensitive welfare laws that were couched as well-intentioned and progressive (the term *'half-caste'* is not only offensive, it indicates the racialized viewpoints of the time).

The official government plan was that the indigenous *pure blood* Aboriginals would eventually die-off and the rest would disappear through a *breeding-out-the-black* plan, and the Aboriginals would cease to be a problem. This was formally known as the *Assimilation Policy*. The colonial government's solution was for the *half-caste* children to be forcibly taken from their *pure blood* mothers by police and sent hundreds of miles away to *mission schools*. There they would be de-conditioned from being Aboriginal, their languages banned, their identities erased. They were given English names and taught to be *useful servants*. The girls were trained as domestics, the boys as *stockmen*. The plan was after several generations of *half-castes* marrying, the *'black'* would be bred out of them and they would be assimilated into white Australian society. In the meantime, they would work as unpaid, or underpaid servants.

What the whites didn't understand was that Aboriginal culture is an entire way of life: *Country* and *Family* is the basis of everything. Unlike secular western culture, there was no division between religion, work, marriage, child-rearing or civic responsibility; it was all one thing, like a tree with many branches. The colonists had cut the roots out from under the Aboriginal people's tree and expected them *to just get on with it*. The children who had been torn from their mothers would never see them or their *Country* again. For these children to grow up without their *Laws* and *Country* was to cut them off from their entire world. They were and are known as the *Stolen Generations*. Many tried to run away. The missionaries who ran the schools were more prison wardens than teachers. This lasted in one form or another for a hundred-fifty years. It is unknown the exact number of children stolen from their mothers and their country, but it has been estimated at around 100,000. By the 1920's the entire Aboriginal population had withered to between 50-90,000, from a pre-colonial population of 750,000. The Brits almost managed to wipe them out entirely.

As these children of the *Stolen Generations* grew up, they were put to work but not assimilated. They were released into shanty towns on the edge of white settlements, forbidden to enter the settlements without written passes, allowed to work in the back of but not enter the businesses, kept out of sight except as their labours required. They lived in abject poverty while the Australian nation, which they were helping build, thrived and was proclaimed *The Lucky Country*. They were subjugated and kept impoverished without any control over their lives. Is there any wonder why alcohol and drug abuse became rampant, or why so many would end up rebelling in their personal lives and ending up in jail?

The total disregard for the wants, needs and desires of the Aboriginal people can be summed up in this fact: even though they'd been here for 60,000 years before the whites arrived, Indigenous Australians weren't given Australian citizenship until 1948. They had no rights until the voters passed a Commonwealth of Australia Referendum in 1967 that granted them the right to vote. They weren't protected by anti-discrimination laws until 1975. But we're getting ahead of ourselves.

By 1900, 90 percent of the Aborigines been eliminated by

disease and genocide and the indigenous population had withered to the point where it looked as if they would cease to exist as a people. But the ones who managed to survive developed a resistance to European diseases, and soon learned to demand their rights. A hundred years later, by 2019, the population had returned to about 650,000, about 2% of the total population of Australia, so they have a very small voice. But they have been heard.

The Pilbara region of Western Australia is desert country, the *country* of the Yindjibarndi, Kariyarra, Nyamal, Ngarluma, Martuthunira, Kurrama, Nyiyaparli and Palyku peoples: hunter-gatherers who for millennia annually migrated through the country. In the mid-nineteenth century white men came to the Pilbara and decided it was good grazing land. Remote sheep and cattle *stations* were established on leased '*Crown Land*', which was already claimed but not acknowledged Aboriginal Country. These *stations* were 'owned' by absentee white businessmen in London, Melbourne and Perth, and run by white managers. The towns of Port Hedland and Marble Bar were built to service the stations. Tax-payers down in Perth subsidized these businesses by building roads, bridges, harbours and a state-owned steamship company to service them.

Meanwhile, the desert people had found it increasingly hard to live the old ways with cattle and sheep grazing dominating their *Country*. They had to feed their families. Lured by the availability of food, their only choice was to move to the stations and go to work for the managers. It started as an easy relationship, the station managers taught the men how to work with the cattle and sheep, they became proficient stockmen, and their wives became domestics as the stations grew. The station owners fed them in return. This system lasted eighty years: generations were born, worked and died on the stations.

Working under white managers, Aboriginal people were the sole labour force. They were paid in tobacco and flour, their families lived near the station in the bush in primitive conditions. As the stations grew and prospered, the Aboriginal workers' conditions remained the same. They came to think of themselves as *Blackfellas*, and their overseers as *Whitefellas*. They were taught to know their place in society, and it was at the bottom. The inequality became oppressive.

Eventually some of these '*natives*' would decide to go *walkabout* and return to the bush. That was when they discovered they no longer had free-will. The police would be sent after them and bring them back in neck chains. Historical research shows that the landowners had planned from the outset to use the native population as unpaid labour, their business models were built on it. It was de facto slavery.

Most white Australians living in cities didn't know this, it was happening in the bush 1000 kilometres away. Those that did, otherwise moral, God-fearing subjects of the Crown, went along with it, thinking that the Aboriginal people were so different from them, with such different appearances, culture and way of life, that it must be OK, that the government must know what it was doing. The government antiseptically referred to this as '*the Native Question*'. To white Australians it was easier to look the other way and accept that that's the way it was, they had their own tough lives to worry about.

To the outside world, Australia was a wonderful far-off place that produced the world's best wool, shiploads of wheat, and had exotic animals like kangaroos and koala bears. The image was of healthy white people working hard and playing hard. Hidden from world view was *The Native Question*.

At Australian Federation in 1901, the new federal government decided that the individual states would have absolute authority over the Aboriginal people. This conveniently avoided the problem of having a national policy on the Aboriginal people, which would might eventually have had to be answered-to internationally. Each state appointed a *Protector of Aborigines* who had absolute power over the natives.

What happened in the Pilbara region of Western Australia is an example of Aboriginal people fighting for, persevering and gaining their own power. Under Western Australian law, the *Aboriginal Protection Act 1897* made them '*Wards of the State*'. *The Native Act of 1898* stated that an Aboriginal person could not leave his employment without permission of the

employer, police or the *Aboriginal Protector*. They were slaves
in all ways except by name.

The Aboriginal people were aware that they were being
taken advantage of, all they wanted was proper wages, better
working conditions and the right to be able to leave if they
wished. This is what they had been promised in the *Western
Australian Colonial Constitution*.

In 1890, as a condition for self-rule of the colony, the
British Government inserted a clause under *Section 70* of the
Constitution that said once public revenue in Western Australia
exceeded 500,000 pounds, 1 per cent was to be dedicated to
'*the welfare of the Aboriginal natives*'. Queen Victoria had
personally insisted on inserting this clause because she didn't
trust the colonials. She was right, but she died in 1901. In 1905
the state Government illegally removed the funding provisions
for 'native welfare'. Aboriginal elders and Lawmen lobbied
for native rights and were denied.

There were scattered small movements through the early
twentieth century to educate and grant freedoms to Aboriginal
people, but the *Protector of Aborigines* would stop most
efforts.

During the world wars young Aboriginal men volunteered
for and were accepted into the Australian army, and while in
the service were exposed to the outside world. After the wars
they returned to their stations and their lives as indentured
laborers, but their eyes had been opened. They told the elders
what they had seen in the army working and living with
whitefella soldiers. These *blackfella* soldiers had learned how
the system worked, and they came to understand how much
economic power they potentially held over the station owners
who were businessmen solely concerned about profits.

The elders searched for a way to organize and use this
power to gain their human rights. In the mid-1930's a maverick
white miner named Don McLeod stumbled onto the cause and,
meeting with the elders in secret (because a whitefella was
forbidden by law to meet with a group of blackfellas), taught
them how to organize. The elders decided a strike was the only
way to go and persuaded MacLeod to lead them. They chose to
wait until after WWII so as to not be considered seditious in

time of war.

On May 1, 1946 without notice, 800 stockmen and workers on all the pastoral stations in the Pilbara Region, along with Aboriginal workers in the towns of Port Hedland and Marble Bar, walked-off their jobs. The *Pastoral Workers Strike of 1946* left the station managers with no workers and hundreds of thousands of head of livestock, crops, businesses and cattle yards to manage. The stations were paralysed.

The strikers' terms were simple: they wished to be paid a fair wage for their work, given decent housing for themselves and their families and allowed to leave if they wished. The basis of their claim was the *British Anti-slavery Act of 1833*, which Western Australia was subject-to as a British colony established in 1829, and the *'Native Welfare'* clause (section 70) of the Western Australian colonial constitution, which in 1905 had been illegally removed by 'gentlemen's agreement' between the WA Premiere (governor) and the Colonial Secretary without notifying the British Parliament or the King. The station owners had built their pastoral business-model on free labour and claimed they could not afford to pay them and wanted the police to force the workers back to the stations. When that didn't work they tried to hire labourers from the southern parts of the state, but no whitefella would work that hard in such conditions in remote regions for so little pay.

For three years the striking workers and their leaders were harassed, threatened and jailed. A sympathetic lawyer in Perth would advise them, pro bono, by wire of their rights and how to proceed. Negotiations with scattered stations settled some disputes, but it soon became apparent the strike had become more about native legal rights than about wages and working conditions. They were forcing the government to enforce the conditions already laid out in the constitution and to eliminate the ones that enabled de facto slavery. The strikers were steadfast, they would not give-in, they would not flinch.

In August 1949 the Seamen's Union got onboard and agreed to refuse loading wool from the stations onto ships for export. The state-owned ship company docked their wages, but the seamen still refused to load. After three days of fevered discussion on the government side they forced the station

owners to cede to the strikers demands. The government later
denied making any such agreement and later went back on
many of agreed-upon demands claiming none of it was ratified
by the WA Parliament.

Many Aboriginal stockmen and household workers never
returned to their former employment in the pastoral industry.
Some workers started their own communities in the regions
and began raising sheep and doing hard-rock mining. Some
pooled resources and sought sponsorships and leased pastoral
stations they had once worked on. Some moved to the cities
and towns and settled there, but for many of those, town life
exposed them to discrimination resulting in alcoholism and
despair. It was a victory, but it was just the beginning of
tackling the larger, deeper issues for native rights.

In the 1960s, after seeing the U.S. civil rights movement,
students from the University of Sydney, led by Charlie Perkins
[more below], the first Aboriginal person to receive a college
degree, formed a group called the *Student Action for
Aborigines*, aka *The Freedom Ride*, and travelled out
to country towns in New South Wales on a fact-finding
mission. They encountered *de facto* segregation. The students
picketed and faced violence, raising the issue of *Indigenous
Rights*. They protested at segregated pools, parks and pubs,
which created consternation in country towns but caught the
attention of the media. The eventual result was that Australia
overwhelmingly passed the 1967 referendum removing
discriminatory sections from the Australian constitution and
enabling the federal government to take direct action in
Aboriginal affairs. The *Assimilation Policy* that mandated
Aboriginal children be removed from their families was finally
abolished in 1973. In 1979, an independent community-
controlled child-care agency was established.

It was another step in an Aboriginal rights movement that
goes on today, and there's still a long way to go to correct the
wrongs, both in a legal context and in the minds of white
Australians.

Torres Strait Islanders   When you hear political or
legal reference to Aboriginal people you will often hear
included the term *Torres-Strait Islanders. Aboriginal and*

Torres Strait Islanders are the native land rights groups representing the indigenous people of Australia.

The Torres Strait is a body of water separating far northern Australia's Cape York Peninsula and the island of New Guinea. There are about 275 small islands in the Torres Strait and are included in the state of Queensland. The people who live there are ethnically distinct from the Aboriginal people, and are known colloquially as the *Torres Strait Islanders*, though they are part of five distinct groups. Today there are many more Torres Strait Islander people living in mainland Australia (28,000) than on the Islands (4,500).

Modern Indigenous Australians   Many *Aboriginal and Torres Strait Islanders* have assimilated and done well. Ken Wyatt, a Yamatji man, was the Western Australian Director of Health, is now a Liberal member of federal parliament and is the first indigenous person to be the Minister for Indigenous Australians. There are indigenous artists, musicians, doctors, lawyers and professors. But many remain in an underclass.

For the latter, they've suffered having been ripped from their *Country*, their families and their traditional *Laws* over a hundred years, which led that generation to despair. The following generations grew up with alcoholic parents, creating a multi-generational chain of problems. They have been discriminated against and undereducated. They've had the wonders of the modern world dangled before their eyes, wonders that are economically out of reach. Many are of mixed lineage and are impoverished, living on the fringe of society on urban welfare or in semi-independent communities out in the bush.

Today Aboriginals make up only 2% of the total population, but represent 28% of the adult prison population. Juvenile statistics are worse: 58% of ten to seventeen-year-old prisoners are Aboriginal. More than 30% of all Aboriginal males at some point in their lives come up against the corrective system.

Most of the problems are due to a lack of understanding by the European-descended people who created and dominate modern Australia. Most of these new Australians don't grasp that the culture of the *First Australians* is so dense and specific as to be almost impossible for whitefellas to grasp.

In order to survive a nomadic life in a harsh country, Aboriginal society had to be communal: if I have something to eat and you do not, I will give you half of what I have. If you have something to drink and I do not, you will give me half of yours. It's not an obligation, it just is how things are done. As modern Aboriginal people have accumulated wealth, relatives have exercised this custom, which makes it difficult for Aboriginal people to lift themselves from poverty.

There is a story about David Gulpilil, the iconic, award-winning Australian Aboriginal actor. He had bought a suit so he could attend a ceremony where he was to receive an acting award, but before he could use it a cousin dropped by and took it for himself, so Gulpilil didn't attend the ceremony. Though he has been in dozens of successful films and is acclaimed as a national treasure, he chooses to be a *long-grasser*, *living rough* (homeless) in Darwin, even though his son has an apartment nearby.

There is a cultural, values-based difference between a non-materialistic culture like Aboriginal, and one that is based almost entirely on materialism like modern Australia.

The term *Aboriginal*, which means *existing from the earliest times*, is itself a construct by the conquering Europeans suggesting that *Aboriginal and Torres Strait Islander* people did not have a history before European invasion, because it is not written and recorded. The name reflects nothing of who they are. 'Aboriginal' people don't usually refer to themselves as such, they call themselves by the name of their specific clan, and by the country their clan is from.

Broome is a wealthy coastal town on the western edge of the Kimberley, three-hours flight north of Perth, Western Australia. There the contrasts are most apparent.

In the dry, warm winter, Broome fills with tourists and *grey nomads* (traveling retirees). It has a rich history as a pearling town and there is still an active pearling industry. There is the famous Matsos brewery and seafood restaurant, the Malcolm Douglas Crocodile Park and the famous Cable Beach where you can ride a camel on the shimmering sand while enjoying the sunset. In the old Chinatown is Sun Pictures, the world's oldest outdoor movie theatre.

Many Aboriginal people have also moved there from the interior communities because the government prohibited *off-site liquor sales* (takeaway liquor stores). Around the town oval most nights are dozens of Aboriginal people inebriated and carrying on, arguing, fighting, passing out. This is a scene replicated in other Kimberley towns: Kununurra, Halls Creek and Fitzroy Crossing. Tourists walk by and try not to stare, it's very upsetting. But these poor, highly visible unfortunates are not indicative of the true Indigenous population of the Kimberley. You don't see the people who are quietly going about their lives.

The *Djugun* people of Broome are an example. The Djugan consider themselves a sovereign people and have never signed-away any rights to the state of Western Australia or to the federal government.

They live in the Broome suburb of Djugun, near the international airport. They are the traditional land-owners of Broome, dating back tens-of-thousands of years to when white Europeans were still living in caves.

They are cultured people. Djugun women Mitch and Eileen Torres run *Wawili Pitjas*, and produce films, documentaries and TV series for SBS and the ABC. Their entire family works on these projects: cameraman, soundman, art department, they have a sound studio and prop-shop on their property. In 2016 Djugun woman Pat Torres published an academic thesis entitled *The Djugun Peoples Sustaining Ideals of Culture and Identity.*

The Djugun, as sovereign people, refuse to sign-off on anything the government presents that they consider compromising to their *Country* or heritage. The government then find another indigenous group that will agree, usually for a price. The Djugan were the *traditional owners* of the Broome area, the other groups moved there when their lands were taken. The Djugan consider themselves *First People*, the term *Aboriginal* is an offensive colonial construct. They point out that all the English language placenames in Australia are actually renaming's of indigenous placenames.

The Djugun have come to learn that the only way they can gain their rights is to embrace Native Title law and pursue them in federal court. They helped lead the successful fight to save James Price Point from destruction for a huge liquified natural gas refinery. The project was planned by the West Australian State Government for a joint-venture partnership with Woodside Petroleum, Shell, BP, Mitsubishi/Mitsui and PetroChina. The Point, on the west coast of the Dampier Peninsula, is a gallery of ancient indigenous people's cave art and has tracks of dinosaur footprints preserved in rock. The waters just off the point are a calving ground for the world's largest population of humpback whales and home to spinner dolphins, endangered hawksbill turtles and dugong (Australasian manatee). The Djugun led the successful fight to stop the project and eventually a giant floating plant was built and moored far out to sea over the gas fields. This was not only a victory for the Djugun culture, but for the environment.

The 1992 Mabo federal court decision established the idea of *native title* to some traditional lands. Eddie Mabo was an Indigenous Australian man from the Torres Strait who fought all of his life for the rights to his lands. The Mabo Decision was a landmark ruling, it overturned the fiction of Terra Nullius.

Around the same time as the Mabo Decision, the Labor government under Prime Minister Bob Hawke set up the *Aboriginal and Torres Strait Islander Commission (ATSIC)*, as an elected body of Indigenous Australians to formally be involved in the processes of government affecting their lives. It lasted until 2004 when it was disbanded by the Liberal-National government under Prime Minister John Howard in the aftermath of corruption allegations and litigation.

Another federal ruling in 2006 gave the Noongar people of Western Australia title to public lands in the Perth area. This allows the Noongar to *conserve and use the natural resources of the area, maintain and protect sites, hunt on the land and use it for traditional purposes*, while not effecting individual landowners' property rights. The ruling is constantly being challenged by the state in federal court, not so much as to have it over-turned, but to more precisely clarify and define it. These fights are likely to go on for years.

To this day if a mineral resources company wants to build a mine on native-title lands, they buy off the local Aboriginal council with a recreational facility and a promise of jobs. If the local Aboriginal council won't agree they find some other Aboriginal people to come in and sign off. If they can't do that, they turn to the government to take control.

During the writing of this second edition in mid-2020, news came out that a 46,000-year-old Aboriginal habitation cave had been blown up by the Rio Tinto Group for the expansion of one of its iron mines. The iron ore goes to China and is the major Australian export, not only providing corporate income and jobs, but also extensive royalties to the government. The large cave was in a hillside in Juukan Gorge in the Pilbara region of Western Australia. The site was well known and had been excavated by archaeologists. Over 7000 artifacts had been removed and it was anticipated there were more to be unearthed. The local Indigenous people, the Puutu Kunti Kurrama and Pinikura, protested. Section 17 of the Western Australian Aboriginal Heritage Act of 1972 bans destruction of such sites. But section 18 of the Act allows anyone to apply to override a section 17 decision. That's what Rio Tinto did, and all it took was a government minister to sign it off. That was in 2013. In 2014 the archaeological dig began. In 2020, when Rio finally got around to mining that area, the execs felt uneasy about destroying the caves so they rechecked with the WA government and was told it was OK. After they blew the cave up there was a huge outcry by the local Indigenous people. The Rio Tinto CEO publicly apologised, and then they began mining. There are an estimated forty such Indigenous sites still threatened. The WA Minster for Aboriginal affairs, Ben Wyatt, himself Aboriginal (a Yamatji man through his father's heritage), denied knowledge of the issue until it was too late, and vowed to change the review procedure. Hopefully this will be the last such site lost.

There is a duality to the way the white majority treats Aboriginal people. Their art is celebrated, their music is enjoyed, most public occasions will begin with a *Welcome to*

Country ceremony that includes blessings in the local indigenous language. But there is also a resentment among some white Australians who feel Aboriginals are given too much welfare and social assistance. Others rationalize that welfare compromises their self-reliance. Some Aboriginal people prefer to *sleep rough*; others have no choice. They are embraced at certain levels of Australian society and marginalized at others, and there still is underlying racial discrimination.

Hope for the future lies in the recognition by the *'Settler Australians'* of the *First Australians*, and their customs, environmental practices and arts.

Dr. Charles Perkins AO (1936-2000), was an example of an Aboriginal man rising through adversity and achieving greatness. Perkins was born in the Alice Springs Telegraph Station Aboriginal Reserve. He was removed from his family when he was 10 and sent 1500 kms away to Adelaide to a mission school where he was trained as a fitter and turner (mechanic). But he was also a gifted soccer player and ended up playing professionally for the Everton club in England, and then back in Australia with the Adelaide Croatian and the Sydney Pan-Hellenic Clubs. Living abroad and in white urban Australia opened his eyes.

Perkins first spoke about Australian/Aboriginal inequality at the Federal Council for Aboriginal Advancement annual conference in Brisbane in 1961.

In 1965 he and Gary Williams, the only Aboriginal students at the University of Sydney, formed *Student Action for Aborigines* (SAFA) and organised a bus tour of western New South Wales towns. About 30 students, led by Perkins, travelled to Walgett, Moree, Kempsey and other towns, exposing discrimination in the use of halls, swimming pools, picture theatres and hotels. In a number of towns Aboriginal returned servicemen were only permitted entry to the *Returned Service League* clubs (like U.S. American Legion) on Anzac Day. This trip became known as *The Freedom Ride* and word spread nation-wide as the students arranged press coverage for the protests and inevitable conflicts. Their effective use of television brought the issue of racial discrimination in country towns to national attention. Perkins' role in this action propelled him to a position as a national Aboriginal leader and spokesman, a position he held until his death.

He continued through his life as a spokesman and leader of Aboriginal equality movements. He managed the Foundation for Aboriginal Affairs in Sydney, and in 1969 to the newly formed federal Office of Aboriginal Affairs. In 1984 Perkins became Secretary of the Department of Aboriginal Affairs, and stayed active in Aboriginal political issues and arts for the rest of his life.

He was given a state funeral in recognition of his dedicated work for Indigenous Australians.

A footnote: his daughter, Rachel Perkins, is a noted film and TV writer/producer/director whose credits include the iconic Australian/Aboriginal musical *Bran Nue Dae*, coming-of-age story *Jasper Jones* and the TV series *Mystery Road*.

Racism   Australia has a dark side. It runs deep in the culture, starting with Aboriginal people but continuing with the White Australia policy aimed at Asians, resentment of the Wogs (southern European immigrants after WWII), and Muslim Middle Eastern, Sudanese and Somalian immigrants in the 1990's.

Some white Australians retain racist attitudes. This does not come out overtly, but rather it is a privately held reaction kept to intimates and like-minded people. They think Aboriginal people should get over the past and just get on with it, that they do not deserve any more special treatment or help. If they see a successful Aboriginal person they attribute it to their 'white blood'. Be aware of deep-seated racism, it is there.

Language differences

Australians speak their own distinct version of English, with a pronounced and quite difficult to imitate accent. The accent has some British cockney with a little Irish and Scottish thrown in, but it has a very distinct sound of its own, with broad 'a's and missing or transferred 'r's. There are regional accents, some are heavier than others, newcomers may have difficulty understanding what people are saying to them.

Here's my take: The country was founded and populated

with regional English, Scottish, Welsh and Irish provincial people so that's the basis of pronunciation. This amalgamated Australian version of 'the Queen's English' evolved in isolation long before the intercontinental telephone, radio and television made voice communication possible. In the mid-nineteenth century, it could take six months for a letter or magazine to make it from London to Sydney. The telegraph sped that up, but it was just dots and dashes. My guess is that when a new word or term arrived, the first people to use it, correctly or not, established Australian pronunciation. Perhaps some of the unique language applications and interesting word pronunciations can be attributed to this.

Australianisms The term *Australianism* is defined in my old Thorndike-Barnhart dictionary as *an English word, phrase, or meaning peculiar to, or first employed in, Australia.*

You can tell a lot about a people by how they treat their language. Australians are fun-loving, intelligent, sarcastic, flippant, irreverent, witty, and vindictive. Give an Australian a word, and in a minute he (or she) will have turned it into a plaything: breakfast becomes *brekky*, wishful thinking becomes *airy-fairy*, waving flies from in front of your face becomes *the Aussie salute*.

Here's what the Australian government has to say about it on an official website:

> *Australians use a lot of colloquial terms (slang). We also have a strong tendency to create a peculiarly Australian, diminutive word form during informal speech. This means that words are shortened and then a vowel is added to the end of the word—usually an 'i' or an 'o.' Although the diminutives would rarely be used in a formal written context, when diminutives are written, the 'i' is usually written as 'ie' or 'y.'*

Here's some examples:

Words are abbreviated with an *ie* or *y* added to the end, so a bricklayer becomes a *brickie*. An umbrella becomes a *brolly*.

Some words are abbreviated with an *o* on the end, so an ambulance driver becomes an *ambo*. A garbage truck driver is a *garbo*. The sound man on a movie crew is the *soundo*.

Names get the same treatment, even in the media. Every Aussie knew Michael Jackson as simply *Jacko*, Arnold Schwarzenegger is *Arnie*, Paul Hogan is *Hoges* (rhymes with 'rogues'). The name Barry becomes *Baz* or *Bazza*, Gary becomes *Gaz* or *Gazza*, Aaron becomes *Az* or *Azza*, Teresa becomes *Tez* or *Tezza*. The Prime Minister, Scott Morrison, is *ScoMo*.

Some words are from *Cockney rhyming slang*: *Yank* rhymes with 'tank', as in 'septic tank'. They grab the word 'septic' and Australianise it to *seppo*, and an 'American' becomes a *Seppo*. A 'lie' is a *porky*. Why? *Pork pie* rhymes with *lie*, so *porky*.

Some terms are from British-English, like *back-to-front*, meaning backwards, or *anti-clockwise* for counter-clockwise. *Ta* means thank you. *Cheers* can mean 'yes', 'thank you' or 'goodbye', besides being a drinking salute. *Whilst* is often used instead of 'while'. A 'jersey' is a *guernsey*. First names are *given* or *Christian* names, last names are *surnames*.

Some words come from other languages, like *abattoir* (slaughterhouse), or *abseil* (to rappel). The snack bar or ticket booth at a theatre is a *kiosk*. Short-term day care is *creche*. They adopted several Yiddish words: *shickered* for drunk, *nosh* for snack, *kibbitiz* for chat, *motza* for money, *shtum* for silent.

Some are just plain unique, like *arvo* for 'afternoon', which becomes *sarvo* for 'this afternoon'. A promoter is a *spruiker*. To defraud is to *rort*. *Strides* are trousers.

Some words are from Aboriginal languages often mispronounced. A *yonnie* is a large rock. A *humpy* is a shack, from the Aboriginal word *yumpi*. A parakeet is a *budgie*, short for *budgerigar*. Many place names are Aboriginal, especially in Western Australia and the Northern Territory.

Sometimes a noun becomes a verb: to 'work hard' is to *beaver*.

Sometimes a verb becomes a noun. To 'wet' something becomes *give it a wet*. I've heard a 'good question' described on TV news as *a good ask*. To try something, you *give it a go*. To decide against something is to *give it a miss*. To say 'goodbye' to some one is to *farewell* them, a *good ask* for a question, *an agree* for an agreement, etc.

Some adjectives become verbs. Clear weather is called *fine*, so to describe improving weather, you'd say, "The weather is *fining* up." If a political situation is heating up, it's described as *hotting up.*

Sometimes things are simply understated, also described as 'British understatement". Instead of saying a particular restaurant was bad you'd describe it as *pretty average*, or *ordinary.* If one is sick they are referred to as *unwell.* During the Covid-19 pandemic this got to be annoying, especially when hearing about someone that is dying described as *gravely unwell.* Another use of understatement is put *a bit* in front of the word: a walk becomes *a bit* of a walk, or you might have *a bit* of dinner, you get *in a bit of a fight*, or *a bit of a biffo.*

Some Australian words are subtly different. You think you know their meaning, but you soon come to realize you were dead wrong. For example:

In Australia, your *partner* is your *mate*, and your *mate* is your *partner.* In the U.S., one's *partner* is a person with whom one shares a project, be it a business, a trip, a boat, etc. In Australia, one's *partner* is their spouse—married or not, gay or straight. In America, you'd call that person your 'mate', but in Australia, your *mate* is your best friend: the tried and true buddy you'd do anything for and who'd do anything for you.

In Australia, this can get sticky if a man introduces you to another man and says, "This is my *partner.*" Without understanding this distinction, you might think they were business partners instead of a couple and might say something unnecessarily embarrassing.

Here's another example: *Pot plants.* As you drive around an Australian suburb, you'll occasionally see a sign proclaiming: *"Pot plants for sale".* This is completely innocent, for it means potted plants, not marijuana.

The lesson from this: <u>assume nothing</u>. Don't let the apparent similarity of the place lull you into a false state of confidence. You're not in Kansas anymore. When in doubt, smile and say nothing, then look it up in this book. If it's not listed here, ask a friendly soul, or Google it.

Everyday Aussie words

'*G'day*' means 'good day,' and is the basic greeting: hello, good bye.

'*Cheers*' means 'yes', 'thank you', or 'good bye'.

'*No worries*' means 'OK.'

'*Onya*' or '*good onya*' means 'well done', or 'good job'.

'*How ya goin?*' means 'How are you doing?'

'*G'day, how ya goin?*' is used reflexively, without forethought, expressing greeting. Learn to say this with an Aussie accent if you want to avoid people noticing that you are a foreigner, and have to answer the same old questions.

Words with opposite meanings   Here are some examples:

Mooted: In America, something which is 'moot' is a statement which is doubtful or self-cancelling. In Australia, to *moot* something is to propose or suggest it. "He *mooted* the idea before the executive board" means he put it up for comment.

Tabled: In America, to '*table*' something, is to put it on hold, to not deal with it at this time. In Australia, to *table* something is to put it up for discussion: to "put it on the *table*" and discuss it.

Punt: In America, to '*punt*' is to give up or get rid of something, while in Australia to *punt* is to try something or gamble on it. In Australia, a 'gambler' is a *punter*. Also, a *punter* is someone looking for a good time, such as a tourist.

On the Nose: In America this describes something that is accurate. In Australia it means the opposite: it stinks. "His unpopular comment was *on the nose*."

Mickey Mouse: In the U.S., something described as *Mickey Mouse* means it's bad. In Australia, it's usually used describing something that's good, though it can also be used describing something bad. This is an instance where you have to consider the context.

Spirit of salts is a seemingly innocuous term. One might think it meant smelling salts or something you'd put in your bath water. It actually means hydrochloric acid, the nasty kind that burns.

Blue or ***bluey*** is what an Aussie might call a person with red hair. This is beyond opposite meaning; this is pure contrariness.

Words to not use: Certain words that are innocuous in North America are improper if not offensive in Australia. Some examples:

Fanny: In America, this usually means one's rear-end. In Australia, it refers to the female genitalia. Call a 'fanny pack' a *bum-bag*.

Root: This can mean the part of the tree that grows in the ground or it can be a coarse way to describe the sex act. Don't ask a girl if she '*roots*' for her favourite team. She might like them, but not that much. You don't *root* for your team, you *barrack* for them.

Map of Tasmania (*Map of Tassie*): Refers to the fact that the island state of Tasmania is shaped like a woman's pubic region.

Stuffed: This isn't a bad word; it just means something that is screwed up, as in "I *stuffed* up" or "My car broke down and is *stuffed*."

Ordinary means bad. You might describe a bad meal at a restaurant as '*rather ordinary*'. Also '*average*', as in, 'that meal was *pretty average*'. It's from British understatement.

Literal-ness   Australian English has developed into a simple say-what-you-mean way. A logger is a *timber getter*. A car accident is a *smash*. An auto body shop is *smash repairs*. The anchor person on a TV news show is the *newsreader*. High school graduates are called *school leavers*, or just *leavers*. When a shop owner takes inventory it's called *stock take*. Payroll withholding taxes are called *Pay As You Go*, or just *PAYG*.

Language usage is based on British English. There are many differences from American English. In Australia:

One lives *in* a street, not on it.

Something doesn't occur during a weekend, but *on* or *at the weekend*.

Time is similar, but 6:30 is written *6.30*, and can be pronounced *half-six*.

A TV show doesn't start at 6:00, but *from* 6.00. *From tomorrow* is a tense-breaking impossibility. *From* is past, *tomorrow* is in the future.

"A week from Thursday" would be spoken "*Thursday week.*"

One doesn't go "*to a hospital*", but "*to hospital,*" as if being in a hospital is a condition, not a location.

A woman *falls* pregnant, as if a stork flew over and sprinkled fairy dust on her.

One doesn't watch cricket; one watches *the* cricket, *the* footy, *the* tennis, *the* golf, etc..

Retrospective means retroactive, as in "the new law was *retrospectively* applied."

A substance labelled "*Not to be taken*" means it is poisonous; it shouldn't be taken <u>internally</u>.

One doesn't take a test; one *sits* a test.

One doesn't 'call' someone on the phone; one *rings* them.

A 'run' in a lady's stocking is a *ladder.*

The number 'zero' is pronounced *nil* or *naught.*

The letter Z is "*zed*".

The letter H is sometimes pronounced "*hay-tch*".

There are a preponderance of British names. You meet more Graemes and Trevors than Bobs and Jims. Many *surnames* (last names) are hyphenates: Worley-Jones, Smyth-Hayter. This adds to the Monty Python feel of the place.

Plurals The British system is used. A company or a team isn't considered a single entity, but as a group of individuals. A newspaper article might say: "Telstra *are* hiring" instead of "<u>is</u> hiring" or "NASA *have* launched a satellite" instead of "<u>has</u> launched." When the Australian cricket team won the World Cup in 2007, the ABC described them in this way: "Australia *are* the best." A radio ad: "Myer *are* having a huge end of year *stock take* sale."

Spelling differences Blame the Brits again: jail can be spelled *gaol*, pajamas are *pyjamas*, tires are *tyres*, maneuver is *manoeuvre*, program is *programme*, airplane is *aeroplane*, dispatch is *despatch*, plow is *plough*, draft is *draught*.

Words than end in '-er' are often spelled '-re': center is spelled *centre*, theater is spelled *theatre*, fiber is *fibre*.

Words that end in '-or' are spelled '-our': humor becomes *humour*, color becomes *colour*, odor becomes *odour*; labor becomes *labour*, although the *Labor* political party is intentionally spelled American-style ending in '*or*.

The ending 'ed' can become '*t*'. Burned is *burnt*, spoiled is *spoilt*, learned is *learnt*. Even "spelled" isn't spared, it's spelled *spelt*.

Some words ending in two L's in American usage get one L in Australian: enroll becomes *enrol*. Installment becomes *instalment*. Willful becomes *wilful*.

The letter S sometimes replaces the letter Z, as "criticize" becomes *criticise*, "cozy" becomes *cosy*.

C's can replace the letter S: "defense" becomes *defence,* though *defensive* is still spelled with an "S" and not a "C".

Hard C's can replace the letter K: "skeptic" is spelled *sceptic*.

Medical terms are spelled more in the Latin style: gynecologist is *gynaecologist*, orthopedist is *orthopaedist*. If you're looking up 'estrogen' in an Australian reference book, don't look under E; look under O. It's spelled *oestrogen*.

"Ass" is *arse*, but pronounced "*ahss*", since the R is silent.

I saw a bumper sticker that read: "Unless you're a *haemorrhoid*, stay off my *arse!*"

Double & triple letters & numbers   When an Australian says a number that has the same repeating digit or letter, they'll say it as *double* or *triple*. For example: the word 'tree' is verbally spelled "*T-R-double-E*". The number seventy-seven is spoken "*double-seven*", 999 is "*triple-nine*". Four repeating numbers are spoken double-double: **8888** is pronounced "*double-eight double-eight*".

This gets confusing when someone is rapidly firing off numbers and spellings. Since the speaker says the *double* or *triple* <u>before</u> they say the number or letter, you have to wait to hear what it's double or triple of, then quickly write down the multiple numbers or letters. By the time you've done that, the speaker is halfway through the next sentence. If it's critical, ask them to slow down or read it back to them.

Punctuation

A period (.) is called a *full stop.*

Quotation marks are also called *speech marks, inverted commas,* or *sixty-sixes and ninety-nines.*

Parentheses are called *brackets*.

Semi-colons are used in place of commas more than in America.

Pronunciation Differences   Accent differences aside, the most common differences are British-isms.

Aluminum is *aluminium*, with an additional letter "I". This comes from the British who discovered the metal in the first place (so they should be able to call it whatever they want). Originally they pronounced it the way Americans do. A few years later, British scientists decided to change the spelling and pronunciation to rhyme with the other metals, such as calcium, sodium, etc. The U.S. followed, but by the 1890s drifted back to the original pronunciation. Australians pronounce it as the Brits do: *aluminium*

Another interesting pronunciation difference is the name for a person who plays a saxophone. In the U.S., he or she is a saxophonist, in Australia they are a *sax-ah-fanist.* Here's some more:

Debut is pronounced *day-boo.*

Margarine is *mah-ja-reen.*

Nikon is *nick-on.*

Adidas is *ah-di-dahs*, with the emphasis on the first syllable.

Nike is *niik*, rhyming with "bike".

Fracas is *frah-kah.*

Debussy is *De-boo-see.*

Houston is *Hooston.*

January is *Jan-yu-ry.*

February is *Feb-yu-ry.*

Rottweiler is *Rot-wheeler.*

Melbourne is *Melbun.*

Cairns is *Kans.*

Schedule is *shed-yule.*

Asphault is *ash-velt*

Derby (as in a horse race) is *darby.*

Tuesday is *chews-day.*

Consumer is *kon-shu-mer.*

Kilometres is *kill-oh-meters.*

Methane is *mee-thane.*

Houghton (the winery) *Horton.*
Oregano is pronounced like the US state.
Nougat is *new-gah.*
Khaki is *kar-kay,* with emphasis on the first syllable.
MacKay (the city) is *mak-kai,* rhymes with sky.
Curiously, pronunciation within words can be inconsistent.
The Australian Banking Authority (the *ABA*) is sometimes
pronounced *ah-bee-ay.* It's subtle; you have to listen for it.

Accent   The Australian accent varies with region and the
background of the speaker. The basic variation sounds like
cockney spoken with a lazy lip, locked jaw and pinched
cheeks. Some accents are so heavy that, when laced with local
words and a few beers, one might as well be listening to
Swahili.   Some   Aussies   sound   British,   which   is
condescendingly attributed to *breeding* and expensive private
schools.

Generally, the vowels O and A tend to pick up an 'i' on the
end ("day" becomes *"die"*). I's, when they occur in the middle
of a word, can be pronounced as a double E ("gig" can be
pronounced *"geeg"*). The combination "ei," as in "eight,"
broadens out to become *"eye-t".* In some rural regions, "no"
becomes *noi.* The eastern states and country folk have stronger
accents.

This   can   lead   to   some   interesting   moments   of
misunderstanding. I recall a story that ran on ABC news radio
shortly after I'd arrived in Australia. The American secretary of
state was to meet with the Israeli prime minister. The word
"meet" is pronounced *"mate",* so it sounded like the
newsreader said, "Condoleezza Rice will be *"mating"* with
Arial Sharon in Jerusalem." This brought up an interesting
image, but both were single and they probably had a lot in
common.

R's are dropped at the end of most words: dollar becomes
dallah, rooster becomes *roostah,* car becomes *kah.* However,
just as in physics where energy is never lost, in Australian
'R's' are never lost. The dropped R's turn up at the end of
words ending in 'A': China becomes *"Choin-er",* Australia is
pronounced *"Straylier",* and idea becomes *"ai-deer".*

I once had a lively discussion about this with an Aussie

mate of mine who chided, "You Americans roll your R's."

I disagreed, "Italians roll their R's; American's just pronounce them." Americans pronounce whatever is on the page.

When the letter A occurs at the beginning of a word, it's pronounced as "ahh", as in "Al Bundy". So the City of Albany, Western Australia isn't "All-bany", like the capital of New York, but "*Al-bunny*". However, this is inconsistent, as the ABC is often pronounced "*Ah-bee-see.*"

S is pronounced like a Z, so the name "Les", sounds like "Lez".

To an American, New Zealanders won't sound much different than Australians. But after living in Australia for the better part of two decades I can easily hear the difference. Kiwi's shorten their vowels. "Ten" becomes "*tin*", "express" is pronounced "*expruse*", "friend" sounds like "*frind*", etc. The number 'six' sounds like "*sex*". My favourite is "fish and chips", which is pronounced "*fush an chups.*"

It's all a matter of perspective. Australians aren't speaking with an Australian accent; rather, you're hearing with an American one.

Verbal Communication   Nevertheless, Australians will sound different to you, and you'll sound different to them. For North Americans, when you go into a shop and ask for something with your accent, you'll probably be asked to repeat yourself. There are three basic reasons for this:

First, the clerk was caught off-guard by an accent they usually only hear on TV and hasn't actually paid attention to what you were saying. Second, they might not have understood everything you said because your pronunciation of the words differs from theirs. Third, you may have used the wrong term for the object you were asking for.

Australians call things by different names: *petrol* means 'gasoline', *flywire* means 'window screen', a *whipper-snipper* is a 'weed-wacker' or 'string trimmer', *the lot* means 'everything', as in "*a hamburger with the lot.*" Relax; don't take it personally. Think of it as a challenging word game: it's better than Scrabble because it's portable and it never ends.

One other reason why Aussies ask you to repeat yourself:

sometimes they just want to hear more of that 'charming American accent.' A North American accent will definitely be noticed and will even carry authority, you can use this to your advantage if you speak with calm confidence and use locally understandable terms.

Pronunciation becomes critical when taking information verbally, especially over the phone. When in doubt, have the speaker spell the key words for you. When I first moved to Perth, I had a job interview on Hay Street, but when the secretary gave me the address on the phone it sounded to me like 'High Street'. I drove around the same block for ten minutes looking for High Street, passing Hay Street each time until my mis-assumption struck me. I once worked for six months with a guy I thought was named '*Tiny*' (he was a big man so I thought it made sense in an Aussie-contrarian kind of way). On the last day I saw his name written out and it was '*Tony*'.

When I first *shifted* (moved) to Australia, I heard a radio ad for a store called "*Maya*", which, coming from California sounded like Spanish. I kept hearing these ads and started wondering why there would be a Mexican store in Perth profitable enough to buy that much airtime when I couldn't find a place to buy a taco. Eventually I figured out the store was '*Myer*', one of the more prestigious department store chains in the country

Once I was telling a car buff friend about an old classic Holden Premier automobile my father-in-law was selling. I pronounced it "<u>*Pree*</u>-*mere*", with the emphasis on the first syllable. He didn't seem know what I was talking about, which surprised me because he was locally born and a motorhead. Finally after three tries he exclaimed, "Oh, you mean a *Pra-meer,*" with the emphasis on the second syllable.

The point is, people are used to hearing familiar words spoken a certain way and to be understood you not only have to learn the words, you must also learn to pronounce them correctly.

Pronunciation of foreign words Aussies seem to do OK with French words, like *abattoir* (pronounced *ab-a-twa*) for slaughterhouse or *abseil* (*ab-sale*) for rappel, but Spanish seems to throw them.

When the Red Rooster fast food chain came up with a spicy Mexican chicken dish, they spelled it *pollo* (Spanish pronunciation: *poy-yo*), but the Aussies insisted on pronouncing it *polo*, like the game on horseback.

It wasn't just a fast food restaurant that was tripped up; When American executive Sol Trujillo (pronounced "True-hee-yo"), took over the privatization of Telstra (the Australian phone monopoly), the then Prime Minister, John Howard, went on live national television and introduced him as *"Sol True Jello."*

Times & dates   Hours and minutes are written slightly differently: 12:30 becomes *12.30*, and is pronounced *"half-twelve"*.

"A week from Saturday" becomes *"Saturday week."*

A *fortnight* is two weeks.

Dates are where things really get confusing. In Australia, the day comes first, then the month, then the year. So 9-11 is *11-9*. If you're doing business with both the U.S. and Australia this can really foul up bills, invoices, and *cheques* (checks), especially when the day is the twelfth or less. If in doubt, write the abbreviation of the month's name instead of the number.

Speaking the dates is similar, and to an American it may sound awkward: October twenty-first is pronounced *"Twenty-one October"*, or *"October twenty-one"*, "March second" is pronounced *"Two March"*, or *"March two"*. Australians rarely use the ordinals "th" or "ist" on the end of the dates: February tenth is *"ten February"* commonly abbreviated, even verbally, to *"ten Feb"*.

Music terms   There are different names for the notes:

A *semibreve* is a whole note.

A *minim* is a half note.

A *crotchet* (pronounced *crotch-et*) is a quarter note.

A *quaver* is an eighth note.

A *semiquaver* is a sixteenth note.

Slang is an expression of humour, it also gives one a sense of belonging and of having a bit of control over your circumstances. Aussies were originally convicts living under police control, thrown onto a hostile, unforgiving land far from home with little hope of return. Slang was something they could own: portable and full of rebellious sarcasm. The police were *the traps*, the property-owning class were *squatters*, Britain was *old blighty*, the Brits were *Poms*.

So much of everyday language is slang that it becomes hard to differentiate from proper Australian English. You could argue that in Australia there is no such thing as proper Australian English, it's all slang. Radio, TV, and print use slang as everyday words. I've heard news commentators on the air call a false statement a *porky* (rhyming slang: pork pie rhymes with lie, hence *porky*). A *newsreader* (anchor person) might talk about a thunderstorm *sarvo* (this afternoon). They'll refer to the St. Vincent De Paul charity as *Vinnie's*. The signs on the Salvation Army's stores read *The Salvos*. Sorting the slang out is a constant source of confusion and amusement. The dictionary in the back of this book has 1800 examples.

Holidays

With tradition stemming from British settlement, don't expect the Fourth of July to get more than a passing glance in Australia. Halloween was barely mentioned fifteen years ago but has thoroughly caught on. People who discounted it as an 'American thing' now decorate their houses and their kids go trick-or-treating, though many older Aussies refuse to give out candy saying "Why should we, this isn't America." Thanksgiving is irrelevant (November is late spring, hardly the time for a harvest festival and a heavy meal). Valentine's day is thought of as a marketing ploy to sell more stuff, though if you want to take your *partner* out that night you'd better *book a table*.

Christmas is the biggest holiday as in the rest of the western world, but it's a summer event, kind of like the Fourth of July but with presents. Almost everybody goes on *holiday* (vacation) from mid-December until Australia Day, which is 26 January, so don't count on getting any serious business done during that period, like having your car serviced or getting a *tradie* out to fix anything at your house. It's also known as the *Silly Season*.

Christmas *Down Under* can be a difficult time for those of

us who grew up in the Northern Hemisphere. Seeing Santa's in shorts and flip-flops and shopping for *Crissy pressies* (Christmas presents) in the middle of summer just seems wrong. Admiring snowman displays as you swelter in the summer heat and hearing Christmas carols about "Jack Frost nipping at your nose" when instead there's sweat dripping off it probably won't inspire you with your accustomed holiday spirit. You're more likely to get invited to a beach party or outdoor barbecue on Christmas Eve than a midnight mass. It truly feels more Fourth of July than Christmas.

Crissy traditions are a family *tea* (lunch) on Christmas Eve or Christmas Day, with the whole family sitting around a big table to celebrate. Next to each setting will be a double-ended party-popper. Your neighbour pulls one end while you pull the other, and when it pops apart, the person that ends up holding the largest piece gets the contents: a cheap toy, a joke on a piece of paper, and a crepe paper crown, which you're obliged to put on your head (looks tacky in a restaurant but everybody ends up wearing one).

If you're visiting Australia for a short stay during *Crissy*, it'll be interesting and fun, but if you're going to be living there a while, you'll learn to suffer through December. Take heart. Transplanted northern hemisphere-born Australians also dream of a white Christmas, and in the dark days of winter there are *Christmas in July* parties.

Boxing Day is the day after Christmas. No doubt you've seen it on the calendar and wondered what it meant. It has nothing to do with the pugilistic sport. It's British, going back to the class system, when servants served the wealthy on Christmas Day and were given the following day off, along with Christmas leftovers in a box. In practice it's an extension of Christmas, the party goes on.

New Year's Eve and New Year's Day are big, a great time to go to the beach, have a barbecue, and drink.

Australia Day January 26, is much like the Fourth of July, celebrating the beginning of British settlement in 1788, when the First Fleet sailed into Sydney Cove and started it all. The day is celebrated with picnics and parties and *sky shows* (fireworks) in major cities. Beware, sometimes these public celebrations get out of hand. If you're on the street that night and hear a group of rowdy drunks yelling "*Aussie, Aussie, Aussie! Oi, Oi, Oi!*", get out of the way.

Invasion Day   also January 26. If you're *Aboriginal or Torres Strait Islander*, this day is considered *Invasion Day*, and commemorates the day in 1788 that 60,000 years of the Indigenous way of life and culture began to end. Not all Aussies go out and celebrate, some march in protest. There is a movement to change the date so the holiday is a celebration of Australia for all people. Most white Australians dismiss this as heretical. Many support the Aboriginal people. This will develop over time.

The Queen's Birthday is celebrated at various times throughout the year, depending on which state you're in. When the Queen ascends to that great throne in the sky and her son or grandson takes over, it'll be the *King's Birthday*. It's sometimes in June in all states except Western Australia where it's in September and coincides with the *Royal Show* (which is the state fair), giving workers a day off to attend.

None of the Queen's birthday dates correspond to when the current monarch was actually born. It was originally proclaimed by King Edward the VII and is a celebration of the reigning British monarch. It wasn't Edward VII's birthday, either. His was in northern winter, but he wished it was in summer and since he was king he could do whatever he wanted, so he proclaimed his birthday to be in June. Of course, in Australia June is in the winter, but *no worries*, the only thing to know is that it's celebrated with a *long weekend* (three-day weekend), so the exact dates change to combine with a weekend, and if you're in Western Australia, it'll be a different day than if you're in the *Eastern States*.

Good Friday, Easter, and Easter Monday combine for a four-day *long weekend.* School term breaks usually occur around then. It's a good time to go out of town on a holiday. Good Friday is bigger than Easter Sunday, just about everything is closed that day. Don't plan on getting much business done around Easter.

Be aware that in some places it's illegal to sell alcoholic drinks without the customer also buying a full meal on Good

Friday and on Easter Monday.

Labour Day is a long weekend (varies by state) and celebrates the coming of the eight-hour workday. Currently, the workweek is thirty-eight hours.

ANZAC Day is April 25. *ANZAC* stands for *Australia and New Zealand Army Corps*. After Christmas, it's probably the most important holiday in Australia, commemorating the 1915 invasion of the heavily-defended Gallipoli Peninsula on the Mediterranean coast of Turkey during the First World War. Australian and New Zealand soldiers performed gallantly, but were defeated by the dug-in Turks during this ill-planned campaign led by arrogant and ignorant British senior officers. The ANZACs lost more than 10,000 men, the Brits lost 22,000, the French lost 27,000, and the Turks lost 57,000. It was a debacle. This wasn't the first or the last time the *Poms* considered their Australian offspring as expendable.

ANZAC Day now celebrates all the soldiers, sailors, airmen, and women who have served in the Australian armed forces in the Boer War, World Wars I and II, Korea, and Vietnam (yes, they were there, too), along with Malaysia, Indonesia, the Gulf War, East Timor, Afghanistan, Iraq I and II, and as part of UN peacekeeping forces. On ANZAC Day there are parades in all the capital cities and there is a nationally televised sunrise ceremony at the National War Memorial in the national capital, Canberra.

There are also ceremonies in small towns. Every Australian town has a war memorial, usually a stone obelisk in a town square, engraved with the names of fallen locals.

Melbourne Cup Day is the first Tuesday in November, when the most important horse race of the year occurs. It's the equivalent of Super Bowl Sunday. If you can't make it to the race in Melbourne, you can watch it on the *telly* with just about everyone else in the country. People generally take a long lunch and often don't return for work that *arvo* (afternoon). Parties and luncheons at *function centres* (banquet halls), taverns, and restaurants are de rigueur. Women traditionally dress up and wear fancy hats. Don't plan on getting any business done that afternoon.

Sorry Day is May 26, the official holiday to remember

and apologise to the Aboriginal people for what the white Europeans did to them. A minor holiday that's more of a protest than a celebration. No time is taken off from work. That week is *Reconciliation Week.*

Other holidays vary by state throughout the year. During *long weekends* the general attitude is that people don't know what the holiday stands for, nor do they care, but they do their best to enjoy it.

Birthdays are celebrated similar to those in North America, with a party, cake, and candles, and the singing of the same 'Happy Birthday' song. Birthday *prezzies* (presents) are often opened as the guests arrive with them.

Money

The Australian currency was originally English style: *Pound*s, *shillings* and *pence.* One pound was equal to twenty shillings, one shilling was equal to 12 pence; so one pound was equal to 240 pence. In 1966 the country went metric and the unit of money changed to the dollar. Like the U.S., there are 100 cents to the dollar. The nickname for the Australian dollar is the *Aussie.* The exchange rate between the Australian dollar and the U.S. dollar varies according to levels of international trade, interest rates, the economies of both nations and the perception of political uncertainty in the world.

The U.S. dollar is the world trading standard. When there is political uncertainty currency traders seek shelter in the U.S. economy by buying U.S. dollars or U.S. dollar investment instruments like bonds, gold shares, etc.

The Aussie is also rated against all the world currencies, the UK pound, the Japanese Yen and Chinese renminbi, etc., though the most common index is the U.S. dollar.

In 1974, one Australian dollar was worth more than the U.S. dollar, $1.43 U.S. In 2001 it was as low as 50 cents U.S. In 2010, with the US in the financial crisis and the Australian mining industry profiting in trade with China it reached parity, or was worth the same. During the initial days of COVID19 2020 it was US$.64. As of this writing Aug 2020, it's US$.72, the increase attributed to the rise in iron ore prices and the decline of the U.S dollar.

A low Australian dollar means exports are more profitable, but imports are more costly. The Reserve Bank of Australia, the central bank and banknote issuing authority, prefers a low *Aussie*, in the 65-70 cent U.S. range.

For international money trading and in dealing with the exchange rate, Australian dollars are written A$ or AUD. Prices within the country will just have the '$,' as all prices are in Australian dollars unless otherwise noted.

U.S. dollars are US$ or $US. Conversion rates are also commonly quoted in euros and yen. A great website for monetary exchange rates is **www.x-rates.com** [also see section on **tourist money exchanging** below.]

Currency   Bills are different colours, depending upon denomination ($50 bills are sometimes called *pineapples*, as per the colour). They also vary slightly in size, increasing with the value of the bill. They're made of polypropylene polymer plastic, not paper, and are water-proof and not tearable.

Denominations are: $5, $10, $20, $50, $100.

Coins are 5-cent, 10-cent, 20-cent, 50-cent, 1-dollar and 2-dollar. The 50-cent piece isn't round, but 12-sided. The $2 coin is about 1/3 smaller than the $1 coin (this is opposite in New Zealand, so beware). The one and two-dollar coins are gold in colour and are called *gold coins* (though they're not made of gold) to differentiate them from the lesser denominations. Charitable and volunteer groups often request a *gold coin donation*.

There is no 1-cent denomination coin. Cash transactions that come to less than 5-cents are rounded up or down to the closest 5-cents. Credit card and *cheque* (check) transactions use exact cents.

A ten percent sales tax, called *GST* for *Goods and Services Tax* is included in the price of anything you buy. So you don't have to add sales tax when you estimate how much something costs, it's already figured in. There's no GST on food from grocery stores or on some medical expenses.

Tourist money exchanging   The best way to get the most for your money is to use your American credit cards, since the exchange rate will be close to market rate that day.

The best way to get cash in Australia is to use ATMs, but

check with your American bank to see which Australian bank has the best deal for you fee-wise. Avoid getting a cash advance on your credit card, interest is charged from day one, along with fees

It's a good idea to have a few hundred dollars in Aussie currency when you arrive in the country, but the exchange rates at airport kiosks can be ridiculous. You can order Australian cash through your American bank before you leave home.

Banking

The four major banks are ANZ (pronounced *A-N-Zed*), Westpac, NAB (National Australia Bank), and Commonwealth. They're known as the *Big Four*. There are also smaller banks and credit unions. Most banks seem to follow a Monty Python approach to business and bureaucracy, so come armed with patience. If you don't like the answer you get, ask someone else (in Australia, an organization is truly a group of individuals). Just when you think everybody there is hopeless, someone will come through for you.

Banking hours are usually 9-5 Monday thru Friday and some branches are open Saturday mornings.

There are smaller banks that offer alternatives. One is Benidgo Community Banks, which are franchises and are the fastest-growing banks in the country. They were started in response to people's unhappiness with the cavalier treatment that the Big Four dish out to little people (and even not-so-little people). Bendigo banks *plough* their profits back into the community, as well as paying modest dividends to their shareholders. They keep charges as low as possible and are responsive to their clientele because the clientele owns the bank.

The equivalent of a U.S. Certificate of Deposit (CD) is called a *Term Deposit (TD)*. Checks are spelled *cheques*. Fees are charged on most transactions.

The Australian Government guarantees deposits up to $250,000 in *Authorised Deposit-taking Institutions (ADIs)* such as banks, building societies or credit unions. This means that if something happens to the bank, this money is guaranteed by the government to be paid back to you.

Identification   To open a bank account, to apply for a driver's license, or to enter into other bureaucratic situations, you'll need ID. Identification has been formalized into a *100 Points System*, i.e. you'll be required to produce *100 points of identification.* Your passport is worth 70 points, a driver's license is 40 points, a credit card or a Medicare card is 25 points, utility bills are 20 points.

Keeping your old American bank accounts   If you're moving to Australia but will still have dealings in your former country, you might want to hang onto your old bank account and credit card to make transactions easier. To do this, you might also have to set up a private post office box in your old country and have the service forward your mail every month. [for more information, see the section on **postal matters**] or use a friend's or relative's address. I kept a post box there for about 15 years but finally abandoned it when I no longer received anything important.

Credit cards work the same as in North America. Credit cards can be used to purchase on credit or *EFTPOS* (*electronic funds transfer at point of sale*), which is a debit card linked to either a *cheque* or savings account. When you put your card into the reader in a shop, you choose account, "credit," "savings," or "chequing." If it's a foreign card, it will probably only work on "credit".

Foreign credit cards may require a signature on the *docket* (receipt). 4-digit PIN numbers are issued with Australian credit cards. At the register you can *Pay Pass* by tapping your card on the icon on the reader, or you can insert the card into the reader, chose credit, or savings, or *cheque* if using it as a debit card, then key in your 4-digit PIN, wait for the prompt to remove the card. If the reader doesn't accept the chip, try swiping the strip-side down the channel on the side of the reader. PIN numbers aren't required under a certain amount, usually around $30, the reader just displays 'remove card' after the amount comes up.

ATMs are available outside banks, in shopping *centres*, in supermarkets, and in some *servos* (service stations). They work the same as in America. You can access an American account at an ATM in Australia, but before leaving home, check to see if your bank has an arrangement with one of the Australian banks to give you a break on fees. Be aware that cash advances charge interest from day-one.

As Australia moves into a cashless economy branches with ATMs are getting harder to find. You can get additional cash with your purchase at a supermarket, but only on your debit account.

Cheques are less common than in the U.S. Most people don't have *cheque* accounts at all. Credit cards, used either as credit or to debit (*EFTPOS*) from savings, are standard. Many people don't even carry cash. Cheques are written the same as in the U.S. Some have "not negotiable" written vertically across the centre, which means they can only be deposited, not cashed. Deposit slips are sometimes in the back of the chequebook and sometimes in a separate book.

Bank Cheques are the same as an American cashiers' check. It's what you use when you need a certified check to buy a car or lease an apartment. You get them at your bank for a small fee.

Internet banking is the standard way to pay your bills It's called *B-pay*, the bank number and reference number you enter are on the bill. You can set up auto-pay for recurring bills and for ones that vary. You can also pay your bills by credit card on line.

Electronic transfers are directly paying from one person's account to another. You'll need the person's name, bank branch name, *BSB* number (usually six digits), and account number (six digits or more). Most businesses pay employees and contractors by this *direct deposit* method.

Phone banking using your credit card is common, with automated systems for paying bills and transferring funds. Phone numbers will be on the bill.

Paying bills at the Post Office is an option if you can't get online. Just go into an Australia Post shop and you can pay your utility bills, car registration, etc with cash or credit card or EFTPOS at the counter.

Wiring funds is the best way for long-term residents to get large sums of money to Australia. You'll need an Australian bank account to receive wired money. You'll give the sending institution your name, account name, *Swift Code*, *BSB* number, and account number. Before you make a move, check with the banks on both ends.

If you're migrating and don't already have your own Australian bank account, you can wire money to a friend or relative in Australia. If it's a large amount, they can open an account in their name and list it *In Trust* to your name. However, beware: they may have to show it on their taxes. *Don't do this if the money will be sitting in their account at the end of the tax year, June 30th.*

Of course, exchange rates constantly fluctuate and you'll want to time your move to your best advantage. A weak Aussie dollar and a strong U.S. dollar means you can buy more Aussie dollars for the same amount of U.S. dollars. When you start the transaction, you'll have to specify an amount in Australian dollars, and when it goes through, the proper amount of U.S. dollars will be deducted from the sending account. There will be fees, and the exchange rate will probably be slightly higher than the posted rate because the banks on both ends will take a cut. Time your move carefully; you can make a bit of pocket change if you catch the cycle—but you can also get burned.

FYI   The *Big Four* Australian banks (ANZ, Commonwealth, NAB and Westpac) have had record profits year after year, charging customers for every little thing they do, and for things they don't.

In 2017 a Royal Banking Commission was established to inquire into the major banks' abusive practices. What they found was astonishing. Banks had been billing estates of deceased account holders for services long after they had died. Commonwealth Bank had been allowing large sums of money to be laundered by drug cartels and terrorist groups. Westpac had to refund A$65 million in benefits to customers they had illegally withheld. NAB refunded millions to customers who had been aggressively market financial services they didn't need. ANZ had been involved in a bank-swap rate-fraud which they settled before the Commission began.

There are a wide range of accounts available, so take the time to shop around before opening one.

Investing

Stocks are called *shares*, the stock market is the *share market* (also called the *Bourse*). Shares are traded through brokers and online brokerages (such as banks, etc.), just as in the U.S.

Preference shares are preferred stocks.

The Australian Shares Exchange is the *ASX*. All publicly traded companies are registered with *ASICS* (the Australian Securities and Investments Commission) equivalent to the U.S. Securities and Exchange Commission. All securities traded online with the ASX are cleared and settled through *CHESS* (Clearing House Electronic Sub-register System), which is owned by *ASTC*, the Australian Stock Exchange Settlement and Transfer Corporation, which is owned by the ASX.

Franking   The *Franking System* refers to the taxation of dividends. *Franking Credits* or *Imputation Credits* are issued on dividends. Companies pay taxes on profits before they pay out dividends, and the reasoning is it would be unfair to charge tax on the dividends because tax has already been paid on them, otherwise they would be double-taxed. Double taxation is avoided by allowing the investor a tax credit for the tax already paid by the companies. In this case, shares are called *Fully Franked*. This applies only to Australian companies and investors who are Australian citizens or legal residents.

What does all this mean? When you have *Franked Shares,* you get a credit on the dividend income on your taxes equal to the amount already taxed.

For retirement funds see *Superannuation*.

Managing American Stock Accounts   Not all American brokerages will allow an American citizen residing in a foreign country to manage a portfolio of American stocks through that brokerage. Post 9-11, the U.S. Congress passed the Patriot Act which, amongst other things, scrutinizes overseas financial transactions and holdings of Americans, and some brokerages just don't an to be bothered. I've had to change brokerages twice since I moved to Australia, after the firms decided that they didn't want to deal with a client with a foreign address, even though I was an American citizen with an unblemished tax history.

Entering the country

Visas   Unless you're a citizen of Australia or New Zealand, or have Australian permanent residency status, you'll need a visa or an Electronic Travel Authority (ETA) to enter Australia. An ETA can be obtained online at www.eta.homeaffairs.gov.au/ETAS3/etas.

The basic tourist visa is good for a year, but you can only stay for three months at a time, though you can re-enter as many times as you'd like. You aren't eligible to work but you can go to school.

For longer stays you can get a twelve-month visa for A$140.

There are also study visa's, skilled worker visa's, refugee and humanitarian visa's, joining your partner visa's, senior visa's. Visit immi.homeaffairs.gov.au/visas for more details.

When you arrive in Australia, you'll find that it's not a third world country. There will be no machine gun-toting soldiers waiting for you in customs. Instead, there will be a nicely dressed immigration agent sitting behind a counter who will check your documents. If all is in order, the agent will direct you to another room where a friendly customs agent may wish to look in your bags.

Quarantine   There are strict quarantine laws. Australia is surrounded on all four sides by large bodies of saltwater which has make it easier to keep out all sorts of unwanted diseases and pests, like rabies, bird flu, and mad cow disease. We managed to keep the COVID pandemic to a controlled minimum. Some things you'll have to declare, have inspected and probably confiscated: honey and honey products, (due to hive diseases), fruit, nuts, seeds, raw food, raw wood products. It's best to not bother with these unless it's really important to you.

Be aware of the friendly dogs strolling on their *leads* (leashes) through the terminal accompanied by uniformed customs agents. These dogs have amazing powers of scent and if there's anything in your bag that shouldn't be there, the dog will smell it and quietly sit down next to you and wait to be rewarded with a doggy treat by the agent. After rewarding the dog, the agent will ask to look in your bag. Don't be foolish; heed the quarantine notices and comply. You will be caught, the dogs love their treats.

Migration   If you want to migrate to Australia you start by applying for Permanent Residency. The best way is to hire a <u>registered</u> migration agent. Make sure they are registered, anyone can claim to be an expert in immigration. The best are lawyers, they know how it works and will get you through much quicker than you could on your own.

The cheapest is a semi-do-it-yourself, they help you file and you follow up on your own, rates vary from $1200 to $2700 per person, depending on their circumstance.

If you want to hire someone to handle the whole process of applying for a business talent visa it will cost about $15,000. We did the latter and got lucky as our move happened as the Aussie dollar rose ten-cents, and we made it back the first year.

There are several schemes to gain residency in Australia, the details are far too involved and boring to go into in this book. Twenty-five years ago there were consulates in major American cities and you started the process through them. Now most are closed and it's all done online. Skilled workers are in demand, successful immigration is possible, and for the right people, very likely. Temporary visas are called 457 Visas. The Department of Home Affairs handles all this, https://immi.homeaffairs.gov.au/ is the place to make contact. Melbourne is very interested in migrants, their website is www.liveinmelbourne.vic.gov.au.

Citizenship   First you become a *Permanent Resident* [see next chapter] and live in Australia on a valid visa for four years and not have been out of the country for more than twelve months in that time, including no more than 90 days in total during the last twelve months. Then you can begin the citizenship process. They try to process the applications in three months.

Once you are accepted you will be interviewed and will take a citizenship tests, which covers an understanding of how Australia works and what Australian values are. You should download '*Our Common Bond*' from the home affairs website and study up on it.

I took it as a good excuse to study it and read the
constitution and Australian history and got a pretty good
picture of the country and how it worked. Eventually we got
called for the interview. My family and I reported to the
immigration office in Perth. After waiting a short time we were
asked to go to a certain window where a clerk checked our
paperwork, then asked me, "Do you understand Australian
values?" I said yes, and he signed us off. I then asked if he was
going to give us some sort of knowledge test. Matter-of-factly
he replied, "That would only show if you were good at
memorizing facts, we want you to understand them." And that
was that. We were sworn in as citizens in a ceremony on
Australia Day at our local shire council.

Permanent Residency

This is the pre-condition to citizenship. It allows you to
stay in the country indefinitely, and many migrants live under
this status their whole lives as it allows them almost all the
rights of citizenships: healthcare, work, study and welfare
benefits. They can even vote in some local elections. They
cannot be issued an Australian Passport.

The most common permanent residencies are family-
related, skilled worker or business investment. There is also
retirement, former resident, distinguished talent and
humanitarian/refugee. For more detailed information and how
to apply, go to immi.homeaffairs.gov.au/visas/permanent-
reside .

My wife and I applied for Permanent Residency in 2002.
We caught the last of the business permanent residency
migrations, I was bringing my movie cameraman equipment
rental business with me. That category ended that year, if I had
applied six-months later I would have had to come in on a
skills visa and I'm not sure it would have worked (and I might
be writing this book about Costa Rica or Hawaii). Knowing
that there was a bureaucratic mountain to climb, we hired a
registered migration agent. We filled out a lot of forms and
faxed a lot of documents. We waited; our lives on hold. We
went to work, the kids went to school, but we were in a kind of
limbo, waiting, imagining our applications slowly making their
way through some anonymous offices somewhere. The

migration agent kept us updated. Finally, after a year, we were asked to do a phone interview. We passed and started the process of selling all our stuff and moving.

Shipping your household goods to Australia
Once you've been accepted, you'll have to send your stuff there. If you can fit it in a few suitcases you're home free. If it's a few additional boxes, just send them by sea through the mail, though this may take a month or so. Shipping by air can be very expensive [see section on **Postal System-Shipping**].

The most efficient way to ship an entire household is in your own sea container. There are many firms that specialize in this. They'll send an agent to your home to estimate costs based on how large a container you'll need and how much time will it will take to pack it, and will give you a bid. Get recent referrals—some of these companies are good, some are bad, some are very bad. Ours was just bad—it got there but with a lot of hassle. If it's very bad you'll never see it again, it'll disappear. Having professional movers pack your stuff is mandatory for post-9-11 security reasons and insurance coverage.

Once you've chosen a shipper, they'll contract to have an appropriate-sized sea container trucked to your home, and contract out for a local moving company to pack your goods into boxes, inventoried, and loaded into the container.

The filled container will be trucked to the closest major seaport and loaded onto a ship. The sea leg takes three to five weeks from the U.S. west coast, a few weeks longer from the east coast.   Transit time also depends on which coast of Australia it's going to. From Los Angeles to Sydney the container will likely travel all the way on the same ship. Shipments to Perth will change boats in Singapore. You'll be able to track the container's progress on the internet, using the container number (painted on the end of the container). Write it down before the truck leaves your house.

The shipper will contract with a local *removals* (moving) company on the Australian end. The container will be trucked to a warehouse and unloaded, and all the goods put into quarantine for customs inspection. Don't ship any kind of raw wood, plants or guns. Once inspection has been completed and administrative fees paid, it will be delivered to your new home.

Generally, migrants can bring in their personal goods and work tools duty-free if they've owned them for one year or more. If it's less than a year old and you declare it, you'll have to pay ten-percent *GST* (*Goods and Services Tax*) on it. Migrants can bring in one vehicle per adult duty-free as long as that vehicle has been in that person's name for at least one year [see **importing a vehicle from America**].

In 2003, when we did this dance, we got estimates from several Los Angeles-based shippers. We chose the one who's salesman convinced us they were the best because they did everything with their own trained, in-house, professional staff. This turned out to not be the case. A contractor dropped off a trailer with the container on it, a crew of non-English speaking day-labourers arrived to pack our household goods, they were rude and not careful. We tried calling the shipper's salesman but he wouldn't return our phone calls. By then it was too late to do anything about it, our plane tickets were booked and the new owners were taking over the house the next day.

The packers mixed up the items, mislabelled the boxes, botched the shipping manifest and left our goods overnight in the unlocked sea container in front of our house. They had three teams packing, so my wife and I could only supervise two of them, and which ever one we weren't watching just threw stuff in boxes. The pièce de résistance was the packers intentionally burying our kids' battery-powered karaoke machine blaring a Mexican radio station in the bottom of the load. As the container was towed away toward LA Harbor, we could hear mariachi music, and imagined it playing deep in the bowels of the ship until it got out of range off-shore, then hissing static for a week until the batteries died. On the receiving-end the manifest was so incomprehensible it had to be completely rewritten to pass Australian customs (almost everything was marked "miscellaneous"). It took us months to sort things out during the unpacking. Amazingly, almost everything survived intact, except for the glassware they'd packed with our garden tools. Learn from our mistake, get recent references.

When shipping in a sea container, weight is usually not the

limiting issue; it's one of bulk, so hang onto those exercise weights and get rid of that stinky old couch. I even shipped a motorcycle over in our container, with its own proper paperwork [see **importing a vehicle from America**]. When I dropped the motorcycle off at the shipper I discovered they were actually in the vehicle-exporting business, they were just experimenting with shipping households as a side-line.

Seasons

Being below the equator in the Southern Hemisphere, the seasons are reversed. Also, curiously, in Australia the seasons don't begin on the solstices or the equinoxes as in America (the 21st day of March, June, September, and December), but on the first day of that month. So winter begins 1 June, spring begins 1 September, summer begins 1 December, and autumn begins 1 March. Notice I said 'autumn', not 'fall'. The term "fall" isn't used interchangeably with 'autumn'. My guess is that it's because leaves don't fall seasonably from eucalyptus trees.

A fluke: on a trip to Australia a few years before we migrated I went through all four seasons in three weeks: I left the U.S. in Northern Hemisphere late spring and arrived in Australia where it was Southern Hemisphere late autumn. A few weeks later, while I was still in Australia, the season changed to winter, and when I returned to the U.S. it was Northern Hemisphere summer. I went through all four seasons in three weeks.

Time difference

Sydney on the east coast is the same time as Vladivostok; Perth on the west coast, is the same time as Hong Kong. Australia is twelve to fifteen hours ahead of the U.S., depending on local time zones and daylight savings. It's ahead because it's across the International Date Line, which lies in mid-Pacific, near Fiji.

Sunday afternoon in Los Angeles is Monday morning in Sydney. Before we moved to Australia, my mother-in-law would call us during her Monday morning commute in Perth and catch us Sunday afternoon in LA.

Because not all Australian states have daylight savings

time, and because not all U.S. states have daylight savings times, a chart would be large, unwieldy, and confusing. For detailed listings, there are several websites: **www.timeanddate.com/worldclock** or just Google search *'what time is it in...'*

Time zones   It can get a bit silly: Sydney and Melbourne are two hours ahead of Perth and one-half hour ahead of Adelaide and Darwin. Yes, there are half-hour time zones, in fact, diving across the Nullarbor plane in the centre of the country there are fifteen minute time zones.

During *Australian Standard Time*, late April to late October (exact dates vary from state to state):

When it's 12 noon in Sydney, it's:

12 noon in Melbourne, Canberra, Hobart, and Brisbane,

11:30 a.m. in Adelaide and Darwin,

10:00 a.m. in Perth.

During *Australian daylight savings time*, October to April (exact dates vary from state to state; see below):

When it's 12 noon in Sydney, it's:

12 noon in Melbourne, Canberra, and Hobart,

11:30 a.m. in Adelaide,

11:00 a.m. in Brisbane,

10:30 a.m. in Darwin,

9:00 a.m. in Perth.

Obviously, this gets confusing. It's possible for it to simultaneously be eight-ten in Darwin and twenty minutes to nine in Brisbane. Since all the states change on different dates, there's a month in spring and another in autumn when you don't know what time it is anywhere else.

Daylight savings time changes at the beginning of April and October for Tasmania, the end of April and October for New South Wales, Victoria, South Australia, and the ACT (Australian Capital Territory). Western Australia, Queensland and the Northern Territory don't have daylight savings time.

When I arrived in Western Australia in 2003 there was no daylight savings time, but in 2006 the government entered into a three-year trial. At the end of the trial they had a referendum and the voters voted it out. The joke was that they didn't want the curtains to fade or to confuse the cows about when to give milk. Now, in December in Perth, first light is at 4:30 am, great if you're an early riser.

Shopping

In the service sector, eye-contact avoidance is an art, you'll learn to wait.

There's a different attitude amongst staff in the Australian service sector. It's common to approach the counter at a store and have the clerk completely ignore you while he or she finishes some other task they've begun. They won't look up to acknowledge you; they'll just let you stand there and wait until they've finished, then they'll turn to you and proceed as if you'd just appeared. If a salesperson does acknowledge you, they'll usually say something like, *"Won't be a sec"* and go about their business, ignoring you until they're ready to help you. After this happens a few times, you come to realize that this is true: it won't be a *"sec"*, it'll be a lot longer.

Other times you'll find two or three clerks waiting on one customer. They know you're there, but rarely will one break away to help you or to even acknowledge you with a *"Won't be a sec."* Americans find this rude but Australians are used to it and they don't expect anything different. If you ask someone about it, they just shrug and say, "That's the way it is." And if they hear your ascent and they've been to the U.S. they'll usually add, "Service *is* a lot better in America." I attribute this attitude to egalitarianism, Aussies don't like to feel subservient to anyone, and if someone is behind a counter they have the power, if for just a moment. (Sometimes they'll say, *"Just a mo,"* Aussie for "Just a moment." Perhaps this is cultural, a resentment stemming from the convict days? Of course, this isn't true for all stores and for all salespeople, some are just as attendant and provide as good service as in any store in North America, but it's common enough to mention, don't take it personally.

On the other hand, salespeople don't seem to be as aggressive as in the U.S., they aren't as driven to make a sale. If they don't have what you're asking for, instead of trying to talk you into buying something else they have in stock, they'll happily direct you to a competing shop that might have what you want.

There are two major supermarket chains: Coles and Woolworth's (aka *Woolie's*). These two giants have gradually bought up the smaller market chains, which is why they are called the *Duopoly*. A distant third is IGA (Independent Grocers of Australia), a franchise owned by Metcash with individual stores independently owned: IGA markets are usually in smaller neighbourhoods and are often the only market in rural towns. European giant Aldi has broken in and created a niche, but most people shop at either Coles or Woolies.

Between the two of them they own, or owned, just about every major retail shop in the country.

Woolworth's is the largest food retailer, with 995 grocery stores nationwide (up from 700 in 2007 when I wrote the first edition of this book). Besides supermarkets, Woolie's owns 1200 BWS liquor stores, 215 Dan Murphy liquor stores, 182 *Big W* (a chain much like Target in the U.S.), hundreds of Caltex petrol stations and the ALH Group which owns 300 old classic hotel/pubs around the country.

Coles has 806 Supermarkets, 712 Coles Express outlets (at Shell petrol stations), 894 liquor stores under the names Liquorland, Vintage Cellars and First Choice Liquor, plus Coles-branded financial services and 88 Spirit Hotels.

Coles also owned Kmart, Target, Bunnings (like Home Depot), and Office Works (like Staples). The Coles group was purchased in 2007 by conglomerate Wesfarmers who, in 2018 spun the Coles food-related businesses off and retained the other retailers.

Target is sometimes sarcastically called *Tar-jay* emulating a French pronunciation as it portends to be an upscale version of Kmart, both owned by Wesfarmers though both have similar motifs. It seemed odd to me that the company was paying rent for two large, similar stores, usually just a few doors apart, on hundreds of shopping centres all across the country. Was Wesfarmers trying to occupy a large space in the centres so other competitors couldn't move in? During the Covid-19 pandemic economic downturn, Wesfarmers took advantage of the situation to resolve this. They announced closing 160 struggling Targets, renaming some as Kmarts. Analysts said Kmarts were out-selling Target stores, the Kmarts were better stocked and organized. The biggest losers are the people in rural towns who will lose their smaller *Country Target* branches, they have few alternatives being hundreds of kilometres from a city shopping centre.

Shopping terms   In Australia a *shopping centre* is what Americans would call a mall, while a *mall* is a shopping street that is closed to car traffic. A shopping centre can also be called a *shoppingtown*.

One doesn't go to the store, one goes to the *shops*.

Supermarkets are often in the *centre* of indoor shopping centres, you can't enter directly into the market but instead must walk through a *centre* past several other shops to get to the market. This can seem inconvenient to Americans, who are used to parking in front of the market and going directly inside.

Supermarkets tend to be scaled-down, about 1/3 smaller than in North America; this includes the aisles, which are narrower and more easily congested when the store is busy. Shopping carts are called *trolleys*, and one pushes them on the left side of the aisle, the same as when driving a car on the road.

Most supermarkets are open until 9pm, though some close earlier and are open limited hours *at* weekends.

Fruit and veg markets offer better produce than most grocery stores, as do butchers', fish stores and bakeries. Most of the larger Coles and Woolies have such sections in the supermarket, but the independent shops, which are usually just outside the markets, are cheaper and have better quality products.

A *chemist* is a pharmacy. Many non-prescription drugs are kept behind the counter and must be requested, even though you don't need a prescription for them. The clerk will question you to make sure you know what you're planning on taking. Conversely, some drugs that need prescriptions in the U.S. don't require them in Australia. Many drugs, like Tylenol and Advil, go by different names [see section on **health care, medical terms**.]

Prescription drugs are a lot cheaper than in the US, because of the *Pharmaceutical Benefits Scheme (PBS)*. PBS is a program of the Australian Government that provides subsidised prescription drugs to residents of Australia, as well as certain foreign visitors covered by a Reciprocal Health Care Agreement. When I pick up my prescriptions at the *chemist* I'm usually pleasantly surprised, based on my previous life in the U.S. I'm expecting a $75 bill, and instead it's $15.

There are family-owned corner groceries and deli's, they are open later and on weekends. Most *petrol stations* (gas stations) have a convenience store inside with basic groceries, snacks and hot fast-food.

Newsagents have a more complete stock of newspapers, magazines, stationary, and phone cards than supermarkets, but their primary business is selling lottery tickets, they're usually only open business hours, 9:00 a.m. to 6:00 p.m.

Beer, wine, and hard liquor is available only at *bottle shops*. Woolworth's and Coles usually have a bottle shop next to their supermarkets. Others are free-standing shops. Taverns and pubs have bottle shops for after-hour and weekend sales. Drive-thru liquor stores are common. When it comes to buying beer from a shop, Australians usually buy a carton (*slab, box*), not a six-pack. Beer is pricey, about $20 for a six pack but $40-50 for a *slab,* which is 4 six-packs. When you drop by someone's house to watch sports or for a BBQ you bring your own beer in an *eskie* (ice chest), and take home what you don't drink. The same with wine.

In many cities there are *markets*, not to be confused with supermarkets or grocery stores. These *markets* are more like a bazaar: a large enclosed area with separate stalls selling various products: meat, fresh fish, produce, luggage, clothes, toys, DVDs, CDs, etc. Often these are only open Thursdays, Fridays, and weekends and are located in old warehouses, military depots, and former train stations. You can get some great deals there, and a lot of junk. Farmers or community markets are often held weekends in town centres, parks, and on streets closed for the day. It's how a lot of people stock up on their fruit and *veg* for the week.

Garage sales are usually held on Sunday mornings (church-going isn't big in Australia, so there's little conflict). Many garage sales are advertised in the Sunday paper or in local classified papers, while some people just put up a handwritten sign taped to a cardboard box on the closest street corner.

Shopping hours

Shopping hours were restricted by law and varied from state to state, but luckily most of that has gone away. Western Australia's 2019 shopping hours for example:

8 am to 9 pm Monday-Friday,
8 am to 5 pm Saturday
11am to 5 pm Sunday and public holidays
Closed Christmas Day, Good Friday and ANZAC Day

This is set and enforced by state law. Restaurants, cafes, short term markets (set up for the day) and shops on Rottnest island are not restricted.

In the past shopping hours were repressive. In *WA* (Western Australia) the hours, dictated by state law, saw most shops closed evenings and Sundays except for neighbourhood deli's and smaller supermarkets (it was based on how many workers the shop employed). Liquor stores were closed Sunday, but you could buy *grog* at a pub liquor store, which had higher prices. Most shops closed at 5 pm weeknights, except for *Thursday late night shopping* when shops closed at 9. I found shopping centres on Thursday night were almost too crowded to get any shopping done. In the sixties, Petrol stations were closed on Sundays, with *rostered stations* (selected stations on a rotating basis) the only ones open, but they were few and far between, and you could run out of petrol trying to find one. By 2010 most shopping hours had been removed. During the mining boom many people had moved to WA from other countries where shopping wasn't restricted, and that brought pressure on the state government. There are still shopping hours but they are much looser.

Car dealership hours are still restricted in Western Australia:

8 am to 6 pm Monday, Tuesday, Thursday, Friday

8am to 9 pm Wednesday
8 am to 1 pm Saturday
Closed Sundays and public holidays

Car dealers closed on Sunday was inconceivable to me, coming from Southern California where car salesmen are just slightly less aggressive than hungry sharks. On a Saturday afternoon, shortly after my arrival in Perth, I walked onto a Toyota lot looking to buy a used Landcruiser for myself and a Camry for my wife. I said *g'day* to the salesman and instead of a friendly reply he curtly informed me they were about to close and I would have to leave. I looked at my watch, it was 12:45 pm. I told him I'd just arrived in the country and was looking to buy two cars, with cash, and expected that to get his attention. He wasn't the least bit impressed, he said they were closing. I asked what time they opened tomorrow, which was Sunday, and he said they didn't, come back on Monday. I said I couldn't believe car dealerships were closed on Sunday and he replied the rationale was employees need family time, and he closed the door in my face. I wondered if his family time was actually on the golf course with his mates. Either way, it was evidence we weren't in Kansas anymore, we were in a different kind of Oz.

Bars once had a 6 pm closing time; workers, mostly men, would drop in after work and drink as much as they could in that hour. It became known as the *6 o'clock swill*. It started during WWI as an austerity measure and was retained into the 1960's as an attempt to improve public morality. It varied from state to state. In those days women weren't allowed in the general pub, they drank separately in a *ladies lounge*. Now bars and pubs can stay open until 3 am or later and everyone can drink. It doesn't mean they have to stay open, some are closed by 10 pm.

So, what does this mean to you? If you're new in town, check out the local shopping hours. And if you're in a bind, you can buy a *pie* (meat pie) and a *litre* (quart) of milk at a petrol station, or a *stubbie* or a *slab* at the corner tavern.

Public toilets

Don't ask for the men's room, ladies room, rest room, or powder room; ask for the *male* or *female toilet.* Sounds crude, but it's what they call it. Other euphemisms for the toilet are: *the loo, the gents, the ladies, the bog,* and *the dunny.*

Ensuite means your accommodation will have a toilet and bathroom. *Ablutions* are the toilet and shower *block* in a *caravan* park (campground).

Not all small restaurants will have a toilet. Don't be surprised if, when you ask for one, you're directed down the street to the public park or library.

Paper towels are not always supplied in public toilets. Electric hand dryers are usually provided but often don't work; otherwise do what the Aussies do, air dry them or wipe them on your pants. It's likely so hot they'll be dry in a minute.

Likewise, toilet seat covers are not found, the only place I've seen them is in the toilets in the Sydney airport.

Food

Australians are blessed with fresh air, clean water and healthy food. Genetically modified food products are generally banned, with the exception of cotton, canola and safflower. Cows are grass-fed and not put into American-style feed lots. That said, most of the salmon available is Tasmanian farmed Atlantic salmon which isn't healthy, Roundup is used on many dry crops, and sheep and cattle are shipped live, up to 50,000 at a time, to Southeast Asia and the middle east. No one's perfect.

But generally, the food here is healthier than in most places in the world. Fast food and processed foods are available, but one can easily find organic, vegan, gluten-free and free-range products.

For a quick lunch you can get McDonalds and KFC, but you can also choose a locally-baked meat or vegetable pie or a *kebab (felafel).* There are lots of locally-owned fresh produce shops, butcher shops and fish markets. Any imported food has to be labelled as such. When it comes to food we're pretty responsible.

However, Australia is the only country I know of where we eat the animals on our official Coat of Arms: kangaroo and emu.

Kangaroo is not an endangered species, where I live I see dozens of them daily, grazing in fields between my house and the freeway. There are an estimated 44 million of them, almost twice the human population. Kangaroo tastes like venison (it has a similar life and diet as deer which are not native to Australia). It is available in supermarkets; I usually marinate it with teriyaki or BBQ sauce to eliminate the slightly gamey taste. The trick is to not over-cook it. It is the leanest red meat, and it'll put a spring in your step.

Emu is similar to an ostrich, and is also not an endangered species. When you drive in agricultural areas you see them out in fields with the cattle. Emu is not regularly eaten, but I have found a specialty market in Perth that makes a nice emu and bush tomato sausage.

Rest assured, we don't eat koalas or parrots.

Eating out

If you want to eat well and inexpensively, go to Melbourne. In the rest of Australia, take what you can get. This might seem like an exaggeration, but it can be hard to find good food and service at a reasonable price.

With no illegal immigrants working as cheap kitchen help, and no custom of tipping waiters and waitresses, and a minimum wage of almost $20 per-hour, inexpensive sit-down-and-be-served restaurants don't exist in Australia. The only exception seems to be Asian restaurants which are usually family-run and seem to have an abundance of newly-arrived relatives.

There are no mid-priced restaurants like Denny's, Marie Callender's, or Coco's. There will be no motherly waitress calling you "hon" and suggesting the meatloaf while topping up your 'bottomless cup of coffee'. Instead of mid-priced restaurants, there are places that serve counter meals [more below].

On the bright side, there are many restaurants that provide *al fresco dining* (outside tables on a veranda or in a partial enclosure).

Licensed restaurant means one that serves alcohol. If the restaurant isn't *licensed*, you can *BYO*: bring your own beer, wine or pre-mixed drinks. There might be a corkage fee. You can't BYO into a *licensed restaurant*. [more below]

There are all sorts of arcane license restrictions. For example, in some restaurants in Western Australia on Good Friday and Christmas Day you can only get a drink when you buy a full meal, and only during the hour that meal is served. In another restaurant a few blocks away this might not apply because they are on a slightly different license.

Australian restaurants fall into three basic categories: fast-food, the mid-priced counter meal, and nicer, more expensive restaurants where a wait-person will serve you.

Service   The downside to no tipping is don't expect the service to be quick or for the waitperson to be interested in whether your meal was prepared to your liking, or if you 'need anything else'. Avoiding eye contact in the service sector is institutional.

Since there is no tipping, there's no incentive for a wait-person to turn over their tables several times during a shift. They get paid the same if they serve four meals or forty. They're happy to let you sit there as long as you like—it's less work for them. At a sit-down-and-get-waited-on restaurant, fast service is something you can't count on, so if you're in a hurry, go to a place that serves counter meals.

The bill   When it comes time to pay your bill and the waitperson is nowhere to be seen or is avoiding eye contact, *no worries*, just go to *reception* (the front counter) and tell the host or hostess you want to pay—but don't expect to see an itemized bill. You'll just get a total. Look on the bright side; you don't have to figure out the tip.

BYO   Some restaurants are *licensed*, which means they can serve alcohol. Some are only beer and wine; some have a complete bar. In *licensed restaurants* you can't bring in your own liquor, and can't leave with an open bottle.

Those that aren't licensed (*BYO*), will allow you to bring your own. You'll see patrons arrive carrying a cooler bag with the night's refreshments. The waitperson will sometimes offer

to put your drinks in the refrigerator. Some places will charge
you a corking fee, others won't

If you haven't brought your own, and the restaurant doesn't
serve alcohol, ask the waitperson where the closest *bottle shop*
is. Chances are one is nearby and you can go there and buy
what you want before the food arrives.

The menu   Nicer restaurants serve several courses. An
entree' is an appetizer, also called *starters*. The *main* is the
main course. Salads often come without dressing.

Fast food works just like in North America. This could be
a McDonalds, KFC, a fish and chips shop, *a felafel shop*, a
corner deli, a *bakery* or a *lunch bar* (also known as a *milk bar*)
or a coffee bar. You wait in line, order, pay, take your food,
then *dine-in* (ironic to call McDonalds dining) or take it away.

Kebabs aren't skewers of meat, they're felafels: lamb,
chicken or fried lentils in a wrap.

Sushi is usually a slice of handroll with teriyaki chicken
inside, not raw fish. If you want fish sushi or sashimi you'll
need to go to a real Japanese restaurant.

Fast food chains   You can have a Big Mac at a
McDonald's in New York, get on a plane, fly halfway around
the world to Sydney, find an identical McDonald's and have
another Big Mac that looks and tastes exactly the same. About
the only difference here is that McDonald's isn't nicknamed
"Mickey-D's", it's *Macca's* (pronounced *Macker's*).

The other major American-style chains are *Hungry Jack's*
(which is the same as Burger King, the name was already
taken), Domino's Pizza, Subway, Baskin Robbins, and KFC.
There are a few Taco Bells in the east. The Aussie chains are
Red Rooster, *Chicken Treat*, *Nando's* (spicy chicken), *The
Kebab Company* (kebabs aren't meat on a skewer; they're
wraps),), *Jesters* (meat pies), and others.

Mexican food was expensive and exotic until around 2005
when *Zambrero* (similar to Baja Fresh) and its imitators, *Mad
Mex* and *Salsa's*, appeared. They serve a limited menu of
burritos and tacos.

Fish and chips are everywhere, serving flake, shark,
barramundi, etc. Don't be surprised when you're asked to pay
twenty cents extra for a packet of *tomato sauce* (sweet

ketchup).

Paper goods aren't handed out to the degree they are in the U.S.; you usually don't get disposable paper placemats, coasters, and promotional handbills. Extra *serviettes* (napkins) aren't routinely given out unless you ask. At fast food chains, they're in the standard countertop dispenser.

There are lots of great independent places that serve pizza, fish and chips, kebabs, noodles, curry, etc., and then there are *lunch bars*.

Lunch bars are the predecessor to fast foods chains. They are independently-owned, order at the counter, fast-food shops, often called a *deli* or a *milk bar*. They'll make a burger, a sandwich, or fish and chips to order, along with pre-made sandwiches and *rolls* (submarine sandwiches), *pies* (single serving meat pies filled with various combinations of meats and vegetables and eaten by hand like a sandwich), *pasties* (a pastry filled with diced meat, potatoes, and onions), and *sausage rolls* (a pastry-wrapped sausage). Chikko Rolls are deep fried mass-produced spring rolls. Hot chips (French fries) are a common treat, served piping hot in a big cup.

The drinks are in the 'fridge, grab one before you go up to the counter or you're going to make everyone wait while you go get one. Try a Coffee Chill or a Barista Brothers Coffee. Lunch bars are usually in working areas and industrial parks.

Coffee bars   Twenty years ago if you asked for a coffee in a restaurant, even a nice restaurant, they'd bring you a cup of hot water and a *sachet* (packet) of instant.

Enter the *barista*. Being from English hot tea-based culture, Australia never established brewed coffee like the bottomless cup at Denny's. They jumped straight to Italian-style espresso/latte'/cappuccino's, like Starbucks. To our benefit!

There are several chains, like *Starbucks* (east coast*), Gloria Jeans*, (major cities nation-wide) and *Dome* (nationwide).

Try a *flat-white* (espresso in frothy milk), a *short black* (espresso), *a long black* (watered-down espresso), or a cappuccino. A *skinny flat-white* is one with non-fat (*skim*) milk. A *long mac* is a macchiato: a double shot of very strong espresso with a little bit of milk, served 'up' in a glass. A *short mac* is a single shot in a demitasse cup. If you don't like coffee, try a chai latte. Aussies have traditionally been tea drinkers, though coffee is taking over.

When you order a basic *cuppa*, you will be asked how you like it. If you want it with milk and one teaspoon of sugar, ask for *white with one*, two sugars is *white with two, etc.* Milk only is *white*. Black is still *black.*

Order an iced coffee and you'll be surprised: besides espresso it will have vanilla ice cream at the bottom and whipped cream on top. If you want just a cold coffee on ice order an *iced latte'*. You won't find iced tea served other than a sugary drink in a bottle. I make my own sun tea at home.

Bakeries have more than just bread and sweet pastries. They also bake fresh meat pies, and there's usually a fridge full of *cool drinks* (sodas and juices). You can grab a *pie and a can* and eat outside. It's the *tradies* (tradesmen's) *favourite* lunch.

Counter meals are served at medium-priced restaurants and taverns. It doesn't mean you sit on a stool at the counter to eat, it means you order at the counter, are given a numbered placard to place on your table, and when it's ready, a wait-person delivers it (no tips). Don't be surprised if you have to order your drinks at a different counter. The only non-fast food American restaurant in Australia is Sizzler, which, of course, serves just such counter meals. Although the menu is almost the same as in the U.S., Australian Sizzler isn't cheap.

Pubs   The corner pub is a fine Australian tradition. Many are in old historic buildings thick with atmosphere and an assortment of friendly locals. You can get a cold *draught* (draft) beer and a good value meal. When you're travelling and find yourself in a new town, you can depend on a good experience at the local pub. Some have sit-down restaurants in the back, but most only serve counter meals, order at the bar.

Nicer restaurants   Except for Italian, Chinese, Malaysian, Thai or Indian restaurants, just about the only time you'll be waited on for a meal in Australia will be in a nicer restaurant. Nicer restaurants have good service, though generally not quite the level of attention you're used to in North America. Dining is more leisurely and more expensive.

But first, before you can get a table, you have to make a *booking.*

Bookings are reservations. You can walk into an absolutely empty restaurant at 5:00 p.m. and the hostess will look down her nose at you and say in her most haughty tone, "Do you have a *booking*?"

You look around—the place is empty—you look back at her and she's very seriously waiting for your reply. Have you wandered into a Monty Python skit? You wait for the laugh, but it doesn't come. She's dead serious.

The reasoning is that, by 7:00 p.m. the place will be full and the restaurant management can't count on you giving up your table by then. This is partially because of the lack of speed of the wait-staff, but mostly it's because patrons have no obligation to leave once they're done eating, they'll linger and drink and chat. That's the style and custom here. Generally, if you've booked a table, it's yours for the evening.

So, don't be surprised if you go into an empty restaurant and can't get a table. You may be able to convince them that you'll leave within an hour. To be sure, make a *booking*.

Tipping   *No tipping is expected,* and in fact if you tip, you'll be looked at like you were from Planet Elsewhere, so don't bother. The tip is already in the price. Minimum wage is $19.84/hr. (2020).

Ethnic food   There are Greek, Italian, Indian, Malaysian, Indonesian, Thai, Vietnamese, and Chinese restaurants, there are Japanese noodle restaurants and sushi bars, and much, much more.

There are nouvelle cuisine Mexican restaurants, but I've yet to find an unpretentious, inexpensive Mexican restaurant with a good goopy cheese enchilada or tamale with refried beans, rice and fresh tortillas. What's served often bears little resemblance to Mexican food from the U.S. because there's never any Mexicans working at these places. And you have to pay extra for chips and salsa. After a few beers, try teaching the waiters how to pronounce the items on their menu. (Pollo is often pronounced like the game on horseback). But refried beans, tortillas, taco seasonings and salsas are readily available in supermarkets, so you can make it yourself at home. Try making fajitas with kangaroo meat, it's pretty good. Prawns are cheap and snapper is available, so you can make camarones and fish tacos. Corona beer is available all over Australia.

A **sausage sizzle** is a simple social gathering, similar to a weenie roast or a hot dog cookout, using Aussie sausages instead of hot dogs. It's also the typical community fundraiser found in a park or outside a shopping centre or hardware store on a weekend.

The *snags* (sausages) are cooked on a griddle BBQ and served on a *roll* (bun) with *tomato sauce* (pronounced *toe-mah-toe*), which is like ketchup only a bit sweeter. Grilled onions are optional. Don't ask for chilli; it'll just confuse them. At best, you'd get sweet chilli from India.

Cheap alternatives If you're travelling or new in town, ask if there's an open night at the local lawn bowling or surf lifesaving club. The food and drink are cheap and abundant. You might need to make a *booking*.

Uber Eats   and it's imitators are available in Australia.

Eating in

If you had to come up with a traditional Australian diet you'd list meat and potatoes, and fish and chips. A *dinki-di, true-blue* Aussie would be happy to eat that for lunch and dinner very day if possible. For *brekkie* he'd have buttered toast spread with *vegemite*, washed down with a cup of tea. If he was living large he might add a baked tomato, a few pieces of bacon and an egg.

Breakfast is *brekkie*, lunch is *lunch*, dinner is *tea*, and a late snack is *supper*. A *smoko* is a smoke break, but it can also be a coffee or tea break, where you'd have a *cuppa*. *Morning tea* or *afternoon tea* is a coffee (or tea) break with a snack. If you get invited to someone's house for *tea* at 6:00 p.m., expect dinner. If you go to a concert and it says "*supper will be served*," that means tea, coffee (usually instant), *bikkies* (biscuits or cookies) and cakes after the show.

Bring a plate   means a potluck. If you're invited to someone's home for dinner or *tea* and are asked to *bring a plate,* that means to bring a dish of food to share.

BBQ   The barbecue is called a *barbie*. It's usually half-grill and half-griddle (older ones may be all griddle). Some may also have a deep iron pan. On the griddle you can cook fish, *prawns* (shrimp), sausages, eggs (in *aluminium* rings), potatoes, onions, tomatoes, etc.; everything else goes on the grill. Most barbies are gas-fired.

Many public parks provide gas-fired barbecues. If you're travelling, you can grab some fresh fish or meat at a fish market or butcher's, some tomatoes at a produce store, and have a cheap, hearty meal in the park. BBQ the tomatoes by cutting them in half and sprinkling some cheese and spices on top, then put them on the griddle next to the meat.

A *mixed grill* is sausages, steaks, and chops (pork or lamb).

Lamb is common, fish is great. Fish, *chook* (chicken), meat, vegetables, and fruit are labelled as to country of origin. In fact all food in Australian markets must be labelled with the 'country of origin'.

A *serve* is a serving, as in 'one *serve* of rice.'

Mushy peas are over-cooked peas served mushy.

Try some Vegemite, it's a dark-brown salty, yeasty paste. Spread it <u>lightly</u> over margarine (pronounced *mah-jah-reen"*) on toast; it tastes like a bouillon cube. Don't be put off by it even though it looks like wheel bearing grease. My first month here I had it every morning for *brekkie*. It'll tighten the muscles around your mouth and help you develop an Aussie accent. Just kidding.

Nutela is a sweet spread made from hazelnuts that can be used like peanut butter (though it looks just like Vegemite).

Jell-O is called *jelly*, and jelly is called *jam*.

Milo is a hot-chocolate Ovaltine-like drink that comes in a jar—like coffee—and can be served hot or cold. There are several brands of pre-made coffee and chocolate-flavored milk drinks that come in small milk cartons, marketed in different regions under different names such as: *Choc Chill*, *Coffee Chill*, *Strong Coffee*, *Iced Coffee*, *Barista Brothers*, etc.

Cordial (pronounced *kor-dee-el*) is a sweet Kool-Aid-like drink that comes as a liquid concentrate—don't embarrass yourself by trying to drink it straight like I did the first time I encountered it. You add a little bit to water to taste. It comes in different flavours and colours. It's a favourite with kids.

Sweets and savouries are terms used to describe types of breakfasts or snacks. *Savoury* snacks are salty things, like *crisps* (potato chips) and *chips* (French fries). *Sweets* are ice cream and cakes. Beware when buying pasties at bakeries, what might look like a cinnamon bun may be a Vegemite swirl.

Aussies like a *savoury* brekkie: bacon or sausage and eggs, baked tomato, cooked mushrooms, and buttered toast with Vegemite. Americans like a *sweet* brekky: sugared cereal, doughnuts, and fruit.

Supermarkets

Supermarkets look much the same as in North America, though the stores are on a slightly smaller scale.

A shopping cart is called a *trolley*. To an American, a trolley is a cute little train that goes "toot-toot," but in Australia, it's anything on wheels that one pushes, such as a shopping cart, a hand truck, or an equipment dolly.

As you push your *trolley* down the supermarket aisle, keep to the left, just as if you were driving on the road.

Many items and products are called by different names.

Aussie food terms

American	Australian
7-Up	Lemonade
Arugula lettuce	Rocket
Bell peppers	Capsicum
Bologna	Polony, devon
Bun	Roll
Candy	Lollies
Cantaloupe	Rockmelon
Cheddar Cheese	Tasty cheese
Chicken	Chook
Cold pancakes (pre-made)	Pikelets
Cookies	Biscuits, bikkies
Corned beef	Silversides
Custard	Pudding sauce
Fine Grain Sugar	Caster sugar
Frosted Flakes	Frosties

Ground meat (any kind)	Mince
Gum	Chewies
Hors d'oeuvres	Nibblies
Jelly	Jam
Jell-O	Jelly
Ketchup	Tomato sauce
Lobster	Crays/crayfish
Meat pie	Pie
New York steak	Porterhouse
Oatmeal (or any hot cereal)	Porridge
Papaya	Pawpaw
Popsicle	Paddlepop, icy pole
Porterhouse steak	T-bone steak
Potato chips	Crisps
Raisins	Sultanas
Rice Krispies	Rice Bubbles
Romaine lettuce	Cos
Scallions	Spring onions
Shrimp	Prawns
Sodas	Cool drinks, soft drinks
Sweet roll	Sticky bun
Tangerines	Mandarins

Meat   Cuts of meat differ. For example, an American porterhouse is called a *T-bone* in Australia. An Aussie porterhouse is just the steak, with no bone or fillet (fillet is pronounced *fil-lett* with a hard 'T'). *Mince* is ground meat of any kind (beef, poultry, or lamb). Hamburger is pre-formed patties of ground beef, often with lamb and filler added.

Chicken is abundant and lamb is cheap. *Crays* (lobsters) are local but very expensive (go diving and catch your own), as well as some fish and *prawns,* but a lot of seafood is coming from Asia. If it's imported, it will be labelled. I don't buy any food from China.

One thing unique to the Aussie supermarket meat section is kangaroo. 'Roo steaks are lean and healthy, and it'll put a little spring in your step. Marinate it lightly or it's a bit gamey, try it barbecued with teriyaki sauce.

Misc.   Australian BBQ sauces have improved in the last few years. I've found that a good place to buy real American-style BBQ sauce is at a kosher meat market, often located near an Orthodox Jewish temple. It's also a good place to get sour pickles (called *cucumbers in brine*).

Aussie mayonnaise is sweet and runny. For American-style, try one listed *with whole egg.*

There are two kinds of mustard: *hot English* and *mild American.* Watch out for the former; it'll clear your sinuses. The latter is what Americans are used to.

Marshmallows look the same, but Australian ones are much sweeter, though my kids tell me that they taste the same after roasting over a fire.

Camping

Caravan parks are private campgrounds. Every town has one. You can park your *caravan* (travel trailer) or motorhome, sleep in your van, pitch your tent, or sleep on the ground. Most also have *chalets* (cabins) to rent and sell provisions in a small store, along with *pies, cool drinks,* and ice cream. There's often a pool and a central cooking or barbecue area. It's the cheapest way to stay in a place with creature comforts like *ablutions* (toilets and showers), which are found in the *ablution block.*

There are books in most states listing *Free Camping Spots.* When travelling, you can also stay next to highways at rest stops or turn-outs. Police policy is they'd rather have someone pull over and sleep in their car than drive tired and risk an accident [see section on **motorhomes** and **camp trailers**].

Public transportation

Capital cities have commuter train systems, buses, and taxis. Smaller cities have just buses and taxis. Melbourne has an extensive system of trams that run on surface streets like a bus system. Urban areas have Uber and its imitators.

In taxis, Ubers or shuttle vans, it's common for a passenger to sit in the front seat (egalitarianism). Even the prime minister sits in the front seat of his security officer-driven car.

Buses   There are inter-city bus systems. For interstate or long-distance ground travel, check **busaustralia.com**. A tour bus is called a *coach*.

Metropolitan trains   Sydney, Melbourne, Adelaide, Brisbane, Perth and Canberra have light rail commuter train systems. Darwin and Hobart do not.

Trains There are several long distance train services.

The *Ghan* is a two-day trip from Adelaide to Darwin through the *Red Centre*, stopping in Alice Springs, where you can take a side trip to *Uluru* (Ayers Rock). The *Indian Pacific* runs from Sydney through Broken Hill and Adelaide, to Perth—a three-day journey—you can put your car aboard and have it with you at the other end. The *Overland* runs from Melbourne to Adelaide, the *Sunlander* runs from Brisbane to Cairns, the *Spirit of the Outback* runs from Brisbane through Rockhampton to Longreach, the *Westlander* goes from Brisbane to Charleville, the *Prospector* runs from Perth to Kalgoorlie. They can be expensive when you compare taking a coach or flying, they are more about the experience and scenery. There are several vintage and tourist trains throughout the country.

Flying   Australia is a large country with the population mostly concentrated around the edges (there are just a few towns scattered through the interior), so flying is the most common long-distance transport. Commercial air transport was invented in Australia in 1920 and safety ratings are among the highest in the world.

Qantas and Virgin fly internationally, along with most major international air carriers, including Air New Zealand, Garuda, Qatar, Emirates, United, Delta, Singapore, Air Asia, Jet Star, Tiger, etc). Before you book a flight to Australia check your frequent flyer program for partner airlines. Qantas is a One World partner with American, Virgin is partners with Delta, Air New Zealand is with United and Singapore.

International flights to North America leave from Brisbane, Sydney and Melbourne. It's about 14-hours from Sydney to Los Angeles, the most commonly used transit points. In 2019 Qantas initiated a non-stop 17-hour Perth to London flight using the 787 Dreamliner. Other flights to Europe stop in

Qatar, Dubai, or Bangkok. There are many routes to Indonesia, Malaysia, Japan, China and Korea. Singapore is a common hub. Bali, in Indonesia, is probably the most frequent foreign destination, being an exotic tourist island just a few hours north of the major Australian cities. Air Asia is usually the cheapest to Bali.

There are many local scheduled and chartered air services serving specific areas. Air commuting within the country is common, with regional airports handling flights to mines and remote towns. FIFO (fly-in, fly-out) work schedules necessitate charter service to distant mine sites. Miners fly out to the site for two-week shifts, then fly home for a week off. On Monday mornings, the domestic terminals are full of skilled labourers wearing *fluoro* (fluorescent safety clothes), carrying tool bags, flying out to *site*.

Qantas and Virgin Australia were the main carriers, with budget airlines Jet Star (owned by Qantas) and Tiger Air (owned by Virgin Australia) bringing up the rear. I say *were*, because the Covid-19 pandemic drastically affected all Australian air carriers and almost all flights were cancelled for months. Qantas is the most solid financially, Virgin went into administration and it's not sure what it will look like when it emerges. Air New Zealand is also solid (the Government of New Zealand owns 52% of shares). Regional airlines serving smaller towns and remote mine sites like REX (Regional Express) were government subsidized through the crisis to maintain an airlink to remote areas. Virgin Australia Regional Airlines, Air North, and Qantas Link may be goners, we'll see.

The *Royal Flying Doctors* is its own specialized airline, providing air-evacuation flights to cities with major hospitals from literally anywhere in the country utilizing airports, dirt strips and even straight sections of highways. It is subsidized by government and private donations. Needless to say, it's the one airline on which you don't want to have to fly.

Driving

Driving on the left side of the road   Australia is a right-hand drive country (the steering wheel is on the right side of the car), so we drive on the left side of the road like Britain and Japan, opposite to that in the Americas, Continental Europe and most of Africa. 75% of countries in the world are left-hand drive while only 25% are right-hand drive.

Even though right-hand drive is in the minority, get it out of your head that it's the wrong side of the road, it was an arbitrary choice made over a hundred years ago by people long since dead, so accept it and deal with it.

Driving on the left isn't that big a deal once you get used to it. Simply follow a few basic principles, the most important of which is *Keep to the Left*. Every time you get behind the wheel of a car in the first few months driving here, repeat these words: *Keep To The Left*. Repeat it several times if necessary—and continuously if need be—while you drive.

Another way to remember it is, as Bert Munro said in *'The World's Fastest Indian'*: "Keep the steering wheel side of the car toward the centre of the road."

Favouring one side of the road over the other doesn't end when you get out of your car. Australians also walk on the left side of the *footpath* (sidewalk) and push their shopping *trolleys* (carts) on the left side of the supermarket aisles.

First steps   Your first attempt to drive will probably be in a *hire* (rental) car. Request one with an automatic transmission. Don't try shifting with your left hand the first time out.

If you do end up with a stick-shift, the pattern is the same, not a mirror image. First gear is still in the upper left, second gear is below that, etc. The pattern will be on the shifter knob. The foot pedal arrangement is also the same, not a mirror image. Piece of cake.

Once in the car, just sit for a few minutes and become acquainted with where things are located. You're now sitting in what, to you, should be the passenger side of the vehicle, but instead there's a steering wheel and a panel of instruments in front of you. Everything inside you says "this is wrong". If you have an American passenger, by now they'll be uneasy because they're sitting on the side of a car that should have a steering wheel, but doesn't, and they'll feel absolutely naked.

Note the speedometer—it goes up to 220! Relax; it's in kilometres-per-hour. Don't worry about kilometres, you won't have to convert them to miles, all the speed limit signs are also in kilometres-per-hour. Just keep the speedometer needle under the number that the signs indicate and you'll do fine.

Normal posted speeds (approximate):
40 kph....25mph   80kph.....50mph
50kph.....30mph   90kph.....55mph
60kph.....35mph   100kph....60mph
70kph.....45mph   110kph....65mph
[More on speed limits later in this section.]

Speed limits in Australia are generally lower than those in North America. Built up areas (neighbourhoods) are 50 kph unless otherwise posted. Freeways are 100 kph. Country highways are 110 kph.

Meanwhile, back in the car...

Note the location of the *turn indicator* (turn signal). It's the stalk sticking out of the right side of the steering wheel. The one on the left is the *windscreen* (windshield) wipers. You can always tell the recently arrived North American or European driver when, as they start a turn at an intersection, the windscreen wipers suddenly start working. To save face in this situation, pull back on the wiper stalk to activate the squirters, thereby fooling anyone watching into thinking you did it on purpose and intended to wash the windscreen. Then you can quickly flip on the turn indicator (the right stalk) and continue your turn without anybody catching on. As you complete your turn, check to see if you ended up on the left side of the road. If not, take corrective action.

The secret to learning to drive on the left is to concentrate while remaining relaxed. Anticipate.

Take along a navigator   When you're starting out, it takes two Americans to drive in Australia: one steers the car, the other points out that they're on the wrong side of the road.

Smart phone map apps have made getting around anywhere easy. Google Maps and Waze work here.

Allow extra time, because you will get lost. This is normal, so don't take it personally.

Australians generally put street signs before intersections

so you can anticipate your turn, but not at cross-streets so they are visible to those already driving on that street. This makes it hard to be sure that you ended up on the right road. The attitude seems to be: if you're already on the road, why do you need a sign? This is compounded by the fact that in some cities the street names change every few kilometres. Pay attention to the driving app, and stay on the left side of the road.

Pedestrians   Don't worry too much about pedestrians unless you are one; then worry.

Even though pedestrians legally have the right of way in most situations, <u>drivers will not slow down or stop for them unless they think they're about to hit them.</u> Australian pedestrians expect nothing different. They patiently stand on the *kerb* (curb) and wait until there are no cars or they dash madly across the street, dodging bumpers. If you're crossing a street on foot in an Australian city, don't assume that drivers will stop for you.

When crossing the street on foot, first look to the right. The first lane of cars will be coming from the right (unless you're on a one-way street). At intersections without traffic lights, be extra careful, as many don't have stop signs. There might be no sign at all or a *Give Way* (yield) sign, and drivers will roll through, assuming no one will cross in front of them (the *she'll be right* attitude).

In some areas there are marked crosswalks: multiple white stripes parallel to the direction of traffic. These are *zebra crossings* (pronounced *zeh-bra*). Some will even have a pedestrian crossing sign. Here pedestrians are grudgingly given the right of way. Pedestrians also have the legal right of way crossing at all intersections, whether or not there are marked cross walks, but this fact is ignored by most drivers, including the police. Jaywalking is common, because legal crossings can be far apart. Some crossings have warning signs: *pedestrians give way to cars*.

When you're driving and see pedestrians waiting to cross the road, proceed carefully, but unless they're in a marked crosswalk or actually step out in front of you, don't disrupt the flow of traffic by stopping for them: it will only confuse them and further endanger them. If you stop your car to let a pedestrian cross the road, they'll usually just stand on the *kerb* and stare at you, expecting some kind of trick, because drivers being nice to pedestrians is outside of their experience. While you wait for them to cross, they'll refuse to move and traffic will back up behind you.

If you do stop and find yourself in this situation, take a moment to notice that—despite the line of cars building up behind you—nobody will honk their horn.

Horn honking and the attitude of tolerance Australians have an attitude of tolerance, which probably comes from their inbred sense of egalitarianism and individualism (aka: the *fair go*). That's why you rarely hear horns honking in Australian cities, in fact it's illegal except in an emergency. It's not just auto-etiquette; it goes deeper than that. Honking your horn means that you're intruding into someone else's life; you're making an overt judgement about them and are trying to force your will upon them. This just isn't done. An Australian has to be really pissed-off to honk his or her horn. With one quirky exception: some people will honk goodbye as they drive away from a friend's house, usually two short taps.

Road rage   The tolerant attitude has its limits. Every once in a while, you hear about some incident of road rage, where two motorists *lose the plot* (go crazy) and jump out of their cars and beat on each other. Road rage is a pitfall of all modern societies and Australia is no different. If you feel yourself *losing the plot* or anger some guy who loses his plot, do yourself a favour: stay in the car and lock the doors, it won't end well.

Keep left!   On all multi-lane *carriageways* (roadways), unless passing slower cars, dll drivers are supposed to stay to the left, in the slow lane. If you're a foreign driver, you'll probably find yourself driving at the speed limit or slower, so stay in the left lane. You'll be passed frequently, because some people just have to speed, despite high fuel costs and sneaky portable speed cameras. They'll probably come right up on your bumper then whip around you and cut in front of you, as if teaching you a lesson for driving so slow. However, oddly enough, while the bastard is cutting you off, he'll courteously use his turn indicators.

Left turns   Woody Allen once observed that the one cultural advantage Los Angeles had over New York was that in California it was legal to make a right turn on a red light. That changed when New York modernized their driving laws, and Woody lost a good one-liner. When it comes to turns, Australians aren't so culturally advantaged. In Australia, the inside turn, kerb lane to kerb lane, is a left turn. It's *illegal to turn left on a red light in Australia.* Just wait mate.

Give Way   Australian *Give Way* intersections are common. They work the same as a Yield sign in America. *Give Way* signs indicate an intersection where you can make a rolling left turn on a red light. Just look to the right, toward the direction of oncoming traffic, and proceed when safe.

Filter lanes   These are the transition lanes, entering or leaving a roadway.

Right turns   This is the equivalent of making a left turn in North America. Making a right turn in traffic, from one divided road to another, can be awkward and difficult at first, since your coordination and instincts say everything you're doing is wrong. Relax. As you wait to make your turn, keep looking at where you want to end up. It's like throwing a baseball, you just keep looking at where you want it to go. When the light turns green and it's safe to move, keep your eye on the target until you finish the turn. It gets easier with practice.

Australia has eliminated many right turns with *round-a-bouts, also called roundy's.*

Roundabouts   The *roundabout*, or *roundy* is common in Australian cities, as it is in some cities on the east coast of the U.S. In Australia, one gives way to cars already in the intersection, which will be coming from your right. When it's clear, you enter the roundy turning to the left, clockwise. You merge into the roundy, and when you come to the street where you want to exit, turn on your left turn indicator and turn left onto that street. Anytime you exit a roundy you use your left turn signal to indicate your intention so other drives won't crash into you.

Beware of two-lane roundy's, where you can enter on the

inside lane, then have to merge to the outside lane to exit. It's really hard to change lanes in a roundy, especially if it's busy, so be in the left lane if possible, though sometimes you'll be forced to exit as that lane will be routed into a side street. If you miss your street, there's no harm in going completely around the roundy again to get back to it. Your kids will love it.

Roundy's are also great if you have to make a U-turn. You can use the next roundy to reverse direction and go back the way you came.

Because of roundy's and *Give Way* intersections, you can drive across substantial parts of Australian cities without ever having to stop.

Hook turns   These are particular only to Melbourne, on streets where there are *trams* that run on tracks. The trams (streetcars) go down the *centre* lanes in each direction. Waiting to make a right turn from this lane would block the trams. Instead, you pull into the far-left lane and turn on your right turn indicator. Then, when the light turns red against you, you make the right turn across all the lanes of traffic. Watch out for trams; they're really big and heavy and they don't stop easily.

Backing up   You look over your left shoulder to back up. Even if you've managed to flop left and right sensibilities going forward, backing up into traffic is an entirely different challenge, trying to figure the direction of right-hand-drive traffic in the near lane in a mirror-image. If you don't take care and plan the move, chances are that you'll end up on the wrong side of the road. Beware in reverse; it's a whole new ball game. Take the time to plan out your move.

One-way streets   These can be another trap. When a North American has to turn right from a one-way street onto a two-way street, the normal instinct is to hug the *kerb*. In Australia this puts you on the wrong side of the road heading directly into oncoming traffic. Don't do this. This usually occurs after you've been driving on the left for a few weeks and have been lulled into a false sense of confidence. You weren't paying attention, your mind wandered, and you forgot to aim at where you wanted to end up.

What if you end up on the wrong side of the road?
For whatever reason, you've found yourself on the wrong side
of the road facing a lot of cars coming at you, you're sure
everyone in the entire world is staring at you, and you think
you're about to die.

Then your navigator, who is supposed to be your ally,
shouts in panic: "You're going the wrong way!" This
compounds things, since your one ally has now deserted you.
About then, your body decides it's a "fight or flight" situation
and dumps a load of adrenaline into your bloodstream. What
do you do? Don't Panic. Stop immediately. Don't try to turn
the car around, you'll get broad-sided.

I guarantee, the oncoming drivers will also stop. They don't
want to get killed, either. Look behind you and carefully back
out of the situation the way you came. Once you're out of the
intersection, calm down, have a good laugh and continue. It
goes without saying after that you'll pay more attention, at
least for another two weeks until it happens again.

Driving in the bush   Another trap is when you're
driving in the outback and haven't seen another car for hours.
One suddenly appears over the horizon coming toward you,
and you can't remember which side of the road you're
supposed to be on. Just remember your mantra: *"Keep Left"*.

A tip: If you're on a single-lane *sealed* (paved) road and
another car is barrelling along at you in the centre of the road
and it doesn't seem like he's going to get over to let you by,
Don't Panic. At the last moment, he's going to swing over to
his left and put his outside two wheels in the dirt as he passes
you, so be ready to do the same.

Outback, dirt road driving is a dusty business, the red dust
gets in everywhere. If you end up following a car kicking up
dust or if you encounter a dust-storm, close the windows,
switch the *air con* system to 'recirculate' and turn the fan up to
full. This will positively-pressurize the inside of the cabin and
keep the dust out. Don't follow too close, it's real easy to have
a rock kick up and crack your windscreen. Oncoming trucks
can do it, too.

If you do venture into the *back of beyond* (middle of
nowhere), be prepared. The Australian bush can be brutal on

people and equipment. Don't wander off if you aren't <u>truly</u> prepared with maps, tools, food, and most important: lots of water. Tell someone where you're going and when you plan to return. 4WDs can get stuck, so it's best to go in a group of vehicles with at least one person who knows what he or she is doing. Training courses are available through 4WD shops.

Important Note: Dozens of tourists get lost every year in the bush (for some reason, most seem to be either German or Scandinavian). Most survive, <u>but some do die</u>. If you do get *bogged* (stuck) or break down or run out of fuel far from help: <u>stay with your vehicle</u>; don't walk off for help. <u>They always find the vehicle first.</u> Please believe me, **stay with the car.**

Road trains   These are really long trucks, sometimes triple trailer rigs more than *thirty metres* (100 feet) long. Be careful when passing them. It takes a long time to get around them and the *hire* car you're driving probably isn't the fastest thing you've ever been in.

If you're on a dirt road in the *back of beyond* and see a plume of red dust approaching and a big truck in front kicking it up, <u>Don't Panic</u>; just get off the road (being careful not to drive into soft dirt and get *bogged*), roll up your windows, turn the ventilation system from fresh air to recirculate and turn up the fan.

Parking   Parallel parking on the left side of the street with a right-hand drive car takes a little getting used to. Practice on a quiet street.

Parking spaces are called *bays*. They are generally smaller than in the US because most cars are smaller. But if you're driving something large, like a 4WD, you may have to squeeze in with compound moves.

No Standing means no parking. Signs that say *1P* mean you can park for one hour, *2P* means two hours, *¼ P* means fifteen minutes. If it says *ticket* or *meter*, it's paid parking, look for a ticket machine—usually a silver-coloured box on a nearby pole—and purchase a ticket for the amount of time you require. Keep a handful of coins in the car for parking. Most machines take credit cards but be careful it doesn't default to the maximum charge. Some will require you enter your car's license plate number. Some operate on a special app you have to download. If in doubt, pay for more time than you need: five minutes late could mean a $50 fine, and just because you're driving a *hire* car doesn't mean the ticket won't get charged to you. The hire car company knows who had that car and they'll just put it on your credit card.

Remember to leave the ticket face up on your dash. Take your valuables with you; what you can't carry, lock in the *boot* (trunk).

On narrow streets, Australians will routinely park on the *verge* (the grassy lawn next to the road), which actually belongs to the *council* (city). It seems strange to park on someone's front yard, but you'll get used to it. Give the bloke a break, try to avoid the sprinkler heads.

Parking structures in cities are expensive.

Speed limits   The basic speed limit in *built-up areas* is 50 kph. If you're driving in a residential neighbourhood or commercial district, that's the speed limit unless otherwise posted. Speed limits are generally posted 50 kph (30 mph) in residential areas, 60 kph (35 mph) in business districts, 70–80 kph (40–50 mph) on parkways, 90–100 kph (55–60 mph) on highways and freeways. Outside of cities you'll see 110 kph (65 mph), and in the Northern Territory, as high as 130 (80 mph). The Northern Territory introduced speed limits for the first time in 2007.

School zones are posted 40 kph during school drop-off and pick-up hours, and in addition there are often flashing red lights or orange flags. Crossing guards wear long white smocks, white cricket hats, carry dual orange flags, and usually work in pairs. They look like refugees from a Monty Python movie. Be nice to them; they're volunteers.

Speeding tickets   With an attitude coming from the convict heritage, disregard for the law and those that try to enforce it is both tradition and sport. Police aren't supposed to pursue speeders at more than 20 kph over the speed limit for fear the speeder might get hurt or crash into innocent bystanders, but it lets the bad guys get away. In order to compensate for this, portable speeding cameras are common, along with fixed cameras on some freeways. They're usually hidden in the buses and they get you before you know it. If you see the flash, they got you. You may tipped off when the drivers ahead of you suddenly hit their brakes in reaction. Oncoming drivers may flash their lights as a warning. If safe, use cruise control to stay at the limit.

There are fixed cameras at intersections to catch drivers running red lights. Police also use hand-held radar and laser speed guns. Radar and laser detectors for your car are illegal in all Australian states except Western Australia. In the other states the police use radar detector-detectors.

There are also elapsed-time cameras on frequently travelled remote highways. You are photographed entering and leaving the section which may be twenty or thirty kilometres long. Your speed is averaged and if you've covered the section too quickly you'll receive a fine in the mail. These sections are good places to stop for a coffee break.

Speeding fines vary from state to state. In Western Australia, as long as you're less than 10 kilometres an hour (6 mph) over the speed limit, a photo-ticket will cost you $75. It's a major source of state income, hence the *truckie's* (trucker's) term: *flash-for-cash*. You fine will arrive in the mail a few weeks after the violation.

The speed cameras can take pictures at a fast rate, so just because the car in front of you is speeding doesn't mean he'll get the ticket instead of you. If you're speeding behind him, you'll both get popped. Speed cameras shoot a picture of the front of the car and also get a photo of your face, so think twice about your excuses.

Motorcycles have no front license plate (by law, so they won't slice up pedestrians in a crash) and most motorcyclists wear full-coverage helmets which obscure their faces, so speeding cameras that shoot the front of the vehicle have no effect on them. New cameras photograph from behind, and the owner of the bike is responsible.

Tourists shouldn't think they can get away with it just because they're driving a hire car and will be out of the country soon. The rental company knows you had that car and they'll bill your credit card.

Speeding cameras have been known to make mistakes, but it's hard to prove. Inaccuracies can result from cars changing lanes toward the camera at the moment the photo was snapped, other vehicles speeding nearby, or the camera being mis-calibrated. These tickets are hard to fight as the police claim the cameras are accurately calibrated each time they are set up. Some drivers have fought and won, but you have to take the time to go to court. And if the magistrate thinks you're trying to pull a fast one, he or she may add to your fine.

Demerit points   There is a *Demerit Points* system, which varies by state. I'll use Western Australia as an example.

If you're caught speeding by a policeman or a speeding camera while going less than 9 kph (about 6 mph) above the limit, you receive no *demerit points*, but you'll be fined $75. Going 10–19 kph over the limit, you get two *demerit points* plus a $200 fine, and it goes up from there. In Queensland it's $174 and 1 demerit point for going less than 13 kph over the speed limit.

Using a *mobile* (cellular) phone while driving is three demerit points plus a $400 fine. Drivers not wearing seat belts is $550, and 4 demerit points. The more people in the car without belts, the more it costs and the more points. Having an unrestrained child under 7 years of age, or allowing someone to ride in the open back of a *ute* (pickup truck) are four points each, plus a $550 fine. Running a stop sign or a red light can mean three points. You can get one point for driving with any part of your body 'protruding' from the vehicle.

If you accumulate twelve points your license will be suspended for three months. If you're a *P plater* (probationary beginner driver), you're only allowed to get 4 points the first year and 7 the second.

On holiday weekends, *double demerit* points are issued. These periods can extend for several days after a holiday—Christmas/New Year's extends until the following weekend. It's possible to have an immaculate record and get one speeding ticket for going 40 kph (25 mph) over the limit while talking on your mobile on a holiday weekend and—with double demerits—receive enough points to have your license suspended for three months. Points expire after three years.

If you're driving recklessly, or speeding excessively, they can impound your vehicle. If you are a repeat offender caught *hooning* (anti-social behaviour in a motor vehicle) they may confiscate your car altogether.

Of course, if you're a tourist, you won't have to worry about points, though if you're way over the limit and get pulled over by a cop, they might just take your license and car for a souvenir and then you can work it out with the hire car company to get them their car back.

Police have laser and radar and will nail you before they see you. I've come over a hill going scarcely ten kph over the speed limit just to see a police car approaching the other way with its red lights already on, pulling me over: they had me before they saw me. Police will also set up hand-held police radar check points at known trouble spots.

Intersections where an abnormal amount of accidents have occurred are called *black spots*. Once designated, they're subject to special funding, used to fix the roadway, to improve the sight-lines, to install traffic lights and as an excuse for hand-held police radar checks.

L, P and E plates   In case you're wondering what the *L* and *P* placards on the front and back of some cars mean, the *L* is for *Learner Driver*, the *P* is for *Provisional* or *Probationary Driver* (depending on the state), *E* is for extraordinary, in this case not a good thing.

Minimum age to get a learner's permit in most states is 16 (16½ in Queensland). In some states, learners must drive a certain amount of hours with a tutor before taking the test, and if they pass and they're over the minimum age (varies with each state), they move up to a *P* plate.

Newly licensed drivers must display a *P* plate front and rear on their car for two years. The first six months they use a white *P* on a *red plate*, and are not allowed to drive between midnight and 5 am except to go to and from work by the shortest route possible. After six months they graduate to a white *P* on a *green plate*. Unfortunately, many *P* plate drivers tend to think the *P* stands for *Permitted to do Anything*. Be wary of vehicles displaying *P* plates. More on this in the section on **Obtaining a Drivers License**.

E plates are *Extraordinary Plates*, issued to drivers in certain circumstances who have had their driving privileges suspended by the courts. *E* plates are issued only by the court that suspended the license and will stipulate the circumstances where and when the person can drive (i.e. to and from work, to the doctor, etc.), and where they can't drive. They are usually issued to someone who has had their license suspended for *demerit points* and/or *drink driving* and are being allowed to begin driving again under supervision.

Hoons   A *hoon* is a hooligan—usually a young male—who sees himself as being above or outside the law. He believes he has a right to do anything he wants to as long as he doesn't get caught. *Hoons* seem to feel this behaviour is perfectly justified, after all, Ned Kelly did it and he died a hero. It's kind of a throw-back to *Mad Max*.

The authorities have given this activity the antiseptically clinical, politically-correct name of *anti-social behaviour*. *Hoons* drive loud and drunk and street race. They've elevated tire burn-outs to an art.

Hoons seem to have a uniform: wraparound sunglasses and a bad haircut, and drive a customized car with threatening stickers on the back window, wide tires, loud exhaust, and a mega stereo. Often they'll be sporting a *P* plate. Sometimes they're in stolen cars.

There are *anti-hoon* laws. Someone caught *hooning* (driving recklessly) will have his or her car impounded and be liable for fines and lots of demerit points. Hoons who have lost their licenses will often continue to drive. I met one bloke who hadn't had a license in years, it had been taken away for too many points, but that little detail didn't stop him from driving. He'd buy an old unlicensed junker and go about his business, and when eventually the police pulled him over for some violation and discovered the situation they would confiscate the car. He'd go to court, promise he'd never do it again, then go out and buy another junker and resume driving. He told me, with a grin, that he'd been doing it for years. Occasionally stories pop up in the papers about hoons getting in a nasty accident while *drink driving* (drunk driving) on a suspended license with an unlicensed or stolen car. Quite often it's young teenagers, and it doesn't end well.

Loyalty to their car brand is an almost religious tradition amongst some people. Holden drivers wouldn't think of being seen in a Ford, and vice versa. You see a lot of old, well-cared for Holdens and Fords, and a lot that aren't well cared for.

Peculiarities driving Australian cars   Some of the safety features standard on American cars are absent on Australian cars. For example, in the U.S., the ignition key locks the steering wheel and transmission and won't let the driver remove the key without the transmission being in 'Park'. In some Australian cars, the steering wheel locks, but the transmission doesn't. Many older Australian cars with automatics will allow you to turn off the engine and take the key out of the ignition with the car still in 'Drive'. With a Holden Commodore, if you accidentally do this and don't set the parking brake, it can roll away on you. Be careful.

In the U.S., a car with a manual transmission won't start unless the clutch is depressed. This is not always the case in Australia, where they had no such requirement. Beware, when driving an older car, if you hit the starter key with the manual transmission shifter in gear and the clutch pedal out, the car may lurch and could hit someone in front of or behind you, it may even start and keep going.

Aussies have a strange way of differentiating car models. Besides going by the year in which it was built, they also go by the model designation. When I needed parts for my Holden, it didn't do any good to tell the counterman it was a 1999 Commodore with a 3.8 litre V6. I'd have to say it was a *Commodore VT.* Likewise, my 2012 Toyota Prado diesel is a *Landcruiser 150 Series with a 1-KD engine.* This is because models run for several years and they change models in the middle of the year. Aussie motorheads seem to know all the model designations. If you work on your car, you might be asked for the model designation when you go for parts.

Maintenance-free batteries are not the rule, many batteries still require adding water. Watch them in hot weather.

Immobilizers   These are anti-theft devices required on new cars and light trucks sold in all states since 2001. This law was instituted to dissuade joyriding thefts which had become a wide-spread problem in the mid-eighties. Newer cars have them built into the key head so you won't be aware of them, so the following is only of interest for people driving older cars.

Immobilizers work by electronically disabling two electrical systems in the car: either starter, ignition, or fuel. This is supposed to make the car impossible to steal. Older cars have added-on systems operated by a separate keychain fob, which is used like an alarm-remote. Others use a sensor on the dash you pass the fob over. Some cars had a kill-switch hidden under the dash.

If you buy an older car that has no immobilizer, the seller is required to have one installed.

Casual thieves out for a joyride choose older cars that don't have immobilizers. Or they break into your house and find your keys and steal the car from your garage, so hide the keys in your house. Professional thieves who are after expensive newer cars to strip for parts or to export intact overseas simply drag them onto flatbed trucks in the middle of the night and take them away without having to start them or damage them breaking open a door.

Tourist drivers can use their driver's license from their home state or country while visiting Australia.

Laws and driving regulations differ from state to state. Carry your current foreign driver's licence and if it's not in English, have a formal translation of the licence into English.

In most Australian states and territories you are able to drive on an overseas licence as long as it is current. The exception is the Northern Territory where you can drive on it for three months. You can only drive vehicles which your overseas licence authorises you to drive and you must drive according to any conditions on your overseas licence.

If you're going to be here for a while, you might want to purchase an International Driving Permit (IDP). This is a special permit established for travellers, which allows motorists to drive in overseas countries without testing as long as their home country driver's licence is valid. Another benefit of an IDP is that it is authorised by the United Nations and is recognised in over 150 countries world-wide. An IDP can also be used as an additional form of identification *whilst* travelling.

If you need it in a hurry go online and apply, they'll email it to you in a few hours.

Migrant drivers will have to get a new license within 3 months of arriving. Get it as soon as possible, you'll have difficulty obtaining Australian car insurance without one. All that's usually required is to go to a local licensing centre, show your old license and take a written test, which is given in English. Study the book as there are peculiarities in the laws.

Previously licensed drivers don't have to go through the *L* and *P* stages, or take the driving test.

Special licenses are required for buses, large trucks, and motorcycles [more on **motorcycles** below]. Your foreign motorcycle license will qualify you to take just the *theory* (written) test.

Larger vehicles may require special training. Five-ton rental trucks which could legally be driven in the U.S. with a standard car license require a special license in Australia.

Obtaining a drivers license for the first time isn't all that easy, whether you're a foreigner or a native. The process has become a formal affair that usually requires hiring an instructor with their car. You could have a friend or relative teach you, but they must have had their license for at least 4 years. The rules and practices are quite fussy and particular, in order to pass the driving test, it's easier and faster to be taught by someone who knows exactly what you'll be tested for. The testing officers also feel more comfortable testing candidates in an instructor's car. You want the testing officer to be happy, they are looking for any reason to fail you. 2018 Western Australian statistics showed 55% fail the first time.

The minimum age to get a *learner's permit* is 16, but you can't take the test for a full a license until you are 17.

The process starts with filing for a Learner's Permit at a licensing centre, paying the fee (around $100) and learning the road rules. The fee includes one driving skills test, if you fail the first time you have to pay for the second test.

There is a different license required to drive an automatic or a manual transmission. Decide before you apply, if you get an automatic license you can't drive a manual unless you retest. The license fees are the same. Your teacher must have a manual license to teach manual transmissions.

You'll take a Hazard and Perception test. Then you can start driving with an instructor.

Learner drivers must display an *'L'* placard on the front and rear of the vehicle. You must log your hours. In Western Australia, if you're under 25, you must log 50 hours before taking your driving test. If you're older there is no requirement. In other states it can be more hours (120 in New South Wales and Tasmania).

Once you pass the test, you'll be a *Provisional Driver*, and carry a red *'P'* placard front and rear on your car for the first 6 months with special restrictions, and then a green *'P'* placard for the next 18 months. During that time, you can accumulate up to 7 demerit points before you lose your license for a year. If you are breathalysed with <u>any</u> alcohol in your breath you are at risk of immediately losing your license. Any time you are pulled over by the police you will likely be given a breath test.

Drink driving (drunk driving).   Don't have more than one drink an hour if you plan to drive. Better yet, use a designated driver or take a cab or an Uber.

If you're driving a car and are stopped by a police officer, for any reason, you'll be asked to blow into a breathalyser—also known as *blow in the bag*. This is routine; everyone who is stopped will be given a breathalyser, we all *blow in the bag*. In Australia there is no requirement of 'probable cause' which in the U.S. comes from the 4th Amendment of the Constitution. Here, if you refuse to be tested, you can be arrested on the spot. The limit in most states is 0.05% *BAC* (*blood alcohol concentration*) for full-license drivers. It's less for *P* plate drivers.

Police sometimes set up checkpoints, often using a *booze bus* (large police van set up as a combination blood lab and holding cell) on busy streets during shopping nights, weekend nights, and during holidays. They block off a lane and route all cars through a line of officers who administer the breath tests.

They're usually set up around a blind turn with no way to turn-off to avoid it, police cars are waiting to chase those who try. You have no choice but to *queue* (line up) and take your turn to *blow in the bag* (they'll let your keep the straw as a souvenir). If you're under the limit, you drive off. If not, they pull you aside and start the process, which involves a second breath test a few minutes later, a possible blood test, and if you fail those, you'll be arrested on the spot and put in the *booze bus* with the other unfortunates to await transportation to jail.

Parking   A parking space is called a *car bay*, *parking bay* or just a *bay*.

Mostly suburban and country areas have free parking. In *CBD's* (*central business districts*), parking restrictions will apply. Timed street parking will have a sign with a large *P* on it with the time allowed in front: *1 P* means one-hour parking, ¼ *P* is a quarter-hour parking.

If the sign says *3 P Ticket*, the longest you can leave your car is three hours, and it is paid parking. There won't be a meter next to each car, but somewhere nearby there will be a ticket machine. Some machines take cash, most take credit cards, some will have you download an app on your phone and set up an account with the local government. On the parking machine you will be asked to push buttons indicating how long you want to leave the car (add a few minutes, if you're running late, it's cheaper than a violation). Once paid, the machine will print out a ticket, leave it on the dash where it can be seen by the *parking ranger*. There are public *car parks* (*parking lots*) in busy areas, and the same rules apply. The first hour may be free, but you'll still have to get a ticket. Sometimes motorcycles park for free in special *bays*, check the signs. Some machines will have you key in your license plate number, so they can check to see if you've been naughty. Memorize your license plate number or you will be walking back to the car to get it.

Private *car parks* can be pricey but may be the only alternative. You drive up to a gate, push a button on a machine, take the ticket and the gate will open. When you leave, before you go to your car, find the pay machine, use your credit card, pay for the ticket, you have a few minutes to get to your car drive to the exit, put the ticket in the machine, the gate will go up and you can drive off.

Car insurance For tourists, chances are your credit card will cover your rental car. Be sure to check coverage and use the credit card that has the best policy. Some cards only cover for a certain length of time, often three weeks, read the fine print. Travel insurance will cover the *excess* (deductible). If you rent a 4WD, the excess can be surprisingly high.

As for people who are staying longer and are purchasing or leasing a car, you get to buy insurance. *CTP* is *Compulsory Third Party* insurance, which is required by law and covers the driver of the other car if you're at fault. In New South Wales it's called a *greenslip*. In Queensland they allow you to chose your provider at the time you register your car, in the other states it's included as part of your registration. This means everyone with a licensed car is insured. CTP doesn't cover collision, fire, theft, etc., that's sold through independent insurance companies. CTP covers the other guy, the one you hit or hits you.

All totalled, with the difference in the dollar factored in, car insurance costs about the same as most places in the U.S.

Bicycles also called *pushbikes*, or simply, *pushies.* All bicycle riders of all ages in all states must wear approved bicycle helmets, except in the Northern Territory where it's not required on footpaths or bikeways, just roads. In reality, compliance isn't very high. This law doesn't apply to riders of three or four-wheel pedal cycles.

An interesting mechanical difference: the front and rear brake levers are switched. In the U.S., the rear brake is actuated with the right hand lever, while in Australia, that lever works the front brake. This is by law. This difference might seem minor to the casual rider, but for serious riders, whether they're road-riders or mountain bikers, it could be hazardous in an emergency where you react instinctively. If you grabbed what you thought was the rear brake and instead locked the front wheel, you'd be launched over the handle bars and there goes your collarbone—or your skull if you've chosen to not wear a helmet.

Signals Australians are very good about using their turn indicator lights. In fact, Australians will conscientiously use their indicators as they blatantly violate other driving laws.

I've had drivers rudely cut me off while courteously using their turn indicator.

Hand signals   Few people use hand signals anymore, in America or Australia, just drivers of older cars, older motorcycles, and bicyclists.

Since the driver is on the right side of a car or truck, the signal will be made with the right hand. The hand signals are exactly opposite of those used in North America. A straight right arm means a right turn, a bent-up arm means a left turn. Motorcycle and bicycle riders may also signal a left turn by pointing straight out with their left hand.

Motorcyclists riding vintage bikes with no turn indicators must use hand signals. But since the signalling (right) hand is also the throttle hand, when you take your hand off the throttle to signal, the bike will immediately slow down, putting you at risk of getting hit from behind. You can signal a left turn by pointing straight out with your left hand, but the laws are vague on right turns. Use your turn indicators if you've got them.

Motorcycles are very popular in Australia, just as in the U.S. and Canada. It's great riding country, with good weather and a million kilometres of open road to enjoy, though only a third are *sealed* (paved). Motorcyclists save on petrol, expensive parking and enjoy the ability to cut through traffic.

Bikes sold are Aprillia, BMW, Ducati, Harley, Honda, Hyosung, Kawasaki, KTM, Moto-Guzzi, Pagsta, Royal Enfield, Suzuki, Triumph, Yamaha; plus scooters like Vespa's, and cheap Chinese copies of Hondas and Yamahas (Chondas and Chammahas).

With a standard car drivers license you can ride a moped or bike under 50cc. To be licensed to ride a motorcycle is a bit more involved.

Learning to ride a motorcycle is a formal affair. One usually takes a course with an instructor or with someone who has been licensed for several years (varies by state). The newly licensed rider is limited lower-powered bikes under the *LAMS* (*Learner Approved Motorcycle Scheme*) If you're a beginner, check models before you buy. It used to be limited to 250cc, but they changed it to a power-to-weight ratio of 150 kilowatts (200 horsepower) per tonne (metric ton=2200 lbs.), and a maximum of 660cc's. That's about 55 horsepower for a 400 lb. bike. Some 650cc dual-sport bikes comply, some 250cc sport bikes don't. A learner approved bike cannot be modified in any way.

As a *learner* you will have to display an *L plate* on the bike or on a *fluoro* (yellow or orange) vest while undergoing training sessions accompanied by your instructor/experienced friend on a separate bike. The learner stage lasts around three months, it varies by state, some states require 50-120 hours of *'supervised riding experience'* (varies by state), including a certain amount of night riding. These supervised sessions will have to be logged on an official form (download and print them from the state licensing website) and have been signed by your supervisor each ride. Then you take an official riding test. If you pass you receive a provisional license and will have to display a red *P plate* on your bike for the first six months, then a green *P plate* for the next two years. During the probationary period, various speed limits apply and you can't *lane filter* (split traffic between the cars to get to the front at a red light). After two years you apply for a full license and can move up to bigger bikes. No further training or testing is required.

The good news for tourists is your foreign motorcycle license will work without restriction. If you're from the U.S. or Canada and are staying long enough to need an Australian license, they'll generally let you bring your current rating with you, so all you need to do is pass the *theory* (written) test.

Helmet laws a strictly enforced, though you occasionally see *bikies* (gang bikers) riding their Harley's without them.

Harleys are as prolific in Australia as in the U.S. In fact, per capita there are more Harleys in Australia than anywhere in the world. Most are owned by nice people who like loud sounds, lots of vibration, and want to be noticed. Some are owned by *bikies*. Bad-guy bikers are called *bikies* and have a nasty reputation. Bikie gangs are as notorious as their American counterparts. Don't mess with them. Even the police are afraid of them.

Crotch-rockets like Ducatis, Ninjas, and Hayabusa's are common. They once had virtual impunity from speed cameras which took the photo only from the front though a motorcycle's plate is on the back. In the early 2000's I saw motorcyclists cut across several lanes on the freeway just to get in front of a speed cameras and flip them off as they flashed. The police came up with dual-shooting cameras that shoot front and back and that era is over.

Dual sport and adventure bikes are popular, used both off-road and as commuters in urban areas. Dual sport is a good choice for Australia because many country roads eventually turn to dirt.

Farmers and *graziers* (sheep and cattle ranchers) use four-wheel ATVs for farm work. There are special agricultural two-wheel dirt bikes with low seats and large fuel tanks for working livestock. My Yamaha AG200 was a prime example (AG being short for agricultural). It had lots of suspension, but I could still easily put both feet on the ground. The *Ags* are built for fat-footed farmers in big boots, so neutral is all the way at the bottom—which makes it hard to bail into first gear to get out of a tough situation—but you get used to it. It has crash bars around both the engine and handlebars, so the farmer can literally drop the bike if he has to get off in a hurry, like when trying to catch a sheep or slipping and falling in fresh cow-flop. It also has a squarish tank so you can lay a lamb across it. It runs all day on a few litres of petrol, needs no battery, and in the rough, pulls like a fourteen-year-old. It was the best (and ugliest) trail bike I've ever owned. I loved it, it was a wreck when I bought it and drove it for years until it died.

The Australian mail moves by motorbike. *Posties* (mailmen and women) deliver to city and suburban homes on little red Honda trail bikes. They drive on *footpaths* (sidewalks) and dart in and out of traffic. They seem to be above the law. [more in the section on **postal matters**].

On your return to the U.S.   When you return home, your automobile driving sensibilities may be confused for a short time. Don't be surprised when you find yourself signalling turns with the windshield wipers.

Fuel

Gasoline is called *petrol* and is bought at a *servo* (service station). It is purchased by the *litre* (about one quart), for estimation it's about four litres to a gallon. The octane is higher: regular unleaded is 91, super is 98. American regular gas is 87 octane. Don't ask for gas, you will get propane, or *Autogas*. In early 2020, petrol cost about the same as in the U.S. once you factor in the currency exchange rate. Petrol stations also sell *Autogas* and *diesel*.

Fuel economy isn't measured in miles-per-gallon or in kilometres-per-litre as you might expect, but in *litres-per-hundred-kilometres*. Ten litres-per-hundred-kilometres is about twenty-four mpg.

Petrol stations work the same as gas stations in North America. They're mostly self-service, though in some rural areas someone may come out and fill your car for you. The gas pumps, called *bowsers*, work the same, though they measure in *litres* (approx. four litres to a gallon). There are few pay-at-the-pump systems: mostly you have to go inside and *queue* (line up) to pay. Petrol stations have convenience stores and snack bars, so once inside, you can buy a *pie* (hand-sized meat pie), a *cuppa* (cup of tea or coffee) and do some light shopping before you pay for your fuel. My guess the reason why there are few pay-at-the-pump stations is they want you to come inside and buy something besides the fuel.

Fuel discounts are common. When you spend $30 or more shopping at Coles or IGA supermarkets your register receipt will have a discount *docket* (voucher) printed on the bottom that will give you a four-cent per litre discount at allied petrol stations. Woolies markets issue a plastic card with a magnetic strip that electronically carries your discounts. Your *RAC* card (Royal Auto Club, like the AAA) card will get you the discount at certain stations. Coles is allied with Shell, Woolies is allied with some Caltex stations (observe the signs before entering). Four-cents per litre is equivalent to sixteen cents per gallon, and on a larger vehicle that can add up enough to pay for your *pie* and *cuppa*.

Australia is a major producer of *LPG* (*liquid petroleum gas*), about 10% of its output is allotted domestically to power homes and LPG-powered vehicles; the rest is exported, so the domestic price reflects the international market price. Petrol and diesel fuel come from Japan, South Korea and Malaysia but usually passes through Singapore, and the wholesale price is based on the Singapore Market Price.

Once in the country the retail prices are up to the retailers. Most of the petrol stations are owned by major corporations: Caltex, BP, Coles, Shell, 7-Eleven, etc. Fuel prices go up and down during the week, often as much as twenty cents a litre, (equivalent to eighty cents a gallon). Currently in Western Australia the cheap day is Monday, though a few years ago it was Wednesday. I'd venture to say if the cost of gas went up eighty cents in one day in the U.S. some people would be tempted to exercise their 2nd Amendment rights. Australians are used to it and don't question it, but it indicates the petrol companies' profit-margins.

A friendly tip: After you've paid your bill and go back to your car, you might get in the wrong side of the vehicle. This is normal at first. You'll sit there feeling foolish with your key in your hand and no place to put it. To save face, open the glove box and pretend to rummage around in it, then get out and go around to the driver's side as if you meant to do that in the first place.

Diesel is widely used, and many 4WDs and utes run on it. Diesel provides better fuel economy since there's more energy in it. The Toyota Land Cruiser Prado diesel uses 8 litres per 100 kms while the petrol version burns 11.6 litres per 100 kms.

In the bush and on farms, diesel is more commonly used than petrol. On *total fire-ban days* during the hot summer, only diesel vehicles are allowed off-road on farms, since there is less risk of starting grass fires. This is because modern petrol engines have catalytic convertors under the car. The convertors get quite hot and if parked in tall grass they can start a fire.

Diesels also have disadvantages. They put out particulate pollution, though this has been greatly reduced with better injector technology. Diesels are more expensive to buy since the engines are built to withstand higher compression. Diesel fuel costs about 10 percent more (it's mostly tax, since diesel is cheaper to refine than petrol) and the vehicles are louder and have slower acceleration. The latter has been solved with turbocharging which use exhaust gasses to spin a turbine that powers a pump that injects more air into the engine. This allows more fuel to be burned more efficiently and boosts performance by about 30 percent.

As you can imagine, this produces a lot of heat, and diesels don't like to breathe hot air, so on newer models an *intercooler* cools the air entering the engine, giving it even more power, so a smaller engine can deliver the power of a larger one, allowing it to get better fuel economy.

There are a few disadvantages. Most noticeably, the engine is weak if run below 2,000 rpm, the point where the turbo boost kicks in. Also, there's a noticeable lag after you put your foot down while the turbo spins up to boost-pressure. Pre-intercooled turbos get so hot if you turn the engine off after a long run, the excess heat can boil the oil and burn the turbo seals, which are expensive to replace.

To reduce heat, on a non-intercooled turbo diesel, a hot engine should be idled for a few minutes until the turbo is cooled. This can be a pain if you're late to work or if you've been driving for a while and have to go to the *loo* (toilet). But if you get off the highway and drive through traffic for a few minutes it will cool down. Some older turbo diesels have aftermarket *turbo-timers* that allow the driver to walk away with the engine idling and the timer will shut the engine off after a specified time.

Biodiesel is a blend of diesel fuel and soybean oils that have been put through a process called transesterification. B5 is a 5% vegetable oil blend and is OK for use on most diesel higher blend has to be clearly marked, check with your vehicle manufacturer's recommendations.

Bio-Eflex 85 (85 percent biodiesel fuel) is so clean it should only be used with Flex-Fuel engines. If used in a standard diesel engine it will completely flush out all the sludge in the fuel lines and clog the fuel filters.

Gas or Autogas In an Australian *servo* (service station), if you ask for *gas*, you'll get Autogas, a blend of propane and butane which is not the same as the same stuff used in a barbecue. Many cars have been converted to run on *gas*, which costs about two-thirds as much as petrol. Gas doesn't contain as much energy as petrol, so it takes about 1½ litres of gas to go as far as one litre of petrol. It's still a significant savings, plus it emits 10–15 percent less greenhouse gases and 20 percent less ozone-forming chemicals. Many conversions are *dual-fuel,* they'll also run on petrol. Conversion installations were eligible for government subsidies, and that, along with the savings in fuel costs over a few years, paid for the conversion, but the subsidies have ended and gas is getting more expensive. Another drawback is that Autogas isn't generally available outside of urban areas. That's why dual-fuel is the way to go instead of LPG-only. Another drawback is that the LPG tank takes up most of the *boot* (trunk).

A bonus: the engine will last a lot longer since gas burns cleaner. It doesn't fill the crankcase with harsh, acidic *vapours* that eventually eat up the bearings. Ford made an LPG-only Falcon that was the favourite of taxi companies, due to its cheap operating costs—the engines would go 600,000 kms (350,000 miles) before a rebuild. Around 2010, taxi companies switched to hybrids.

Some large truck fleets converted their diesels over to *LNG*, Liquid Natural Gas.

There are LPG Gas injection systems that piggy-back onto diesel vehicles that boost economy and performance 20-40%.

Eco and economy-wise drivers now turn to electric vehicles.

Charging stations   Electric cars have been slow to catch on in Australia so there aren't many charging stations. A location map can be found at myelectriccar.com.au .

Tesla's are sold, as are the Nissan Leaf, BMW i3, Hyundai Kona, Mercedes EQC, Mini, Jaguar I-Pace, but you don't see many. Hybrids are more common, but not to the extent as in the U.S.

Australian cars

Common Car Terms

Aussie	American
All the fruit	All the extras
Autogas	LPG for cars

Blow the bag	Breathalyzer test
Bonnet	Hood
Boot	Trunk
Bowser	Gas pump (at a service station)
CTP	Compulsory third party insurance
Footpath	Sidewalk
Gas	Propane
Give Way (sign)	Yield
Hire car	Rental car
Kilometer	1000 meters, or .6 miles.
Immobiliser	Automatic security system that makes vehicle inoperable
Laneway	Alley
Litre	Measure of liquid, about one quart (four per gallon)
LPG	Liquid petroleum gas, propane, Autogas
L plate	Displayed on learning driver's car
No Standing (sign)	No Parking
Peak hour	Rush hour
Petrol	Gasoline
P plate	Probationary driver, displayed for first two years licensed
Roundabout (roundie)	Circular intersection, traffic flows around it clockwise
Servo	Service station
Skimmed	refers to turning the brake rotors
Windscreen	Windshield
Witch's hat	Orange safety cone (because of shape).

Cars overview   Roads are smaller and things are more expensive than in North America. That's why Australian cars tend to be about 2/3 the size of American cars. You won't see many Chevy Suburbans or Ford Expeditions. The largest passenger vehicle normally sold is a Toyota Land Cruiser or Nissan Patrol, which is about two-thirds the size of a Suburban.

Suburbans, powered by diesel V8s, were briefly imported badged as Holdens in the mid-nineties, but were too big to be practical and were discontinued. Ford sold dual cab F250 pickups built in Brazil, but stopped in 2008 when the CAFÉ emission standards came in. Full-sized American trucks: Ford F250, Chevy Silverado, RAM (Fiat-Chrysler), are imported left-hand drive and converted to right hand drive, but are very expensive, about $150,000 new. They are great towing and work vehicles, but good luck trying to park one in an Australian city where the parking bays are small and the lanes between them narrow.

Being a former British colony, the early cars were from Britain, so right-hand drive was established. But Australia is a vast country with rough roads that ate up the fragile British cars. Early-on, more robust American cars were imported, though in smaller numbers. Being so far from North America, shipping entire cars on the relatively small ships of the day was expensive. An import tariff drove the price up further, so Ford and GM shipped chassis-engine sets and had the bodies built by Australian companies.

In the early 20th century there were a few small Australian car builders but they couldn't make a product like the Ford Model T, which was shipped flat-packed and assembled here. After WWII as the population approached 10 million, Australia developed its own car industry though under ownership by foreign auto-giants such as General Motors (which made Holden), Ford, Chrysler, Studebaker. VW, Renault, British Leyland, Toyota and Mitsubishi. They built or assembled vehicles in-country. These cars were beefed-up versions of existing cars, with the exception of Ford and Holden, which made distinctive Aussie models.

In 2018 about a million new cars were sold, both imported and Australian-built. That's an amazing number since the Australian population is only 25 million people. In comparison, China sells more than 25 million cars each year but with a population of 1.5 billion.

In the mid-fifties, half the cars sold were Holdens, and they were exported to 17 countries. In 1969 they made 200,000 cars.

Eventually import tariffs were removed and, with an upsurge of imports from Japan and Korea, domestic vehicle manufacturing folded. By 2015 only three automobile companies were building cars in the country: General Motors

Holden, Ford of Australia, and Toyota. But General Motors was losing money on each Holden they sold. How could they do that? The industry was government subsidised, which was the only way it could exist.

Holden and Ford had lines of uniquely Australian cars, designed, engineered, and built in the country, mainly the larger more expensive models, plus lines of foreign-produced smaller cars re-badged under the Ford Australia and Holden names. Toyota made Camry Hybrids and imported the rest of its products.

That ended in 2015 when the *Liberal* (Republican-like conservative) Government announced they would discontinue subsidies. Ford, Holden and Toyota responded by announcing they would cease manufacturing cars in Australia in 2017 and would begin importing foreign-built vehicles to sell. It was odd that the pro-business party would eliminate an entire manufacturing sector. Not only would those jobs be lost, but also those of the associated parts-manufacturing industries.

To those who believed in Holden or Ford with a religious loyalty, the ending of Australian-manufactured cars was a crushing blow. Many vowed to keep their old cars going forever, and I believe they will.

Holden and Ford began importing vehicles from their other markets, cosmetically designed for Australia. Ford ended the venerable Falcon series, Holden rebadged GM's German Opel's as Commodores. The Holden Captiva SUV was a rebadged Korean Daewoo, the Ford SUVs were made in Thailand. It's now odd to see a Kia police car, where they had once all been Holdens. Taxi's are imported Chinese copies of London cabs.

In 2020 GM dealt a crushing blow to the already-wounded Holden drivers when they decided to get out of the right-hand-drive market entirely and end the Holden brand completely.

Ford still exists but makes no cars in Australia, though they maintain a design centre in Melbourne for imported Ford products. Toyota continues to import products and dominates vehicle sales. Dozens of other brands are imported, but the end of domestic automobile manufacturing killed off many associated manufacturing businesses in South Australia and

Victoria where the factories and suppliers were based. Tax payers save subsidies but the supporting businesses and their employees are no longer paying taxes, and Australia lost manufacturing capability. Now Australia has no vehicle manufacturing industry other than small niche markets converting imported left-hand-drive cars to right-hand drive.

The wisdom in eliminating the automobile manufacturing industry is questionable. Might Australia need a manufacturing capability in a future when imports may become unavailable and reliance upon other countries might be necessary? Time will tell.

There is a silver lining. The next generation of Australian submarines are to be built in South Australia, in the same region where the car manufacturers were based, with the idea of employing the same workforce. It's a A$50 billion-dollar project that will last until 2050. Back to cars…

The 8 top selling cars (2020):
Toyota Hilux mid-sized *ute* (pickup truck).
Ford Ranger mid-sized ute.
Toyota Corolla hatchback/sedan.
Mitsubishi Triton mid-sized ute.
Toyota RAV4, 4-door mid-sized SUV.
Mitsubishi ASX, 4-door mid-sized SUV
Hyundai i30, small hatchback/sedan
Isuzu D-Max mid-sized ute.

If you're interested, here's a brief history of the Aussie motorcar industry:

Early years   The earliest cars were imported from Europe. In the 1890's a few local Aussie inventers created steam cars, the first being the *Thompson Motor Phaeton*. In 1899 Col. Harley Tarrant began building petrol-powered cars in Melbourne. Various manufacturers hand-built cars and trucks, the most successful was Felix Caldwell, who invented a four-wheel drive system in 1907 and used it in his first truck in 1911. They built 50 four-cylinder trucks which were sold to the Government and private firms. The price was £1250 each, which is about A$17,000 today.

WWI brought about a world-wide reset in auto and truck manufacturing as the introduction of mass-production by large corporations dominated the industry. The Australian auto and truck industry was serving such a small domestic sales market that it couldn't compete, and contracted to foreign manufacturers who imported engines and chassis from Europe and North America, assembling them in Australia with locally built body components.

Holden started as a saddlery in 1856, then made horse wagon upholstery and eventually car bodies. General Motors started exporting engines and chassis to Australia in 1919, contracting with Holden Motor Body Builders in 1924 to make bodies and to assemble them into finished cars. In 1931, GM bought the company and formed General Motors-Holden LTD.

After WWII, Holden began designing and building cars in-country specifically for Australian tastes and conditions, starting with the FX model in 1948. The FX looked like a 2/3 size 1948 Chevy 4-door with a toothy grille. It had a 2.1 litre (130 cubic inch) 60 hp straight-six and featured an early unibody construction. It was beefier than the British or American imports and held up better in rougher Australian conditions. At one time Holden exported thousands of engines each year to GM factories around the world.

The last Holden Commodore, made in 2017, was a large four-door sedan the equivalent of a Chevy Impala, though like the first Holdens, built tougher for Australian conditions. It was the quintessential full-sized Australian car: powerful, durable, comfortable, and rear-wheel drive.

Holden also had a smaller sedan/hatchback, the Astra, which was based on the Chevy Cruze, and the 4WD Holden Trailblazer and the Colorado Ute (based on an Isuzu) which were made in Thailand. When domestic production ceased in 2017, Holden imported German Opel's rebadged as Commodores. That ended in 2020 when GM announced Holden will cease to exist and close all its dealerships by 2021. It will retain staffing to support Holden vehicles for ten years.

A last gasp: in 2004, when General Motors decided to revive the Pontiac GTO (famously rear-drive) for the American market, they realized they no longer made a rear-drive platform in the U.S. Instead of designing a new one, they imported the Holden Monaro, an iconic Aussie two-door, V8 super-car. They redid the trim, swapped the steering wheel to the right and called it the *'New GTO'*. Similarly, the full-sized four-door Holden Commodore was imported briefly into the U.S. in 2008 as the Pontiac G8. In 2010 GM ended Pontiac.

Ford   The Model T arrived in Australia in 1908 as a knock-down kit that was assembled by local dealers. It became affordable to a whole new class of potential motorists like farmers and tradesmen who were far from wealthy. It was useful on a farm or in the city. Ford of Australia was founded in 1926 as a subsidiary of Ford Canada.

Curiously, Australia is where old American Ford names went into exile. The *Falcon*, *Fairmont*, and *Futura*, American Ford names of the '60s and long-since killed-off in the U.S., continued on *Down Under* into the mid-2000's. Even the *Maverick* name made it down here, though not like in the US as a cheap version of the Mustang but as a heavy-duty, re-badged Nissan Patrol 4WD. It was replaced by the Ford Explorer in 1997.

It was the Falcon that was the star of Ford's line-up for almost sixty-years, having won *'Australian Car of the Year'* many times in a row. It was originally the same 1960 Falcon that was America's first economy car, but beefed-up for the rough Aussie conditions. Many of those old '60s Falcons are still plying Australian roads.

In 1970, the Falcon, discontinued in the U.S., became its own unique car, entirely Australian-designed and built. It was available with a straight 6 or high performance V8. *Mad Max's* car was a 1973 XB Falcon GT Pursuit Special, *'...the last of the big V8 Interceptors'*. Smaller Ford cars and trucks are re-badged Mazda's and European econo-boxes.

In a case of the tail wagging the dog, Ford Australia redesigned the Ford Ranger so well that Ford made it their world truck, building it in Michigan, Thailand and Argentina. It's the first time in 60 years an Australian design was built in the US, instead of vice-versa.

The biggest and most powerful pickup trucks available in Australia are the Ford F250 and F350, identical to the U.S.

models though right-hand drive. In the 1990's they were built in Brazil, but that ended when they couldn't meet European CAFÉ emissions standards. Now they are shipped-in from the U.S. and the driving system is remanufactured to right-hand drive, at an additional cost of about $40,000. They are powered by a 6.7 litre turbo-diesel engine with a 6-speed auto. They're the best choice for pulling very large loads on the farm, or a fifth-wheel *caravan* (travel trailer) or a large boat. They dwarf all other light trucks on the road, but they're not cheap, they go for A$150,000.

Chrysler once had a large presence in Australia, starting by importing complete cars from the U.S. in 1935. In 1951 they started building bodies in Adelaide for imported American chassis and drive trains. The cars were based on the American Plymouths, but with Australian restyling. The Chrysler Royal, Plainsman, and Wayfarer cars and *utes* were the main models and looked similar to their American fin-mobile cousins. By the 1960s, models were available with V8s and TorqueFlite transmissions. Aussie drivers like performance, and they got it with Chrysler.

The Plymouth Valiant that was sold in North America as Chrysler's economy car answer to Ford's Falcon was introduced to Australia in 1962, called simply the *Valiant*. Chrysler opened an assembly plant in Adelaide, along with an engine foundry. The Valiant soon became an Aussie icon, having almost twice the power of the Holden and a third more than the Falcon. The Valiant followed American styling and was built into the late '70's. From '71 through '73, they built the *Charger*, which was a short-wheelbase Valiant V8 muscle car that looked similar to the American Dodge Barracuda. Many 1960's Valiants, wings and all, are still on the road today.

Big Chrysler sedans from the '60s are still around, though they look strange being big American cars with the steering wheel on the right. Dodge pickups and utes are objects for restorers, and rusted old Dodge 2-ton trucks can still be seen plodding farm fields and country roads.

Chrysler Australia stopped production in 1981 because they couldn't compete with Japanese imports. They sold the

Adelaide plant to Mitsubishi.

Daimler (Mercedes) bought Chrysler in 1998 and ran it as Daimler-Chrysler. They were already importing Mercedes, so they brought in Dodge, Chrysler, and Jeep. The Mercedes line—cars, trucks and buses—were marketed separately.

In 2014 Fiat bought Chrysler and formed *FCA, Fiat Chrysler of Australia.* The conglomerate now sells Fiat, Alfa, Jeep, Dodge, RAM (Dodge pick-ups), and Chrysler.

Chrysler sells the 300c Luxury and the 300 SRT with a 6.4 litre. Hemi and an 8-speed transmission. Jeep sells the Cherokee, Grand Cherokee, Compass, and the Gladiator ute.

Mitsubishi had two assembly plants in South Australia in the old Chrysler factories. They now import everything, from tiny econo-boxes, mid-sized sedans, *utes* (pick-up trucks), to heavy haulers.

Misc. Aussie auto manufacturing   Several other car manufacturers assembled vehicles *Down Under*, including VW, Renault, and British Leyland, but all have since ceased.

Electric cars and hybrids

Australia lags way behind the U.S. in numbers of hybrids and electric vehicles (EV's). In 2019 there were only 12,700 EV's on the road. The cheapest plug-in is the Hyundai IONIQ EV at A$50,000. The cheapest Hybrid is the Hyundai IONIQ Hybrid at A$33,900.

Toyota began building hybrid Camry's at their plant in Victoria in 2009, but ceased manufacturing vehicles and engines in Australia when Ford and Holden shut down at the end of 2017. Toyota sells imported Prius, Corolla hatchback and Camry hybrids.

Holden sold the Volt, a right-hand driver version of the Chevy Volt from 2011 to 2019, but sales were soft because it was expensive, A$60,000, and Aussies wanted 400 horsepower Holden Commodores, not some high-tech greenie tree-hugger car. Holden discontinued selling the Volt and announced the new Chevy Bolt EV won't be made in right-hand drive.

In early 2019 there were only about 6000 electric cars in Australia, and most of them were Teslas. Commensurately, there are few charging stations along highways to charge them. The Nissan Leaf is available, the starting price is A$54,000.

Jaguar, BMW, Audi, Hyundai, Kia and Renault sell electric cars but sales are low. There is a huge need for electric cars and infrastructure in Australia, unfortunately the Aussies haven't realized it yet.

The pitiful fact is that seventy-three percent of Australia's electric power comes from coal, so unless you charge your EV off your rooftop solar panels during the daylight hours, your EV is actually burning coal...just like the Titanic which was built in 1912.

Imports include Bentley, BMW, Citroen, Chery, Chrysler, Daewoo, Daihatsu, Great Wall, Honda, Hyundai, Jeep, Kia, Land Rover, Lexus, LDV, Mazda, Mercedes, MG, Nissan, Proton, Renault, Skoda, SsangYong, Subaru, Suzuki, Tata, Toyota, Volvo, VW, and special makes like Ferrari, Porsche, Alfa, Rolls.

Many imported models are the same as those sold in the U.S., but with different names. The Mitsubishi Montero is called a Pajero (pronounced *Pah-Ger-O*), earlier Holden Colorado's were the Isuzu's. Acura doesn't exist as a brand, but are marketed as high-end Hondas. The Mazda Miata is called an MX-5 and isn't marketed as a mild-mannered 'hairdresser's car' like in the U.S., but as a semi-aggressive, British-styled sports car, with a price tag to match. There are MX-5 racing events around the country, along with high-performance mods available.

Nissan and Toyota of Australia have almost entirely different product lines from what they market in America, with the exception of the Toyota Camry and Corolla and the Nissan Maxima. There are many third world models, notably the large Toyota Troop Carrier (also known as the *Troopy*) and the potent Nissan Patrol (arguably the best production 4WD in the world). There are four-door utes (pickup truck chassis with flatbed trays) and large diesel utility vans. The SsangYong Rexton is a Korean-built full-sized luxury 4WD powered by a cloned Mercedes engine. Proton is a Malaysian manufacturer that has development deals with VW, and Mitsubishi and sells a full line of cars. There are also lots of small Asian and European cars too tiny to market in the U.S.

U.S. Imports   With the demise of Holden, American-made Chevrolets will be imported and converted to right-hand-drive under GMSV (General Motors Specialty Vehicles), though it's unclear now that Holden dealers are going to close who will sell them.   The models should include Camaro, Corvette, Suburban, Tahoe and Silverado pickups.

Utes   The *ute* (utility vehicle) is a generic name for pickup trucks, but more specifically, ones that have had the bed replaced by a flatbed *aluminium* tray with short fold-down sides. You can carry a lot more with this configuration.

A popular car-style that has vanished in America but was still being built in Australia up until Holden and Ford closed local production in 2017 is the sedan-based pickup, like the old Chevy El Camino and the Ford Ranchero, based on full-sized Holden Commodores and Ford Falcons. They were V-6 and V-8 powered, rear-wheel drive, available in two- and four-door models with beefed-up chassis. Many were set up as work trucks, others as sports-trucks and family cars. Some have pickup beds, some have flat trays. They are no longer being built but Aussies will keep them going for a long time.

4WDs and driving in the bush   There are many four-wheel-drive vehicles sold in Australia, but when it comes to serious outback performance and durability, there are only a few worth mentioning, and all are diesels: the Toyota Land Cruiser and the Nissan Patrol, with the Land Rover Defender and Mitsubishi Pajero a distant third and fourth. Anything else is just a *soft-roader.*

Americans don't appreciate how tough outback conditions can get. The normal American SUV wouldn't make it through the first day on some of the more serious routes. On trips like the three-week Canning Stock Route, travellers routinely get several flat tires per day and have to pull the tires off the rims to fix them each night (that's why they use tall skinny tires on split-rims, you don't need a tire mounter to replace the tubes). Snorkels on the trucks aren't just for going into deep water, they're to scoop cooler, less-dusty air from high above the road surface. Serious off-road explorers have *air-lockers* that lock the transfer case and both differentials for unbelievable traction. Bush-welding is an art: hooking several car batteries in series to stick your vehicle back together. You have to carry all your water, food, and fuel.

My Land Cruiser Prado diesel has an 1100 kilometre (700 mile) cruising range, which I needed it when I drove the *Great Central Road*, an 1100 km dirt highway across the *Red Centre* with only 3 remote Aboriginal settlements along the way. Outside of the settlements I only saw one other car in two days of driving. I did see herds of wild camels and brumby's (mustangs), and some wonderful wide-open vistas.

Australia is serious 4WD country—and not just for recreational explorers—miners, *pastoralists* (cattle and sheep ranchers), and anybody who has to *go bush* knows it's serious business.

Even in normal highway driving in the outback, you can hit a kangaroo or an emu. This is most common at dawn and dusk, what I like to call '*roo o'clock*. That's why many cars and trucks have the beefy bar-work around the front end, called '*roo bars*. Heavier-duty versions are called *bull bars*. The 'roos, and emus come out at dawn and dusk, it's not in their instinct that anything can move as fast as a car, they see headlights coming and can't judge the speed, they just freeze or suddenly panic and leap across the road in front of the on-coming car. Try not to drive in the bush at dawn or dusk. When driving country highways, you see dead kangaroos laying alongside the road every few kilometres. If your kids ask why they're lying there, tell them they're just resting.

Seriously though, hitting a 'roo is no laughing matter, not only can they damage your car and themselves, but there have been instances where a struck 'roo has come over the *bonnet*, through the *windscreen*, into the passenger cabin and kicked the driver to death.

Towing and trailers   *Box trailers* are the true workhorses of the Australian fleet; it seems like everybody has one. They are usually an inexpensive six-foot by four-foot trailer that instantly turns the family car into a *ute* which can be used to haul furniture, dirt bikes, livestock, firewood, mulch, or to take a load to the *tip* (dump). It's the perfect complement to the DIY (do it yourself) attitude.

Many *tradesmen*, like *chippies* (carpenters) and *sparkies* (electricians), use enclosed versions of the box trailer to carry their tools and supplies, towing them with the family sedan or 4WD, which is far cheaper than buying and maintaining a work truck. When they're not working, they unhitch the trailer and it's back to being a family car.

Aussies will tow with pretty much anything. Family cars tow horse trailers, which is why the big Fords and Holdens had rear-wheel drive. Small pickup trucks tow large boats. You see tiny Daewoo's, Honda's, and Suzuki's towing box trailers as large as them loaded with yard trimmings headed for the *tip*. People also tow behind fancy cars like BMWs, Jags and Audis; they'll tow literally with anything someone will weld a hitch onto.

Motorhomes and Caravans   Motorhomes are small by American standards, using cab-chassis designs. They are usually diesel-powered. More people are more prone to buy a *caravan* (house trailer) and tow it with the family car or a ute. This is very popular with the *grey nomads*. Grey nomads are retired folks who travel north during the winter to warmer climes.

There are many *holiday hires* (vacation rental) motorhomes available for overseas travellers, pick it up near the airport in one city, drop it off at another when you fly home.

There are holiday hire self-contained campers built into small vans or pop-top Toyota Land Cruiser Troop Carriers. These *Troopy* Campers are great for travel into the bush. And once the odometers hit 100,000 kms. (60,000 mi.), they're sold from the fleet and locals snap them up. Australians also convert small buses like the Toyota Coaster into motorhomes.

A budget tourist's alternative to the motorhome is the *Wicked* vans (**www.wickedcampers.com.au**) and their imitators: funky second-hand vans with outlandish hand-painted decorations, designed for the backpacker traveller. They're cheap, they carry a lot of people, and you can sleep in them. They can be hired in one city and dropped off in another.

Camp trailers, etc.   are heavy-duty off-roaders designed to be towed by a 4WD. Lighter versions are designed to be towed by a small family car. They have fold out tents and pull-out kitchens and can carry an aluminium boat on top.

There are roof-top tent systems that go on top of 4WD's.

These are popular with people who don't want to tow a trailer yet want a safe sleeping spot up off the ground, a good idea up north in croc country. Combine this with an interior pull-out drawer system for 4WD's that turn the back into a chuck wagon and you've got a versatile camping system.

People often tent-camp, in a typical *caravan park* (campground), tents will outnumber motorhomes, caravans and tent trailers.

Hitches   Standard tow-balls are 50mm, one mm smaller than the standard two-inch American ball, which is enough to prevent an American ball from going into a standard Australian trailer hitch. There's a smaller 47mm size (not very common) that's slightly smaller than the standard American 1 7/8-inch ball.

Receiver hitches work the same as in the U.S., and an American two-inch bar will generally go into an Australian receiver, but the bar part may need the corners ground off, since the receivers are 50mm, about one mm too small. I brought my hitch along and still use it, I ground the corners and replaced the ball.

Why bother to bring your American stuff, like I did? Why not? If you're migrating and planning on towing boats or *caravans*, and are shipping down a sea-container full of stuff, bring your hitches. The limiting factor in a container isn't weight, it's bulk [see section on **shipping your household goods to Australia**]. It'll save you some money since parts are expensive *Down Under*.

If you plan on towing a car behind a motorhome, the towbar that is mounted on the car is called a *towing A-frame*.

Importing a car from America

You can't just ship any car into Australia from another country, many rules and conditions apply. Currently you can bring in an older car. In 2019 the rules changed from pre-1989 vehicles to a rolling 25-year-old rule.

If the car is newer than 25 years, and same year, model, and configuration was sold new in Australia *it is ineligible*. There are two exceptions: if you have owned the vehicle for twelve months while living overseas and you are returning home permanently as an Australia citizen or a permanent resident. The other is if it is being imported for racing only.

Importing a vehicle temporarily for racing or rallying purposes requires proper racing licences and homologation with the FIA (Federation Internationale de l'Automobile). The vehicle can only be used for practice and competition.

A separate issue is whether the vehicle must be converted from Left Hand Drive (*LHD*) to Right Hand Drive (*RHD*). Each state has its own requirements on how old the vehicle must be to waive conversion, if considering this check with the state the car will be registered in. Generally only cars older than 25 years can be exempt from LHD-to-RHD conversion. Conversion is very expensive.

There is another scheme for newer cars and trucks: the *Special Enthusiast Vehicles* (*SEV's*). Under the *Registered Automobile Workshop* (*RAW's*) scheme, certain popular new cars and trucks like new Corvettes, RAM pickup trucks, etc. are imported and converted to RHD. These workshops rebuild the vehicle from the dash forward. They have completely re-engineered the vehicle at great expense and even destroyed one in an official crash-test, dummies and all. As you can imagine it is expensive, adding about A$40,000 to the price of the car. Check online to see if there is a *RAW* that does your model car.

You may find an older American car in Australia that is already RHD. Some American cars were built that way or converted new: some Pontiac, Dodge, Studebaker, Chevrolets, etc. were built and sold here. Some 1970's Corvettes were imported, already converted, from Japan (which also is a RHD country). Be vary if you buy a converted car here, have it inspected by a conversion specialist, and make sure the registration papers show it's legal. I've seen some early conversion jobs on 1965 Mustangs that had the steering and brake controls run across the engine compartment using chains, levers and pulleys and looked unsafe. A good conversion sees the entire front end of the vehicle remanufactured, from the dash forward.

Aussie car enthusiasts want American cars. They can buy one online or go there and pick one out. There are companies that handle importation of older vehicles from the U.S. They ship from the west coast of the U.S., packing four cars into a sea container using a temporary wooden shelf system, sometimes fewer if they're large pickups. Cars cost about US$3000 to ship. Once in Australia the vehicle will have to go through an engineering inspection and have things like lights, tyres and seat belts converted to *Australian Design Rules* (*ADR*) standards. This can cost as much as A$1000 plus parts. The finished vehicle will be fitted with an *Australian Identification Plate*, on older imports it's called an *Australian Compliance Plate.*

Before you ship your vehicle, get all your approvals from *The Department of Infrastructure, Transport, Regional Development and Communications*, which used to be called *The Department of Transport and Regional Services,* or simply *DOTARS* (Australian departments change their name every few years as they shuffle the bureaucratic chairs around).

Whatever it's called, don't try to ship your vehicle until it has been approved. No reputable shipper will accept it if it isn't approved. This may take a month or two. I knew an American Navy sailor who mustered out in Australia. He had his very fancy Vespa scooter shipped in without paper work. It was confiscated on the dock by the inspector, sent to a wrecker's and crushed.

Shipping by sea-container will take five to six weeks. Shipping by airplane takes three to five days, but it's very expensive and there are lots of technicalities—like draining all fuel and scouring the tank with alcohol and dry-ice before it will pass hazardous materials certification. Shipping by airplane is usually only done for race cars or motorcycles.

Once the vehicle has arrived in Australia, it will have to go through *Customs*. Customs doesn't have anything to do with the *Department of Infrastructure, etc.* so have duplicate documentation on-hand of all forms you sent for your shipping approval. Once Customs approves the vehicle and collects their fees, you can take it home *on a trailer* or flatbed tow truck.

But you're not done. Depending on the vehicle you may have to get above mentioned engineering certificate and modifications to receive an *Australian Identification Plate* that says it meets the *ADR's* (*Australian Design Rules*).

Next you get to take it *over the pits*: an inspection at a state government licensing centre to make sure it's roadworthy. Inspectors will pick and probe, and if it's not too bad, will eventually pass it. Then you get to pay for registration and it's yours to drive.

I've done it. Here's my story:

When my family and I began planning our move to Australia in 2003 I decided to bring my 1971 Norton Commando motorcycle along in our sea-container. There was going to be plenty of room in the container. I'd owned lots of motorcycles before, but the Norton was special. Being a bike, I knew there would be no LHD/RHD issues, and being a British bike, and Australia being a former British colony, I figured it would be a cinch.

As soon as we heard we'd been accepted for migration I began the importation process. Under our migration scheme I was allowed to bring in one vehicle as long as it complied with the *ADR's* and had *DOTARS* approval. I emailed *DOTARS* and got the paperwork and required document list.

Since it was pre-1989, I merely had to install turn signals and a second rear-view mirror.

I emailed DOTARS copies of my importation form, California pink slip (title), registration, purchasing receipt, insurance records, etc., showing I'd owned it more than a year. About a month later I received my approval form. I then prepared the bike for shipping: removing the battery and draining and thoroughly airing out the fuel tank. I left the oil in it.

Though it would be in the sea container with our personal belongings, it had to ship on completely separate paperwork. A week before our container was to be packed, I trailered the bike directly to the shipper's warehouse in LA Harbor. There it was strapped onto a pallet and shrink-wrapped. When our container arrived, it would be bolted to the floor. I left wondering if I would ever see it again. A week later the movers packed our personal stuff into the container and trucked it away to the harbor where I assumed the bike would be put inside. Placated by the knowledge that everything was insured, we got on a plane and flew to our new home Down Under.

The sea-container travelled on a huge container ship, east across the Pacific, through the Java Sea to Singapore where it was shuffled around a container depot and eventually transferred onto another ship that sailed down the Indian Ocean to Perth, Western Australia. I was able to track its progress online (make sure you record the container number before it leaves). The container was off-loaded in Perth and trucked to our Australian receiving company, who unloaded all our stuff into a locked cage in their warehouse where it awaited the import broker to pass it through Customs.

We were notified the container had arrived. By then five weeks had passed since the container had shipped. We set a date for everything to be delivered to our rental house.

The next day I received a separate call from the import broker asking for the motorcycle paperwork. I told him I'd already sent everything to DOTARS. He said this is for Customs, not DOTARS. I asked if Customs could get the paperwork from DOTARS, he said Customs and DOTARS didn't share paperwork, and didn't talk to each other. Customs needed copies of all the same documentation I'd sent to DOTARS before they'd release the bike. I told him the originals were in a file cabinet with our stuff in their warehouse.

I drove across town to the importers. The broker took me into the warehouse and pointed to a long row of container-sized locked cages: inside one I saw all our stuff and my Norton. It looked like it was in one piece.

I pointed to a file cabinet inside the cage and said the paperwork was there, top drawer, filed under 'N', could I get it out? The broker said he couldn't possibly let me do that, *it hadn't been released by Customs yet*. So close but so far away.

A few days later they released everything, except the bike, and our stuff, including the file cabinet, was delivered to our newly rented house.

The next day I took the paperwork to the importer, paid my import fees and Customs released the bike. I took it home on a borrowed trailer.

So, the lesson is, keep a copy of all your importation paperwork with you and not in your shipped possessions.

But…I'm not finished with my Norton saga yet. I had the bike but I still had to get it licenced for the street with the State of Western Australia.

Now I had more to worry about: it was an old bike, there was no guarantee it would pass. What then? Undeterred, I installed a new battery and fuelled it. I got it running, which was no small feat with a thirty-two-year-old British motorcycle that had been travelling for over a month in a damp steel container across half the world's oceans.

I called the Licensing Centre and found that, since it was still currently licensed in California, I could get a one-day permit to ride it to their office. I'd been tipped off by a vintage motorcycle collector about a licensing centre that was friendlier than most, and headed there.

I hopped on the Norton and rode off to meet our fate. After years of riding it on the right side of the road in Los Angeles, it felt very strange to ride it on the left side of the road in Perth.

The licensing office was on a tree-lined side street in a pleasant suburb. In the office I waited as the inspector, a tall quiet man in his fifties, read through my paperwork. Saying nothing, he walked out to the bike. I warily followed. He looked it over thoroughly and pointed to the turn signals, "These aren't far enough apart." Then he examined the front brake, "This doesn't have an Australian part number on it." He shook his head.

I knew all this. The bike never had turn signals, I'd put them on before shipping just to pass this inspection. As for the brake hose, it had come off a reel of hose, my mechanic made it when we converted the brake from drum to disc (typical of British bikes, the original drum brakes were for slowing down, not stopping). The brake had been working perfectly for years.

Instead of arguing or explaining I played dumb, I just stood there saying nothing, smiling pleasantly.

The inspector abruptly turned, walked away and disappeared into the office. My heart was in my throat. Had we failed? Then he reappeared holding his helmet and asked if he could take it for a ride. I said sure. I kick-started it for him, and told him about the backwards shift pattern using the wrong foot. He just nodded and smiled, hopped on and roared off.

After fifteen minutes I began wondering if I would ever see the bike again, had it broken down? Had he taken it to a confiscation lot? Had it already been crushed? Then I heard the distinctive sound of Dunstall exhausts approaching. He rode onto the lot, got off the bike and put it on the side stand. He pulled off his helmet and said with a big grin, "Did you want to register it now?' Hiding my anxiety, I nodded. Ten minutes later I rode away with a brand-new Western Australia license plate tucked in my jacket.

Looking back, I realize he'd been *having a go* at me. His usual work day was spent inspecting rusted old trailers and broken-down old cars, today he'd gotten to ride a British classic.

I still have that Norton, it's almost fifty-years-old, we regularly roar around the Australian countryside, it never fails to put a grin on my face. Importing it was more than worth the trouble.

A footnote to importing vehicles   Adult migrants to Australia can each bring in one vehicle, be it a car, truck, motorcycle, etc., but it has to have been registered in that person's name for twelve months. If you want to bring in two vehicles, register the other one in your spouse's name and allow a year to qualify.

Even though migrants won't be charged Customs Duty, they may be charged some additional fees and 10 percent *GST* (*Goods and Services and Services Tax*) on the value of the vehicle including all shipping costs and transport insurance.

Imported Travel trailers and Boat trailers can have additional complications besides importation issues. American trailers are wider than the legal Australian width.

U.S. maximum width for trailers is 8-foot 6-inches, while the Australian maximum is 2.5 metres, or 8-foot 2½-inches, so a maximum-width American trailer could be 3.5 inches too wide. This varies from state to state, but if it's wider than 2.5 metres, you might need a *wide load permit* to tow it, and will have to display *Wide Load* signs front and rear. You can probably get away with towing without them but if you had an accident the insurance company could invalidate your coverage. Not only would you be out for the cost of your rig, but you might face millions of dollars of liability for the other party.

The wider you go, the more restrictions there are, like not being allowed on highways at certain times such as at night, *peak hour* (rush hour), or on freeways. Do your homework.

If your rig is over a certain weight, usually 3 *tonnes* (a metric tonne is 1000 kilograms, or 2200 pounds), you will have to convert your American hitches. Trailers over three tonnes need electrically-actuated hydraulic brakes, operated by a sensor in the towing vehicle. A typical American hydraulic hitch with a surge brake actuator won't be legal in Australia, even though it works fine and is legal in the US. To be legal in Australia you'll need to convert it an *electric-over-hydraulic actuator* on the trailer. Remember, if you don't have a legal system your insurance is void.

Tourists' can bring a vehicle into the country under certain conditions for a period of one year, so you may be able to bring a camper or motorcycle into the country to tour with. It'll be on a *Carnet de Passage en Douane*, and will have to be out of the country by a certain date. Check with https://www.infrastructure.gov.au/vehicles/imports/faq/import_options.aspx

Grey market refers to a vehicle model imported into the country that was not originally marketed in that country. Currently grey market, or parallel imports were banned in 2018. The ban was pushed through by the Australian Auto Dealers Association (AADA).

Grey market car favourites already imported are the Mitsubishi Delica, a sleek 4WD turbo-diesel van built on the heavy-duty Pajero 4WD chassis, the high-performance Nissan Skyline turbo and the Toyota Supra Twin Turbo. The Toyota Prius wasn't imported into Australia until 2001, so any older than that were imported grey market.

Many almost-new cars were available for grey market export from Japan. The Japanese have strict emissions laws, rigorous yearly road test requirements, high depreciation, and strict environmental laws that make it expensive to drive cars that are just a few years old. Also, Japan is a right-hand-drive country so little or no conversion work was required.

Imported cars had to go through *Australia Design Rules* (*ADR*) complacence, change to Australian approved *tyres* (tires) and had the air conditioning gas changed.

But at present, early 2020, the Grey Market is closed.

The metric system

It should be of no surprise that Australia is on the metric system; the entire world is, with the exception of the U.S., Liberia and Myanmar. Australia converted in 1966.

The metric system is more logical than the U.S. system of feet, pounds, and gallons. Think about dealing with twelve inches to the foot, three feet to the yard, 5,280 feet to the mile—and that's just measuring distance. What's the difference between a fluid ounce and a weight ounce? How many ounces are in a quart, a gallon, or a cup?

In the metric system you just keep adding zeros, and it's designed so that linear and volume measurements mesh. At first it seems foreign to those from the U.S., but once you're forced to live with it you'll find it's incredibly simple and well thought-out.

The metric system was proposed in 1791 by Gabriel Mouton, a French astronomer and mathematician. The standards of measurement were set by the French revolutionary assembly in 1799. The treaty of the Meter was signed in 1875 by 17 countries and became the world standard of measurement.

Since they were starting from scratch they had to pick a known value and put a number on it. The first unit was arbitrary, the distance from the Equator to the North Pole, which they decided to value as 10,000 kilometres, and it went on from there. All the measurements are cleverly interchangeable: a litre of water weighs one kilogram. A *cubic metre* (cum) of water contains 1,000 litres. A *hectare* contains 10,000 square metres. A *tonne* is a metric ton, and contains 1,000 kilos.

To break it down:

Meter means measure. The prefixes: *kilo* means thousand, *milli* means thousandth, *centi* means hundredth.

Distance is measured in *metres* (mtr), which is a little over a yard. In one *metre* there are 1,000 millimetres (shorthand: *mm*) or 100 centimetres (*cm*). 1,000 metres make a *kilometre*. You just keep adding zeros.

Liquid is measured in *litres* (l) which is a little under a quart. In one litre, there are 1,000 millilitres. One millilitre (*ml*) is equal to one cubic centimetre (*cc*).

Weight is in *grams*. A thousand grams is a *kilogram*, or simply a *kilo*, about 2.2 pounds.

OK, you can see the metric system is more logical and you're willing to give it a try, but you've only known the U.S. system of feet, pounds, and gallons: how can you estimate what you are buying, building, or driving? Here are some quick and dirty equivalents:

Quick metric conversions

A litre is about a quart. Four litres are about a gallon.

A kilo is 2.2 pounds (if you went through the sixties, you already knew that). Roughly a pound is half a kilo, minus ten percent. A *tonne* is 2200 lbs.

A metre is a little bit more than a yard (39 3/8 inches or roughly 3.3 feet). Figure 3+ feet to a metre. Three metres are almost ten feet. These are approximations; the easiest way to deal precisely with metres is to buy a tape measure that reads in both feet and metres (most come like this) and use it as a handy converter, like an old-fashioned slide rule.

A kilometre is .6 miles. Multiply the kilometres by six, then move the decimal. Example: 50 kilometres an hour is 50x6=300; move the decimal, it's 30 mph.

But don't worry about converting, speedometers in Australian cars (built after 1966) are in kilometres. Just watch for the speed limit signs, put the speedometer needle on that number, and you'll be fine. Here's an idea of what the speeds are:

> Normal posted speeds (approximate):
> 40 kph....25 mph   80 kph.....50 mph
> 50 kph.....30 mph 90 kph.....55 mph
> 60 kph.....35 mph 100 kph....60 mph
> 70 kph.....45 mph 110 kph....65 mph

A hectare is 10,000 sq. metres, or about 2.5 acres. 1,000 sq.

metres is approximately one-quarter acre, about the size of a suburban lot. To roughly convert square metres to square footage, just add a zero to the metres and add 7 percent (i.e., 100 sq. metres would be approximately 1,070 sq. feet).

An important note, these are approximate conversions: as amounts go up, the error from the approximation increases. I find it's easy to *estimate in feet and build in metres.* If accuracy is critical, use a calculator and do a precise conversion. NASA missed Mars with the Climate Orbiter because someone forgot to convert miles to kilometres.

Temperature is measured in Celsius (originally called centigrade). Celsius is more logical: freezing is 0 degrees, boiling is 100 degrees (in Fahrenheit, freezing is 32 degrees, boiling is 212 degrees). There's no easy way to convert, since Celsius degrees are larger than Fahrenheit degrees and the zeros are in different places. You'll have to stoop to rote memorization:

Roughly:

0 C	=	32 F
5 C	=	40 F
10 C	=	50 F
15 C	=	60 F
22 C	=	70 F
27 C	=	80 F
32 C	=	90 F
37 C	=	100 F
41 C	=	105 F

Power is measured in *kilowatts* (kW) and torque in *Newton metres* (Nm), even in cars. It's hard to get excited about a car with 100 kW and 250 Nm (that converts to about 135 horsepower and 185 foot-pounds of torque). A kilowatt is about 1 1/3 horsepower and a Newton metre is about 3/4 foot-pounds (precisely, one kW is 1.341 horsepower, and a Nm is .738 foot-pounds).

Calories aren't just a way of making you feel guilty about eating things that make you fat, but are a measurement of heat energy. Metrically, this is measured in *joules.* A joule is one Newton metre, or the amount of energy required to lift 100 grams one metre, or warm one cc of water ¼ degree C, or create one watt of power for one second. Pretty neat, huh? By way of conversion, a joule is .22 calories. A calorie is about 4.2 Joules. Large amounts are expressed as *kilojoules*.

Stationery

Paper size   Often it's the subtle things that get to you, lulling you into a false sense of confidence, leading you to think you have this Australia thing under control, and then 'wham': gotcha again.

Take a simple thing like stationery. How could anybody change anything about the size of a piece of paper that would have any international significance? They can and they did, and the difference is just enough to make American stationery accessories like notebooks and multi-hole punches incompatible in Australia. But don't blame the Australians, it's because America is out of sync with the rest of the world—it's that darn metric system again.

The standard letter-sized paper in Australia—and most of the world—is called A4. A4 is slightly narrower and slightly longer (210mm by 300mm, or 8.27" by 11.69") than American letter-sized paper which is 8½" by 11". It's just different enough so that business envelopes are a different size, as are manila folders, notebooks, and binders. Ring notebooks (called *files*) use A4 paper with two punched holes instead of three (though some paper is punched for both systems).

Here's where the metric magic kicks in: A4 is half the size of A3, A5 is half the size of A4, A6 is half the size of A5, etc. The larger the number, the smaller the paper. By folding a piece of paper in half you can make it exactly the next smaller size.

The American computer printer you brought will have to be reset to print A4 paper.

Misc.   A ballpoint pen is often called a *biro* (pronounced *bye-row*). It's from a brand name, which came from the inventor, Laszlo Biro.

In the U.S., one signs important documents in blue ink so it's easy to tell an original from a photocopy. In Australia, one signs everything important in black ink.

A *diary* isn't just something you write your deepest thoughts in. In Australia, that's what you call your appointment book or Day Runner.

Pencil erasers are commonly called *rubbers.* I'm not making this up. Imagine my reaction the day my ten-year-old daughter came home from school and asked me if she could borrow a *rubber*.

Postal system

The postal system is run by a government-owned corporation called *Australia Post.* Some post offices are corporately operated while others are franchises.

Mail A mailbox outside your home is called a *letterbox.* A mailbox outside a post office is called a *post-box.*

Mail is delivered to homes and businesses five days a week, Monday through Friday *with no Saturday delivery.*

Letters will not be picked up from your home *letter box*; you must drop them in a *post-box*. Post-boxes are red, with "POST" written on it in large white letters, mounted on a pole in front of post offices, petrol stations, newsagents, etc.

Posties (mailmen) are the men and women who deliver the mail. They don't go on foot or in a Jeep or mail van like in the U.S.; instead they buzz around on little red Honda trail bikes loaded down with huge orange bags *chockers* (full) with mail.

Posties are generally nice people, but with the excuse of delivering the mail they perform the most outrageous moves on their little bikes, darting through traffic, cutting between parked cars, and dodging pedestrians on the *footpaths* (sidewalks). They jump *kerbs*, take shortcuts over lawns, and roll backward down steep driveways. I've seen them drive part way into shops to drop letters on the front counter. So if you hear the putt-putt of a small motorbike approaching, watch out; the *Posties* are above the law.

Postage costs seem to change yearly. In 2020, a domestic letter mailed within Australia cost A$1.10, a business letter to the US was A$3.20. Normally, air mail to the U.S. takes about five days, a day or two longer from WA (Western Australia). If sending an item to North America, be sure to write *AIR MAIL* prominently on it or it will take four to six weeks to travel by sea. Stamps can be bought at a post office or newsagents.

Shipping   The easiest way it to use Australia Post, you'll get tracking, insurance, etc. For larger items or urgent or valuable deliveries, you can go with FedEx or DHL, though usually you'll have to go to a freight terminal at an airport to find the office. For large or heavy items I use an independent shipping service like Pack and Send. They'll shop around and get you the best rate, I've had them beat DHL by 75% when shipping oversized professional camera gear cases across the country.

Shipping into Australia can be pricey. When buying online from the U.S., some shipping rates are deal-breakers. Also, due to a trade agreement with the U.S., anything over A$1000 in value is subject to customs and *GST* (*Goods and Services Tax*). If you're shipping something over A$1000 expect to hear from the shipper asking you to pay customs duty and GST before they'll deliver it. If it's less it usually just arrives, nothing said.

Some items are duty-free if there are no comparable items manufactured in Australia—professional motion picture equipment falls under this category—but you have to know to ask for your exemption. Check the Australian Customs website, **www.customs.gov.au**, for more information. If you find that your item is listed as duty-free, write down the number of the section that covers it to quote to the shipping company who calls to arrange delivery.

If your shipment is coming from the U.S. by UPS, FedEx, DHL or the US Postal Service, it will be delivered by a contracted mail service like Star Track, so don't expect to see a FedEx or UPS truck at the *kerb* (curb).

Receiving mail from the U.S. and Canada   If you're moving to Australia, notify your senders and put in a change of address form in your old post office, just as if you were moving across town. For greater volumes of mail, you might want to rent a private post office box with a forwarding service in your old hometown and have your mail sent weekly, biweekly, or monthly, as needed. Once you've settled in and everyone has your new address, you can cancel the service. In situations where you're required to have an American address in order to retain American credit cards, bank and brokerage accounts, you may want to keep this forwarding system going indefinitely. This is also the best way to receive your favourite American magazines, which may otherwise be unobtainable in Australia.

Telephones

OK, so you've been using telephones since you were five years old, what's the big deal, a phone is a phone. The problem is: in Australia phone numbers are so different that until you catch on you probably won't be able to make a simple phone call without asking for help. You're going to have to learn a new system.

Australian phone numbers, briefly: They differ in the sequence and number of digits used. In America, phone numbers have long been standardized: you dial 1, then the three-digit area code, then a three-digit prefix, then four numbers. (Example: 1-800-555-1212.) It's the same pattern for landlines and cell phones, businesses or residences; anywhere you go in the U.S. or Canada.

This logic doesn't apply to Australian phone numbers. Australians use different amounts of digits in different groupings in different situations. If you're calling within your area code, a home number might look like this: 9999 9999, a *mobile* (cellular) number might look like this 0499 999 999, a *free call* 800 number would look like this: 1 800 999 999, while a *1300* (business line) might look like this: 139 999 or this: 1300 999 999.

Plus, there are the area codes:

02 New South Wales, ACT (Australian Capitol Territory)

03 Victoria, Tasmania

07 Queensland

08 South Australia, Western Australia, and the Northern Territory

(There's some overlap in the corner where Victoria, New South Wales, and South Australia meet).

When calling normal land lines from another state you put the area code first, so calling Sydney from Melbourne you'd dial 02 9999 9999.

All *mobile* (cellular) numbers start with **04**, and are

sequenced like this 0499 999 999. This makes it easy to know if you are calling a *mobile* or a landline.

Using a phone   The Australian telephone system uses a completely different calling scheme.

Emergency is <u>not</u> 911, it's *000*, which is spoken "*triple zero*".

If you dial '0' nothing happens. Directory assistance is 1223, and an actual human will answer and assist you, but your mobile will be charged 50-cents. International directory assistance from inside Australia is 1225, you'll be put on hold and have to wait until someone answers.

The pound sign (#) is called the *hash key*. Calling card users will be prompted to use this key to signal they have finished dialing their number.

An 800 number is a *free call,* but is called a *one-800 number* and is followed by three numbers, then another three numbers: 1-800-801-800.

A *1-300* number, or any number that begins with 13, is called a *thirteen-hundred number*. It's an inquiry number for a business and you will be charged the rate for a local call. These *1300* numbers are sometimes 6 digits, sometimes 10 digits. For example: The Western Australian State Emergency Services information number is 132 337. The business line for Telstra (the largest Australian phone company) is 1 300 476 984. 6-digit numbers are easier to remember, other than that there is no difference in how they work.

There are *1-900* numbers for specially-charged services, like psychic hotlines, sport lines, weather, etc.

All *mobiles* start with the prefix *04*. They use 10 digits and are sequenced like this: 0499 999 999.

All landlines are eight digits, usually written four and four, such as 9999 9999. The first number (in this case, the 9) varies by city. In Brisbane, the first number in a landline is always 3, Townsville is 4, the Gold Coast is 5, Canberra and Hobart is 6, Melbourne and Adelaide are 8, Sydney is 9, and Perth is mostly 9, though it also uses 6.

But that doesn't include the area code. When calling a landline from another state <u>inside</u> Australia, you put the area code before the number. If you were calling that same number in Perth from Melbourne, you'd dial *08* 9999 9999. The area codes are listed in the previous section.

International calls By far the best, easiest, cheapest way to call overseas from Australia or vice versa, is to use an online service, like Skype or Facebook Messenger. But that's not always possible, sometimes you have to call a bank, a business, or your dear aunt Mabel who can't figure out how to use a computer, so:

To call to Australia from overseas. dial the International Code (*011*), then Australia's country code (*61*), plus the area code (minus the zero), then the number. To call the Perth landline number we used above from the U.S., you'd dial 011 618 9999 9999.

To call an Aussie *mobile* (which in-country looks like this 0499 999 999), you drop the first 0 and insert the country code. It becomes: 011 61 499 999 999.

To call overseas from Australia first find the country code, at https://countrycode.org/ . For example, if calling North America (country code 011). You dial 0 to get out of Australia, then 011 (the North American country code), then 1, then the number. Example: 0011-1-800-555-1212.

If you're travelling in Australia your phone service may have a calling card that works off an Australian 1800 number, enquire with them.

The cheapest way to call an overseas phone number from Australia and back to the U.S. is to buy a pre-paid calling card from a newsagent. You can replenish it by calling a 1-800 number and charging it to your credit card. I've been using the same one for 17 years.

A final note about phone numbers: If someone gives you a number and it seems as if it can't be right because it has the wrong amount of digits, try it anyway, it'll probably work.

Cellular phones A cellular phone in Australia is called a *mobile* (pronounced "*moe-byle*"). All *mobile* numbers start with *04*. They use similar, if not identical, handsets as those in America. It's illegal to use a hand-held *mobile* in Australia while driving a motor vehicle. You must use a hands-free kit, consisting of at least a headphone/earpiece, or use Blue Tooth through the car audio system. This law is enforced, the penalties are steep. Starting 1 July 2020, the fine in Western Australia will increase to $1000 and 4 demerit points.

Mobile calls are billed differently. In American cellular phone systems, both outgoing and incoming calls are charged to the cellular phone owner. In Australia, only the outgoing call is charged to the mobile owner. The incoming call is charged to whoever is calling. There's usually a connection fee and a charge based on airtime. It all ends up on the caller's bill at the end of the month.

Plus, there's Data charges for your internet use.

Most plans include a certain amount of calls and data for a flat fee.

Bring your American cell phone   If you're travelling in Australia bring along your cell phone. If it's a relatively current unlocked model it will probably work. Your home service may have international roaming but that can be expensive, check before you use it. Once in Australia you can buy a prepaid SIM card and have easy communication. The major companies are Telstra, Optus, and Vodaphone; shop for the best deals. Remember to bring a plug adapter for your charger or bring your car kit [see the section on **electricity— cell phone chargers**].

For international calls back home, you can use a prepay mobile phone in conjunction with a prepaid calling card, which you can purchase from a newsagent. On your *mobile* put the calling card access number in the memory, after you key in the calling card number the card company's software will remember it. Then you just speed-dial the local access number for the calling card, it'll tell you how much credit you have, then dial the International Code and then the number back home. After you've done it a few times, it'll be easy.

Phone etiquette   People often answer the phone by stating their name instead of saying "hello", even at home. Being a paranoid American, I don't do this, since I don't necessarily want a stranger to know who they've called, in case it's a wrong number, a sales call or a scam. Ask an Aussie why they answer that way, and they'll generally say "it's more businesslike".

Caller ID is very common, especially on a mobile, so if you call someone and don't leave a message or change your mind and hang up before they answer, there's a good chance they'll call you back, because they have your number on their phone and figure you got cut off.

Internet

Almost everyone is on Wi-Fi, your hotel will have a password as will your friend's home or apartment. When I have visitors, I make my iPhone into a hotspot and let them piggyback off it so they have data even when we're out and about doing tourist things.

Phone plugs are the same, so your laptop will plug into a wall jack if there is no Wi-Fi.

Australian websites usually end in .*au*.

DSL is called *ADSL* (for *Asymmetric DSL*, meaning the data comes in at a faster rate than it goes out)—the same as in the U.S., but just a different name.

There has been a major nationwide internet upgrade over the last 10 years called *National Broadband Network* (*NBN*), but the roll-out was long, slow and frustration. Unfortunately, it has resulted in us having what is in effect 10-year-old capability.

Wi-fi hot spots are in many airports and public business districts, internet café's Some small towns have *telecentres* or internet facilities in, or adjacent to, their libraries.

Electricity and appliances

Australian household voltage is 240 Volts at 50 Hz (abbreviation for '*hertz*'), in comparison:

America is 110-Volts at 60 Hz,
Japan is 100V at 60 Hz,
UK, Europe and China are 230V at 50 Hz,
Hong Kong is 200V at 50 HZ,
Taiwan is 100V at 50 Hz.

You'd think electricity would be standardized by the 21st Century, but it's not. Modern electronic equipment manufacturers have learned to compensate for this. Most electronic devices manufactured in the last 20 years can handle 100 to 240 volts, and 50 or 60 Hz, they sense and adapt the incoming voltage, then step it down to the voltage and Hz the devices uses. The little boxes on the power cables that go from the wall to the device have convertors built in that do it automatically. BUT, please note I said <u>electronic</u> equipment, not <u>electrical</u> equipment. An iPhone or notebook computer charger will adapt to different currents but a refrigerator, toaster or hair dryer won't.

What does this mean to you? If you were to plug most American, European or Japan-sold electronic equipment into an Australian *power point* they will work fine, but if you plug your American or Japan-bought microwave directly into an Australian wall circuit it'll blow up and trip the main circuit breakers in the entire building (believe me, I've done it). To prevent the possibility of doing this, Australian plug ends are different than those from other countries (except New Zealand). You can't just plug any device from another country into an Australian *power point*. More on plugs later.

FYI: most notebook computers work on 19 volts, so the charger box drops the wall voltage to 19 volts. Other devices may be 7.2 volts, or 9 volts or 12 volts, etc. Anything that runs on a USB plug is 5 volts. The logic is, the manufacturer can make one electronic device for the world, changing only the external transformer box with the appropriate plug for each country, and by having the converter be external they can make the device smaller. Take a close look at the label on any of those little boxes, it'll have the input voltage and output voltage. If the box reads: '100-240V, 50-60Hz', that means they are universal. If it says 110 volts, don't plug it into an Aussie power point, or wham!

Hz means *cycles*. Voltage is the amount of electricity; Hz is how fast the power alternates from positive to negative. This is crucial to regulate the speed of an electric motor since a motor relies on changing fields (positive-negative) to make the motor spin. That's why anything with a motor in it like a clock, food mixer, refrigerator, microwave, washer or dryer, vacuum cleaner etc., will run only at the Hz it was designed for. So, bring your computer, phone charger, camera charger, etc, and leave your 110-volt 60 Hz appliances behind. If you plan on using heavier amperage like 110-volt power tools, bring a 300 or 500 watt, 110-240V transformer with a 50-60Hz frequency converter. More on this later.

Where Voltage is the amount of electricity, Amps is the amount of power behind it, and Watts are how the final combination of these are measured, i.e. the amount of work it will do. Here's the basic formula:

> Amps = Watts divided by Volts
> Volts = Watts divided by Amps
> Watts = Volts times Amps.

Most household circuits in the US are 20 amps. Most in Australia are 8 amps.

So, if you had a device that drew 1000 watts, in Australia with 240 volts wall current it would draw 4 amps, in the US, with 110 volts, it would draw 9 amps. Both systems supply the required watts, they just do it different ways.

Bottom line is, high volts with low amps won't hurt you, but low volts with high amps will. The US arrangement draws more amps so it is more dangerous.

Plugs   Here is an explanation and a set of solutions to keep you and your gear out of trouble.

Australian wall plugs are two or three prongs. The two-pronged plugs are the same spacing as North American plugs, but are splayed at an angle, 'pigeon-toed.' The third prong is flat-bladed like the other two but below and in the *centre*. Plug adapters are available to convert most foreign plugs to Australian power points, get some before you leave home because they'll be hard to find in Australia, the ones here will go the other way. *But before you plug something in, make absolutely sure the voltage will be corrected by your device.*

If you don't have a plug adapter there is another way. Since the two-prongs are exactly the same distance apart as an American plug, by using a pair of pliers you can carefully bend them to fit the power point. Just be sure your device will handle 240 volts/50 Hz, or WHAM!, you'll see fireworks.

Power points   You might have gathered a plug outlet in Australia is called a *power point*. Australia is very safety-conscious; that's why each power point is individually switched. The switches work the same as Australian light switches, opposite of those in America: down is on, up is off. If you can see the little red indicator on the top edge of the power point switch button, it's on.

Why is each *power point* switched? Safety. With every power point switched individually, you can turn off the power point before you plug-in or unplug the cord.

Most circuits, especially those around water, like in a bathroom, kitchen or outdoors, are fitted with an *RCD* (Residual Current Disrupter), to minimize the hazard. In the U.S., this is called a 'ground fault interrupter', or GFI.

Some basic terms: in Australia, a power cord is called a *lead* (pronounced *leed*). The electrical term for 'ground' is *earth*. A circuit isn't 'grounded', it is *earthed*.

Electrical converters   For older devices that aren't 100-240 volt compatible, small electrical converters that bump the wall voltage down from 240 volts to 110 volts are available in the U.S. from places like Radio Shack and travel stores. Get them <u>before</u> you come over; the converters available in Australian stores are designed to change the voltage in the opposite direction.

When shopping for a converter, check the wattage it puts out: a battery charger for your cellular phone or iPad draws little current, but a hair dryer draws a lot—special converters are made for hair dryers. Make sure you get the proper plug adapters for Australia as described above. A tip: don't put anything on top of a converter; they can put out a lot of heat.

If you're bringing along a lot of electronics for work or are moving to Australia for an extended time, you can get a heavy-duty 300 or 500 watt converter at an electronics supply store (buy them in North America before you leave, they're very expensive in Australia), then you can set up a 110-volt station in your home or business. This way, you can use larger 110-volt electronics, like your sound system, turntable, computer accessories, or your power tools. You'll need to bring North American-style 110-volt power strips and 110-volt extension cords for that station. Be aware, *not all converters change the cycles from 50 to 60Hz*, so anything with a motor, including electric clocks, turntables etc., might not run at the proper speed.

Don't bother bringing large appliances like washers, dryers, refrigerators, vacuum cleaners, etc. They draw too much current for a converter or transformer and aren't worth the trouble. Buy or rent them locally. You can rent appliances like refrigerators, washers, (referred to as *white goods*), TV's, computers and even furniture by the week in Australia.

If you have an electronic device with a wall box that won't work with 240-volts, you can swap the 110-volt box for a comparable 240-volt version These can be purchased at an electronics store like *JB HiFi* or *Jaycar*. These come with a variety of output plugs to fit various devices. However, just getting a unit that supplies the correct voltage isn't enough. It's crucial that the amperage output of the new wall box matches that of the 110-volt unit it's replacing, or is close. If the amperage is too low, the device won't work; if it's too high, it will burn it up. Read the label, write down both the output voltage and amperage, and match it with a 240-volt model, or just bring along the 110-volt wall transformer and have the salesperson match it. It's a bit of a hassle, but it's cheaper than buying a complete appliance. Electronics can be expensive in Australia, and some things aren't available at all.

Computers Windows-based PC's are the same as in North America. The operating systems and software work the same.

A Mac is often called an *Apple Mac*, and uses the same OS systems. Apple has the same relative market share as in North America: professionals who specialize in graphics, video editing, and people who like to be different.

USB 3.0, Firewire, Thunderbolt, HDMI, and all the various sizes of each are all standard. Bluetooth and Wi-Fi are standard. Monitors, keyboards and mouses work the same. The same brand printers are available as in North America, but not all ink cartridges. Bring a supply or be prepared to buy a new printer.

Australian websites end in *.au*. [more in the section on the

internet]

Notebook computers will handle 100-240 volts, all you need is a plug end adapter, get them before you leave the US.

Desktop computers may have to be manually switched from 110-volt to 240-volt. In the back of the computer, there may be a red recessed switch marked 110v-240v. Switch it to the proper voltage before plugging it in. In either case, you'll still need a plug adapter to convert your plug or buy a new cable.

Australian power cables are available that will plug directly into each unit that have the standard plug on the device end and the Australian splayed prong wall end, but they're expensive (A$10-A$20 each). If you have a lot of components, that will add up fast. It's a lot cheaper to put an adapter on the wall-plug end of the old cable. They're cheap (about US$1 each), but you need to buy them before you leave North America. Try Radio Shack or travel stores.

Again, beware! Make sure the device can handle 240v or has had the power supply switched to the 240v position before you plug it in!

Cell phone chargers If you're staying only a short while and will be *hiring* (renting) a car, just bring your car kit and charge the phone off the cigarette lighter.

FYI: It's illegal to talk on a handheld *mobile* (cell phone) while driving a car anywhere in Australia unless you use a hands-free kit, which consists of at least an earphone. Starting 1 July 2020, the fine in Western Australia will increase to $1000 and 4 demerit points.

Lightbulbs are called *globes.* Australia has banned old-fashioned tungsten filament globes, now all are either *flouro* (fluorescent) or LED. Exceptions are some ornamental globes and oven globes.

There are two kinds of standard-sized household 240v globes: *screw base* and *bayonet base.*

Newer lamps use the conventional American-style screw base—but don't try screwing in an American 110-volt *globe* into an Australian lamp: as soon as the switch is thrown, it will pop.

Bayonet bases are found on older lamps. The globe itself

looks the same, but the metal part that goes into the socket doesn't have threads; it instead has two small pins that positively lock the globe into the base.

Fluorescent tube fixtures work pretty much the same as in North America, but one clever addition is an external '*starter*', a little can-shaped component about the size of your thumb that twists into the side of the fixture. If your *fluoro* light doesn't work and the tube is good, pick up a replacement starter at the hardware store. It's cheaper and easier than replacing the entire ballast.

110-volt lamps   If you're moving to Australia, you can bring and use your American lamps. The wires are identical, as are the screw bases for the bulbs, so all you need to do is swap out the 110-volt bulbs for screw-base 240-volt globe and change the plug ends or use adapters.

Light switches   In America, you turn on a switch by flipping it up. In Australia, you flip it down.

Radios   Digitally-tuned North American radios can have problems with Australian stations. The same frequency bands are used, but the intervals between stations are different. Some can be adapted, some can't; check the manual. Older analogue styles don't have this problem.

Older Australian multi-band radios were called *radiograms*. Early AM radios didn't have frequencies printed on the dials, just the name of the cities, as the only thing broadcasting in those days was the ABC. Aussie component stereos from the '70s and '80s had separate tuners and amplifiers.

Video Formats   Australia and America use different electronic signals for video. America uses a system called 'NTSC', while Australia uses 'PAL'. Australian TVs are multi-format and play both systems, but American TVs aren't, so won't so don't bother bringing your set.

Australia changed over to digital in 2013, so analogue sets won't work. Since then the number of free-to-air stations increased from six to several dozen.

Though most broadcast signals are High Definition, they are still based in the native format, either NTSC, PAL or SECAM.

NTSC is the electronic standard for TV signals in the U.S., Canada, Mexico, and Central and South America (except Argentina and Brazil), along with Japan, South Korea, Taiwan, and the Philippines. The SECAM signal is used in France, Russia, and western Africa. Almost everyone else (including Australia and New Zealand) is on PAL. Each uses completely different electronic methods of reproducing a video image and playing sound.

Your American TV may work on Australian voltage, but the digital tuner is completely incompatible with the Australian system, so leave it behind

UK-bought TVs may work through an HDMI set top box, depending on the make. It is probably better to sell your old one and buy a new one in Oz, that way it will have full capability.

American DVD players will only play NTSC. If you're moving *Down Under*, sell your American TV equipment or put it in storage until you return.

Australian TVs and DVD players are '*multi-format*', they'll play anything: PAL, NTSC, and SECAM. Blue Ray decks can be a bit fussy. Australian multi-format VHS tape decks (remember VHS?) will play NTSC American videos, so your NTSC home movies and old films on tape will play in Australia TV and a Australian multi-format VCR (if you can find one).

Unfortunately, this is not the case when going back to the U.S. PAL videos won't play back in the U.S., since U.S. video equipment plays only NTSC.

DVDs are a different story. Though multi-format DVD players found in Australia will play NTSC as well as PAL, there's also a '*Region Code*' electronically imbedded in most commercially produced DVDs. This only allows them to be played on machines sold in that region, making it harder to produce counterfeit DVD's.

If you're interested, here are the regions:

Region 1   U.S. and Canada
Region 2   Europe and Japan, south Africa, Middle East
Region 3   Southeast Asia

Region 4   Australia, New Zealand, Central and South
           America, Mexico
Region 5   Russia, Eastern Europe, India, Africa
Region 6   China

So, what does this mean to you? If you buy a DVD in
Japan, you figure it should work in the U.S., because Japan and
the U.S. are both on NTSC, but it won't work, because they
have different Region Codes. But if you're in Australia, again
you're in luck: most DVD players sold in Australia are multi-
format and multi-region, so they'll play everything. If you're
buying a new DVD machine in Australia, make sure you get
one of these.

Either way, if you're moving to Australia, you can bring
your old NTSC DVD player, run it off a 240-volt to 110-volt
transformer, and play your old NTSC Region 1 movies on your
new Australian multi-format TV. The cables will plug right in.
No worries.

Hard drive video recorders appeared much later in
Australia than the U.S., around 2005. They're called *hard drive
digital recorders*, they are cheap, about $50. I use one to record
NFL games that are broadcast on free-to-air TV (on 7Mate)
early Monday morning in Perth (Sunday afternoon in the U.S.).
I watch them during the week with little chance of hearing who
won since NFL scores aren't mentioned in the news.

Streaming services available are Netflix, Stan, Disney+,
Apple TV+, Foxtel Now, Amazon Prime, Video, Kayo Sports
(ESPN content), 10 All Access, etc. Hulu may launch in 2020.

If you live in a huge, self-centred media market like the
U.S. you might not realize there is a digital firewall around
countries. In Australia we can't just subscribe to an American
or European media stream. Sometimes we click on a U.S.
video on Facebook and get a black screen with a notice saying
"this video is unavailable in your country."

To get a streaming service that is unavailable in Australia
you can subscribe to a *VPN* (*Virtual Private Network*) which
sets up a proxy address in the U.S.

Netflix Australia is a completely different steam than the
U.S. version and doesn't have the breadth of content as the

U.S. version. Before Netflix was available in Australia I used a VPN called Unblock US and streamed Netflix, but when Netflix Australia arrived it pre-empted my U.S. Netflix and forced me onto the Australian service.

Stan is an Australian service, owned by the *Channel Nine TV network*. It carries movies, TV shows and Showtime content like '*Get Shorty*' and '*Better Call Saul*'.

The two Australian government broadcasting services, *ABC* (Australian Broadcasting Corp) and *SBS* (Special Broadcast Service), have streams. ABC has a 24-hour news service plus a video library of its recent shows called *ABC iView*. SBS has a similar service called *SBS On Demand*.

There are edited MSNBC, CBSN, Fox, CNN, etc. available, though in abbreviated versions, mainly highlights and stories that can be a day or to old. YouTube is a great resource for foreign news content and will stream live foreign news. A smart TV will have direct access to many services plus an eclectic library of videos, and weekly NFL game highlights.

Cable & satellite TV (see **media**)

Health Care

Medicare   Australia enjoys universal health care, called *Medicare*. Everybody in the country can get medical care at little or no cost, depending on the doctor or hospital. The overall level of treatment is good, though waits for elective surgery can be lengthy. There's *private coverage*, which is supplemental to Medicare, for those who can afford it. More on *private health coverage* later.

The bottom line is that all Australians have basic health care. It's paid for through taxes, and though it's a major national expense, it doesn't bankrupt the treasury because everyone pays, and everyone is covered. Since the majority of medical treatment and medicines come through the government, prices are kept down. Supplemental private coverage is available for those who want private hospital rooms and greater choice of specialists.

Americans have been conditioned to think of this as evil Socialized Medicine. To them I say think of it this way: from a business standpoint there is a great advantage to have a system where everyone has health coverage and the business owner doesn't have to pay for it. He or he can concentrate on running their business instead of trying to pay their employees' healthcare premiums. Since everyone pays, it's a level playing field.

Medicare coverage. If you are an Australian citizen, a New Zealand citizen or an Australian Permanent Resident, you get Medicare.

Tourists can use medical services but will have to pay. If you have travel insurance you will have to apply to your insurance company to be reimbursed, keep your receipts. Some U.S. private medical insurance will pay for Australian services. My kids got their orthodonture paid for in Australia by my U.S. Motion Picture Industry Health Fund insurance.

Some doctors *bulk bill*, which means they'll bill Medicare directly and accept whatever Medicare pays as total payment, so the patient pays nothing and owes nothing. Only 23% of doctors take Medicare's payment as payment-in-full. This isn't just generosity, as a doctor friend has informed me, the advantage of *bulk billing* is doctors are guaranteed payment and don't have to chase deadbeats who don't pay their bills.

Most of the other 77% of doctors will credit what Medicare pays toward the bill. The difference between what Medicare pays and what you're charged is called *the gap* and is usually about 1/3 of the bill. About 85% of treatments are done this way.

Public hospitals work the same as bulk billing. X-rays are covered one-hundred-percent; a CT scan is about sixty-five percent.

An eye exam with most optometrists is covered *bulk billed*, but glasses aren't. Some states offer a subsidy.

On the surface, the health care system looks a lot like the U.S. system: doctors have private offices (called *surgeries* or *rooms*), by themselves or in groups. You book an appointment over the phone, you wait in a waiting room, you see the doctor. After the appointment, if they *bulk bill*, you just leave. If they don't *bulk bill*, at the payments desk you pay *the gap* and they do a debit card transaction. Medicare will deposit their portion of the payment electronically into your bank account. If you don't have a bank account they will give you a form to turn in to a Medicare office, where you will be reimbursed in cash.

General practitioners and specialists An important protocol: *you can't just book-in to see a specialist, you must first go to a GP and get a referral, otherwise Medicare will not cover the visit.* The GP's are the gate-keepers to the system.

The hierarchy is: doctors, physicians and surgeons. The first two are addressed as *'doctor'*, the latter as *'mister'*. If you find yourself *in hospital* and are introduced to a doctorish looking person who is referred to as *'mister'*, he's your surgeon. The doctor above him is called *'professor'*.

In Australia, there are fewer specialists, so GP's handle a lot of the load. A woman is more likely to go to her GP for routine female check-ups and to see a *gynaecologist* only if there is a complication. If you're suffering from clinical depression, you'd see a psychologist for counselling and your GP for an antidepressant. The GP may refer you to a psychiatrist.

Pharmaceutical Drugs The *Pharmaceutical Benefit Scheme* (*PBS*) covers prescription drugs with a deductible. This is automatic at the *chemist's* (pharmacy) when you pay for the prescription. Medicine is cheap, much cheaper than in the US.

Private health coverage 45% of Australians have supplemental private health coverage, which uses private specialists and hospitals with shorter waits for elective surgeries. Private coverage can also be offered as a job perk.

Typical private policies are about $2,500/year for a family of four—about what you'd pay per month in the U.S. These policies can partially cover dental and optical with limits.

The *private health insurance rebate* is an amount the government contributes towards the cost of your private health insurance premiums. The rebate is income-tested, which means your eligibility to receive it depends on your income. The rebate is a tax offset refundable against your income tax.

If you chose an elective surgery, your doctor will enter you into the private system directly.

What's the immediate difference between *Medicare* and *Private Coverage*? If have a medical emergency like a car accident or heart attack, whether you have private insurance or not, the ambulance will take you to the nearest public hospital emergency room and you'll enter into the public health system. You will be given expert emergency treatment, and once stabilized, if you need to be hospitalized and you don't have private insurance you'll stay in a public hospital, if you do you can choose to go into the private system.

One difference I've seen from the American system, is in post-natal treatment (private or public). After giving birth, new *mums* are allowed to stay *in hospital* a few more days to get the baby feeding and allow *mum* to regain her strength before sending her home.

I've had experience with Australian Private and Public systems, both as a patient and as a visitor.

The private hospitals are nicer with fewer patients in a room. The public hospitals are larger with more patients to a ward and more patients per staff. But from what I've seen the public hospitals provide excellent care, they are just a bit busier.

Bottom line: Private Coverage or Medicare, everyone in the country is covered for health care.

Healthcare terminology   One doesn't go '*to a hospital*' they go '*to hospital*', as if being in one was a condition, not a location.

A *junior doctor* is one who has completed his/her twelve-month internship and is undergoing further training to receive *fellowship* from the medical training college. This is similar to a 'resident' in the U.S.

A *registrar* is a doctor with a few years of training beyond his or her residency.

A *consultant* is a doctor who is a specialist.

A surgeon is called *mister*, not doctor.

A nurse is sometimes called a *sister*, with no religious implications.

Normal body temperature is *37 degrees C.* which is 98.6 degrees F.

Australians tend to call any cold the '*flu*'. You'll hear people say, "I'm feeling *fluie*."

Crook also means sick, as in "I'm feeling *crook*."

If a medicine or other substance is labelled *Not to be taken,* it means it isn't to be taken <u>internally</u>.

An intravenous injection is called a *jab* or a *needle*.

Out-patient surgery is called *day surgery*, or *same day surgery*.

Ibuprofen (Advil) is called *Nurofen*.

Acetaminophen (Tylenol) is called *Panadol.*

Aleve is called *Naprosyn* or *Naproxen* and requires a prescription.

Mononucleosis is called *glandular fever*.

Estrogen is spelled *oestrogen*.

A Caesarean section is also called a *Caesar*.

Women who opt for Caesareans because they don't want to go through normal childbirth—for whatever reason—are sometimes referred to as *too posh to push*. *Posh* means elegant.

Mental Health is as much an issue for Australians as for residents of other countries. This is more prevalent in regional areas where the remoteness sometimes brings feelings of isolation and despair.

As you travel the regional areas you may see an old dead tree standing in a field that is painted bright blue. They are a reminder that people care and you should seek help if you are having a rough time emotionally.

Health care for travellers Visitors to Australia should have traveller's insurance. If you have a minor medical problem get a recommendation for a local GP, book in, go and pay.

For serious emergencies, call *000* (*triple-zero*), or go to an emergency room. You might have to pay up front and later get your medical policy or travel insurance to cover things. Make sure you get receipts for everything and submit a claim to your insurer when you get back home. Make sure your travellers' insurance covers medical costs, trip cancellation, lost luggage, and the *excess* (deductible) on your hire car. If you are scuba diving, get diver coverage from DAN (Divers Accident Network), which is international, arrange coverage through your home country. DAN will cover air-evacuation from a dive boat, which is required on some live-aboard dive boats on the Barrier Reef. If you have a diving-related medical problem there is a 24-hour number for consultation, and in an emergency, they will coordinate your evacuation and treatment.

If you have Australian permanent residency or have a parent, spouse, or child who is an Australian citizen or resident, you'll automatically have Australian Medicare coverage. If you're from Ireland or New Zealand, you have full reciprocal coverage. If you're from the UK, Sweden, the Netherlands, Finland, Norway, Italy, or Malta, you're covered for *immediately necessary* treatment.

If you've migrated on a permanent residency visa or are on a work visa and have applied for permanent residence, you can get a Medicare card. The latest info is on the Medicare website: **www.medicare.gov.au**.

Australian diseases   Coronary heart disease is the leading disease in Australia for all ages combined, followed by lung cancer for males, and arthritis and other musculoskeletal conditions (such as back pain and osteoporosis) for females.

Melanoma is skin cancer. Skin cancer is Australia's most common cancer, with almost a million cases in 2015. It's primarily caused by excessive exposure to ultraviolet (UV) radiation from the sun, causing DNA damage to skin cells.

Australia is the melanoma capitol of the world. The ozone hole sits over the continent and lets through powerful sunlight. I've been in the tropics where a tour guide warned us of the tropical sun. The tropics have nothing like the Aussie sun, it's so strong you can feel it pressing down on your shoulders on a hot day.

Take melanoma seriously: *Slip Slap Slop* was the motto for the media campaign in the 90's: *slip* on a long-sleeved shirt, *slap* on a hat, *slop* on the sunscreen. If you see something abnormal growing on your skin, like a scab that won't heal or a scaly patch, get it checked out.

Ross River Virus is endemic to Australia, Papua New Guinea and other islands in the South Pacific. It is responsible for a type of mosquito-borne non-lethal but debilitating tropical disease known as *Ross River fever*, aka: *epidemic polyarthritis*.

It feels like flu plus possible swelling and joint stiffness, sometimes with a rash that lasts about a week. Symptoms appear about a week after being bit and last about a week. Sometimes joint stiffness will last a few months.

There is no vaccine, best practice is to avoid getting bit by *mozzies* (mosquitos), wear long sleeve shirts and pants and use mosquito repellent.

If you think you've got it, go see a doctor, they will give you anti-body tests.

Murray Valley encephalitis (MVE) is a rare but potentially fatal disease caused by the MVE virus which is carried by mosquitoes. *Kunjin virus* is a related virus that is also carried by mosquitoes, but generally causes less severe symptoms. It is limited to the northern parts of the country during the wet season. It can be serious, debilitating and fatal. Both *MVE* and *Kunjin* viruses are very rare. Approximately only 1 person in 1000 will develop MVE symptoms after being bitten by an infected mosquito. People who live in the affected area build up an immunity. Symptoms will vary from person to person. While many infected people will not develop any symptoms at all, children and adults who develop symptoms can become seriously ill.

The Covid-19 Pandemic As I was completing this second edition the pandemic hit. Surrounded by water with a small population and a strong public health system, the country had a distinct advantage, and the government responded quickly and decisively. The flip-side of the Australian curse of the *tyranny of distance* is *the safety of distance.*

The Prime Minister Scott Morrison, recently embarrassed by not responding quickly to the massive eastern bushfires of late 2019-early 2020, took Covid-19 very seriously, especially after seeing the virus tear through northern Italy. He quickly summoned a national cabinet meeting with all seven state premiers and devised a plan: close the national borders, shut the state borders, close businesses, institute social distancing, start testing, get personal protective gear and ventilators.

Australians watched in dismay as first Italy, then then the UK, both homelands for many Aussies, were ravished by the virus, and then in horror as it spread virtually unchecked, across the U.S.

The first outbreak was from the Ruby Princess cruise ship which docked in Sydney and disembarked passengers without testing them, and they disbursed across the country. The first wave was well under control by July.

All repatriating Australians coming in from overseas had to go into a mandatory 14 day quarantine, in a hotel specifically used for that purpose. The weak point in the system occurred in Melbourne, Victoria when the private security personnel who were hastily hired and given little training, let some of the quarantined go out for coffees and drinks.

The resurgence in late June of cases in Victoria shook things up. Victoria and New South Wales never shut their mutual border. The rest of the states had, and by mid-June had no cases and reopened.

By early August a strict stage 4 lock down had been put in place in Melbourne and surrounds, and the rest of the states closed their borders.

The danger of additional waves will remain until a vaccine is available and has been administered to 7 billion humans. Until then, Australia will be isolated from the rest of the world.

The first edition of this book had a shelf life of 13 years, hopefully by an additional 13 years this virus will be a footnote in history.

Pando **(pandemic) slang**   In typical Aussie irreverence, slang developed almost as fast as the virus spread.

Comedian Josh Hawkins: '*Me boss tested pozzi for the rona so now I'm in iso. Popped down to Woolies for some sanny but it's been bloody magpie'd.*'

Translation: "My boss tested positive for the Corona virus so I'm in isolation. I went to the market for some hand sanitizer but the hoarders had bought it all."

Flying doctor service

This is an Australian icon. The Royal Flying Doctor Service was established in 1928. It's partly funded by the state and federal governments, but the air fleet is supported entirely by charitable donations. It maintains a network of shortwave radios at remote settlements and pastoral stations throughout the Australian bush and provides communication, health care, advice, and air-evacuation when necessary. There are thousands of designated landing strips around the country. The brave doctors, nurses, and pilots have saved thousands of lives in the ninety years since it was founded.

Social assistance

Australia has a social welfare system that helps citizens with lower incomes, seniors, the unemployed, the disabled, and families that need counselling. There's also a system of allowances and benefits to supplement working people with low wages. There is a family tax benefit if you have kids, that helps with the cost of raising children.

It's a safety net, most people who need help receive help, it is a socially responsible system, however there are still some people who find themselves homeless and without food. There are food banks that distribute food. Many of these unfortunate people are waiting for public housing, and some find themselves *living rough*. The centralized welfare, employment, and family assistance agency is called *Centrelink*. There are Centrelink offices throughout the country. It is a part of the Department of Human Services, and can be contacted on the web at https://www.humanservices.gov.au, or you can hear a recorded directory by calling 132 468

Public housing for low-income and disadvantaged families is provided by the individual states. There are high-rise U.S.-style projects in Sydney and Melbourne, and low-density detached bungalows on master-planned estates located in the suburbs of other eastern cities and towns. In Western Australia (population of 2.72 million in 2020), the state housing authority *Homeswest* owns about 37,000 properties, including many houses in mainstream neighbourhoods. Homeswest provides varying rent subsidies to families who would otherwise be on the streets. It's not perfect, in 2017 there were 16,500 families and individuals on the wait list. These people could be living with friends, relatives, in their cars or '*rough*', on the streets.

The homeless problem in Australia isn't as widespread as it is in major American cities. You see people sleeping on the streets, but not in the numbers as in the U.S.

Pensions   The *Age Pension* is a scheme which pays a
steady income to eligible Australians to help them cope with
the costs of living when they're retired. If you're eligible, you
can receive up to $926.20 a *fortnight* (2 weeks), $1,396.20 for
couples.

To be eligible you must be over 66 and have your assets,
excluding your home, *deemed* at under $50,000. [See **Taxes** for
an explanation on *deeming*.]

There are also widow, *carer* (caregiver) and disability
pensions.

Concessions/concessionaires

Concessions are special rates that seniors and the disabled
receive on pharmaceuticals, transportation, car registration,
phone bills, utilities, and admission to entertainment events.
One needs to apply for a *concession card*.

Students can also qualify for some concessions for reduced
prices to events, train tickets, etc., by showing their student ID
cards.

A *Seniors Card* is state-issued discount card that gives
discounts at businesses including cinemas, some utilities, and
some free public transportation. Qualification varies from state
to state, in some states it's 60, some it's 63, some it's 65. When
you turn 60 contact the *Seniors Card* on your state's
government website to apply.

Education

The school year runs from February to December. There's
a six-to-eight-week summer break from Christmas until after
Australia Day (Jan. 26). There are two-week breaks around
Easter, another in late June and a third in October.

Terminology varies from state to state. Elementary schools
are called *Primary schools*. *Kindergarten* (or *kindy*) is
preschool. *Pre-primary* is equivalent to American kindergarten,
and depending on the state, might instead be called *reception*,
preparatory or *transition*. First grade is called *Year One*, and
so forth to *Year Six or Year Seven* (depending on the state.
There is no middle school.

High school is Years Seven or Eight through Year Twelve. Years eight through ten are mandatory until a student reaches age seventeen. Some students leave after year ten for independent apprenticeships or to train for a trade at a TAFE (Technical and Further Education), which is a state trade school where you can learn bricklaying, hairdressing, engineering, filmmaking, fashion design, etc. Some students drop out of high school after they turn 17 and get a job, some finish and then go onto apprenticeships, or TAFE, or university.

For those students who plan on going to university, Years Eleven and Twelve are spent studying for university entrance exams: *ATARS* (*Australian Tertiary Admissions Rank*).

In the typical non-judgemental Aussie way, people leaving school, whether graduating or dropping-out, are called *School Leavers*, or just *Leavers*.

Students in the last month of their twelfth year are called *Schoolies* and go on a raucous celebration much like spring break in the U.S. There are resort areas you might want to stay away from in late November when the *Leavers* are on the loose.

High School Education Certificates High school *Leavers* who pass their final exams receive a *HSC Higher School Certificate* (*New South Wales and Victoria*) *or a WACE* (*Western Australian Certificate of Education*), *SACE* (*South Australia Certificate of Education*), *TCE* (*Tasmania Certificate of Education*), *QCE* (*Queensland Certificate of Education*), *(NTCET) Northern Territory Certificate of Education and Training,* The Australian Capital Territory has something similar and it's tied to the New South Wales certificate. These are equivalent to a high school diploma, but Australians don't use that term regarding high school, a *diploma* is an advanced level of course completion at a TAFE.

ATARS (*Australian Tertiary Admissions Rank*). There are no SAT's. Students take classes and are tested in subjects that directly apply to their chosen field of university study. University admission is based on grades and scores on the applicant's *ATARS score.* Students who wish to go on to post-high school (tertiary) education, study the required subjects for their exams in years 11 and 12 and then *sit* the ATARS tests. Everything rides on getting a good score, so the pressure is on.

The Ranking is by percentage. If you get a '75', you are in the top 25% of the high school *leavers* taking the ATARS exams for your year.

Seems simple so far, but this is where it gets complicated. There are other factors such as a *Scaled Score*. For example, a score of 89 in Psychology might be scaled to 77, while a score of 89 in Physics might be scaled to 84. This is based on mapping each score to the national averages.

Then some voodoo math is applied to figure each student's standing. There are a fixed number of positions available, so each state then allocates entrance positions at its universities accordingly.

If this seems confusing, you're right.

School terminology

Semesters or quarters are called *terms*.

Grades are called *years. Year One* is first grade, *Year Two* is second grade, and so on.

Form room, or just *form* is home room.

A high school is sometimes called a *college* (example: Trinity College is a high school).

The American equivalent to college is *university* or *uni*.

The *head boy* and *head girl* are the popularly elected student leaders of a school, like student body presidents.

Dux is the honour awarded to the top student in the school.

A *cohort* is a group of students at the same level.

The *Parents and Citizens (P&C)* is the equivalent of the PTA.

VET is *Vocation Education Training*.

LOTE means *Language Other Than English* (a foreign language program).

Mathematics is called *maths*. They put an '*s*' on the end which makes sense since it's mathematics, not mathematic).

Substitute teachers are called *relief teachers*.

Alumni are called *ex-students*.

S&E stands for *Society and Environment*, the equivalent of Civics or Social Studies.

Rock Eisteddfod is a bi-yearly modern dance/drama competition held between schools as part of the Global Rock Challenge to promote healthy lifestyles.

Steiner Schools are innovative education systems, similar to Montessori Schools.

Government schools in Australia are generally pretty good. They aren't completely free, there are yearly student fees of about $250 (it increases as the student progresses), which cover expendables in cooking, science, physical education classes, etc. Though fees aren't mandatory, the money has to come from somewhere, and the students that pay end up paying for those that don't.

There are no local school districts, government schools are run from the state level. This means there's less local control over assigning of teachers and required curricula, though individual schools have a good amount of independence when it comes to day-to-day operations and programs. A *school council* is a board consisting of parents, teachers, the head boy and girl, and administrators that act as the public consultants for the school.

There's a different air about Australian high schools. Where American schools are the usually the centre of activity for teenagers (and often entire communities), with weekend football or basketball games, marching bands, cheerleading squads, proms, dances, after school clubs and weekend fundraisers, Australian schools do little of that. There are sports, like a school *footy* team, but the games take place after school with little fanfare and there's no big Friday night football or basketball game, and everything that goes with it. There might be a school play or orchestra concert, and there is a *Year Twelve Ball* (prom), but that's about it. Once school is out for the day, the campus is like a ghost town.

Private schools are a common alternative to public schools. Unlike American schools, Australian private schools receive government subsidies. This includes religious schools. There is no Bill of Rights in the Australian constitution guaranteeing religious freedom (or of press, speech, search and seizure, etc.), so there is no formalized separation of Church and State.

Private schools are run by, or affiliated with churches: Catholic, Methodist, Anglican (Church of England), are the most common. The Catholic schools are most numerous (and least expensive). The others are called *Independent Schools*. The most prestigious of the independents are usually Anglican. Private schools can be pre-primary-through-twelve or just high school. Some are all-girls, some are all-boys, some are co-ed.

Many parents believe it's easier to get into a university from a private school and they feel it's worth the trouble and expense. They would rather put the money into high school knowing the hard part is getting the good *marks* (grades) to be accepted into *uni* [more in **university tuition**].

A good education is just one reason to send your child to a private school, especially the more prestigious and expensive ones. Just as important—at least in the minds of the parents footing the bill—are the 'contacts' the kids will make. It's assumed that the friendships made at a private school will be essential later in building a career. Keep in mind, Australia has a relatively small population and many people stay in the city in which they were educated. Once in their careers they'll be running into many of the same people with whom they went to school. Important alliances developed in a private high school are expected to benefit one in later years, or so the theory goes. In practice, the '*Old Mates*' networks do work, and it makes it difficult for an 'outsider' to break in to some fields.

Catholic schools tend to be cheaper, and if you have more than one child at a Catholic school the prices go down considerably. *Independent* (non-Catholic) schools are more expensive. Yearly fees for private primary schools range from A$1,500 for Catholic schools to A$13,500 for the most prestigious schools. Private high schools range from A$5,500 per year for Catholic schools to A$22,000 for the most prestigious private high schools.

Private schools in Australia receive generous government subsidies. For example: in 2019 the government, state and *Commonwealth* (Federal) chipped in an average of A$13,000 per student in public schools, A$10,000 per student in Catholic schools and A$9,000 per student in independent schools.

The guiding principle is that subsidizing private schools

takes the burden off the public schools. In practicality, every tax dollar that goes into a private school is one that doesn't go into a public school, and not all parents can afford to send their kids to a private school—even a cheaper Catholic one—and while private schools can be selective in accepting only the students they like while rejecting problem students, public schools have no choice but to accept all students, including the ones the private schools have rejected or expelled. It also makes private education elitist. My feeling is this goes against Australian egalitarian principles, but don't try to convince an Aussie of that. When I've had the *cheekiness* to point this out, I'm usually dismissed as a *bloody Yank*.

Uniforms   All students in primary and high school—both public and private—wear uniforms. It simplifies the choice about what everyone is going to wear to school.

State schools usually have polo shirts and *jumpers* (long sleeve jerseys) with school crests on the breast as tops; shorts or long pants for the boys, and shorts, long pants, or skirts for the girls.

Private school students wear shirts, ties, and blazers; long pants or shorts for the boys, skirts for the girls, and knee socks for both. They look very formal, regimented and English. Despite the formal school-wear, as soon as classes are out the ties come off, the shirt tails come untucked visibly below the blazer, the knee socks fall. Nothing is sloppier than a private school kid five minutes after school is out.

A **gap year** is a year taken off school between high school and university, to travel and work. This is a common tradition. There are many programs in Australia and abroad that cater to young people out to expand their horizons before settling into the serious business of going to *uni* and building careers. American ski resorts are full of Aussie kids working and enjoying their *gap years*.

Universities   (commonly known as *uni*)

There are forty-four universities in Australia: thirty-seven public, five private and two international. There are 21 medical schools. There's no equivalent of an American junior college or community college. However, the closest thing is *TAFE* [next section].

The tuition average price for a bachelors in science is about $9000 per year, but there is a program called *Commonwealth Supported Place (CSP)* that offers assistance that significantly lowers tuition for qualifying Australian students who are citizens or permanent residents. By U.S. standards, the tuition is cheap, and much of it can be covered by student loans. In the U.S., you save your money for university; in Australia, many parents spend the money on private high schools because they know the hard part is getting into *uni* and the easy part is paying for it. This is because, for Australian citizens, there is the *Higher Education Contribution Scheme (HECS)* which provides cheap loans (compared to America) that are repayable once the graduate's income reaches a certain level. Permanent residents and New Zealand students are not eligible for *HECS* loans, but enjoy the same domestic tuition prices.

Foreign students attending Australian *uni's* is big business, the overseas students pay full-price tuition which fills the school's budgets and off-sets lower tuition for local students. Foreign education is a major Australian export, injecting $32 billion into the Australian economy in 2017. That year there were about 800,000 foreign students attending educational institutions, including 350,000 in higher education. Universities charge foreign students between A$20,000 and A$30,000 per year tuition, as opposed to about A$9000 (before CSP assistance) for domestic students. The Australian government estimates that typical international PhD fees are between A$18,000 and A$42,000 (USD $12,300-$28,750) per year. It is big business for uni's to recruit and educate foreign students. The Coronavirus of early 2020 cut into that when most foreign students, were refused entry due to quarantine. If these programs don't recover, budgets will suffer significantly.

To cope with that, the federal government, which pays for most of the universities' budgets, announced a realignment of tuition costs. Instead of prices being standard across disciplines, they will now reflect the cost of delivering the courses. Humanities degrees are going to become expensive, while science and engineering degrees are going to get cheaper.

The typical undergraduate course is three years for a

bachelor's degree, with an optional fourth year for *honours,* which is advanced study in the graduate's field. It's kind of like half of a master's degree.

The reason for three-year undergraduate programs in Australia versus four years in the U.S. is that there's a different attitude about general education courses: they expect that you should have had them in high school.

After graduating with a bachelor's degree, if your grades are good enough, you can do an *Honours Year* in your major, and then you have the option to do a master's degree. PhD's differ in that you do an oral presentation in your first six-months to defend your premise, and then do the work and publish your thesis over the next 3+ years without an oral at the end.

PhD's are free tuition for Australian citizens, permanent residents, and citizens of New Zealand. Scholarships are available on top of that for living expenses for citizens and those with Permanent Residencies.

TAFE   Since not everyone intends to go to *uni,* many students leave high school early to learn a trade, either through a private apprenticeship or at a *TAFE (Technical and Further Education).* They're set up like community colleges, but without the general education classes (which one is supposed to have already had in high school).

There is a standardized national curriculum with a system of *Certificates* and *Diplomas* awarded to different levels of skill and knowledge. You may need a *Certificate III* to be able to drive a forklift, or an *Advanced Diploma* to cut hair.

Depending on the size and location of the TAFE, specialized programs are offered in a wide choice of professions including: art, hair dressing, fashion design, auto mechanics, computer programming, computer repair, carpentry, business, electrical contracting, drafting, engineering, public relations, plumbing, video production, brick laying, radio announcing, pottery, operating heavy equipment, farming, livestock-raising, welding, etc.

An alternative to government TAFE's is *RTO's (Registered Training Organizations),* that use the same standardized national curriculum but are private organizations offering more specialized courses or ones with smaller, personalized classes.

Media

TV   Australia is a relatively small market. Television broadcasting began later and advanced more slowly than in North America or Europe. Australia is catching up but you won't find as many channels at your beckoning. As in other markets, we get TV several ways: *free-to-air* via commercial and government networks, on paid cable/satellite services, and by internet streaming.

While American television began in 1948, Australia began broadcasting eight years later in 1956, but only in the major cities. Regional television began in 1962 and *colour* TV began in 1975. The switch-over to digital TV in 2013 made previous equipment obsolete, but made a lot of bandwidth available and now each of the networks has multiple digital channels in the upper reaches of the tuner.

Free-to-air TV   There are six commercial networks: three in the capital cities, and three that serve rural and regional areas; and there are two government networks.

Government networks are more prominent than in U.S., more on a par with the BBC. *ABC* (*Australian Broadcasting Corporation*) and *SBS* (*Special Broadcast Service*), reach most of the populated areas of the country. Both are government-funded but independent, paid for from general taxes, not by a TV licensing fee as in the UK, or grant and viewer funded as in the U.S.

The ABC is sometimes called by the nickname *Aunty*. The ABC is completely non-commercial. ABC News has a history of balanced reporting, often challenging government policies and is sometimes vilified by right-wing politicians who keep chipping away at the budget. But the ABC also provides essential communication to the otherwise underserved rural areas, with several channels specializing in news, music and public interest broadcasting. The ABC particularly demonstrates its value in time of emergency like during the bushfires of 2019-20, storms, floods, and cyclones. It also broadcasts important sessions of federal parliament.

The ABC 2020 budget is about A$1.1 billion, out of a

national federal budget of A\$4.4 trillion. In June 2020 the Liberal/National government announced further cuts to the ABC, after promising during the 2019 election that it wouldn't.

The ABC has several channels: a dedicated 24-hour national news channel, an entertainment channel that also carries local news, a kids' channel and one that carries comedy/entertainment in the evenings and kids' programming during the day. It covers most of the country via conventional transmission, satellite and internet.

The ABC produces its own high-quality dramatic, documentary and entertainment shows. As important as the ABC is on television, it is just as vital on AM and FM radio with news, public interest, sports and music channels (more on this in **Radio**). The ABC also broadcasts digital music channels: country, classical, jazz, etc. tuneable on the upper TV channels. *ABC iView* streams an online library of recent shows. While not snobby, it's a more intelligent alternative than the commercial networks, the thinking person's channel.

SBS (Special Broadcasting Service) tends to service foreign language and indigenous audiences. It is also government-owned but only partially government-funded. The 2019 subsidy was A\$295 million, but SBS is allowed to sell commercial time to make up the difference. The content is also independent from government control.

SBS operates five TV channels: SBS, SBS Viceland, SBS World Movies, SBS Food and *NITV (National Indigenous Television)*.

The main SBS Channel broadcasts SBS World News each evening, independent from the ABC. During most of the daytime hours it carries news programs from countries around the world for the large immigrant population (in 2017 29% of the population were born overseas, 7.3 million migrants, including me—I watch PBS). These programs are broadcast in the originating languages without subtitles. I find this unfortunate as it would be fascinating and enlightening to be able to follow so many diverse international perspectives even if I had to read subtitles. A few programs are English language foreign broadcasts such as the English language version of DW (German news), and the American PBS News.

The other channels are *SBS World Movies* (with subtitles when needed), and *SBS Viceland* which carries alternative content mostly from the U.S., and *SBS Food*, a cooking channel. SBS also streams recent shows online on *SBS OnDemand*.

NITV (*National Indigenous Television*) is an SBS channel that carries Aboriginal and Torres Strait Islander broadcasting. There are news, sports, music, drama and cooking shows, from an Indigenous point of view. Besides serving the indigenous population, it's a great way for foreign visitors and recent immigrants to get a feeling and appreciation for contemporary Indigenous culture.

Commercial networks   There are three commercial networks in the major cities, and three more in regional and rural areas.

Channels Seven, Nine, and Ten are available in *the capital cities*: Brisbane, Sydney, Melbourne, Adelaide, Darwin, and Perth, and are on the same channel as their names imply (Simple, eh? Not. See the section on **tuning a television**). Hobart has Channels 7 and 9, and gets 10 on a regional carrier.

After analogue changed to digital and made additional bandwidth available, the networks began broadcasting additional, digital channels.

All three commercial networks and their assorted digital offspring carry Australian drama, news, gameshows, sports and *chat* (talk); plus various current popular shows from the U.S. and the UK. The networks are based out of Sydney and Melbourne where most of the Australian production originates. Their individual stations in the capital cities of each state produce a local half-hour nightly news program.

There once was a law that required local broadcasting to originate from each capital city. Local production of drama, variety and children's shows thrived, creating lots of production jobs and local on-screen representation. Though it was expensive it created a common experience, local identification and intimacy. The networks (which are part of huge media conglomerates) lobbied the government to change the laws. Local production ended and commercial TV is now Sydney-Melbourne-centric.

Regional TV   Australia is a huge geographical area with most of the population concentrated in just seven cities along the coasts, so there are vast areas where people are sparsely spread out in regional towns, on remote pastoral stations or mine sites. These rural areas are served by regional networks that are affiliated with the city commercial networks and carry those network's programming (the ABC and SBS also serve these areas).

WIN, *Southern Cross*, and *Prime7* are the rural and regional TV networks, covering remote areas and regional towns. This becomes apparent when you're in a hot, arid mining town in the far-north and see a TV ad for a dairy equipment company in the cool, lush far-south.

Some regional networks also own radio stations around the country.

Streaming   There was a time when American TV series aired in Australia a year or two behind the U.S. Now, with streaming services, they are available on the same day as in the U.S.

NBN (National Broadband Network, a government-funded countrywide broadband system) brought increased streaming speeds, though it has proved disappointing: it used contemporary technology when it was begun ten years ago and is now far behind the rest of the developed world.

Services available are Netflix, Stan, Disney+, Apple TV+, Foxtel Now, Amazon Prime, Video, Kayo Sports (ESPN content), 10 All Access. Hulu may launch in 2020.

YouTube streams same-day portions of shows otherwise unavailable, such as CBS Late Night with Steven Colbert, CNN, BBC, MSNBC, Fox, etc.

Cable & satellite   *Foxtel* is the main Pay-Tv provider in Australia, it absorbed all the smaller cable and satellite companies over the past ten years. But that business is shrinking as more viewers stream online. In the cities it comes in via cable, and in the rural areas by satellite. Foxtel has 5 million subscribers. It's a partnership, owned 65% by Rupert Murdoch's News Corporation, 35% by Telstra (the largest telephone company).

On *Foxtel Now* you can buy packages that have CNN,

BBC, Fox News, Sky Channel, Sky News, Disney, Arena, Nickelodeon, Discovery, Showtime, Comedy, two Nat Geo's, Animal Planet, ESPN, FOX Sports channels, many channels of Foxtel Movies. Most carry U.S. content with Australian announcers that make it seem a bit less American.

A recent merger with Netflix will allow Foxtel subscribers to tune into that streaming network without having to go online. *Fetch* is also a streaming service on cable or satellite for a fee. It comes in through a box you rent.

Radio   There are AM, FM and Digital stations.

The ABC, the Australian Broadcasting Corporation, is normally referred to as *the* ABC (just as football is referred to as *the football*), has several AM networks, devoted to news, talk, and features.

The ABC has a locally-produced station based in each state's capital city and covers that state's issues and activities. It's a middle-of-the-road talk-radio station that is distributed live state-wide via repeaters.

A twenty-four-hour national news network broadcasts mostly Australian news, but also broadcasts BBC and the English language editions of Deutsche Welle (German), Radio Netherlands (Dutch), plus National Public Radio's 'All Things Considered' (American). It also carries live coverage of Parliament when it's in session.

The ABC's third AM network is *Radio National*, a country-wide arts and journalism network. ABC National is more than just entertainment. In such a vast, sparsely settled country, it is a major communication link to the far-flung areas of the country, and it is heavily relied-upon for news, weather, entertainment and basic companionship.

All three networks carry cricket: if WWIII breaks out during a cricket match, Aussies won't hear about it until tea break.

There are also regional stations with local programming.

ABC has several FM nationwide stations: *ABC Classical, Triple J,* for listeners of 'alternative music', *Double J* was spun-off from Triple J as a hipper version.

The *SBS* radio network carries foreign language programming in 68 languages online, plus four dedicated on-the-air networks: *PopAraby*, *PopAsia*, *PopDesi* and *SBS Chill*, the latter of which is interesting background music.

There are various commercial AM and FM stations, mostly Top 40 rock, and a few country stations. These are owned by national media conglomerates and can originate from central studios in the eastern states or from local studios in state capitals and regional cities.

There are also *community stations* of various sizes. Some have major listenership: *RTR FM* in Perth is one of the hipper, trend-setting stations. Some are small niche stations, broadcasting in Russian or Greek, and are often run by unpaid volunteers. Some are quite large and sound commercial. These community stations are allowed to play limited commercial advertising which must be identified as *station sponsors*, while maintaining non-profit status. These stations have varied programming.

Music stations are required by their license to play a certain hourly quota of Australian-produced music. This is so they don't just play American and British hits, and we can maintain our culture and music. '*Mainstream adult contemporary*' and '*classic rock*' stations have a 20% quota; '*soft adult contemporary*' and '*hits and memories*' stations have a 15% quota; and '*easy listening*' stations have 10%.

And then there's *Racing Radio*—the bookie's dream—twenty-four-hours a day of horse and dog races [more in **gambling**].

Digital Radio in Australia uses the DAB+ standard and utilizes a higher standard codec for better sound. Available in *the capital cities* (Sydney, Melbourne, Brisbane, Perth, Adelaide, Canberra, Darwin and Hobart), it carries more than 20 ABC and SBS channels, plus dozens more local commercial stations. You will need a special radio to tune it in. It is available on newer car radios.

To listen to digital radio on my old, much-loved *analogue* stereo system with big speakers, I bought a cheap digital radio, and use it as a tuner by plugging a stereo mini-jack cable from the headphone jack to the back of the amp.

Streaming Radio For those hankering for stations from beyond Australia's shores, there's radio on the Internet. Use your computer to tune an app such as *Simple Radio.* You'll have thousands of international stations at a mouse-click. I use an old iPod Touch plugged in from the headphone jack via the same cable I use on my digital tuner, plugged into the to my analogue stereo. I can listen via Wi-Fi to stations from all over the world: jazz from New Orleans, LA, and New York, local 80's rock stations out of heartland America, pop music from France, Samba from Brazil, etc.

I also listen to those stations via Bluetooth from my iPhone when I'm driving around. It's a hoot to be driving on a country road in Oz hearing traffic reports from New York City. On my sailboat I plug the phone into waterproof speakers and listen to soft jazz while sailing blissfully on the local inlet.

Newspapers There are two nation-wide daily newspapers in Australia, and each of the seven capital cities has at least one major daily. There are also over 450 regional papers, including more than 100 ethnic language papers that serve urban immigrant communities, though, the numbers are diminishing post COVID 19

'*The Australian*' is the only nationally distributed daily newspaper aimed at a general readership. As of September 2019, its readership, including online, was 2,394,000 million. It is owned by Rupert Murdoch's *News Corp Australia.* The other national paper is the financial daily, '*The Australian Financial Review*', owned by the Nine Entertainment Co., owners of the Nine TV Network. Both are published Monday-Saturday.

News Corp Australia owns the sole daily newspapers in Brisbane, Adelaide, Hobart and Darwin, and the highest circulation papers in Sydney and Melbourne. That means Murdoch owns all the major papers in all the major cities except Perth. The Perth daily, *The West Australian*, is owned by *Seven West Media* which also owns the *Seven TV Network.* Perth's Sunday Times was owned by Murdoch, but he sold it to Seven West in 2016.

Many of the major papers are tabloid-style: opinion blended with fact…the reader has to figure where one ends and the other begins. There are two major papers in Melbourne: *The Age* is a serious paper, but more people read News Corps *Herald Sun*, which is a tabloid and is Australia's biggest selling daily.

A good example of a tabloid *The West Australian*, the only major Perth daily. Objectivity is secondary to selling papers, and opinionated headlines are common. A frontpage headline about then state *Premier* (Governor) Geoff Gallop read: "Fat cats flourish under Gallop." Another one read: "How scam scumbags rip us off." These aren't on the editorial page or labelled as opinion, but are presented as straight news, and since it's the only major paper in town, there's no alternative for state-wide news in Western Australia. Also, notice that Australian papers don't capitalize all the words in headlines, just the first word.

In the tabloids, *the cricket* often bumps major news from the front page. A bad car accident is described as a *horror crash*, *road carnage,* or as *chaos*. A sex-offender is a *sex fiend*; and the word "alleged" is rarely used. Some cover photos are shocking, if not completely disgusting. The inside front cover is opinion, gossip columns, and political cartoons. Car crashes, murders, political gaffes, and scandals fill the next ten pages, followed by two pages of world news, then the actual opinion pages, then business, racing, and *sport*.

Ironically, most of the news on the commercial Perth pop radio stations is lifted from the first five pages of that morning's *West Australian*, so people who get their news between music sets only know the paper's take on the news that day. As an alternative, many people in Perth read the national daily, *The Australian*, and get their local news from *the ABC*.

Rupert Murdoch and News Corp own all the major newspapers in Australia except the one in Perth. Plus he owns *Sky News* and *Fox News*, and 65% of the Foxtel Australia cable/satellite system.

Murdoch's worldwide media empire started in Australia when, at the age of 22, he inherited a chain of newspapers after his father died. In fifteen-years he'd built it into a major media empire. In 1968 he moved to the UK and built an empire there, inventing the tabloid newspaper style, and in 1973 he moved to the U.S. In 1985 he gave up his Australian citizenship to become a U.S. citizen to satisfy the legal requirement to own a

U.S. television network. He bought 20th Century Fox movie studios and began building the Fox TV network, which includes Fox News. In 2019 he sold 21st Century Fox to Disney for US$71.3 billion. Murdoch is known for using his media power to manipulate governments...and not just in the U.S. and U.K. Australia is no exception, his manipulation via his media empire contributed to the unexpected Liberal/National win in the 2019 Federal elections. This could have the effect of changing the course of Australia for a generation when it comes to climate and immigration.

News Corp Australia's revenues have been falling, -6% in 2018, continuing through 2019. Some experts attribute the loss in print media to the unpopular political positions News Corp media takes. Subscribership to Foxtel cable is falling due to the inevitable shift to online streaming services.

Magazines Australia is like the rest of the world, many magazines are being driven out of business by internet content. The best place to shop for magazines is at a *newsagent's*, where you can also buy lottery tickets.

Australian has its own versions of *Vogue*, *Men's Health*, plus specialty magazines on travel, photography, cars, motorcycles, cycling, fishing, guns etc. *TV Soap, Australian Women's Weekly* and *New Idea* are some of Australia's magazines for lovers of TV soaps, drama, gossip and glamour.

Many imported magazines are available from the UK and the U.S.   The *Time* magazine sold in Australia is the Singapore/Hong Kong edition, half as thick as the U.S. version with mostly international stories. If you're moving to Australia and want true American editions, rent a post office box in the States and have the magazines forwarded [see section on **receiving mail from the U.S. and Canada.**]

Gambling

Gamblers are also called *punters*. Gambling or *tipping*, is an Australian tradition and is promoted by the government and legally advertised by legal bookmakers on TV, radio, online and in print. There is legal gambling in many forms in all states: state lotteries, casinos in capital cities, betting parlours in neighbourhood shopping centres and pubs, and horse and dog tracks.

Gambling in the form of lotteries is prominent in schools, clubs, shopping centres. It is a part of the social fabric.

Horse and dog racing are so prominent that there are *Racing Radio* stations throughout the country that carry nothing but races and results.

Each of the capital cities and some of the smaller cities have at least one Las Vegas-style casino.

Gambling is state regulated, and the states rely on profits to fund many community programs, including arts, state film boards, drama groups, walk trails, and exercise equipment in parks.

TAB   If you can't make it to one of the big city casinos, there are opportunities right in your *neighbourhood*: *TAB (Totalizator Agency Board)* betting shops. TAB operates in over 4,400 venues across Australia, in shopping *centres* throughout cities, in neighbourhoods, and PubTAB in local taverns and eateries. Here one can place bets on horse races, dog races, sports games, etc. In Australia, TAB generates A$5.5 billion annually. It takes 1.1 billion bets annually and has 57% revenue market share of gambling.

TABs were originally government-owned, but are now largely privatized. It is a publicly-traded, dividend-paying company listed on the *ASX (Australian Stock Exchange.* In financial year 2018-19 it delivered $1 billion in returns to industry partners. In Australia, the bookies not only bet on the stock market, they are traded on it, too.

TAB also delivers multi-platform, market-leading racing vision through the *Sky Racing* brand, and owns racing radio stations across the country.

In 2019 TAB gave A$9.6 million to charities and community services. TAB also sponsors a program called *Betcare* for people who can't control their gambling, which, of course, is most of their customers.

Betting Methods   *Pokies* is short for *poker machines* (slot machines). Australian slot machine designs are used worldwide. The second largest manufacturer in the world is Australian: *Aristocrat*. Just about every pub and private club in Australia has *pokie* machines.

According to the *Australian Gambling Statistics 35th edition*, Australians bet more than $242 billion in *financial year* 2017-18. Averaged out across all 19.75 million Australians aged over 18 that's more than $12,000 per person: $25.8 billion was spent on racing ($1,340 per capita), $181.4 billion was spent on gaming like casinos and the pokies ($9,419 per capita), and $11.6 billion was spent on sports betting ($603 per capita).

Not every dollar spent on gambling is lost, wins can offset losses, but in the long-run *the house always wins*. The 2018-19 national gambling losses were $24.88 billion, that's more than $1,260 lost to gambling every year, up 5% from 2016-17.

Lotteries are the most common form of gambling. There are various games: randomly selected computer-generated tickets, state-wide big draws and national draws. You can play online games or go to a newsagent. Saturday afternoons you'd think selling lottery tickets was all newsagents did, I always feel a bit silly waiting in line to buy just a birthday card. There are local lotteries that benefit surf lifesaving groups, schools, etc. Winnings aren't taxable.

The simple reality is that people (especially Aussies) are going to gamble, so if it's government-regulated the profits are funnelled back to the community.

Western Australia's *Lotterywest* (est. 1932) is owned by the state government It took in A$985 million in 2019, and after paying out A$455 million in winnings, gave A$281 million back into the community: for health programs, sports, the arts, plus helping fund 682 grants to 613 non-profit organizations, local government authorities, the Perth Festival and Screenwest (the state film board). This made possible conservation projects, the Opera, local movie productions, sports teams, etc.

A typical Casino is Burswood, across the Swan River from the Perth *CBD* (*Central Business District*). Picture a medium-sized Las Vegas strip casino/hotel/resort. It's about halfway between the CBD and the airport, next to the new 60,000 seat Optus stadium and just across the freeway from the Belmont Horse Track. Burswood not only attracts Perth locals and visitors from around *WA* (Western Australia), but lures

tourists from Asia who want to holiday in a western country.
Like a Vegas hotel/casino, Burswood has a convention
centre, two hotels, a half-dozen restaurants and bars, a golf
course, a pool and spa, tennis courts, night clubs, a legitimate
theatre, and of course, a casino. Curiously, unlike American
casinos, the slots don't ding and chime; it's a relatively quiet
casino. The games are poker, baccarat, blackjack, craps and
Two Up.

Two-Up is a traditional Australian gambling game,
involving a *spinner* (dealer) throwing two coins or pennies into
the air. Players bet on whether the coins will fall on the ground
with both heads up, both tails up, or with one heads and one
tails. It's as basic as a game can get—kind of like pitching
pennies against a wall—more at home in a bush camp (where it
originated) than a casino.

When you first come upon the *Two Up* game in the casino,
it looks a bit strange. Between tables of *punters* playing on card
tables, roulette wheels and craps tables, you'll see a crowd
standing in a circle and assume there's another gaming table in
the middle. But when you get closer, you notice there's no
table at all, they're standing around an open carpeted space in
the middle of the casino floor. You notice how intent everyone
is. One of the players puts two large copper-coloured pennies
tails up on a small flat piece of wood called a *kip*. He or she
throws them up a certain height—the pennies must turn
properly—if not, the *ringkeeper* will make the player do it
again—when the pennies fall to the floor the ringkeeper leans
over them and reads them to see if they're both heads or both
tails. He then picks up the coins, everybody pays off, and they
toss again. Pretty basic.

Ban gambling???!!! The social fallout from gambling
is a concern to some, but the dependence on generated
revenues that benefit charities and community programs seems
to far outweigh any remorse. Gambling is deeply ingrained and
accepted in the Aussie way of life and is unlikely to ever be
eliminated.

Tobacco

Australia has one of the lowest proportion of persons aged

15+ years who were daily smokers (12.4%). Tobacco usage has halved in recent years, and smoking has been banned in, and near, most public buildings throughout the country. Smoking in restaurant *alfresco areas* (semi-enclosed outside dining patios) is still allowed (varies from state-to-state). Queensland has even banned smoking on patrolled beaches (ones with lifeguards).

The only bright spot for smokers is that Havana cigars are legal—but not cheap.

Alcohol

Beer   Australia is famous for beer—drinking it, as well as making it. Amongst some social classes, beer is almost a religion. Beer drinkers tend to be loyal to their brew.

One major misconception is that Australians drink *Foster's*. Chalk that one up to advertising, in America. Fact is, you rarely see actual Foster's, and it's not even made in Australia. Fosters was sold few years ago to Anhueser Busch-InBev. Aussies do drink a lot of former Foster's products: *VB* (Victoria Bitter), *Crownies* (Crown Lager), *Carlton, Sterling, Cascade*, etc.

Other major beers are *XXXX* (called *4X*) from Queensland, *Boags* from Tasmania, *Tooheys* from New South Wales, *Victoria Bitter* (VB) from Victoria, and many more. There are many smaller breweries, like Western Australia's *Little Creatures* and South Australia's *Coopers*. Coopers is the oldest Aussie brewery (1862) still producing, plus it's the largest Australian-owned brewery. There are micro-breweries, like *Feral, Bootleg, Mountain Goat* and my favourite local, *Thorny Devil*, brewed in a vineyard next to the beach not far from where I live. Hundreds of boutique breweries have sprung up throughout the country, each making their own brew to their own recipes, served fresh to locals and tourists.

In the U.S. one buys beer by the six-pack. In Australia we buy it by the *carton* (or *slab,* or *box*). In Australia six-packs are expensive, and buying it by the carton (which is 4 six-packs) works out cheaper. In the U.S., when you drop by a friend's for a BBQ or to watch a game, you bring a six-pack. In Australia you bring our own *esky* (ice chest or cooler bag) with your own particular beer (because everyone is particular and not everyone drinks the same *piss*). When you leave you take your *esky* along with the bottles you haven't consumed. Domestic beer isn't cheap—about twice the U.S. price. You can expect to pay A$40–60 for a *carton* (case), or A$15–20 for a six-pack, depending on the brand. If you hanker for the taste of home, Budweiser, Miller, Coors and Corona are available as expensive imports, along with many beers from Europe. When it comes to a good brew, what's a few dollars? Besides, one doesn't buy beer; one just rents it for an hour or so.

Beer terms   A *stubby* is a bottle of beer. A *stubby holder* is an individual bottle cooler made of wetsuit material that keeps the contents cold. The stubby holder is another Australian icon; Aussie males travelling abroad make sure to pack theirs because you can't count on finding one just anywhere. If hosting a group and you want to fit in, have a supply of *stubbie holders* on hand. Most Aussie males don't drink beer out of a glass unless drinking *draught* (draft) in a pub. *"Out of the bottle is just fine, mate. Ya got a stubby holder?"*

When you do go into a pub, tavern, or hotel and ask for a glass of beer, you'll need to know the correct terms, which vary from state to state and city to city. A small (eight oz.) glass is called a *pot* in Queensland, a *middy* in Western Australia, and a *schooner* in South Australia; while a large glass (sixteen oz.) can be a *schooner* in Queensland, but a *pint* in WA .

And then there's a *yardie*. A yardie is a yard-long beer glass, spherical at the bottom, with a narrow neck that flares to a wide horn at the top, and holds up to a half gallon of beer. If you Google *yardie,* you'll find the first two pages of listings are websites about how the former Australian prime minister (1983-91), Bob Hawke, once held the world speed record for drinking a yardie. It's truly something all Aussies can be proud of, and indeed, most Aussies hate politicians, but they loved Bob Hawke.

Besides being a stubby, a bottle of beer can be a *coldie*. A big bottle can be a *tallie* and a small bottle can be a *throwdown*.

A can of beer is a *tinny*. It's all confusing, but don't be intimidated. The first time you order at a pub in a region, you're bound to get it wrong; just ask the bartender for the right term and by the second round you'll be ordering like a local.

If you want to buy the next round, you say *"it's my shout,"* which means "the beer is on me." A *Yankee shout* is where everyone pays for themselves.

A case of beer can be a *carton, box,* or *slab*. If you make a stupid mistake at work you might get *slabbed*, which means you have to bring a case of beer to share with your work mates the next day.

A pitcher can be a *jug* or a *handle*. I once went into a pub after a hot twelve-hour drive up the west coast from Perth to Exmouth and ordered a pitcher of beer. The bartender didn't seem to understand what I was talking about. We went back and forth over it for a bit, and were both starting to get *a bit aggro* (aggressive) when a young woman sitting at the bar next to me said quietly, "Ask for a *jug*."

I asked for a *jug of beer*.

The bartender looked at me and said, "Why didn't ya say so in the first place? I thought ya wanted me to get a camera and take a picture of beer," and he served me my *jug* of beer. Had he just been *havin' a go at me* or was he serious? At that point, I didn't care, I was thirsty.

In the great Aussie *DIY (do-it-yourself)* tradition, you can also make your own beer with home brew kits available at supermarkets. There are also shops that cater to do-it-yourself brewing. They provide the materials and tanks, you do the work, and when it's all done, you bring home a large quantity of your very own concoction.

Wine   Australian wines are world class and relatively inexpensive. Eighty percent are from the Barossa Valley in South Australia and the Hunter Valley in New South Wales. There are cottage industries in almost every state. In Tasmania there's Piper River, Derwent Valley, Tamar Valley, in Western Australia there's the Swan Valley, the Southwest, and Margaret River.

Almost all varieties are grown. Sirah is called *Shiraz*

(pronounced *sheer-azz*). Blends are common, such as Cab-Merlot (Cabernet Sauvignon/Merlot) and Cab-Shiraz (Cabernet Sauvignon/Shiraz). Whites include Chardonnay, Chenin Blanc, and blends like Chardonnay/Sémillon/Sauvignon Blanc.

Dessert wines are quite good. Try *cane dried*, which means the cane is cut leaving the bunch in place on the trellis for a few weeks to intensify the sugars.

Chateau Cardboard is the *bogan* (redneck) favourite: wine packaged in a foil bag in two or four-litre cardboard boxes. Also called *a bag of wine*.

Mixed drinks in a can are called *RTDs* (*Ready to Drink*), slang: *alcho-pops*. You can get Jack Daniels and Coke, and various flavours of *Bacardi Breezer*. *Vodka Cruiser* has eight flavours: Wild Raspberry, Pure Pineapple, Lush Guava, Zesty Lemon-Line, Sunny Orange Passion fruit, Bold Berry Blend, Ripe Strawberry and Juicy Watermelon. They are consumed like any canned drink, they're easily transportable and handy for barbecues, beach picnics, and BYO restaurants, and they go down way too easily for young drinkers.

Hard liquor   North Queensland is sugarcane country, and that's what rum is made from. Bundaberg (*Bundy*) is the most famous rum, made in the town of the same name. There are several types and ages of Bundy rum, some so smooth you'd almost think you were drinking scotch. Bundy makes *RTD's*, the specialty is *Bundy and Coke*.

Various small label whiskeys are produced throughout the country. Imported booze is expensive—grab some duty-free on the plane or at the airport. Jack Daniels seems to be the most popular American whiskey, though I don't know why. Bogans wear shirts emblazoned with the logos.

The *esky* is an ice chest (from Eskimo cooler). They come in all shapes and sizes.

When Australians are invited over to a barbecue, they might show up with a small *esky* full of their regular brew and perhaps, if the misses is along, a bottle of wine. In America, when one brings a six-pack of beer to someone's home as a guest, one usually leaves what's left at the end of the night. Aussies, at the end of the evening, will take any unconsumed bottles home in their *esky*.

Bottle openers   Who needs one? Aussies use the bottom of a cigarette lighter. When camping I use the back door hinge on my Land Cruiser

Drink driving in Australia is what Yanks call drunk driving. My advice: don't. The police are extra-vigilant. Any time you're stopped by a cop—and they don't have to have probable cause like in the U.S.—you'll be asked to *blow in the bag*. There are police road blocks for *RBTs* (*random breath tests*) in major traffic areas on shopping and weekend nights. Pick a designated driver or take the train, taxi or Uber.

Drugs

Abuse of non-prescription drugs is very similar to North America, and to make a laundry list of them would be tedious and undoubtedly of little interest to the readers of this book.

Marijuana   Getting caught with a small amount of marijuana will result in a caution or minor fine, depending on the cop and the state. Every state has different laws and different consequences. In Western Australia, if you are caught with a few joints or residue on a smoking device, you might fall under the Cannabis Intervention Requirement Scheme or CIR and have to go to counselling. If caught with more than 100 grams (3.5 ounces) they might consider that you had it for sale and that would get you into court with a possible fine and jail time. Selling to underage people will get you into court and up to two-years in prison, plus a fine. In Victoria or New South Wales simple possession you will get the equivalent of a traffic ticket, and after two or three of these you may go to court and face jail time.

Cultivation In the ACT (Australian Capital Territory) you can grow 2 plants and have up to 50 grams legally, but you can't sell it, or share it.

In Western Australia growing, even for personal use, can get you 2 years in prison and a $2000 fine. More than 20 plants they will consider you growing for sale and you could get 25 years.

This isn't California or Colorado. Heed the warning.

A laugh: if you see a hand-painted sign in front of someone house that says, '*Pot Plants*', it is referring to potted plants: marigolds, not marijuana.

Heavier drugs (coke, heroin, speed, ice and ecstasy) will see you in court.

Meth is a major problem. 1 in 70 Australians have used Crystal Methedrine, or ICE in the past year. 10% of those used it once a month, while 20% of those used it weekly or daily. Part of this can be blamed on *workplace drug testing*. THC, the active ingredient in marijuana, can be detected in your system for up to a month with a urine test. ICE is undetectable in 3-5 days, so someone who works *FIFO* (*fly-in fly-out*), 2 weeks on, 1 week off, which is common in the mining industry, can binge for a few days when they get off, then abstain for a few days before flying back to site. If they smoked marijuana they would have it in their system for a month and be detected. Most mine sites require workers to take a urine or saliva test when they go back to site.

Real estate websites offer ICE testing kits to detect if your rental property has been used as a lab.

Petrol sniffing   One option among the poor was solvent sniffing: *petrol* (gasoline) or paint. This was prevalent on remote Aboriginal communities, young people fell into despair, with few opportunities and little hope. To combat this, remote communities switched to a non-sniffable petrol called *Opal*, which costs 33 cents/litre more to produce than standard petrol and is paid for with a government subsidy. These remote communities do not sell standard petrol.

The prevalence of petrol sniffing in selected Indigenous communities was reduced 95.2 per cent since *Opal* arrived in 2007.

Dress

Business attire   Australians are generally casual dressers, they dress up for business as required, but on weekends dress like they just came from the beach, even if they're a thousand kilometres inland in the desert.

In the *CBD's* (*Central Business District*), business suits are common for lawyers, accountants, and businessmen. This is usually a two-piece or vested suit, black or with an understated stripe, two-button or double-breasted, with tapered trousers. Once in the office, the coat comes off but the tie stays on.

Engineers and less-formal white-collar workers will wear slacks and a pressed, button-front shirt. Tan slacks and a light-blue shirt is common. Ties are rare.

Many workers who come into contact with the public wear uniform shirts. Real estate reps, bank workers, etc., wear ironed, button-front shirts or blouses with the company logo embroidered on the breast, name tags are common. Salespeople, counter clerks, car dealers, etc., wear golf or polo shirts with printed or embroidered logos on the breast. The colour is usually the same for everyone in a particular shop, so finding staff is easier.

One possible reason for the widespread use of uniform shirts is because Aussies are very casual dressers, and with required uniforms they are forced to dress presentably.

Tradesmen will commonly wear *hi-vis fluoro* (florescent) yellow, lime, or orange-coloured shirts, for high visibility and safety; and work pants with horizontal reflected strips around the thigh and knees, This is especially true for *truckies* (truck drivers), heavy machinery operators, road crews, construction workers or anyone on a mine site. These will commonly have the company's logo on the breast. Work clothes are UV-resistant (the southern sun is merciless). Shorts are common for working men. *Blokes* (men) under fifty wear long ones that go below the knee. Older blokes wear them short, just below the *bum* (butt).

School kids wear uniforms, too. Public schools use a polo shirt with the school logo, a heavier *jumper* (sweater or sweatshirt) with logo for cooler days; matching shorts, long pants, or skirts for girls, and shorts or long pants for boys. Private schools often require school blazers, button-front shirts, and ties; slacks or shorts for boys, skirts for girls; knee-socks for both.

After work   Perhaps because of the uniforms, both at school and at work, when Aussie males are on their own time, they usually dress very casually. The standard fashion seems to be beach togs, no matter where they live. *Boardies* (boardshorts: sloppy and loose-fitting), untucked T-shirts, or a *singlet* (tank top) are common. For footwear: thongs, or in the case of Western Australians and Queenslanders, barefoot. Dark socks worn with *joggers* (sneakers) are the norm. Faux racing shirts with Holden or Ford logos and sponsors emblems are always in vogue.

Many Aussie males seem to be impervious to rain and cold and dress lightly in singlet, shorts, and thongs, even on the coldest days. In deference to a bad storm you might see a bloke wearing a jacket or a hoodie with shorts and thongs. Few people dress differently for the rain; most ignore it. Don't worry about them, *they'll be right*.

Going out   In the cities, many businessmen and women will dress up to go out. Black seems to be the colour of choice. In the suburbs, many men go out in beach clothes, and it's common to see a well-dressed woman in a nice cocktail dress and heels accompanied by a man wearing baggy shorts, thongs, and a T-shirt printed with a car logo, or an off-colour saying. This has become institutionalized to the point where it's intentionally used in the wardrobe on TV commercials—I know this for a fact because I've worked on them and asked the Agency people about it.

Footwear deserves mentioning. I've seen people at the *tip* (city dump) wearing nothing but thin rubber thongs on their feet, up to their shins in debris. At least they weren't barefoot.

Nikes and Adidas (pronounced ah-dee-dahs) can be pricey, over A$200 for a fashionable pair, though Chinese imports are cheaper.

The traditional work boot is a short, pull-on with elastic sides, water and oil-proof leather, often with steel toes. Rossi's (Rossiters) are still made in Adelaide, Blundstones were made in Tasmania, but now in China. They're relatively inexpensive and sturdy. Great on a farm as you can easily slip them off when going in the house so as not to track in dirt. Mine sites require lace-up steel toes, so boot manufacturers make laceups with zip-sides which are easier to get on and off.

Younger business people who wear suits and slacks often choose a leather lace shoe with an exaggerated long toe.

Multi-story buildings

Again, things are different.

The bottom floor is the *ground floor*, the floor above that is the *first floor*, and on up. The area below the ground floor, as in a building on a hillside, is called an *undercroft*.

Some office buildings are wholly owned, some are *strata-titled* (co-ops), with individual offices separately owned. This provides investment opportunities for owner-occupiers or small investors [see section on **real estate**]. Shops in centres can also be *strata-titled*.

Australians like to formally name otherwise ordinary buildings. Sometimes it's after the original builder, sometimes after the occupant. The Asthma Foundation in Perth is in a modest office building called *Asthma Foundation House*. Wesfarmers, a multi-billion-dollar corporation, is in a fifteen-story skyscraper called *Wesfarmers House*.

The Australian home

A tour Most Australian homes have several smaller rooms instead of fewer, larger rooms. One reason is that it's easier to heat in winter and cool in summer, as most homes don't have central heating. A typical home might have a *lounge* room (living room), a family room, a games room, a screened-in veranda, a kitchen, bedrooms, bathroom, and a toilet or two.

The toilet itself isn't always in the same room with the sink, bath and shower, but often is in a separate room. This makes sense for a family, as one person can be washing in one room while another person is using the toilet in the other.

Toilets and bathrooms have tile floors with drains in the centre; useful if there's an overflow or when it comes time to mop, but short on aesthetics as the sink and shower drains are plumbed common with the floor drain, which means the stuff that goes down them can be heard gurgling and seen passing under the floor drain. Thankfully, toilets are on separate lines.

To save water, Australians use two-speed toilets: one button for a half-flush, the other for a full-flush. On some toilets, it's pull for half, push for full; on others, it's by duration—hold it down two seconds for half, longer for full. Don't forget to observe if the toilet water spins the opposite direction as in the Northern Hemisphere.

Bedrooms in older homes don't have built-in closets; instead they'll have a freestanding *wardrobe*, often called a *robe*. If you rent an unfurnished older home, you might have to buy a *robe* or two.

Electric blankets in Australia are heated electric pads that are placed <u>under</u> the sheets, immediately on top of the mattress. American-style electric blankets that go on top are unavailable, and if you ask for one and describe how it works, you'll receive puzzled stares.

Kitchens typically have a meals area in addition to a separate, more formal dining room. In the kitchen, you'll find most of the *mod cons* (modern conveniences) you're used to: double sink (usually stainless steel), microwave, and lots of appliances, like toasters, juicers, ice cream makers, etc. The stove (sometimes called the *hob* or a *cooker*) can be gas or electric or both: a gas top and an electric oven. Refrigerators tend to be about two-thirds smaller than those in North America; some have an ice maker and cold water spout. Often there's a second fridge on the back porch (the *beer fridge*), and sometimes a deep-freeze.

Dishwashers aren't as common as in the U.S., and there are no garbage disposals or trash compacters, but you can be certain of finding an electric kettle in every kitchen. This is just what the name implies: a vessel you plug into a power point, flip the switch in the handle and it heats the water for you. When it's boiled, it switches off automatically. These are as common in an Aussie kitchen as the sink itself.

When hand-washing dishes, Aussies use soap, but typically don't rinse the dishes with fresh water before putting them in the drying rack.

Garages   Aussie houses often have carports instead of garages. Some of these have lockable garage doors, but are open to the sides and back.

The shed is another Aussie icon. Located in the backyard, it can be the garage or a simple corrugated galvanized steel structure for tools and storage. This is where Dad retreats when he's had enough pleasant family life. It's no surprise that this is also where a *beer fridge* is commonly located.

Air con (*air conditioning*) can refer to both cooling and heating. There are several kinds used.

Window-mounted units have largely been replaced by *reverse-cycle* (also called *split-systems*) installed in individual rooms. A vented box is mounted high on an interior wall with hoses going through the wall to an outside heat pump. These units can run in one direction as an air conditioner and, at a touch of a button, can be run in reverse as a heater. Most have TV-set-like remote controls.

Large centrally-located forced air systems (called *ducted systems*) like those found in suburban American houses are rare in Australian homes. Some newer high-end homes are being built with them

You'll find many homes will have a whole-house evaporative cooler, aka 'swamp cooler' as was prevalent in the U.S. many years ago. They're simply a big blower box on the roof with water plumbed to it. The water soaks into pads in the sides of the box, an electric fan pulls air through the pads, evaporation cools the air, which is then blown throughout the house via ducts. The trick is to leave a few windows open so the air can flow through. These don't work well in humid regions.

Water heaters   Though conventional hot water systems using gas or electric-heated holding tanks are available, *instant-on* water heaters are still common. It's a box about half the size of a microwave, mounted on an outside wall near a bathroom. It super-heats the water in a small (about a half-gallon) copper tank before delivering it into the house. This system is energy efficient but can produce an irregular hot water mix in the shower. The trick is, turn on the hot water, then once it's at full heat, blend in the cold water to the desired temperature. Properly set-up, these systems work as well as the large water heaters used in North America, but with considerable savings from not having to keep a large amount of water constantly heated.

Another energy-efficient alternative to the instant-on systems are solar water heaters mounted on the roof. Normal city pressure pushes the water up to the heater where it flows through a solar collector (a radiator made of copper pipes in a black box), then into a large water storage tank where it continues to circulate by convection. They also have an electric or gas booster to heat the water on cold or sunless days or at night. Older systems had time clocks, so heat can be boosted automatically for early morning or late-night needs. For newer systems a small time-clock the size of a breaker can be substituted as a timer, obtainable at an industrial electric supply shop. Otherwise you can switch the boosters off at the main power panel during summer months to save energy.

Washing machines are as essential as in North America, but dryers tend to be smaller and only used in the winter or in rainy weather, as Aussies line-dry most of their wash. Because of this, dryers are often kept outside on the back porch or in a nearby shed.

The *Hills Hoist* is a four-sided, rotating clothesline on a central pipe with a crank in the middle so you can lower it to hang the clothes and then raise it so the kids and the family dog can't get at them. It's a homegrown invention Aussies are proud of.

Misc.   Window screens are called *flyscreens* or *flywire*. Security screens, heavy gauge flywire, are common to prevent burglaries.

An inside trash can is called a *rubbish bin*. An outside trash can with wheels is called a *wheelie bin*.

The kids' playhouse is called a *cubby*.

A hand rail is called a *balustrade*.

Hanging pictures   When attempting to hang pictures on plaster walls, don't use nails. Unlike *gypboard* (sheetrock), plaster crumbles and leaves big holes. Use a masonry drill and a wall anchor insert. For heavy items, use *Dynabolts*.

House   architecture   in   Australia   developed pragmatically. Early *humpies* (native shacks) led to mud brick cabins, then corrugated galvanised steel shacks, then timber plank homes. Today there's a *hotchpotch* (hodgepodge) of styles.

Australian cities are huge suburbs, and there comes a point where it is impractical to keep building out. As cities build-in instead, older homes on larger inner suburb blocks are knocked down and replaced with duplexes and triplexes, which have little set-backs from the street, no backyard and fill the block with buildings, the only open space is the driveway.

Inner city multi-story apartment buildings are sprouting up. The apartment is often owned by the occupant on a strata title [more on this in **real estate**].

Cookie-cutter tract homes aren't common; homes are generally individually built [see **real estate**], so there's more variation than in suburban America. That said, the basic suburban brick home is relatively boring, but there are some interesting styles if you look for them.

Federation refers to the house style built at the time Australia federated into a nation, around 1900. It's generally red brick and white mortar, with high peaked roofs covered in corrugated steel, often *bullnose* (curved down over the veranda), with Queen Anne filigree around the corners. The windows are tall, slim, multi-panelled, often with *leadlight* (stained glass) patterns and artwork. There are many examples of these still standing, plus new versions being built reminiscent of the age.

Italian immigrants built brick houses with a series of arches across the fronts, often supported by Roman columns. Short columns support *balustrades* (handrails).

Some homes are split-level with the garage and a few rooms on the lower floor. Broad exterior steps lead up to second-floor entrances where the living areas are. This split-level style is called a house with an *undercroft*.

Scattered in the older big city suburbs are colonial farmhouses, English country cottages, Mediterranean villas with tile roofs, Californian Craftsman bungalows, and ultra-modern white cubical homes in multi-story arrays.

However, most newer suburban homes are practical, double brick, but *rendered (plastered over)*.

Construction   Older houses were made of wooden planks, *cladding* (siding) or *weatherboard* (also called *Hardiplank,* after the manufacturer, the John Hardie company). Weatherboard is a fibre-cement plank still in use today and used like shiplap. Some were made of pressed asbestos sheets—called *fibro*—which has been illegal since the late 1980's.

Asbestos was a common building material until its cancerous side effects were discovered. Corrugated asbestos fencing was common throughout Australia, and a lot of it is still around. They say it's safe as long as you keep it sealed in a coat of paint. Beware: don't break up old *fibro* boards or fence materials.

In the southeast and west, brick construction is now very common. Some brick houses in the eastern states are merely a veneer of brick. True brick houses have outer walls that are *double brick* (two layers with an air space in the middle), which keeps inner walls dry and insulated. The inside walls are single-thickness. Masonry is un-reinforced, since earthquakes are uncommon. The inside of brick houses is often left raw brick or *rendered* (plastered). In very dry weather, the mortar in brick homes can crack, and homeowners are advised to water their walls.

Timber (wood) framed houses aren't as common as brick. As wood studs become more expensive, hollow steel beams for framing are being used. Wood is also subject to *white ants* (termites), which are a major problem.

Rammed earth (which looks like poured concrete) is a new trend: cool in the summer, warm in the winter. *ECO block* is concrete poured into four to eight-inch wide hollows in foam forms with rebar inserted. It's energy efficient and sturdy [also see **real estate, new homes**].

In the northern tropics, homes with broad verandas are built on poles called *stumps*. This construction allows air to circulate underneath and provides additional storage. It's also good in a flood and to protect the houses from termites. Queenslander houses typically have lots of air circulation and sometimes fancy filigree around the verandas.

Deep sewerage refers to sewage systems piped to a municipal treatment plant, as opposed to on-site septic systems.

Roofing is either fired-cement tiles in various shapes and colours, or sheets of corrugated galvanised steel. The steel can be either factory painted (*Colourbond*) or left with the shiny galvanised finish.

Tile roofs are supported by narrow toe-rails. Tiles interlock and rest on top, and a lip on the tile hooks over the top edge of the rail. Only about every fourth tile is nailed to the rail, so be very careful walking on these rooves; it's easy to crack a tile and fall through. Step where the tiles overlap; it's the strongest part. The advantage of these rooves is that they ventilate well and are waterproof, and it's easy to remove a section to replace tiles if needed or to gain access under the roof.

A *timber and iron* house refers to a wooden house with a corrugated galvanized steel roof. To Americans, corrugated steel roofs might seem cheap, like they belong on a mining shack. Indeed, they go back 150 years in Australia. Early settlers would build their entire houses, including the walls, out of it, since it was easily transported and lasted a long time.

It still is and does. Many new houses are roofed with corrugated sheets of steel, in galvanized finish or *Colourbond*, resting on sturdy wooden support beams. *Bullnose* sheets are pre-curved sections that give a classic *Federation* look.

Corrugated steel sheets are relatively inexpensive, light, sturdy, and easy to work with. One man can roof a house in two days, and the sound of rain falling on it is pleasant, especially in dry country. When installing it, put in a lot of screws through the steel into the supporting timbers to hold the panels down in strong wind. If you have to walk on the roof, walk where the screws are; the support beams will be directly underneath.

White ants (termites) are virulent in Australia. They'll eat through unprotected pine in a few months. Anything wood should be off the ground on steel footings and the bases painted with creosote if possible. In the northern regions of Australia, termites will make mounds that can grow to two and a half metres high (eight feet).

Wood dimensions come in either metric or imperial.

When you refer to a wood size, the order of the dimensions is reversed. The common two-by-four is called a *four-by-two*, a one-by-eight is an *eight-by-one*, etc. Dimensions are also in millimetres, so 19mm is about ¾ inch, and 40mm is about 1½ inch. Most tape measures are in both metres and inches and can be used as a handy converter. I find it easier to estimate in feet and then build in meters. Millimetres are easier to read on a tape measure and better than having to add fractions of an inch.

Lumber is called *timber*. Be wary when you price timber in the shop, as it's sold both by the length and by the metre. Look closely; shelf placards will read $X per *len.* (length) or $X per *mtr.* (metre). A metre is about 3.25 feet.

Pine, spruce, or fir is also called *oregon*, though it usually refers to Douglas Fir which was imported and grown as a forest crop. Plywood can be expensive. Native woods like jarrah are also expensive, though incredibly hard and strong.

Jarrah, a eucalypt native to southwest Western Australia, is such tough wood it is often recycled, salvaged from demolished homes. It is so hard you have to drill a hole before you can nail into it. Hundred-year-old wharf pilings have been made into beautiful table tops. You can mill off the weathered-grey outer layer revealing a beautiful polished red surface ready for another hundred years of life as furniture.

Wood glue, like Elmers, is called *PVA* glue.

Gardens   Aussies love their backyards. The Australian dream is a four-bedroom house on quarter-acre *block* (lot) with a Holden in the carport, a wide-screen TV in the lounge, a shed out back, and a lawn all around.

They love their lawns and their flower beds. Unfortunately, the climate trend is countrywide drought. The 'El Nino' that brings rain to the U.S. robs it from Australia. Australia likes 'La Nina', which brings winter rains. Water rationing is normal, with watering days mandated and fines levied if violated.

Garden hoses, sometimes called *hose pipes,* are innovative. Instead of having the American screw-in fitting on the ends, they have plastic quick-releases. Any hose will pop onto the fitting at the faucet and any nozzle will pop onto the other end. If you're migrating, don't bother bringing the hoses; buy them there.

Sprinklers are also called *reticulation*. Drip irrigation is common. Many suburban *blocks* (lots) have *bores* (wells). *Reticulated sewage* is a sewage treatment system on the property that uses the treated wastewater, or the *grey water* from sinks and showers to irrigate the landscaping.

Nuts & bolts   Though Australia has been on the metric system for forty years, standard or Imperial (USA measurement in fractions of an inch) nuts and bolts are still as common as metric, so hang onto your tools.

Nuts, bolts, screws, and nails are called *fixings*.

Tools   A wrench is a *spanner*. A C-clamp is a *G-clamp*. Power is 240v 50 Hz, so don't bother to bring your wall-powered tools. But do bring your battery powered tools, which can be expensive here. You can put a plug adapter on the battery charger to make it work.

Swimming pools

In 2012 two-thirds of Australian backyard pools were saltwater. It's not seawater, but fresh water that has had salt added to it; ocean water is eight-times saltier. Saltwater pools are far superior to normal chlorinated ones. The salt is actually good for your skin and is a recommended treatment for eczema. Most noticeably, it's much nicer than stinky, eye-stinging chlorine.

How do saltwater pools work? If you remember your high school chemistry, salt is a molecule containing sodium and chlorine, NaCl. An electrical unit in the pool's filtering system *electrolyses* the NaCl molecule, producing NaOCl, sodium hypochlorite, a safe form of chlorine that purifies and sterilizes the water. Instead of pouring jugs of chlorine into the pool, you occasionally add an eight-kilogram (twenty-lb.) bag of non-iodized swimming pool salt, just pour it into the shallow end and let it dissolve. The sodium pulls the acidity down, so you also have to add small amounts of hydrochloric acid to keep it balanced, but it's still easier to maintain and better for swimmers than chlorine-only systems. Get a simple ph test kit and follow the instructions.

Public pools, because of their size and the large numbers of people that use them, utilize the same conventional chlorination systems common in North America.

Real estate

Methods of land ownership   *Freehold, leasehold* and *Crown land* are the basis of land ownership in Australia.

Freehold means privately owned land. This can be bought and sold.

Crown land is government owned land and can be used for parks, utilities, airports, government facilities, granted to individuals or corporations, sold as *freehold* land, or leased. The *Crown* originally referred to the Royal Family, but it now applies to any government land ownership, be it state or federal. The land is held in the *right of the Crown*, and *the Crown* has legal rights as an individual land owner. About half of all Australian land is *Crown* land, including ninety-three percent of Western Australia.

Leasehold is where an individual or corporation buys a long-term lease on Crown land, usually ninety-nine years, and can treat the lands as if they owned it privately. Throughout the interior, huge tracts consisting of hundreds of square kilometres of Crown land are leased as cattle and sheep stations. The backbone of the economy—the mining industry—is entirely on leased land.

All the privately occupied land in the *ACT* (*Australian Capital Territory*) is *leasehold*. This was done to avoid speculation in undeveloped land. In 1908, the city of Canberra was created as the nation's capital from scratch in the bush because a compromise couldn't be reached to base the capital in either of the two major cities, Melbourne or Sydney. Cheap leases were issued to stimulate home building to jump-start development of the city. An individual was issued a lease and had to build a house on it within a year. The leases are now sold as if they were private land, and a nominal annual fee is paid to the government.

Real estate terms   The equivalent of a U.S. real estate agent is called a *real estate representative* (or *rep*), while the equivalent of a U.S. real estate broker is an *agent*.

Escrow is called *settlement*. An escrow officer is a *settlement agent* or *conveyancer*. Minimum settlement time for a cash sale is about three weeks.

Home loans work similar to those in North America.

Mortgage payments are called *repayments*.

A lien is called a *caveat* and can be placed against a property without the owner's knowledge.

A *Dutch auction:* an auction where the price is lowered until it gets a bid, as long as it is over the reserve.

Agreeance means agreement.

Countersign means counter-offer

Strata refers to condominium-style ownership, either private residential or commercial [more in **strata titles**].

When land is condemned for public use, it's called *resumption*. The land is said to have been *resumed*.

A model home is a *display home*; model homes are in *display villages*. A housing tract is called a *housing estate*.

Buying off the plan means buying anything that hasn't been built yet. This can be an unbuilt tract home, *strata* (condo-style) development, office, or commercial building.

A *greenfield project* is a previously undeveloped site.

A *brownfield project* is modifying or developing an existing site.

Reno means renovated or renovations.

An open house is called a *home open*. *Home opens* are generally held on Saturdays or Sundays, are advertised in the papers, and last only about one hour. The short session means a *rep* can open several homes that day, while *stickybeaks* (looky-loos) are minimized and homeowners aren't inconvenienced for the entire day. Temporary signs are posted at cross streets to lead you to the house.

House and *block* (lot) size are expressed in square metres. For an approximate estimate, just add a zero to the square metres, plus a little (i.e., 200 sq. metres is about 2,000 sq. feet). A quarter acre is about 1,000 sq. metres. Another common measurement is the *hectare*, which is 10,000 sq. metres, or about 2.5 acres.

Foreign investment in real estate   Only citizens, legal permanent residents, citizens of New Zealand, and foreign nationals married to an Australian can automatically buy residential property in Australia. All others must apply to the *Foreign Investment Review Board* (*FIRB*). With approval, foreign nationals may be able to buy new residential property, but when they eventually sell it, it will have to be sold to an Australian. This has created a problem as foreign investors—mainly from China—have driven up house prices beyond what most Aussies can afford. Commercial property is easier for a foreign national to purchase.

Under the *Australia-United States Free Trade Agreement* (*AUSFTA*), it's easier for U.S. citizens to buy commercial property. For specific information, try the website at **www.firb.gov.au.**

Home sales   Just like in the U.S. and Canada, owning your own home is the Australian dream. The process of buying a home is similar.

Commissions are around 2–3%. Usually there's <u>no</u> buyers' rep, only the sellers' rep serving both buyer and seller. Since the seller's rep is by definition biased toward the seller, the buyer is at a disadvantage: <u>buyer beware</u>! Occasionally the buyer can get a seller to agree to a split commission so the buyer can use a rep, but this is rare. When commission splits do happen, they're called a *conjunction*.

On the east coast of Australia, homes are often sold by public auction. The auction is held on the front lawn with open bidding, and if the minimum price isn't met, there's no sale. On the west coast, auctions aren't as popular, but do occur. If a home at auction doesn't meet its minimum it is called *passed in*.

In some areas, home prices are listed in a *price-range*, not at a fixed price. For example, a house might be listed as $450,000–$480,000. This might seem a bit strange, and it doesn't necessarily mean the seller will take the lower amount. It means the seller will entertain offers in that range, hoping for offers from several potential buyers that will push it toward the upper end. It also gets buyers to look up into the next price bracket. Sometimes commercial realtors won't state a price, but will ask for *expressions of interest* or *price on application*. This means you make a blind bid; the highest bid over the seller's minimum (which they're not making public) gets it. In a hot market this can really drive the prices up.

An important aside: Buyers are on their own when it comes to researching their properties. There's some requirement of disclosure by the seller and the rep, but buyers should make an effort to research the property during the *due diligence period*, which can be a week or two, negotiated in the *purchasing offer*. During this period, the potential buyer can check out the titles and contracts, talk to the local shire or city governments to find out what's planned for the area, talk to the neighbours to find out what's not visible or apparent (i.e., a loud road nearby, airplane noise, a bad smell from a factory when the wind shifts, a neighbour who races dirt bikes in the back yard, etc.), and read the association agreements if strata-titled [see **strata titles**].

Australian developers can be every bit as cutthroat as American ones. People have purchased land to build their dream home next to what was listed on the developer's plans as a 'water conservation reserve'—envisioning a placid marsh or lake—only to discover it meant a future sewage plant. Likewise, people have been sold rural land only to discover that a high-density subdivision was planned nearby and their quiet country lane would soon be a busy thoroughfare. Buyer beware!

Home financing   As in North America, home loans come from banks, credit unions, and mortgage companies. Privacy laws prohibit buyers from being pre-qualified for loans, so the seller won't know whether a buyer will actually be able to borrow the money to buy their home until the financing is either approved or disapproved. A buyer can obtain a verbal or written pre-approval, but banks usually won't be held responsible in case conditions change.

Most loans are for part of the purchase price, but 100% loans are available at higher interest rates.

In some states, first-time home buyers can receive a grant to help make their purchase or can have the *stamp duty* waived.

Stamp Duty is a pseudo-tax that applies to home buying in some states, similar to an American Luxury Tax. I say 'pseudo-tax' because, unlike a true tax, it is not tax deductible from the buyer's income taxes. But it is a government tax in the sense that it can add several thousand dollars to the purchase price and you have no choice but to pay it. Stamp duty can be tiered, meaning the percentage increases as the house price goes up.

New homes Housing tracts aren't common as in America; most homes are individually built on sub-divided land. A developer will purchase and clear several hectares of land and put in the basic infrastructure, like roads, water, power, and sewers; and sell it ready to build upon. Instead of signs proclaiming 'New Homes', you see signs advertising *'Land Sale'*.

Buyers buy the land and build once they're funded and ready. They hire an architect to design a house and a builder to construct it. The upside is that every house isn't identical, each is an individual design reflecting the requirements and taste of the inhabitants. The downside is that homes aren't mass-produced in an assembly-line system, and therefore cost more and take longer to build.

Strata titles refer to condominium or co-op style ownership, where one has title to the space but not necessarily to the land. Owners control a share of the total area, proportionally based on how much of the total property they own.

Strata titles can be on a townhouse in a residential development, an apartment in an apartment building, a retail store in a shopping centre, a warehouse or factory in an industrial centre, an office in a business centre, a floor or a portion of a floor in an office building or skyscraper. It's a *scheme* (system) that allows a small investor to get into a bigger market. It also allows a developer to maximise profits and move on to another project.

A suburban strip mall with a half-dozen stores might not be owned by one person or company. Each individual shop might have a different owner—and not necessarily the proprietor of the business in that shop. In large office buildings, individual floors and offices can be owned on a *strata* basis by separate small investors who either occupy the space themselves or rent it out.

It's a kind of investor egalitarianism. One might not have the leverage to buy a $35 million high-rise building, but you might be able to put together $500,000 to buy an eighth of a floor of that building. The investor then rents it out at a 6–10 percent annual return, hoping for a long-term financial appreciation of the property.

That doesn't always work. In Perth, the business centre of the mining industry, the double-whammy of the financial crisis of 2008, and the ending of the mining boom in 2012, caused entire office buildings to become vacant. Some have been empty for years while fixed costs: utility bills, insurance, management fees, and *rates* [property taxes] have continued. These properties are unsellable as no one wants to invest in an empty building.

Strata companies manage properties with ten or more units, and there's a set of rules and regulations. Each title is assigned a *unit equivalent,* to be used for voting, tax and maintenance levy purposes, in proportion with the percentage of the property owned. There's an *annual general meeting (AGM)* and minutes are kept. If you're planning to buy a unit in a strata building or complex, ask for a copy of the minutes to see the current situation and what's planned for the future.

Commercial real estate   There are real estate investment trusts. A lot of real estate is foreign-owned, especially by Japanese, Chinese and European offshore investors. Commercial leases are usually five years, and most improvements, *rates* (taxes) and building management fees are paid by the lessee.

Renting   *For Let* means either 'for rent' or for lease'. Month-to-month renting is called *periodical tenancy.*

At first glance, house and apartment rental rates look really cheap. On closer examination, you'll discover the symbol *p/w* after them, meaning *per week*. You can also pay per *fortnight* (two weeks) or per month.

Property owners usually have management companies handle rentals. These companies are often part of a real estate company, and take the job very seriously. When you apply for a rental you'll think you were buying the place, not just renting it. The *property managers* screen new tenants scrupulously and will often request references. They may meticulously photograph the property before you move in, and you'll be asked to put up a *security bond* (deposit), which is put in a government-controlled escrow account. You may even be restricted as to how many pictures you can hang on the walls or whether you can hang towels on the outside veranda railing. Managers are allowed to occasionally inspect the interior—they'll make an appointment first—and when this happens you may feel like you're being treated like a criminal. When you move out, you'll be required to return the place to immaculate condition to the point of having the carpets commercially cleaned. And then you get to fight for your security deposit. Australian renters don't question this, it's just normal.

Labour (labor) and business

The Australian minimum wage is about twice that of the U.S., and the basic work week is thirty-eight hours. Employees get nice workplace benefits: an average of four weeks per year of *holiday* (vacation), paid *sickies* (sick days) long-service benefits, and *superannuation* (also known as *super*—what Aussies call retirement funds—like an American 401K). There is no Social Security, there is an *Age Pension* but only for people with few cash assets, but they are allowed to own a house.

The 2019-20 national **minimum wage** is $753.92 per week, for a 38-hour week, or $19.84 per hour. The national **minimum wage** is a starting point, most employees are covered by this *award rate*.

Basic wages agreed upon though negotiation are called *award rates*. These are set by the government *Fair Work Commission* with a list of entitlements and minimum wages for specific jobs. One can check to see if the job they're seeking is covered by an *awards rate* or what the *historical rate* has been for that job. The *Fair Work Commission* website is: fwc.com.au .

Penalty rates are higher than normal rates paid for work performed outside normal working hours—this can mean for overtime or for working on a weekend or holiday.

An employee isn't fired; he or she is *sacked*. One isn't laid off; one is *let off*, *stood down*, or *made redundant* (the latter meaning your job has disappeared due to restructuring). *Rationalisation* means eliminating staff or equipment to make a business more efficient. An employee who feels they were wrongly *sacked* or *made redundant* can usually appeal to a state appeals board. Information can be found at the *Fair Work Commission* (fwc.com.au) or through the individual states.

At one time the unions were very strong. They overplayed their hand in some major work stoppages in the 1980's, especially airline employees and dockworkers, who brought the country to a standstill. The government stepped in and legislated limits to their powers. In 2006, under the Howard Government (Liberal Prime Minister John Howard), the federal government pushed through *Industrial Reforms* which created the *Australian Workplace Agreements* (*AWAs*), further eroding the strength of the unions and tilting power toward employers. The idea was to make the Australian workforce internationally competitive. Instead of collective bargaining, Individual workers had to negotiate their own deals, but not everyone has the bargaining skill to get themselves a good deal. Imagine a twenty-year-old fresh out of his apprenticeship negotiating with a sixty-year-old businessman for a first job. Workers in commissioned sales, like real estate, had to be paid a wage and have it deducted from their future commissions, which can be difficult for the employer.

When Labor defeated the Libs in 2009, the *Rudd Government* (Labor Prime Minister Kevin Rudd) went back to an awards system. The Morrison government wants to return to an AWA-like system, but post-Covid , this is still unsettled.

Unions   The Australian workplace has been transformed in the last thirty years. The unions are still formidable and frequently flex their muscles, but have decreased significantly in size and clout. Management can now sue a union if workplace disruptions can be proven unjustified. The government can also levy fines on unions and deny their representatives access to workplaces. In some cases this has tamed the unions, in others it has made them more defiant and aggressive.

The *Australian Council of Trade Unions* is the largest body representing workers in Australia. It is a national trade union centre of 46 affiliated unions, and eight trades and labour councils. The *ACTU* was founded in 1927 in Melbourne and is a member of the *International Trade Union Confederation*.

The nation's largest union is the *Australian Nursing and Midwifery Federation* with about 300,000 members. There are police unions, aircraft engineers unions, etc. My favourite Australian union name is the *Liquor, Hospitality, and Miscellaneous Union.*

Religion

By number of members, they are: Catholic, Anglican Church (the Church of England, same as the Episcopal Church in the U.S.), Uniting Church (a merger of Methodist, Congregational Union, and Presbyterian), Presbyterian, Greek Orthodox, Baptist, Pentecostal, Jehovah's Witnesses, Church of Christ, Salvation Army Church, Seventh Day Adventist, Latter Day Saints (Mormon), and Brethren. Other Christian religions are present and represented in smaller numbers. Non-Christian religions include (in order of numbers): Islam, Buddhism, Judaism, Hinduism, Baha'i and others.

The 2016 census identified that about 52% of Australians classify themselves Christian. 23% of the total population identified as Catholic and 13% as Anglican.

Identification doesn't mean practice. Australians aren't particularly religious as a nation, especially when compared to the U.S. This can be partly traced to each country's original settlers: in the U.S., many immigrants were religious refugees, in Australia they were mostly convicts.

Australians love to question authority, such as government, the legal system, the police, etc. Religion is no exception. Church attendance isn't high, only six percent attend regularly. A lot of people will proudly proclaim their atheism. Julia Gillard is an example.

Julia Gillard was Prime Minister 2010-13, and was an atheist, she didn't make a big deal about it, she just was. She also lived with her partner Tim, and they weren't married. They are still together and are still unmarried.

Many couples are together in a family without benefit of a formal marriage, they'll say they don't need a piece of paper and a prayer, it's between the two of them.

It's also been said that in the absence of religion, Australians have turned to their sport teams as repositories of their faith.

Islamaphobistics Though there is isolated agitation within the Islamic community, most Muslims consider themselves solid members of the greater Australian community, and most non-Muslim Australians remain typically tolerant. There have been a few exceptions on both sides. Some

clerics have made volatile statements. There were the so-called
anti-Muslim beach riots in Cronulla, near Sydney in 2005, and
the Lindt Cafe siege which occurred on 15&16 December 2014
when a lone gunman, Man Haron Monis, held ten customers
and eight employees hostage, resulting in the deaths of two
hostages and the gunman. These were isolated instances and
generally everybody gets along.

A curiosity: You might occasionally see a six-pointed Star
of David displayed or used in advertising, especially on
handwritten signs. This is not a reference to Judaism. In
Australia, the six-pointed star is as commonly used as
Americans would use a five-pointed one—for decoration or to
attract attention.

Jews are in such a small minority that most Aussies aren't
aware of their presence. In fact, in the last census Jews weren't
specifically listed as a religion, Jews had to check 'other'. This
is despite the fact that the most famous war hero of WWI, Gen.
John Monash, was a Jew, as was a chief justice of the high
court who became Governor General, Issac Issacs, and the
current treasury minister, Josh Frydenberg.

Weddings & funerals

Many Australian weddings are held in churches, with
ceremonies performed by appropriate clergy, but since a large
percentage of Aussies are non-religious, many marriages are
performed outside the church by a *celebrant*. A *celebrant* can
be described as a justice of the peace with a major in charm
and a minor in philosophy. They also lead non-religious
funerals. Celebrants are specially trained and are registered
with the government. Some celebrants are justices of the peace,
but not all JPs are celebrants.

Weddings are big events just as in North America (if you
want a primer, watch a movie called '*Muriel's Wedding*'). A
bachelor party is a *bucks night;* a bachelorettes party is a *hens
night*. Both involve much alcohol and as much embarrassment
for the honoured person as can be arranged.

Marriage, de factos, partners, & divorce

Marriage is treated a bit differently than in North America.
While traditional marriage still exists, many good, enduring

relationships have never had the blessing of the church or the legal system, which is why the term *partner* is widely used.

It's common to meet families where the couple has been together for years and have had several children together, but have never chosen to formalize the relationship with a ceremony. The feeling is that what exists between the couple is no business of the state or any religious organization.

Same-sex marriage was legalized in 2017.

De facto relationships are partners who have lived together for two years or more, or have a child together. These individuals are legally referred to under the term *de facto*, as in his *de facto wife*, or her *de facto husband*. A de facto couple have all the legal rights of marriage if the relationship breaks up: child custody, support payments, division of assets, etc.

Divorce   It's sad and unfortunate that one-third of all marriages end up in divorce. The good news is that it used to be about one-half, so divorce is in decline. This can be attributed to fewer couples getting married, and more people living together before actually tying the knot. The average Australian marriage lasts 12 years.

Divorce and separation are handled by a special *Family Court*. All the details are at familycourt.gov.au.

Separation is different than divorce. Australia has *no-fault divorce*, one partner doesn't have to charge the other with infidelity or mental cruelty or anything like that, they just say the marriage is over and the other partner has no choice but to go along.

In Australian Family Law, *Separation* is defined as '...the bringing to an end of a marriage or de facto relationship'.

Separation is more like breaking up a business than a marriage. Divorce is the emotional side, separation is the financial side. All the assets in the marriage: house, cash, shares, debts, etc. must be fairly divvied up. Future care of underage children must be accounted for, which means determining child support responsibilities and visitation.

There is no need or ability to register a separation under Australian Family Law. One partner merely tells the other partner the marriage is over and that they are separating, then calls a friend or relative and tells them as a witness. Then the clock starts ticking. One year later they can file the divorce papers, if they choose to, but they don't have to.

It's the separation that causes problems, not the divorce. If things get emotional and there is acrimony, then that's when lawyers come in, and lawyers get expensive—multiplied by two—one for each side.

Some people are more passive. There are some separated couples who never get divorced, and some divorced couples who never fully separate the assets. I had neighbours who had a 40-acre property. They split-up but never separated or divorced, he just built a house on the opposite side of the property and connected a new driveway onto an adjacent road. They haven't spoken in years.

You can download forms from *familycourt.gov.au* and download a *Divorce Service Kit* and do it all yourself: the divorce is lodged online.

There is support, *Relationships Australia* is community-based, not-for-profit, non-religious. *Legal Aid*, can offer mediation.

Prostitution

Prostitutes are also called *sex workers*. Prostitution is subject to state laws. Though not exactly legal in most states, it is tolerated.

In Victoria, Queensland, New South Wales and the ACT it has been decriminalized or regulated. Brothels in South Australia are illegal but prostitution is not. In Western Australia it's technically illegal but '*informally tolerated*' by the police.

Brothels tend to be small and are often called *massage parlours*. In Tasmania, only *sole operators* are legal, no one can profit off of someone else's prostitution. It is legal in the Northern Territory.

Generally, street work is illegal but there are not many violations since a lot of solicitation is now done online. Most states require health checks and supervision.

Taxes

Income tax   Australia has a reputation of having high taxes, though there are frequent noises in Parliament about lowering them—usually just before an election. There are no state income taxes, just federal income tax.

The federal government collects income tax and *GST* (*Goods and Services Tax*). It sends tax money back to the states to fund the state budgets. The states also receive royalties on mining profits.

The federal government has been known to withhold funds to pressure states to get its way on issues. In the mid-2000's it held back billions of dollars from Western Australia because WA wouldn't loosen its weekend trading hours ban, and because WA hadn't eliminated the stamp duty on cars and homes. Eventually WA loosened weekend trading but retained Stamp Duty.

Income Tax returns The tax year is 1 July to 30 June. Tax forms need to be filed with the *ATO* (*Australian Tax Office*) by October 31, unless you're using a tax agent, but you need to have consulted with the tax agent by that date. If you work for yourself and you're not on *PAYG* (*Pay As You Go*— withholding tax), you pay quarterly *instalments on a BAS* (*Business Activity Statement*), which is based on your previous years taxes (like estimated tax in the U.S). First payments are due 21 November, or if that's on a weekend or holiday, the next business day after.

Taxes seem high, but once you factor in that there's no state income tax it's not as bad. Plus, your health care is included, with no pre-existing conditions.

The U.S. equivalent of a CPA is called a *Chartered Accountant*.

Income Tax Table

This is the 2018-19 and 2019-20 tax schedule (in Australian dollars):

$0–18,2000	No tax	
$18,201–37,000	$0	plus **19%** of amounts over $18,000
$37,001–90,000	$3,572	plus **32.5%** of amounts over $37,000
$90,001–180,000	$20,797	plus **37%** of amounts over $90,000
Over $180,000	$54,096	plus **45%** of amounts over $180,000

Tax deductions can be claimed for business, farm, work, and vehicle expenses, plus real estate loans on investment properties. If you have deductions for expenses you should use a tax agent to best take advantage of them.

Real estate deductions are different. In the U.S. the interest on the mortgage of ones' primary home is a tax deduction. In Australia this is not so, but a second home that is an income property will have its mortgage interest deducted.

Negative gearing is borrowing money to make an investment where the interest and allowable deductions exceed the investment income. It may be possible to claim a deduction against other types of income. If you have a high income, this is a way to offset taxes and build a real estate portfolio.

Deeming rate Of course, if there's a system, an Aussie will figure a way around it. Retirees once parked their money intentionally in low-interest-paying accounts to fudge their way around the income qualifications for pensions and allowances. The Tax Office decided to counter that by setting their own rate for what the market minimum should be and called it a *deeming rate* (the government *deems* what the minimum market rate should be). *Deeming rates* are set below market rates, so *pensioners* (retirees) can still achieve a high return on their investments while qualifying for allowances. For tax purposes, actual income is still assessed.

GST is *Goods and Services Tax*. It's a national ten-percent sales tax on everything. *GST is included in the price* so you don't have to calculate it like sales tax in the U.S. It's on everything *except* medical expenses and food bought in grocery stores (except hot takeaway food and beverages). It brings A$70 billion into the treasury and funds 13% of the budget. It was introduced in 2000 and was supposed to eliminate other taxes, like Stamp Duty (a non-deductable tax on cars, houses, insurance), but those weren't eliminated. There are proposals in the works to increase GST to 15% and include everything, including medical expenses and fresh food, and finally do away with Stamp Duty.

GST is levied on everything along the supply chain, from manufacturing   through   distribution,   sales,   and   even installation. Retailers generally include GST in their prices, so there's no figuring at the counter; the marked price is the final price.

Tradies (tradesmen) charge GST: carpenters, mechanics, pool cleaners, etc. When taking a bid from a tradesman, be sure to ask whether he's including the GST. When you receive a bill it will have **Tax Invoice** written prominently on it to make it a legal GST document. Anyone with a business can register for GST, but unless you're grossing over $60,000 it is probably unnecessary.

Businesses registered for GST can deduct the GST they pay when they buy products and services used in that business. Businesses have to register with the *ATO (Australian Tax Office)* to collect GST. Likewise, when a business issues an invoice as a result of a service provided, or a product sold, the invoice must have **Tax Invoice** written on it.

Businesses owe the ATO the GST they collect on sales, minus the GST they paid for the merchandise, materials, and services to make the sales. In this way, the GST is passed down the line. At the end of the line, it's the consumers who end up paying the tax, because they have nothing to charge GST on.

GST is paid monthly, quarterly, or yearly, depending on the business. The form is called a *BAS (Business Activity Statement)* If the business turns a profit it will owe the ATO GST, if not, the ATO will owe the business. Creative bookkeeping applies.

Why GST? The rationale was to create a new revenue stream so other taxes could be eliminated: taxes that were perceived as holding back economic growth, such as *Stamp Duty*. Plus, a sales tax taxes people who spend a lot of money, and not people who don't. The fallacy is people who spend a lot of money have a lot of money, and people who don't have to pay more for essentials.

But many of these taxes like Stamp Duty haven't been eliminated. The states don't want to give up Stamp Duty and other indirect taxes. The states and the federal government have been fighting over it for *yonks* (a long time).

The other problem with it is the GST money a state sends the ATO isn't the same as what it gets back. That amount is determined by a formula that gives money to poorer states while penalizing richer states, and it's figured on a several-year delay.

Western Australia powers the economy because of all the mining that goes on there. During mining boom in the early 2000's, it sent the ATO a lot of GST and got little back. When the boom ended and the GST stopped flowing in, WA still owed GST money to the ATO at that high rate, even though it was no longer taking anywhere near that much in, plus the ATO was sending WA back a fraction of what WA paid. WA was going broke. After ten years of fighting, the ATO finally agreed to pay a large lump-sum back to WA.

Stamp duty is a state tax paid on official documents. It's not a sales tax a buyer pays when purchasing a house, it is a *duty* on the document that makes the house sale official. To be specific, it's for the stamp on that document, which, in actuality, is a virtual stamp. The more expensive the item, the more duty you pay for the virtual stamp on the document. That's the logic. It's a tax straight out of Monty Python, only no one is laughing.

Stamp duty is not just on documents for buying a house, but also on things like cars, motorcycles, and insurance policies. And since it's a *duty* and not a *tax* it isn't tax-deductible on the buyer's income tax.

Stamp Duty differs in each state. On a $400,000 house in Western Australia is $13,015, in Victoria it would be $16,370, in New South Wales it would cost $13,719. In some states first-time home buyers have their Stamp Duty waived, so on that same $400,000 New South Wales house, a first-time home buyer's stamp duty would be $0. There is a home price calculator is at iselect.com.au .

Vehicle purchases are also affected by Stamp Duty. In Western Australia for example, there's a sliding rate for stamp duty on cars and trucks based on the manufacturers list price of a new vehicle, on a used vehicle it's *a reasonable market value*. For cars under $25,000 it's a flat 2.75%. For cars from $25,001 to $50,000 it's a rather bizarre formula: R% of the dutiable value where R = [2.75 + (dutiable value − 25000)/6666.66)]. Singing the Spam Song yet? A $30,000 car would have a 3.5% stamp duty on it. Over $50,000, it goes back to a straight percentage, 6.5 percent, with a ceiling of $3250.

As you can see, Stamp Duty creates a significant increase in the price of an already pricey item, and can be a factor in a buyer deciding that something is unaffordable. The use of that product is lost to the consumer and the sale is lost to the merchant. Everyone (except the state treasurers) hates Stamp Duty. Stamp Duty was supposed to be eliminated by the introduction of the *GST* (*Goods and Services Tax*), but that was in 2000 and it hasn't happened yet.

PAYG stands for *Pay As You Go*, the Australian term for tax withheld from a worker's pay check, like the U.S. federal withholding tax. It is applied toward the worker's income tax at the end of the year.

Payroll tax is a state tax that businesses pay on their payrolls. It only applies to businesses with annual payrolls over a certain threshold. Depending on the state, the tax is between 5-7% for companies that make between A$800,000 and A$1.5 million. It can be seen as a dis-incentive to grow a company. Details: pwc.com.au/taxtalk/tax-rates .

Business tax is a federal tax. The tax form is called a *BAS* (*Business Activity Statement*). Commonly called '*the baz'*. The BAS is required from businesses and people who are registered for GST. They use it to determine quarterly payments on business profits, plus payments of GST and PAYG withholding. Depending on how big your business is, you may want to do it yourself or have a bookkeeper do it.

Rates in Australia are property taxes. They work the same as in the U.S.: you receive a bill from the local government or council (shires, towns, or cities) who use the money for local roads, civic improvements, etc.

Superannuation is the national retirement system, introduced in 1992. There is no American-style Social Security, instead there is *Superannuation,* a privately-administered system commonly called *Super.* It is similar to a 401k. Paying *Super* is mandatory: the employer contributes an amount equal to 9.5% of the employee's income and deposits it directly into the employee's *superfund* of choice.

An employee can add more, as can the self-employed. This is called *salary sacrifice*.

In 2020 A$2.7 trillion dollars was held in Australian superannuation accounts.

Super Funds Most workers contribute to a *Administered plan*, which is like a special mutual fund, but if they have considerable assets, over $300,000, there are advantages to running their own *Self-Managed Superfund*. *Superannuation* is in addition to any government pensions.

An *Administered plan* is basically a mutual fund. Your employer's weekly contribution is deposited directly into your fund of choice where it is invested in shares, cash, real estate or whatever strategy the fund chooses—you have no say over it other than removing your account and putting it into another plan. Over time it grows through employer contributions, dividends and capital gains, minus management fees. It is taxed at a lower rate (15%) than your income and when the fund owner reaches *preservation age*, 55-60 (depending on when you were born), they can start withdrawing funds tax-free.

When you start a job you will be asked for your superfund *details* (personal information). There are many funds to choose from, compare them online. A Superfund company may have several different funds to choose from.

Check each funds fees and investment histories, some funds are stinkers. There have been some scams and *rorts* (theft schemes). *AMP Super* charged such high fees that even a fund with $100,000 in it wouldn't make a profit. It was cited in a *Royal Commission* investigation (independent special investigator) and fined heavily, and forced to compensate A$5 million amongst 50,000 investors whose funds were short-changed. Another angle they play is some funds will automatically issue the owner a life insurance policy and automatically deduct the payments. Check your statements, you can opt out of the policies.

There are *ethical funds* that invest in Green industries and these do quite well.

A common pitfall with *Supers* is people losing track of them. This happens to people who change jobs frequently. If they don't specify that their new employer deposit their contribution to their current fund, the employer will choose a fund for them. Some people end up with many funds and lose track of them. Since all funds charge a management fee, it is in your best interest to have all your super contributions paid into one fund and pay one fee, instead of having many funds paying many fees. If you end up with several funds you can consolidate them into one. Choose the one you want to keep and ask them to help you transfer the others to it.

If you have a fund that doesn't get regular contributions, the management fee will eventually eat it up. If the balance is under A$200, or you are over *preservation age*, you can withdraw it by contacting the fund.

If you are wealthy you should have a ***Self-managed superfund***. You can manage it yourself and buy and sell *shares* (stocks), real estate, collect rents, etc. One proviso is it requires *administration by a licensed administrator*, usually an accountancy firm which is audited annually. This administration will cost about $2000/year, which is why only larger asset superfunds, over $300,000, can afford this.

If you are a couple you can co-contribute to a self-managed fund so you can have more to invest. The administrator will keep track of each person's contribution so they can pay taxes on it separately, and if there is a divorce settlement, they will apportion the amounts to each according to their contribution.

Superannuation can be thought of as an independently managed Social Security system, but with one major difference: American Social Security is guaranteed where a private Superannuation system is not. Investments can go down as well as go up. In an *Administered* plan the share market can go bust just as you reach *preservation age*. In a *Self-managed Fund* investments can go bad, and you end up with no retirement.

You can apply for a *compassionate early withdraw* of from A$1,000-10,000 once a year before your *preservation age* for certain hardships: medical bills, or if you are about to lose your house due to debts, etc. During COVID 19 the government allowed a one-time maximum withdrawal of $10,000.

Trusts   If you have substantial assets, look into forming a trust. Trusts are more financially flexible and they aren't taxed, instead the beneficiaries are, and at a lower corporate rate. There are many advantages to having a trust; check with an accountant. However, under U.S. tax law a foreign trust is a foreign corporation and it may complicate U.S. tax situation.

U.S. taxes in Australia   Yanks, sit down for this one. U.S. taxation is *Citizenship-based*. The rest of the world, including Australia, is *Residency-based*. The U.S. is one of only two countries that makes their citizens who live overseas pay tax on their foreign, worldwide income (the other is Eritrea). This means American citizens owe the U.S. Internal Revenue Service taxes on their income wherever they live.

An Australian living and working in the U.K., Germany, Kenya, or wherever, would owe taxes to that country, but no taxes to Australia. But an American working in those countries would owe taxes in those countries and to the U.S.

If you have dual citizenship, U.S. and Australian, and reside in Australia, your primary tax country is Australia. [More on this below in ***Double Taxation***]

U.S. tax law is pernicious. It doesn't matter if you were born in Australia and your father was an American citizen who'd left the U.S. many years before, you, as a child of an American citizen, are legally an American citizen and are required to file U.S. taxes. This is true even if you've never even been to the U.S. Chances are, if this is your situation, they'll never find you, but you have been warned.

Besides U.S. citizens, U.S. Green Card holders are also subject to U.S. tax law. Even if your Green Card has expired, you still owe U.S. taxes. To avoid this you have to go through a formal rescinding of the status. There are a lot of retired Canadian NHL players who wish they'd known that.

Americans living abroad receive an automatic filing extension to October 15th.

Double taxation   Australian income tax law provides protection from *double taxation* if you owe taxes on assets in the U.S. and Australia.   In theory, since Australian taxes are usually the higher of the two, one deducts their U.S. tax bill from their Australian tax bill and most people end up owing the U.S. nothing. Unless you're wealthy.

Americans living abroad have to file IRS Form 1040 and any relevant schedules for the previous year if their income was above a certain threshold. These thresholds are the same as for U.S. residents: under 65 and single US$12,200, 65 and over and single US$13,850, under 65 and married US$24,400, 65 or over and married US$27,000.

Americans living abroad will have to file special forms if they own, or are signatories, shareholders, officers or directors of a non-U.S. corporation. That may include a big business, your family trust, your Superannuation Fund and even mutual funds.

There are taxes applicable for Americans that aren't charged in Australia: Social Security, pensions, inheritance taxes and taxes on capital gains on real estate sales.

Dual-taxation for Americans living in Australia (or any country outside the U.S.) can be complicated. I use an Australian Chartered Accountant who is also a U.S. CPA (Certified Public Accountant).

So, you might wonder, you're in a far-off country on the back-end of the Earth, how will the IRS find you? It's simple. the Australian Tax Office will *dob you in* (inform on you), using FATCA.

FATCA (Foreign Account Tax Compliance Act) is a U.S. tax program that requires other countries to provide them with financial records of American citizens living abroad. Why would other countries agree to this? The U.S. coerced them.

According to the ATO (Australian Tax Office): '*FATCA generally requires financial institutions and certain other non-financial entities that are foreign to the U.S. to report on assets held by their U.S. account holders or be subject to withholding on withholdable payments.*'

It's a system the IRS initiated to ensure Americans living abroad file their U.S. taxes. The ATO complies with the IRS and requires all Australian financial institutions to supply the IRS with your financial accounts, and since everything is digital, it's easy, FATCA even specifies the software they use.

When you open a financial account in Australia you will be asked if you are an American citizen. If you say no they will cross-reference and figure out who you are and 30% of your income from that institution will be withheld until you comply. FATCA started in 2014, and in that year supplied the IRS with over 44,000 accounts. By 2016 it was 862,000. They stopped bothering to report after that.

As of 2018, 94 countries were signed up with FATCA. Why are they helping the U.S. collect taxes? The U.S. threatened to not allow them to trade with the U.S. so they had no choice. The only countries that don't comply are North Korea, Cuba and Iran.

FBAR (Foreign Bank Account Report)   American citizens living overseas also have to declare any cash holdings in foreign banks over US$10,000. On your IRS FBAR form, required yearly when you do your U.S. taxes, you list each banks name and the highest amount you had in it during the tax year. You will not owe tax on this; it's how the IRS keeps track of Americans living abroad and their funds so they won't launder money.

It can get complicated, when in doubt, hire a good accountant who knows both systems.

Rescinding U.S. Citizenship   If you haven't paid your U.S. taxes in a long time and have considerable assets, you may be in trouble. You should consult a qualified, experienced U.S. tax attorney—not an accountant—an account won't have attorney-client privilege. You may even want to look into renouncing your U.S. citizenship, which is complex but not unusual. You have to seriously consider if it's right for you.

If you decide to rescind, you pay your past five-years taxes and fill out a lot of forms and go through an exit interview, it could take over a year. You need a lawyer specializing in citizenship renunciation who will charge US$10-15,000 to begin with, which could double if extensive filing of back-taxes is required. If you're worth multi-millions you may want to consider this. You don't want to screw this up, the IRS could come after you to repay anything you owe plus penalties and interest, and may even blacklist you from ever entering the U.S. again.

Government

Australia is a Commonwealth, formed by the six former British colonies on the Australian continent and the island of Tasmania, plus the Northern Territory. It is a parliamentary-democratic monarchy. Like most of the former English colonies, Australia uses the Westminster system of government, which means it's ruled by an English-style Parliament elected by the people. The Royal Family of England has statutory power, but it's mostly a stabilizing presence and is very rarely exercised. Australia is also an independent member of the Commonwealth of Nations (the successor to the British Empire): a league of fifty-three former British colonies, including Canada, South Africa, India, Bermuda, etc.

The National capitol is Canberra, in the *ACT* (*Australian Capital Territory*). The city is patterned, in concept, after Washington D.C., in that it was created from scratch as a national capital city. Like Washington, it is laid out with parks and malls between the government buildings. Where Washington was built on the banks of a river, Canberra was built on the shores of a lake, be it an artificial lake that was created for the city. The lake is Lake Burley Griffin, named after the man who planned the city, an American, Walter Burley Griffin of Chicago, Ill.

Canberra lies halfway between Sydney and Melbourne and was the result of a compromise between political forces in the two dominant cities of Australia, each of which wanted to be the capital. Canberra is the only major city in Australia that isn't on the coast. By law, all states and territories must have access to the sea, so the ACT has a 3,000-acre non-contiguous holding at Jervis Bay, where the Naval Academy is located.

The Westminster system of government means the government is a body of popularly-elected members, representing geographic electorates. In the Westminster system there is no President. The loose equivalent in the UK is the Queen, who in the unwritten British constitution is a figurehead. In Australia (which has a written constitution) the equivalent is the *Governor General* who is the *Vice Regent* for the Queen. The *Governor General is* another figurehead who's power is mostly ceremonial.

This system isn't that different from the U.S. except, since there is no president, the equivalent of the Speaker of the House, the Prime Minister, is head of government.

The equivalent of the U.S. president's cabinet is the *front bench*—made up of the minsters of defence, treasury, foreign affairs, etc.—who themselves are elected members of Parliament. This gives them direct accountability: if they screw-up they won't get re-elected in three years. They also have more independence than an American cabinet secretary.

If anything, the Westminster system is a more direct representation of the people in government, at least in theory.

Levels of Government   In the U.S., there are four levels of government (federal, state, county, and city); in Australia there are three levels (federal, state, and local). We'll start at the top and work our way down.

Federal The federal government is also known as the *Commonwealth*. Governmental power lies in the Parliament, consisting of a House of Representatives (150 members) and a Senate (76 senators). Members of the House represent districts called *electorates,* which are established by population. Members of the House each represent about 110,000 voters. The Senate has twelve senators from each state, regardless of population, and two from each of the major territories (the Northern Territory and the ACT).

Members of the House are elected by popular vote from their *electorates* using a *preferential* method. Senators are also elected *preferentially*, and then the numbers go through a *proportional* voting count within each state, so smaller parties can elect a senator [more on this in **elections**].

Whichever political party ends up with the most *MPs* (*Members of Parliament*) in the House of Representatives forms *the Government* and elects the *prime minister* (*PM*).

So, unlike the U.S., where there are three branches of government (executive, legislative, and judicial), in practicality Australia has only two, with the executive and legislative combined into one. Technically, the Queen and her *Governor General* (the *vice regent*) are the executive branch, but most policy is led by the prime minister [more about this in **the Queen of Australia** and the **Governor General**].

After forming Government, the prime minister appoints other MPs to head the various ministries, such as Foreign Policy, Treasury, Defence, Education and Training, etc. Collectively, these are known as the *frontbench*. Ministers can also be from the Senate. In the Westminster system there is no appointed executive cabinet, the cabinet is the frontbench ministers and they are elected members of the parliament. There is no need to confirm them as in the U.S., they have been confirmed by election to the parliament.

Parliament: Either the House or the Senate can originate bills, but only the House of Representatives can propose or amend legislation on any bill that authorises expenditures or imposes taxation. In effect, the Senate is an advisory body, but both houses have to pass all bills before they become law. Since the head of government is also the head of the Parliament (the prime minister), veto power is unnecessary, though technically the Queen or King, acting through the governor general, can veto bills or laws.

Checks and balances are called *swings and roundabouts*.

Elections have to be held three years after the previous election, though there is no fixed date on exactly when, the prime minister can call it whenever it is convenient.

There are no term limits, as long as they get re-elected to Parliament and have the seats to carry the majority, a prime minister can keep serving. Prime Minister Robert Menzies served over twenty years. Prime Minister John Howard served thirteen.

An interesting feature of the Parliamentary system, if the prime minister, who is leader of the majority party, decides to resign, or if the rank and file members have *lost confidence* in him or her, they can take a *spill vote* and change party leaders, and the new leader becomes the new Prime Minister. This means they can change the leader of the country without holding an election. This has happened four times in the last ten years, two for Labor, two for the Liberal/National Coalition, in all cases a successor was in place within the week. Sometimes a retiring prime minister chooses to step down a year before the next election to give his successor a chance at establishing himself as a worthy incumbent. After a losing

election the losing party leader usually resigns as leader, but
often stays on in their seat, if they've been re-elected to the
seat.

Confused? A party wins the election if their members win a
majority of their seats. So a party leader can win his individual
seat but if his party's members don't win a majority of their
seats they don't get to form a government. Likewise, if a party
wins more seats but the leader loses his seat, then they'd have
to pick another leader since the prime minister must be an
elected member of Parliament. That is why parties will
parachute members into *safe seats*. A member of parliament
doesn't actually have to live in his or her electorate in order to
run in it.

The three major national political parties are, in order of
size: the *Labor Party* (intentionally spelled American-style
with an *o* instead of an *ou*), which is liberal and *labour*-based
and roughly equivalent to the U.S. Democrats; the *Liberal
Party*, which is conservative and roughly equivalent to the U.S.
Republicans; and the *National Party*, which is the rural-based,
conservative country party, and represents farmers and
pastoralists (ranchers). The *Liberals* and *Nationals* formed a
coalition many years ago in order to have enough seats in
Parliament to take on *Labor*. The *Coalition* usually has the
Liberal leader as Prime Minister and the Nationals leader as
Deputy Prime Minister, and the cabinet ministers are split
between the two parties.

Smaller parties are the *Greens Party*, which is left wing and
pro-environment; *One Nation*, which is anti-immigrant, openly
racist and virulently right wing; and *Family First*, which is
conservative Christian. Due to the *proportional voting* scheme
in the Senate these parties usually get a certain number of seats.
The Greens currently (2020) hold six seats. This might not
seem like many in Senate that has 76 seats, but in a close vote
they can hold *the balance of power* and play a key role if they
decide to back either Labor or the Coalition.

Smaller parties have little direct power, but as Don Chipp,
a founder of the now defunct *Democrats*, once said, "Our job is
to keep the bastards honest."

There are about twenty small fringe parties, like the

Australian Shooters Party, the Fishing Party, The Communist Party, the Sex Party, etc. With proportional voting some of them were actually getting seats in the Senate, but that has been changed.

Naming the conservative party the *'Liberals'* was unintentional irony. Robert Menzies, who was Australian Prime Minister 1939-41 and again in 1949-66, founded the party in 1944. At that time the semi-socialist Labor party was dominating Australian politics. Menzies wrote about forming a new party that had "...*a liberal, progressive policy and are opposed to Socialism with its bureaucratic administration and restriction of personal freedom*". He meant 'liberal' in the sense of freeing individuals and companies from socialist restrictions and governmental meddling. So the Liberals are the conservatives...only in Australia. You might over hear someone describe themselves as "*liberal small 'l'* ", meaning one who is liberal politically, as opposed to "*Liberal uppercase 'L'* ", which means they identify with the Liberal party, which is conservative.

The nickname for the Liberal party is *the Libs.* The nickname for the Australian Labor Party is *Labor,* or the *ALP.*

The Commonwealth Government is currently (2020) run by an alliance of the *Coalition* (Liberals and the Nationals), and has been in power since 2013, having been returned to power in 2016 and 2019.

Since there's no executive branch, the various *ministers* (Defence, Foreign Office, Treasury, etc., equating to the U.S. President's Cabinet), tend to be the most powerful members of the party(s) currently dominating Parliament. These ministers are called the *frontbenchers.* All the other ministers are *backbenchers.* Ministers can be either from the House or the Senate. A minister does not have to be a member of either house, but Section 64 of the Constitution requires the minister to become a member within three months. Someone from that party would have to step down to vacate a seat and a by-election would be called. This is rare.

The lesser party is called *the Opposition,* and they elect a *shadow government,* minister by minister. The *shadow ministers* attend all the meetings of their respective ministries as observers and speak out—often just knee-jerk criticism—about what goes on in each ministry. The advantage of this shadow system is that there's constant oversight of each ministry, as the unwritten duty of *the Opposition* is to keep putting pressure on *the Government* to deal with issues properly. And if the government were to call a sudden election and power shifted to the other party, the new ministers would already be up to speed on administration and issues.

Senators serve a six-year term. Elections for the House of Representatives have no set date, but must be held some time before the end of the third year since the last election. That election is called by the prime minister and is usually timed to his advantage, like when things are going well, before things are about to go bad, or when the opposition is in disarray. Because of this, the official campaign season is short, about 6 weeks, though *pollies* seem to be constantly campaigning.

Throughout the three-year term, the ruling party—which controls government spending—strategically withholds funds. Then, just before the election, they free those funds and lavish generosity and largess upon the electorate by announcing popular programs and tax cuts, hoping it will be fresh in the minds of the populace just before they go to the polls. Everybody knows they do it, but it still works.

The parties also make lots of promises that, as soon as the election is over, they quickly forget. The popular line is: "How do you tell if a pollie is lying? It's when his lips are moving."

Campaign funding   Political parties in Australia are theoretically publicly funded to reduce the influence of private money upon elections in shaping public policy. But it doesn't work out exactly like that.

After each election, the *Australian Federal Election Commission* (*AEC*) distributes a set amount of money to each political party, *per vote received*. After the 2013 election, political parties and candidates received $58.1 million in election funding. Of that, the Liberal Party received $23.9 million in public funds while the Labor Party received $20.8 million.

But private money does get in legally. Private donations are allowed from individuals, corporations, trade unions, etc.

Anyone who contributes over a total of A$13,800 to one candidate or a number of candidates must file an *annual donor form*. Foreign donors cannot contribute more than A$1000. The AEC monitors donations to political parties and publishes a yearly list of political donors. Despite that, it is not difficult for donors to make undisclosed donations to political parties hiding behind *associated entities* such as think tanks, industry foundations and advisory boards.

And rich pollies can pay for their own campaign. Billionaire Clive Palmer spent A$5million on his 2019 House of Representatives campaign...and lost. But he swayed the election away from Labor and the Liberal/Nationals won a third term, which many suspect was his intention.

Parliament meets a few weeks a month. Aussie lawmakers in session make the U.S. Congress look like a bunch of chaste librarians. Parliament is really a debating society, decorum is like the British model, where members argue and harass and interrupt each other's speeches with shouts and jibes. The presiding officer of the House of Representatives is the *Speaker of the House*, usually a member of the majority party, but not the Prime Minister. The *Speaker* is elected from that body and acts as a referee, constantly telling members to sit down and be quiet. He or she runs the house, directs the members through the day's schedule and tries to keep a semblance of order.

Before each vote in the House, a bell is rung. Exactly four minutes later, the doors are locked. No members are allowed in or out until the vote is over.

A verbatim transcript of all Parliament debates is called a *Hansard* and is available shortly after each session. *Hansards* are kept by all countries that use the Westminster form of government. It's the U.S. equivalent of the Congressional Record. By checking the *Hansard* on the day of a key debate, one can see which side of an issue any representative took.

One of the most interesting things in Parliament is a session called *Question Time*, where the MPs can ask the ruling Government ministers questions about policy, projects or programs that must be answered publicly. Questions from the *ruling party* MPs are merely set-ups for self-congratulation or promoting policy, while questions from *the Opposition* can be vicious ambushes. Members of Parliament are exempt from slander laws while in the *House Chambers*, so they can get away with saying almost anything. They frequently harangue each other with shouted interruptions from the opposing sides.

You can watch Question Time live on ABC iView, and listen to a delayed broadcast that evening on ABC radio. Many people tune in to Question Time as entertainment—a reality show with a notable, clever, dependably contentious, cast.

The carryings-on can sometimes sound so childish that you wonder if *Question Time* should be followed by *Nap Time*, *Milk and Cookies Time*, and *Make Up and Be Friends Time*.

States   There are six states: New South Wales, Victoria, Queensland, South Australia, Tasmania, Western Australia; and two territories: The Northern Territory and the Australian Capital Territory (ACT). They're all run by parliamentary systems consisting of two houses: an upper house and lower house. The exception is Queensland and Northern Territory, which each have just one house.

The upper house is called the *Legislative Council* (elected members have the title *MLC* after their names), and has a review function for the laws created in the lower house.

The lower house is called, depending on the state, the Legislative Assembly or the House of Assembly, and has the power to authorize expenditures and levy taxes. Members of the Legislative Assembly have *MLA* after their names. Like the Commonwealth level, the states work by the Westminster system: the majority party in the Legislative Assembly elects a *premier* (the American equivalent of a state governor). He or she forms a cabinet—*frontbenchers*—just as the prime minister does in the federal Parliament, and the opposition elects *shadow ministers*.

The states have a great deal of autonomy when it comes to urban planning, roads, utilities, education, law enforcement, basic infrastructure, and levying stamp duty, but the federal government has been chipping away at the states' powers. Since the feds collect and control income tax and GST and issue it back to the states, they have control of a lot of programs. In 2000 the *Commonwealth* passed the *GST* (*Goods and Services Tax*) into law with the proviso that the states eliminate many of their taxes. The states refused, so the ratepayers get double-taxed. It's a constant battle.

The states run the police force. There is no local city police or county sheriff departments. The police are state, run by a police commissioner and overseen by a police minister who is a state parliament frontbencher.

Likewise, there are no local school boards: public schools are run by the states.

Local government also differs than in the U.S., where there are counties, and within them, cities, each with its own government and police force, plus local schoolboards, park districts, flood control districts, etc.

In Australia, there's only one level of government below the state. These can be called *shires, cities,* or *towns,* and the government is commonly referred to as *the council. Shires* tend to be rural, *cities* are suburban, and *towns* are urban. They can be vast shires in remote regions or suburban towns in metropolitan areas. The desert Shire of East Pilbara in Western Australia is 154,000 sq. kms (about the same size as Oklahoma), with a population of about 10,000. The city of Nedlands, in the middle of the Perth metropolitan area is 20 sq. kms, with a population of 23,000.

These are run by elected councils, headed by a president or mayor, and managed by a CEO (Chief Executive Officer). They are funded by *rates* (property taxes).

These *councils* handle local roads, building permits, recreation facilities, rubbish collection, libraries and community festivals. They regulate urban planning and development to some degree, but the states supersede them. There's a state Minister for Local Government who can overrule or suspend councils if they act illegally.

There is no local police force, local governments have unarmed *Rangers* who do not have arrest authority. They function as code-enforcement officers, meter-maids and dog-catchers.

Rate Payers and Progress Associations are neighbourhood or community groups within the shires, towns or cities. Since the councils are often governing such large areas, local groups form within these to deal with local issues. They advocate for their communities to the shire councils.

These groups can report to the council about traffic problems and pot-holed streets, lobby for parks, promote historical sites, etc. These associations operate under formalized constitutions regulated by the states, and as such they must hold yearly *Annual General Meetings (AGMs)*

Another type of local organization are *Friends Groups*: volunteers who care for natural reserves, rivers, estuaries and and parks.

Some groups form to advocate for or against controversial planning issues like urban development or zoning change issues, and have the option to incorporate so individual officers can't be sued if the group steps on the toes of developers, businesses, or council members.

Police and crime   Police need no probable cause to stop and question you. If a police officer stops you, he/she can ask your name, address, and date of birth. If you withhold this information or get caught lying about it you can be arrested. If you are driving a vehicle, you will be breathalysed. If you refuse a breathalyser test, you can be arrested.

The U.S. has 18,000 police departments and over 800,000 sworn police personnel. Australia has 8 police departments and about 70,000 sworn police personnel. There are no local police, each state has a state-wide police department, and there is the *Australian Federal Police (AFP)*. This simplifies things dramatically.

Australian Federal Police handle interstate and international duties, counterterrorism, national security, and are the police force for the ACT (Australian Capital Territory) and major airports.

State police   Each state has one centrally-controlled police force that is deployed throughout that state. There are no separate city forces, nor are there county sheriffs or state troopers like in the U.S. One state police force serves all communities: dense cities, sprawling suburbs, rural farmland, remote indigenous communities, and some of the most sparsely settled regions on Earth.

There are advantages and disadvantages to this system.

Administratively, it's efficient, since all elements can easily communicate. and resources are maximized with little duplication or waste. Conversely, there's little local control over how many officers will serve an area, since those decisions are made by state officials at the state capital which might be 2000 kilometres away.

In mainstream Australia, day-to-day crime is mostly non-violent burglaries and car thefts. Robberies are usually committed with non-firearm weapons, like knives and clubs. A recent Perth liquor store hold-up was typical: the local newspaper reported that the robber used a green shovel to threaten the shop owner into emptying the till. The robber got away with a few hundred dollars and a bottle of Jim Beam. The police put out a bulletin for a drunken man carrying a green shovel.

Australians have a different attitude toward policing: less is more. Unlike the U.S., where off-duty officers are armed and always ready to go into action, Australian police leave their weapons and attitude at work. They're far less gung-ho and militaristic. It isn't that the officers are lazy or cowardly, they're trained to be less aggressive. Rules prohibit high-speed auto pursuits. Though the cops are armed, if one pulls out a gun, it's a big deal. They first resort to non-lethal methods, like *capsicum* (pepper) spray and Tasers. They're more apt to shoot someone in the leg to disable them instead of in the chest to kill them. The state governments are always asking for more officers on the street, but want to keep the level of conflict low. This isn't a completely baseless idea.

An example: during the G20 conference in November 2006 in Melbourne, protestors attacked the police guarding the conference venues. I happened to be working in Melbourne at the time, and was surprised to see news footage of police officers in regular uniforms—no helmets or chest protectors—going toe to toe with club swinging rioters who were wearing helmets and padded jackets. A local explained to me that the police once wore riot gear in these situations, but found that it escalated the situation. If the police looked like bullies, more protesters joined in. By using minimum force at the G20, the police not only kept the protestors at bay and defused the situation, but they also won the sympathy of the citizenry.

It's not always that easy. In rural Aboriginal communities, white officers often get a bad reaction. Take the riots of December 2004 on Palm Island, off the coast of Queensland. An Aboriginal man died under suspicious circumstances while in police custody, and a white officer was accused of beating him to death. Islanders became enraged. They burned down the *watch house* (police station) and the few officers on the island had to barricade themselves in the hospital until reinforcements arrived from the mainland. The fresh officers had little riot training and clumsily returned the island to order. Resentment continues to this day.

In 2020, Aboriginal deaths in custody are still occurring and a Black Lives Matter movement is gaining traction.

The police in remote communities learn to work with the Aboriginal leaders who have their own systems of justice, punishment and retribution, a system developed over 60,000 years.

In Western Australia there are Aboriginal police specialist units that are deployed in areas with large indigenous populations. They handle problems with greater sensitivity before they get out of hand.

For a wealthy, educated country, Australia surprisingly suffers with a significant number of idle and angry youth. Young Australian men will sometimes get so drunk they commit unmotivated violent and vicious attacks on each other. The attackers get off by pleading they were so drunk they didn't know what they were doing. Judges seem to buy this as a valid excuse.

It's hard being a cop in Australia. Due to the convict heritage, some people tend to instinctively side with the underdog, and that's usually the bad guy. The judges are notoriously lenient, and often the criminal is out of jail before the police officer is finished with the paperwork. Many officers retire early.

Individual rights   The Australian Constitution contains no Bill of Rights or any equivalent. Personal freedoms like freedom of speech, religion, assembly, gun ownership, etc., are determined only by convention and precedent, not by statute.

These freedoms are *assumed* but not *guaranteed* Rights, and if push comes to shove, individual cases would have to go to court.

The rationale I've been given is that if you specifically list a Right statutorily, it could actually limit that Right through clever argument in a court or by a *Government*. And unlike the U.S., where cabinet members—who are the heads of most of the government bureaucracies—are appointed, in Australia all equivalent ministers are elected members of parliament, and if they were to violate the basic assumed freedoms, they'd be ejected from office at the next election. In a parliamentary system, if there's a major deadlock, parliament can be dissolved and early elections can be called. There's also the assumption that the members are all basically decent Englishmen who'd do no wrong, and if they did, the impartial Monarch would *still the troubled waters*. In actuality, Australian personal freedoms are guaranteed on faith.

Despite that (or because of it), there's a mild desire to enter a Bill of Rights into the Constitution, but it isn't seen as a national priority and is seldom mentioned. *She'll be right* seems to apply here, too.

The Queen of Australia is not Priscilla; it's Elizabeth II of England, and eventually her successor, Prince William.

Australia is a *Constitutional Monarchy*, which means the Queen (or King) of England is the actual head-of-state, and the Parliament exists at the pleasure of the Monarch. When Australia became an independent nation, it didn't sever all ties with Mother England—they never threw the figurative tea into the harbor.

All elected members of Parliament have taken an oath to *"...be faithful and bear true allegiance to Her Majesty Queen Elizabeth the Second."* Also in the constitution is this: *"...the Queen may disallow any law...and annul the law."* All she has to do is notify both houses of Parliament of her decision.

Yes, the Queen of England still technically owns the place. Her picture is on all the coins and her photos are on the walls of all government offices, but tradition deems a hands-off policy, and that's what the *governor general* is for.

The governors general   The prime minister, his

cabinet and elected members of Parliament run day-to-day matters, but over them is the Queen's representative, the *governor general*, the Queen's *vice regal,* the executive. The Constitution of the Commonwealth of Australia, Section 2, reads: *A Governor General appointed by the Queen shall be Her Majesty's representative in the Commonwealth.* Therefore, if the Queen has total power, so does the governor general.

The governor general is technically the executive branch: the commander-in-chief of the armed forces, he or she has the power to approve the results of elections, allow the appointment of ministers, ratify treaties, appoint ambassadors and federal judges, form commissions of enquiry. This is all a formality. Legally, they also have the power to overrule anything the elected rabble in Parliament might decide upon and even dissolve parliament, but governors general never exercise this power—except once—but I'm getting ahead of myself.

In actuality, the governors general almost never act on their own and generally follow the lead of the prime minister who actually appoints them with the Queens approval, which she always does because she has little concern about far away Australia. When it comes to the day-to-day functioning of the government, you rarely hear anything about either the governor general or the Queen.

Technically, the Queen appoints the governor general on '*advice*' of the prime minister. The PM can also advise the Queen to dismiss the governor general and appoint someone else. This has never been done, though they came close in 1975—again, I'm getting ahead of myself.

So, who are governors general? They are prominent public servants who have led distinguished careers. Many have been *knighted* or are *peers* (Lords) and are former judges, archbishops or high-ranking military officers. In the last fifty years, ten out of the fourteen governor's general were Australian-born—the rest were English. There has been one woman, Dame Quentin Bryce. Two, Sir Issac Issacs and Sir Zelman Cowen, were Jewish, which is a good example of multi-ethnic attitudes (Issacs was the first Australian-born governor general). Governors general traditionally serve a five-year term. Each state also has a state governor general, serving the same function on a state level.

Though the governors general (both federal and state) are mainly ceremonial positions, *they can wield the ultimate power and dissolve parliament*, effectively dismissing the elected Government. This only happened once, and will probably never happen again. It was a double-dissolution of parliament, known historically as *The Dismissal.*

In 1972 Gough Whitlam's Labor Government had been elected on a narrow majority, and the balance of power in the Senate was held by the small Australian Democrat party. In 1975 a key appropriations bill came before Parliament. The Democrats sided with the Liberals and refused to pass the bill. This threatened the complete financial shut down of the government. The Liberals decided to use the impasse to coerce Labor into calling an early election in the *lower house* which they thought they could win. Labor wouldn't budge. After a month the Prime Minister Gough Whitlam decided to call for an early election for the *upper house*, where the hold-up was. Things totally deadlocked.

Finally, in desperation, the Governor General Sir John Kerr fired the prime minister before the prime minister could ask the Queen to dismiss him. The governor general then appointed the Opposition Leader, Malcolm Fraser as caretaker prime minister. Later that day, when Fraser couldn't get a consensus to pass the bills, the governor general fired him, dissolved Parliament, and called for new elections.

This was earth-shaking, it had never been done before, and there's doubt as to whether it would ever be allowed to happen again. But it was legal, permitted by the Australian Constitution.

In the election held the following month, Malcom Fraser and his government were elected with a massive majority. Governor General Kerr resigned and lived the rest of his life abroad.

Monarchists & Republicans   Aussies have a love-hate relationship with the Royal Family. They like being part of the historical tradition, but dislike and distrust anyone held over them, especially ones who receive a lot of money just for being born into the right family. What probably irks them most: they hate having the same ruler as the *Poms* (British).

Why not change to a republic and throw the Royals out? It's not that easy. You'd have to rewrite the Constitution and change the entire method of government.

Monarchists are people who believe in the constitutional monarchy. They feel the Monarch is a stabilizing force, a non-political influence that keeps things on an even keel. They point to the simple fact that the current system has worked in the UK for centuries. The UK doesn't even have a written constitution.

Republicans are people that believe in chucking-off the reins of the Royals and replacing them with an elected President.

In 1999 there was a referendum in the general election to do just that, but it was narrowly defeated. The government wrote the referendum in such a way as to make it difficult for the referendum to win, they wrote it so *yes* meant *no*, and vice-versa. The proposal was also written so instead of holding a general election for a president, it would instead be determined by a two-thirds vote of the members of Parliament.

This split the pro-republic vote, half were OK with parliament voting in the president, half wanted a general election. This led to the referendum's defeat.

In the end, the electorate chose to stay with what they had: a known quantity. The fear is, once you open the cage and start changing the Constitution, a monster could emerge and you could end up with something unintended. In 2007, the Labor leader intimated if elected he will hold another referendum on the subject. He was elected and it never happened, the Global Financial Crisis hit and there were more important things going on. The Liberal PM that followed was a self-avowed *Republican*, but he never pursued it either. In 2020 it's rarely mentioned. It's one of those things that end up in the *too-hard bin*.

The bottom line is that the Royals are a stabilizing force for the Australian ship of state: the people are the sails, Parliament is the rudder, the Monarchy is the keel.

Elections

Australia had two important electoral firsts: the secret
ballot (1856) and allowing women to vote (1894), though the
Kiwi's seem to want to grab the latter as their own *first*.

The country is broken into states and within each state are
electorates, with one parliamentary seat per electorate. The
electorates can have place names like Ballarat and Bendigo, or
names honouring some past official like Pearce or Hasluck.
Each electorate represents about 110,000 voters.

Voting age is eighteen. *Voting is mandatory* in all
national, state, and some local elections, and a $20 fine is
levied if you don't show up to get your name *ticked off the list.*

Polling is always done on a Saturday, and it becomes
somewhat of a community festival. The political parties set up
colourful booths outside the polling station, and happily hand
out *how to vote cards*. A local community group sets up a
sausage sizzle (hot dog BBQ). Since voting is mandatory
everyone in the area drops by to do their duty and neighbours
and old friends chat and there is lots of laughter and sausages.

Though voting is mandatory many people resent that they
have to take the time to come vote, and once you've been
ticked off the list, you're free to either vote, not vote, throw
away the ballot, deface or eat it. Many people vote for Mickey
Mouse or something equivalent, and this is called an *informal
vote*.

So, in actuality, voting isn't mandatory; showing up at the
polls is.

Political parties   As mentioned before, the *Liberals*
aren't liberal, *Labor* is, the *Greens* are more so, *One Nation* is
ultra-right wing, and the *Democrats* say they're in it *"...just to
keep the bastards honest."* The *Nationals* are supposed to
represent the rural voters, but they're the minority part of a
coalition with the Liberals, so they're the caboose on that train,
though a noisy caboose.

The *Centre Alliance* and Pauline Hanson's *One Nation*
have two elected members each, the *Jacquie Lambi Alliance*
has one elected member (Jacquie Lambi), as does the *Country
Liberal Party* which has the sole senator from the Northern
Territory and has voting rights within the National Party and so

is part of the Coalition.

Not every voter who votes along party lines is a <u>member</u> of that party. Just because you say you vote Liberal doesn't mean you're a voting member of the Liberal party. There's a formal admission process to each party.

In the U.S., it's a lot looser. You're a member of whatever political party you say you are. You could be a Democrat on Monday and decide to be a Republican on Tuesday.

In Australia, it's much more formalized: you can vote for whomever you wish, but in order to actually be <u>in</u> a political party, you must apply, and the party members then decide if they'll accept you. Once in, you pay yearly dues and can vote, but you must also do what the party leadership says. If you cross them, they can throw you out.

Take what happened in Western Australia in early 2007. There was a huge scandal involving an ex-Premier (equivalent of the state governor) who'd gotten caught ten years earlier taking bribes from big business and had been thrown out of office and into jail. In 2007, he got caught again, this time doing the bribing. The State *Corruption and Crimes Commission (CCC)* released the findings to the public and it all blew up in the press, resulting in a lot of high-level resignations and possible indictments. There were daily leaks about who knew what when and what was coming next. The current Premier realized his administration was failing. He put out a gag order on all the members of his party, decreeing that no member could talk to the press, that everything would come from the official spokesman and any violation would mean instant expulsion from the party. The order was instantly effective; the leaks stopped immediately and so did the scandal's momentum, all because nobody wanted to risk being thrown out of the party. If a member was expelled from the party they would still remain in Parliament as an independent, but at the next election they wouldn't be able to run for their seat in their old party and the party would run someone against them and they couldn't be elected. Stopping leaks instantly like that could never happen in the U.S.

Preselection of candidates is what the Westminster system uses instead of holding primary elections.

The winner is effectively chosen by a small number of people behind closed doors who may or may not be electors of that district and may, in some cases, not even be Australian citizens.
Brian Costar, Professor of Victorian Parliamentary Democracy, Swinburne University

Australians argue that it makes for a more dependable, stabile election environment. For an American observing this system, it rankles one's sense of independence.

Australian political parties have more control over their members and proceedings than parties in the U.S., and not only about who says what to the press, but also about who gets to run for office. In the U.S., almost anybody can declare their candidacy, get enough signatures to qualify, and run in a primary election for the nomination of their party. They might not get many votes, but they can run. In Australia, there are no open primary elections, just the final election. Potential candidates must put their name up before a closed party committee (called a *council* or an *executive*) for *preselection*. These committees have total control over who gets to run for office, and therefore who can get elected, and who ultimately runs the government.

One can run as an independent, but without a political machine behind you it's difficult to get elected. In some electorates that are *safe seats* (securely one party or the other), whichever candidate the *preselection* committee chooses is guaranteed to win. The candidate doesn't even have to be from or live in that *electorate*. The term for this is *parachuting into a safe seat*. If a party wants to get someone special into parliament, they *parachute them into a safe seat*.

In 2006 Liberal MP Judy Moylan, the *Federal Member for Pearce* in Western Australia, broke with Liberal Prime Minister John Howard over an immigration detention reform bill she thought was cruel and immoral This was called a *back-bench rebellion*. Despite taking a moral stand, Moylan came close to losing her seat over it because she'd gone against the PM. The Liberal party leadership was going to *stand her down* for preselection for the next election and replace her with someone more loyal. That new person would be *parachuting into a safe seat*. It made no difference that she was the incumbent, was very popular with her electorate and could easily win re-election. The party wasn't going to let her run as a Liberal because she'd pissed off the PM. She could have quit the party and run as an independent, but Pearce is a secure Liberal seat and she would have lost to anybody the Libs put up against her because they control the votes (through the leverage system of *preferences*—more about this later). She narrowly beat the challengers for preselection and was allowed run again as a Lib in 2007. She held the seat until 2013 when she retired. Her successor, WA State Attorney-General Christian Porter, was *parachuted into the safe seat*, and is now Federal Attorney-General, and involved in a nasty sex scandal.

Preferential and proportional voting   The way votes are counted is complex and unique to Australia. It's called *preferential voting*. It is fair, representative and egalitarian, and it is starting to be imitated by other countries. In the U.S. it's called Ranked Choice voting and is used in many cities, and in 2020 it will be used for the presidential election in Maine.

Preferential Voting   On the ballot there is a list of candidate's names with a blank square next to each. Instead of putting a check in the box next to the voter's choice, the voter instead numbers the boxes next to the names in order of their preference.

The counting of the *first preference* votes is called the *primary vote*. If the candidate with the most votes doesn't have an absolute majority, then the candidate with the least number of votes is eliminated. The votes on the ballots that have been eliminated are then awarded to the candidate who was listed on those ballots as #2, and then they're recounted. If there still isn't an absolute majority, they keep going down the line until someone has a majority. It's complex but logical, and there are no ties causing run-off elections.

With *preferential voting* close votes are resolved automatically. Think how Ralph Nader split Al Gore's vote in the U.S. presidential election of 2000, resulting in the Bush/Chaney presidency. If there had been preferential voting and Nader's voters had listed Gore as a second preference, Gore would have been elected and history would have taken a different course.

Proportional Voting is in addition to *preferential voting*, and is used to determine the members of the Federal Senate and the *upper houses* of NSW, Victoria, South Australia, Western Australia, and the lower houses of Tasmania and the ACT.

The idea is that the seats in those houses are divided *proportionally* between the parties based on the percentage of votes they received. First there is the *preferential vote* process, the winners of that must secure a *quota* of the vote which is the basis of the *proportional vote*.

There are twelve seats available in the Federal Senate from each state, so in a theoretical election, by party, if Labor gets 33% of the vote, the Liberals get 25%, the Greens get 15%, the Liberal Democrats get 10%, the Justice Party gets 9%, and Family First gets 6%, here's how they divvy up the 12 seats: the magic formula is applied and Labor would end up with four seats, the Liberals get three seats, the Greens get two seats, the Liberal Democrats, The Justice Party and Family First each get one seat. That way the smaller parties have representation, at least in the upper houses.

Rigging the preferential vote is inevitable since Aussies are great schemers and they always find a way to game the system. It's done by *exchanging preferences* for political favours. Political parties not only tell their voters to vote for their candidate as the *#1 preference*, but whom to vote for as the *#2 preference*, the *#3 preference*, etc. Of course, that can be a lot to remember, so that's why on *polling day* there are representatives from each party outside the local polling stations handing out *how to vote* cards with the preferences listed. In fact, on the ballot you can just check one of the parties and their list of preferences will be automatically counted.

So, why rig preferences? To trade for favours. For example: say you want to vote Greens, but you know they can't possibly beat the Liberals (remember, they are the conservative party), only Labor has a chance. In conventional voting, if you don't vote for Labor the Liberals will win. But with preferential voting, if the Greens tell their voters to put Labor as their second preference, and the results are close, Labor will get that vote. The underlying effect is that Labor owes the Greens a favour, plus the Greens will get credit for your vote for their cut of the subsidized funding for the next election. So, in effect, you get two votes. And even if your candidate loses but your second preference wins, they will play ball in Parliament with your other winning candidates because they owe them.

Preference trading is an open process reported in the press. It can be an opportunity for dirty dealing and strange bedfellows. It's politics and not for the faint-hearted.

In some states the parties form *tickets*, which have a *pre-formed list of preferences*: you actually vote for the list and not the candidates. It can get dirty: in 2001 in Western Australia, the minor right wing ultra-conservative party *One Nation* wanted to counter the power of the two big parties (Labor and the Liberals), so they put the smallest party, the ultra left-wing *Greens* on their *ticket* in the number-two position just to spite the two big parties, not figuring it would matter. They underestimated their own popularity and the left-wing Greens ended up with five seats in the state's upper house, the exact opposite effect One Nation wanted.

Why should it matter that a small party can get a few seats in Parliament when the big parties hold the rest? The small parties can become the deciding or blocking factor on tight votes and can trade power in such situations by getting the big parties to back the small party's otherwise unviable issues. For example, in Western Australia in 2007, during a period of notorious scandals, there was a move by the Labor Government to lessen the power of the commission that administered the *Freedom of Information Act* (*FOI*), the instrument that counters secrecy in government. The Greens Party, with only two seats in the upper house and none in the lower house, effectively blocked the move by siding with the opposition (the Liberals), and the right-wing Liberals ended up owing the left-wing Greens a favour.

So the smallest minority parties matter, they can hold a

balance of power: '*Keeping the bastards honest.*'

Election Day is held on a Saturday. Local elections can be on a fixed date, federal elections are called by the Prime Minister, at his/her convenience as long as it's within three years of the previous election. The Constitution stipulates the House of Representatives lasts no more than three years after it first meets, but may be dissolved sooner. The Senator's terms are six-years, but half the senate is elected every three-years.

The Constitution requires that in half-year elections, the election of senators must take place within one year before the places become vacant. State elections work similarly. Usually the senate election is on the same day as the House of Representatives, so a new senate might not convene for months. If a vacancy occurs between elections, a *by-election* is called.

When the Prime Minister or Premier call the election, the voting date is six-weeks from then, on a Saturday. Parliament goes into care-taker mode until the election result is clear. No major legislation is considered.

Polling stations are usually at primary schools or volunteer bushfire stations. Since it's mandatory voting, everyone in your suburb will turn up that day. Political parties are allowed to put up booths or tables distributing how-to-vote flyers which are necessary since there are so many parties on the ballot. The local P&C (like the PTA) will have a benefit *sausage sizzle* (hot dog BBQ) and it takes on a festive atmosphere.

Election advertising is nowhere near the level of the US. Since elections are only six-weeks long the active campaigns don't go on for years. There are TV, radio, print and billboard ads as in the US. All advertising must end the Wednesday before the election.

Legal system

The legal system is similar to the U.S. and Britain, with the accused being innocent until proven guilty. Juries, drawn from voter rolls, decide major trials, just as in the U.S. On the other hand, in some states, judges and *barristers* (trial lawyers), wear flowing robes and little white powdered wigs, just like their predecessors did a hundred-fifty years ago.

Courts are arranged in a hierarchy. The *High Court of Australia* is equivalent to the U.S. Supreme Court. The *Federal Courts* decide tax laws and federal violations. *Magistrates Courts* were designed to ease the large caseloads on the Federal Courts.

Each state has a *Supreme Court* that deals with serious crime, like murder, armed robbery, etc., These are called *indictable offences*, which equate to felonies. Below them are the *District Courts*, which hear crimes except murder and treason. From there on down are *Magistrates Courts* (also known as *Courts of Petty Sessions*), which were designed to deal with the overburden on the higher courts, and *Family Courts*, which deal with divorce and child custody issues. Serious crimes are heard by judges and juries; less serious infractions by magistrates. In rural areas, uniformed police officers (called *police prosecutors*) present the state's case to Magistrates Courts.

Though crime is every bit as serious as in North America, the names of some of the offences are straight out of Monty Python. Arson is called *Lighting a fire likely to injure or damage*. Kidnapping is *Deprivation of liberty*. A police officer may detain an intoxicated person who is *behaving in a disorderly manner or in a manner likely to cause injury to the person or another person or damage to property*. If you give someone an illegal drug you can be charged with *administering a drug of dependence*. If you attack someone you could be arrested for *an unlawful act with intent to harm, assault occasioning bodily harm*, or *assault by kicking*. And there's the charge of *going armed in public to cause fear*, or *possessing a firearm with circumstances of aggravation*.

There is no capital punishment, and sentences are notoriously lenient by American standards. Rights of *self-defence* are restricted. An example: in Sydney in 2003, three men robbed and terrorized a disabled man in his home on several occasions over a period of months. On the last occasion, they murdered him. The trial took three years and they were found guilty. They got an average of twelve years in jail, with the possibility of early parole. In the U.S. they'd be on death row. Ironically, if the victim had obtained a gun and used it on his attackers to defend himself, there's a good possibility he would have been charged with using *unlawful force* [more on this in **guns**].

Another case: a man slashed and stabbed another man with a metre-long (3-foot) sword. He was charged with *attempted murder*, but it was reduced to *unlawful wounding with intent to cause grievous bodily harm.* He was given the maximum sentence of 20 years, and served 4½.

A person sentenced to life-imprisonment in Australia can be paroled in 20 years. Some are released sooner.

Aboriginal tribal law is still practiced in some remote communities. The state police allow elders to try, judge sentence and administer punishment to some degree. When the crimes get serious, police step in and the perpetrator goes into the traditional court system.

Lawyers   There are two types of lawyers, *solicitors* and *barristers*. *Solicitors* are contract lawyers, *Barristers* are trial lawyers. Barristers of prominence are appointed *Queen's Counsel* (or *QC*). In New South Wales, the Northern Territory, and the ACT, QCs are called *Senior Counsel*. They're also known as *Silks*, after the silk robes they wear in court.

So, if you find yourself in need of legal help, you start with the *solicitor* for advice. If you end up in court, you'll have a *barrister,* and when the guy in the powdered wig and red robe walks in, don't laugh at his get-up; he can put you away—but probably only for a little while.

Military

European settlement of the Australian continent began in 1788 as a penal colony. The first armed forces were English Marines who came as guards with the convicts, they were more a police force than a strategic military. English regular troops came in 1810. Colonies and towns formed volunteer corps in case the convicts revolted. Convict *transportation* ended in 1868.

Being an isolated colony surrounded by oceans, there wasn't much need for a large organized military force. Through the nineteenth century local volunteer units grew and participated in Britain's various wars. Gradually, volunteer groups became more organized, with professional soldiers as leaders. Periodically there were miners' revolts and shearers strikes, and citizen-soldiers were mobilized to deal with them.

There were no large-scale indigenous revolts as in North America or South Africa; the Aboriginal actions were sporadic and localized, with few people involved on both sides. Since the police had guns and the Indigenous people had spears, the police won. Rarely were there overt battles in the open. From the Brits' point of view, most were small scale guerrilla acts and they didn't see a sufficient threat to bring in troops. These were dealt with as police actions, often involving indigenous trackers from other *country* who had no connection and little regard for their prey.

As Australia developed through the nineteenth century, she formed six independent colonies, each responsible for their own defence. From 1788 until 1870 this was done with British regular forces: twenty-four different British infantry regiments served in the Australian colonies. Between 1855 and 1890 the Australian colonies became self-governing, though the Colonial Office in London retained ultimate control and the colonies were still firmly within the British Empire.

The Governors of the Australian colonies had the authority from the Crown to raise military and naval forces. These militias supported British regular troops until 1870 when the colonies assumed their own defence. Colonial forces, including home-raised units, saw action in many of the conflicts of the British Empire during the 19th century: India, Afghanistan, the New Zealand Maori Wars, the Sudan conflict, and the Boer War in South Africa. The separate colonies maintained control over their respective militia forces and navies until 1 March 1901, when the *Commonwealth of Australia* was formed and the colonial forces were amalgamated into the *Commonwealth Forces*. The officer corps was British-trained.

For a country with a relatively small population, Australia has always punched well above her weight in military affairs. First as a colony, then as an independent member of the *Commonwealth of Nations* (the former British Empire), she, like Canada, supported Great Britain's military adventures, providing men and material to the British Imperial Forces.

Australians distinguished themselves on the African Veldt in the Boer War; on the bloody beaches and cliffs of Gallipoli, and in the trenches of France in WWI, across the deserts of North Africa and in the defence of Singapore in WWII.

Then came the Japanese War in the Pacific and it all changed. For the first time Australia itself was threatened, war was no longer a distant adventure, it had come home.

On December 7, 1941, when the Japanese bombed the American bases at Pearl Harbor, Hawaii, they also invaded Northern Malaysia. This began a two-month advance down the Malay peninsula toward the British fortress of Singapore, manned by 130,000 troops, including 20,000 Australians. Most of the Australian Army was half a world away in the North African desert fighting alongside the British against Rommel.

In February 1942 Singapore fell to the Japanese who took thousands of British, Indian, and Australian troops prisoner. This act, more than any other single incident, signalled an end to the British Empire.

Then the Japanese invaded New Guinea, at that time Australian territory, just 150 kilometres (90 miles) from the Australian coast. Darwin, the capital of the Northern Territory, was bombed.

These weren't just a few token raids, but repeated strikes by the same large Japanese fleet that had attacked Pearl Harbor two months before. Darwin was levelled, more than a dozen ships were sunk, 250 civilians were killed, thousands were wounded. It was so bad that the news was kept secret from the rest of Australia for fear of causing panic. Britain was busy fighting Germany and couldn't help, Australia, always the dutiful child of Britain, always first to volunteer to fight for the *King and Country*, was left on her own.

For the first time, Australians were fighting alone on their own doorstep, backs against the wall. The situation was dire: the entire population of Australia was only about seven million, not enough to occupy the vast continent let alone defend it. Most of the regular army was in North Africa, thousands of soldiers had been captured at Singapore and there were scant forces left at home to defend against invasion.

The *Top End* (northern Australia) was evacuated as the Japanese bombed north Queensland, the Northern Territory and the north coast of Western Australia. Australians reasonably considered they were about to receive a full-scale Japanese invasion, and they had neither the manpower nor equipment to do much about it. Things were looking very grim.

What the Aussies didn't know was that the Japanese move against Australia was a feint, they were really after the Dutch East Indies (now Indonesia) and its rich rubber and oil resources, and then onto Siam (Thailand) and eventually India. By then, they reasoned, Britain and the U.S. would have been defeated and they could come back and take Australia at their leisure. But the Japanese leadership, as cunning as they were, hadn't heeded what Admiral Yamamoto, who had led the bombing of Pearl Harbor, had warned: "I'm afraid we have awakened a sleeping giant." The giant he referred to was the United States.

By early 1942 American forces were retreating out of the Philippines. In desperation they asked to base forces in Australia, and Australia wisely welcomed them. The continent soon became an impregnable citadel from which to counterattack. Younger Australians might not want to hear about it, but *oldies* gratefully remember that the U.S. saved Australia from being invaded. Since then, the U.S. and Australia have maintained close defensive ties.

Australia recalled her army from Africa and hastily retrained and deployed them in New Guinea. There, against odds, and with American help, they heroically stopped the Japanese. Eventually the American juggernaut began pushing the Japanese forces back up the Pacific.

Australia emerged from WWII bloodied but battle-tested, wiser, and more worldly. She realized that Great Britain could no longer help her but the U.S. could. During the last 75 years Australia's defence strategy has reflected that.

Since the Second World War, Australia has maintained an active, independent presence both politically and militarily in the region: campaigning in Korea, Vietnam, Malaysia, Indonesia, East Timor, the Solomon Islands, Iraq, and Afghanistan. Australia supplies forces for UN peacekeeping missions worldwide. Australia is a regional power but contributes to world efforts such as contributing ships and planes patrolling the Persian Gulf.

The latest threat is Chinese military dominance of the South China Sea, and the use of loans to developing nations to secure bases in the region. The Australian/U.S. alliance is evolving to answer that threat.

Since 2014 the U.S. has had forces stationed in the Top End near Darwin, with a cache of pre-positioned weapons and material, and U.S. Marine brigades rotating-in to the base under the guise of 'wargames'. In early 2020, Australia announced a large military upgrade, including state-of-the-art anti-ship missiles. Also included was lengthening the runway at the *RAAF* (*Royal Australian Air Force*) base at Tindal, near Darwin in the Northern Territory, to accommodate aerial tankers and U.S. B-52 long-range bombers. The upside is Australia would have greater U.S. protection; the downside is, she is now a major target of a possible Chinese attack on RAAF Tindal,. Ironically, the Australian government allowed a Chinese company to secure a 99 year lease on the Port of Darwin.

ADF   The Army, Navy and Air Force are collectively called the *Australian Defence Forces*, or *ADF*.

National Service or *Nasho* (the draft) ended in 1972. All Australian forces are now volunteer. As for officer training: the Royal Australian Naval College is at Jervis Bay, the Army's Royal Military Academy is at Duntroon, and the Royal Australian Air Force Officer Training School is at Pt. Cook. College degrees for officers are optional; the Australian Defence Force Academy at the University of New South Wales provides Officers in Training with academics for college degrees.

Navy   Australia is an island nation, so having a potent navy is fundamental. The *RAN* (*Royal Australian Navy*) has fleet of 45 ships and is authorized for 14,500 personnel. The centrepieces are two 27,000 tonne amphibious assault ships, HMAS Canberra and HMAS Adelaide, which each can carry 1000 troops deployed on landing craft from internal docking wells and on helicopters from full flight decks. They are not currently configured for F35 jump jets, though they could be upgraded as the ships have ski-jump launch ramps on the bow.

The rest of the fleet consists of three Aegis guided missile destroyers, eight frigates, fifteen 187-foot Armidale fast patrol boats, mine warfare, and support ships, plus six deep-water non-nuclear submarines. The Navy no longer uses aircraft carriers; the *HMAS Sydney* and *HMAS Melbourne* were retired in the 1980s.

The submarine fleet consists of six Collins-class diesel/electric attack boats. The fleet is in the process of being replaced with French-designed, Australian-built vessels.

In addition to its own duties, the *RAN* provides forward support to U.S. Navy vessels operating in southeast Asian waters. U.S. Marines are reportedly stationed aboard the assault ships.

The naval air arm is currently limited to a fleet of helicopters, mostly Sea Hawks, Sea Kings, and Super Sea Sprites. The *Royal Australian Air Force* handles fixed wing duties.

Air Force   The *RAAF* (*Royal Australian Air Force Air*) Combat Group consists of 259 aircraft including 110 combat aircraft: American F18A/B Hornets, F18F Super Hornets and F35A attack bombers, British Hawk 127 close support fighters (which double as trainers), and PC9/A and PC 21 trainer-reconnaissance aircraft, plus unmanned UAV's.

The *Airlift Group* flies C-17 Globemasters, Boeing 737's, C130 Hercules transports, DHC-4 Caribou, and various other support aircraft, with Airbus A330 aerial tankers.

The *Air Surveillance and Reconnaissance Group* is gradually replacing its P3 Orions with P-8A Poseidons and P-8A Maritime Patrol planes capable of anti-ship and anti-submarine warfare. The group also operates ground-based radar.

The RAAF helicopters have all been transferred to the Army.

Army   The *Royal Australian Army* consists of about 31,000 men and women on active duty and 19,850 in reserve units.

The Army has fifty-nine American M1-A1 battle tanks,

268 A Survival Guide to Australia

plus M113 armoured personnel carriers, eight-wheel armoured fighting vehicles, Bushmaster and Hawkei utility vehicles (similar to Humvees), tactical military trucks and Land Rovers. The Artillery consists of fifty-five 155mm howitzers and a number of mobile surface-to-air missile systems.

The Army flies several kinds of helicopters: the Blackhawk, Chinooks, Kiowa, and Eurocopter EC135, Airbus ARH Tiger and MRH-90.

SAS stands for *Special Air Service* and is the special forces. This experienced, highly respected unit is the match of any on the planet. They are based in Western Australia and deploy around the world.

ASIO stands for the Australia Intelligence Organization, the equivalent of the CIA. It's based in Canberra, has a staff of about 1,700 and is growing. They are hiring, check their website.

Australian intelligence originally was a branch of the British *'Central Counter-Espionage Bureau'*, as part of a British Empire-wide system. In 1949 ASIO was formed in response to the Cold War and is entirely Australian, though one can assume it cooperates with allied countries' counterpart services.

The *Five Eyes* intelligence alliance of Australia, Canada, New Zealand, the UK and the U.S. are parties to an agreement treaty for joint cooperation in signals intelligence.

Pine Gap is located near the geographic centre of Australia, not far from the town of Alice Springs in the Northern Territory. Pine Gap is a top-secret U.S.-Australian base called the *Joint Defence Facility* (note the Australian spelling of *defence*, with a 'c').

Pine Gap is a large complex of buildings and huge satellite dish antennas, operated by about 1,200 Australian and American personnel. It's top secret so few people know what goes on there, and those that do aren't telling. The Netflix drama series *'Pine Gap'* will give you an idea what it's about—or what they want you to think it's about.

Rumours as to its purpose and activities know no bounds: everything from a UFO base, a five-mile deep hole to tap the earth's magnetic field, a huge nuclear generator to power death-ray space weapons, or a new headquarters for a World Dictatorship. Is probably master control for ASIO/NSA electronic surveillance for the southern hemisphere.

One thing is certain: it's a very secure base in the middle of nowhere.

Defensive Strategy   The idea is to keep any fight offshore. Australian forces, though not large in number, have a reputation as an able fighting force and are technologically superior to any in the region. The Navy is based in the Pacific and Indian Oceans, and along the north coast. The Air Force has pre-supplied bases around the country and can deploy air wings of fighters and attack bombers as needed. The Army, Navy, and SAS usually have (or had) forces overseas running operations as peacekeepers or working with allies in active theatres, such as Afghanistan, Iraq, and East Timor. The rest of the troops are in training or in support.

Out of curiosity, I once asked a friend who was an Australian Reserve Army officer what would happen if one of the large Asian nations to the north managed to fight their way past the Navy and Air Force and invaded somewhere along the vast northern coast.

"We'd let them penetrate into the red centre," he said smugly, "then cut them off and wait for them to die of thirst."

Another friend suggested if Indonesia wanted to invade, all they'd have to do is load up cruise ships with thousands of refugees and crash them into Australian ports.

However you want to think of it, Australia, population 25 million, is geographically directly below Asia, population 2 billion. If anything goes down, all the ADF will be able to do is try to hold the fort until the U.S. Navy's Seventh Fleet arrives.

China is the obvious challenge. Though China is Australia's major trading partner, in 2020 China threatened Australia for criticising Beijing's on-going attempts to take-over the South China Sea, the political crackdown on Hong Kong, and causing Covid-19. China placed tariffs on Australian products, has threatened preventing Chinese students from attending Australian Universities (a major source of income), has been caught harassing Chinese-Australians in Australia, and has refused to discuss these issues with

Australian government ministers. Western countries think short-term: earnings quarters, financial years, political terms. China thinks in 10, 50, 100-year plans. And the Chinese Communist Party has total control over their government, they have allowed their people the benefits of capitalism but not allowed any political freedom. The Chinese don't have to invade, they are *buying* Australia. They own nine-million acres of farmland, a regional airport in Western Australia, the Port of Darwin, and coal and iron mines. And there is evidence they have infiltrated the Australian government, including getting their people elected to Parliament

And what of Indonesia (population 267 million), Australia's immediate neighbour to the north? Will they standby if China starts to threaten Australia? If world-affairs go *pear-shaped* over the next fifty-years, and Australia loses the protection of the U.S., might Indonesia not decide to take Australia to prevent China from doing so, the way Nazi Germany took Norway in 1940, with the excuse they were doing it to prevent Britain from doing so?

Australia might provide forward-support for U.S. Navy ships, Marines and the U.S. Air Force, but she must have her own defence.

Antarctica

The Australian Antarctic Division claims and manages almost half of the 14 million sq. km. (5.5 million sq. miles) Antarctic continent and maintains several bases. There are three permanent research stations at Casey, Mawson, and Davis There are several temporary summer stations and a sub-arctic marine station at Macquarie Island. The Division regularly charters a research icebreaker ship, the *Aurora Australis*. As the only continent completely within the Southern Hemisphere, Australia feels she has a right and duty to occupy and protect the fragile frozen land.

Since 1947, Australia has had a presence on the continent, performing research and scientific studies, living year-round, inventing techniques and technology to survive the harsh environment.

A vital air link was opened in 2007 when Australia initiated regular air service between Hobart, Tasmania, and Casey station via the newly constructed Wilkins Runway. This was built 70 km. from Casey station, carved out of blue glacial ice and capped with pavement made of compressed snow. It's a fully-certified aerodrome, so it can potentially handle future commercial flights.

The runway wasn't the only technical achievement. There is a specially-built Airbus A319 which carries 20–40 passengers plus cargo and enough fuel to fly round-trip without refuelling. An Australian Air Force C17A flies in heavy equipment, like vehicles and helicopters that are too big and heavy for the A319, and can air-drop cargo from its aft-facing loading ramp to remote locations.

New Zealand or *Aotearoa*

New Zealand is the sister country to Australia and therefore deserves some mention in this book. Geographically and historically they are as close as two countries can be, even closer than the U.S. and Canada.

New Zealand is the size of California and consists of two islands, North and South, and a population of five million. Where Australia is closer to the equator, is flat and mostly dry, New Zealand is closer to Antarctica, is mountainous, and receives a great deal of rain. The mountainous South Island gets quite a bit of snow. Australia is an old continent with smooth, worn topography, New Zealand is newly-formed with jagged peaks, fjords and active glaciers.

Aotearoa is the *Māori* name for New Zealand. The *Māori*, ethnic Polynesians, were the first human inhabitants of the islands.

New Zealanders are also known as *Kiwi's*, named after an iconic, native flightless bird. There is also a native fruit called a kiwi fruit.

Aussies and Kiwi's enjoy quasi-citizenship in each other's countries: citizens and permanent residents from each can travel between the countries without visas, and can obtain jobs, own real estate and receive health care in either without legal complications. But while the countries are similar, they are not identical, nor are the people.

When Australia separated from the rest of the continents 180 million years ago, it already had numerous plant species, mammals, birds and reptiles. When New Zealand was thrust up from the ocean depths about 25 million years ago it had no native land mammals at all. Over the years vegetation and insects drifted on currents to the islands, birds found their way, and even a strange lizard called a tuatara. Plants and animals adapted and evolved: the Northern Island is lush and tropical, the Southern Island is mountainous and temperate.

The Australian Aboriginals migrated to Australia 40-60,000 years ago, while the Polynesian Māori settled New Zealand merely 1,500 years ago. The British settled Australia in 1788 as a penal colony and met only token resistance from the scattered Indigenous people as they took control. The first British in New Zealand were sealers and whalers, and they encountered an established Polynesian civilisation—there was no attempt at *Terra Nullius* here. New Zealand was settled by free British pioneers starting in the 1830's, who encountered well-organized, fierce warriors. Several wars were fought for control of the land, the British pioneers eventually buying much of it from the Māori. The problem that ensued was that the land had been communally-owned and that started many fights between Māori over what could and couldn't be sold. By 1869 the fighting had ended and British rule had been established.

New Zealanders seem to have an inferiority complex toward Australia. Australia is larger and richer, and traditionally dominates the relationship. New Zealanders have nothing to feel bad about: the scenery is breath-taking, the food is good, the culture sophisticated, the people well-educated.

Being a smaller economy, jobs are not as plentiful and a lot of Kiwi's migrate to Australia to work. But they never leave their Aotearoa spirit behind, they are still Kiwi's and they maintain their identity. If you see a car with a silver fern leaf decal on the back window, there is a proud Kiwi inside.

Politically, New Zealand is more left-wing than Australia, and has declared a non-nuclear status. After the Christchurch Mosque shooting they banned semi-automatic weapons, magazines and parts, and initiated a weapons buy-back scheme.

Over 56,000 firearms were turned in, a substantial number for such a small population.

Australia and New Zealand have historically combined militaries in time of war, forming the *ANZAC* forces (*Australia New Zealand Army Corps*) in WWI and continuing through various conflicts through the Viet Nam war. They are separate countries with separate forces, but still operate closely, though New Zealand is less likely to project power in the region, leaving that up to her big sister, Australia.

The modern Aussies and Kiwis' are steadfast rivals and love to make fun of each other, especially over their accents. To an American ear they both sound like a derivation of British, but the Aussie accent is full of broad vowels and sounds cockney, while the New Zealand accent has clipped vowels and sounds a bit Scottish.

Rugby union is the national sport, and the Kiwi *All Blacks* and the Australian *Wallabies* fight out as bitter a grudge match as the Dodgers and the Yankees. Though rivals on the sports fields, they fought as a unit as *ANZAC's* in both world wars.

International relations

Recently, Australia had a limited role alongside the British and American forces in Iraq and Afghanistan. Closer to home, she has projected her limited, though high-tech power [see section on **military**] into the Pacific and Asia, intervening militarily in Indonesia, East Timor, and the Solomon Islands. She also provides advisory, leadership, and economic assistance to the poorer countries in the Pacific region.

Economic realignment from American and European markets to Asian-Pacific trade has been successful. Australia is western historically, socially, and demographically, but geographically she's in Asia.

Of late, China's reversion to hard-line rule has hampered trade, though the bulk of it seems unaffected. Australia has angered the Chinese government over criticism on Beijing's crackdown on the Hong Kong freedom movement, the freedom of navigation in the South China Sea, on attempts to infiltrate and influence Australian society, and the harassment and arrest of Australians living or working in China. In 2020, Beijing imposed a steep tariff on Australian barley, which was Australia's chief market for the grain, forcing Australian growers to find other markets. China is threatening to embargo Australian coal, though she owns many of the mines.

Fitting into Asia is important for more than economic reasons. Just to her north are two billion Indonesians, Malaysians, Chinese, Vietnamese, Japanese, and Koreans: all going about their lives indifferent to what goes on in Australia. To maintain her security, she must be both socially and economically useful to her neighbours.

Trade with China   China is Australia's major import and export market. Though twenty-five percent of Australia's manufactured imports come from China, Australia sells more than it buys and in 2018 had a A$38 billion surplus.

Annually, Australia sells China billions of dollars of raw materials: iron, alumina, nickel, copper, coal, gold, etc. Thirteen percent of Australia's exports are thermal coal to China. Australian schools and universities educate 200,000 Chinese students annually (post-Covid 19 this may change), which adds up to billions of dollars in tuition. In return, Australia imports billions of dollars of Chinese manufactured goods. Chinese companies, many state-owned, have invested billions of dollars into Australian mines, farms, and real estate.

ChAFTA is the *Chinese Australia Free Trade Agreement*. It isn't free, there are small tariffs on many items. You can find out more at https://dfat.gov.au/trade/agreements.

Ninety percent of Australia's merchandise imports are from China. Imports of textiles, clothing and footwear were replaced by household appliances in the 1990s, today fifty percent are engineered products, including office and telecommunications equipment.

China could militarily envelope Australia and take control—and that may happen one day in the distant future—but at present it would be disruptive to the international order and is unnecessary—as long as Australia is useful to China.

Besides external trade deals, the Chinese government also applies internal leverage by owning large amounts of Australian real estate: almost 2% of the land (22 million acres), several large coal mines, and the Port of Darwin (Australia's major north coast seaport).

The Chinese monitor Chinese Australians, especially Chinese students studying in Australia. In 2019 they allegedly attempted to infiltrate federal parliament by running a candidate for the seat of Chisholm in Melbourne (the man, Nick Zhao, was mysteriously found dead in a motel room after alerting *ASIO*, the Australian equivalent of the CIA).

Ostar Media is a Chinese media group established in Australia in 1995. It is part of the CAMG Media Group Pty Ltd, an international media holding group covering Oceania, Asia and along 'The Belt and Road' (China's international investment scheme). In Australia CAMG Media operates 5 branches in Sydney, Melbourne, Canberra, Adelaide and Perth, including 39 radio broadcasts, 12 weekly newspapers, lifestyle magazines, events, webcast, television and online media. The purpose is to promote and spread the PRC (People's Republic of China) party line by projecting Soft Power.

As long as Australia is a reliable source for the materials she needs, China will allow Australia to manage them, probably because Australia would be easier to deal with as a client than as a captive colony.

The inescapable fact is that the Chinese play by 100-year plans, while the Aussies (like most western nations) are only looking as far as the next financial year and the next election cycle. In the long run the best Australia (and the rest of the world) can hope for is that China becomes liberalized by the newly affluent and educated masses, who would turn the country democratic.

Living in a bad neighbourhood After the Bali bombings in 2002, Australia awakened once again to the reality of living in a bad neighbourhood. With a small population and a wide, mostly unoccupied northern coastline, Australia is under constant threat of illegal immigration, and with it the side effects of smuggling, degradation of the environment, and the possible introduction of disease.

Australia realizes she must maintain good relations with Indonesia and Malaysia, her immediate neighbours to the north. Indonesia seems to be unable (or unwilling) to control its fishing industry, which constantly poaches into Northern

Australian waters, decimating fish stocks and killing reefs. Australia has had to increase sea and air patrols. Negotiations with the Indonesians are ongoing.

A victory for the whales: starting in the mid 1980's, the otherwise rational Japanese annually sent a whale-hunting fleet into southern waters to harvest a few thousand whales under the guise of 'research', the meat ending up in Japanese meat markets. Australia officially objected but did little to stop the practice. A non-profit animal rights group called *Sea Shepard* ran a twelve-year battle of harassment and eventually drove the Japanese out, though they still 'harvest' whales in Japanese waters.

Economics and the future

As a former-British colony, Australia was habitually linked by trade with the mother country. What wasn't manufactured domestically was imported from the UK, and to a lesser extent from the U.S. Being so distant, local manufacturing was essential. In the first half of the twentieth century this allowed Australian goods to be sold domestically and throughout the Pacific and Southeast Asia. That started to change after WWII.

In 1950 the Australian population was just eight-million, not exactly a vast market. Meanwhile, its Asian neighbours were developing manufacturing industries, and with cheaper labour and mass-marketing, were about to envelope the Australian market. Australian governments placed stiff tariffs on imported goods to protect Australian industry, making Japanese cars and electronics prohibitively expensive. But protectionism is a double-edged sword: it might have protected Australian manufacturing but it limited Australian consumers to mediocre products, and made exports uncompetitive and unwanted. This eventually became an existential problem.

By the early 1990s, Australia was in danger of becoming what one Chinese premier described as "...the poor white trash of Asia." What he meant was—through protectionist economic policy—Australia was stagnating and falling behind. Labor Prime Minister Bob Hawke and his Treasurer, Paul Keating, forced unpopular reforms on the country, reducing all import tariffs to five percent while phasing out protection for the textile, clothing, and motor vehicle industries. This was both risky and out of character politically, because the Labor Party was the party of the workers, not the capitalists. Australia reluctantly went into what Keating called *"The recession we had to have."*

By the end of the decade, the reforms had been successful, and to quote Gregory Hywood, former editor-in-chief of Melbourne's *The Age*: *"Hawk and Keating had transformed the Australian economy from closed and protected to open, vibrant and global."*

Keating succeeded Hawke as prime minister in 1991, but was defeated by John Howard in 1996. The economic good times continue because of those reforms. Australia was the only western country that didn't go into recession during the Global Financial Crisis of 2008.

A major factor driving the economy is the mining industry. Australia has huge deposits of raw materials: iron, nickel, *aluminium*, gold, lead, uranium, oil, and natural gas. The Chinese have invested billions of dollars in Western Australian iron mines, and huge super-carriers transport millions of tons of ore to Chinese, Korean, and Japanese steel mills. As sophisticated as Australians consider themselves, to Asian business people, the country is merely a quarry and a source of grain and meat, and to a lesser extent a market in which to sell electronics and cars, and someplace '*close-but-western*' to go on holiday.

Though Australia produces substantial oil and natural gas, domestic oil is priced at international rates, so fuel costs are higher.

Comparing prices between the U.S. and Australia: petrol is 27% higher in Australia while rent is 20% lower. Grocery prices and local purchasing power are about the same. Australia has the world's 14th largest economy with just one-third of one-percent of the population. The GDP (2020) was US$1.42 trillion.

Free trade agreements   Australia has free trade agreements (*FTA's*) with the U.S., China, Japan, South Korea, Hong Kong, and Peru. Peru buys a lot of Queensland sugar, along with beef and dairy products, and it's a straight route across the Pacific. In 2018-19, Australia's two-way trade with Peru was worth A$656 million.

Exports   If mining is king, agriculture is queen: wheat and sheep and cattle (processed and live) are exported on a large scale.

Wheat is still a major export, but U.S. government-subsidized exports are squeezing Australia out of many markets. Australia exported 22 million *tonnes* in 2016–17 valued at A$6.1 billion, produced on mostly family-owned farms.

Besides processed meat products, there is a *live animal export business*. Australia ships significant amounts of live sheep and cattle to the Middle East. Strict Muslim Halal and Kosher laws require the local slaughter of animals for religious purity reasons. Giant transport ships with twelve-story high pens holding upward of 10,000 sheep, make regular runs from Western Australia to the Arabian Gulf. This industry is highly unpopular with animal rights groups, and restrictions have been imposed to improve conditions on the ships and to prohibit shipping during the northern summer hot months.

Because Australia is an island, it's been able to keep out diseases like Mad Cow Despite this, the Chinese are beginning to undercut Australia's market with cheaper production costs.

Education is a major export. In 2018, 870,000 foreign students studied in Australia, making up 22% of total enrolment. This not only helps to fund Australian universities, it also brings in millions of dollars in associated student living expenses. Foreign students pay considerably higher tuition than Australian students, and the universities depend on this to fund their budgets. COVID-19 has restricted foreign students attending Australian universities, and this could have an adverse effect until a vaccine is developed.

The Australia-United States Free Trade Agreement

AUFTA, was established in 2005. It eliminated tariffs and duties on American goods coming into Australia, and Australian goods going into the U.S. This included manufactured and agricultural items.

The United States is the largest and most significant investor in Australia, accounting for 27 per cent, A$939 billion, of Australia's total foreign investment stock (2018).

In 2018, the United States was our third-largest two-way trading partner in goods and services. Australia's exports to the United States were $23.1 billion, and imports were $50.8 billion. The U.S is also Australian investors largest overseas trading destination, 28 per cent (A$719 billion) of Australia's total overseas investment stock as of December 2018 is invested in the U.S. Two-way investment has almost tripled since the Agreement came into force. Those are the official Australian Government statistics.

There is an alternative view, from Shiro Armstrong, Co-Director of the Australia-Japan Research Centre at the Crawford School of Public Policy, Australian National University:

"The lead-up to the agreement was accompanied by heated debate. AUSFTA marked a departure from the primacy of unilateral and multilateral trade and investment liberalisation in Australia's foreign economic policy strategy. ...the arrangement gave American goods, services and investment preferred treatment and gave US exporters better access to Australian markets than that enjoyed by exporters from other countries. The drawback...is that it can change the mix of Australian imports away from the most efficient suppliers towards suppliers who are only competitive because of the special treatment they receive...

This discrimination is part of the design of these agreements and is meant to encourage other countries to join the game and negotiate preferential deals of their own. Preferential agreements only create efficient trade if the lowest-cost suppliers are included.

Our analysis shows that trade between Australia and East Asian economies would have grown more – to the tune of $53 billion for both the United States and Australia – if AUSFTA had not been put in place.

As a minor trading partner, Australia had to settle for whatever it could get. The AUSFTA agreement opened

Australia for the entry of U.S. products and investors, but ignored Australian exports like Queensland sugarcane and West Australian wheat.

Australia is the third-largest sugar producer in the world, and in 2015 wanted to export 500,000 tonnes to the U.S. under the AUSFTA, but has to apply each year to import there. The U.S. limited it to 152,000 tonnes that year. Australia was promised eventual parity, but has had to settle for whatever the U.S. decides.

An interesting trade tale: the innocuous *Ugg boot*. The ankle-high fleecy sheepskin boot was an original Australian beach classic, made from abundant sheepskins and worn by surfers worldwide. An American company, Deckers Outdoor Corporation, discovered that the name was considered generic in Australia and hadn't been copyrighted.

Deckers registered the name and forbade anyone, including Australians, from using it. This prohibition wasn't just in America, they had the *cheek* (gall) to bring a lawsuit forbidding Australian manufacturers selling Ugg boots in Australia from calling them Ugg boots.

It gets worse: Deckers had cheap imitation Ugg boots mass-produced in China and opened stores on U.S. malls marketing them using images of kangaroos, boomerangs, and a huge Australian map on the wall. Some Aussie manufacturers tried an end-run and continued making and selling Uggs as '*Ughs*', Deckers went after them again. Backed against the wall, a small family-run Western Australian company took them on and beat them in the U.S. courts. The name is back as a generic; anybody can use it. It was a rare victory.

The environment

Australia was one of the first nations to institute a wide-ranging tax on carbon dioxide pollution. It then became the first to revoke one. The country is a gluttonous consumer of fossil fuels and has some of the highest per capita greenhouse-gas emissions among industrial nations. Petrol is cheap, and people drive a lot. GlobalPetrolPrices.com

Per capita, Australians are the world's highest carbon polluters. Australia is the world's largest exporter of coal, mostly to China and India. Some remote towns have wind generators, but out of pragmatism, not conservation. Solar panels are on roofs throughout the country but state power companies have tried to hamstring the solar industry at every turn. Very few electric and hybrid vehicles, which require government tax incentives to be affordable, are sold. There are relatively few charging stations, and even if there were, since renewables make up just 13% of energy sources, if you drive an electric car in Australia you are actually burning coal.

With unlimited sunlight and heaps of wind, you'd think Australia would be a shoo-in for renewable energy. Not. The coal and natural gas industries have shackled the economy to fossil fuels. The re-election of the *Liberal/National Coalition* in 2019, in an election manipulated by Rupert Murdoch's Australian newspaper monopoly and a A$5 million-dollar media blitz by mining billionaire Clive Palmer, kept the climate change deniers in power. The right-wing faction of the *Coalition*, despite the massive fires and droughts, still doubt that 250 years of mankind burning fossil fuels have caused the spike in carbon in the atmosphere and oceans.

The Liberal/National Coalition, which has held power since 2013, mocks climate change as an anti-business conspiracy, as fake news. On February 24, 2020, during Federal Parliament Question Time, there was a telling exchange between the Prime Minister, Scott Morrison (Liberal), and Leader of the Opposition, Anthony Albanese (Labor). Albanese proposed that Morrison and he debate climate change. Morrison said, "I'll debate you on climate change—at the next election!" The next election would be two years away. The Prime Minister grinned triumphantly as his side of the aisle cheered and the Labor side just shook their heads.

In 2015, prior to becoming Prime Minister, Morrison, who was then Treasurer, brought a chunk of coal into the lower house chamber (against the rules as no props are allowed) and held it up while answering a question, saying: "This is coal, don't be afraid."

What is needed is national leadership. Until Australian

exports of coal are curtailed and a carbon price system is initiated, Australia will not be participating in the survival of life as we know it on Planet Earth.

Bushfires

A drying climate, increased temperatures, longer summers, forests full of oily eucalyptus trees and people living amongst them is a formula for bushfires. The disastrous summer of 2019-20 will not likely be the last.

Backing up *career firefighters* are 250,000 volunteer members of bushfire brigades.

The trend of people leaving suburbs and living in the beautiful bush has the downside of making them and their homes potential bushfire victims. Controlled burns lessening fuel loads are effective but difficult to do over millions of acres of forest, during the short period after bushfire season ends and the rains make it too wet to burn.

Guns

Like the U.S., Australia had a frontier history. Unlike the U.S., a U.S.-style gun culture doesn't exist in Australia. That's not to say there aren't any guns and there isn't violence, but someone is more likely to hold up a convenience store with a knife or a cricket bat than with a gun.

From the first day Captain Cook stepped ashore at Botany Bay in 1770 and had his men fire warning shots over the heads of protesting natives, guns were a factor.

"Without guns the British would not have succeeded in taking the entire continent," author Nick Brodie wrote in *Under Fire*. Aboriginal people weren't allowed to own guns.

During the *bush ranger* (outlaw) years, guns were used by criminals and the police chasing after them. In the Australian goldrush of the 1850's, miners arrived from California heavily armed and ready to defend their diggings. In the frontier days, no one would venture into the outback unarmed.

After WWI soldiers brought home their service revolvers, many fell into criminal hands and a *pistol crisis* developed. At one point the Australian government asked the City of New York for advice on gun regulation. Gun laws tightened up.

After WWII there was a surplus of .303 Enfield rifles, and

they were used to hunt 'roos and crocs. New gun laws regulated gun ownership to a by-need basis, if you were a *'primary producer'* (farmer, pastoralist, grazier, miner) and needed one on your station you could get a gun license, otherwise they were restricted to a licensed gun range or gun club. Another limiting factor is there isn't a gun manufacturing industry in Australia with a powerful lobby restricting laws.

Australia's modern turning point on guns occurred in Port Arthur, Tasmania, on April 28, 1996, when a lone gunman with an assault rifle opened fire on innocent tourists and townspeople. He killed thirty-five people and wounded two dozen more that afternoon, many of them were women and children. Australians were shocked and appalled and the government re-examined the gun laws. Gunowners were encouraged to turn in their weapons, which they did in huge numbers. A system of tightly regulated gun licenses was introduced. Each state has its own system of gun regulation.

In 1996, at the time of the shooting, there were 3.2 million guns in Australia. After the buy-back there were 2.5 million. Now it has gone back up. In Australia in 2019 there were 3.6 million guns in a population of is 25 million. In the U.S. there are 393 million guns in a population of 330 million. In Western Australia (population 2.75 million), the Police assess about 10,500 firearm licence applications each year, and approve over 99% of them.

Handguns are tightly regulated. The purpose of a long gun is to shoot game and vermin, the purpose of a handgun is to shoot people. If you can obtain approval to own a handgun it will most likely be restricted to staying at the gun range, you won't be taking it home and 'hiding it' in your bedstand.

Handguns can be owned only by members of approved gun clubs, and then only after a police background check, six months of training, and the approval from the applicant's *partner* (spouse, live-in boyfriend or girlfriend, etc.).

Rifles and shotguns can be obtained for a specific purpose, either for target shooting or to shoot varmints. For the former, you have to be a member of a qualified gun club. For the latter, you must either be the owner of a large property or have the owner of such a property write a letter stating that you'll be using the rifle to control pests on that property. Self-loading (semi-automatic) rapid-fire rifles are prohibited. Pump action shotguns are allowed only for *primary producers* (full-time farmers who must control pests). Therefore, only bolt-action rifles and single or double-barrelled shotguns are available to the public. A state licensing fee is assessed annually, and the gun must be kept unloaded in an approved and inspected gun safe, with the ammunition in a separate, locked compartment. Here's the procedure I went through in Western Australia to get a bolt-action .22 calibre rifle to shoot varmints (mainly foxes) on my father-in-law's 1000-acre cattle farm.

First, I obtained a signed letter from my father-in-law stating what the firearm would be used for. I filled out an application with the local police stating what calibre gun I wanted to buy, paid an administrative fee and passed a written gun owner test. Then I went to the gun dealer and bought the gun, but the gun stayed at the shop. I went back to the police with the receipt and a form listing the specific weapon by serial number. I paid the licensing fee, then purchased and installed an approved gun safe in my home (bolted to the floor and a wall) and had it inspected by the police. Then I took the police paperwork back to the gun shop and they released the gun to me. I took the gun back to the police station, they inspect it and verified the serial number. Then it was mine.

Gunowners need to carry their gun license whenever transporting their gun outside their home. They will need to bring the license to the gun shop in order to buy ammunition. You can only buy ammunition for your specific calibre gun.

If that isn't enough to put you off, guns are expensive to buy. They cost about twice what you'd pay in the U.S., plus the mandatory safe and a yearly A$80 licensing fee.

In 2016 there were an estimated 260,000 unregistered guns in Australia: 250,000 long arms and 10,000 handguns. Most of these were in the hands of organised crime groups and other criminals. These guns seem to be used mostly on other criminals. Street violence is usually not committed with guns. Most Australians are appalled by guns and don't understand the acceptance of them in the U.S.

Laser pointers are classified as a *controlled weapon*, as are crossbows, spearguns, swords, and imitation firearms. Stilettos or any self-opening knives are illegal in all states. In Queensland the only knife you can legally carry on your person is a Swiss-Army knife, in Western Australia you can carry a pocket knife but only if you need to use it for purposes other than self-defence. BB guns require full gun licenses.

Sport (sports)

Sport is very serious stuff in Australia, and people's support of their teams is deeply felt. It's been said that because Aussies aren't very religious, they put their faith into their sports teams. American football (called *gridiron* or *NFL* in because *football* means soccer in much of the world) and baseball are played peripherally, but not commonly.

Women's Cricket, Footy and Basketball are mainstream. They are televised and the scores are covered on the nightly news.

Cricket, when played amongst friends in the backyard, is just cricket, but when it's played professionally, it's *The Cricket*.

The Cricket is a major sport, enjoying a status much like baseball in the U.S. It's a British game, played throughout the Commonwealth. In Australia, there are leagues in each state, and the Australian national team plays in *test matches* (five-day games) and the more modern *one-day* form of the game, against the British, Indians, Sri Lankans, South Africans, Kiwis, etc. The two types are called *Test Cricket* and *One Day Cricket* (or *One Day International*).

A game is a *match*. the traditional long form of the game is called a *test* and is played across a five-day period on a oval-shaped field called an *oval* or *cricket ground* about 140 meters (460 feet) long. In the centre of the oval is a strip of grass *one chain* (22 yards) long, with a *wicket* at either end. A *wicket* is three waist-high sticks called *stumps* that have a piece of wood called a *bale* balanced on top.

There are twelve players on a side, although only eleven may take the field at any time. The player designated as the twelfth man is used only as a substitute for fielding and may not bat or bowl.

A *batsman* (batter) *faces* the *bowler* (pitcher). The bat is about the length of a baseball bat but with flat sides. The ball is like a baseball hardball with different stitching. The object is for the *bowler* to throw a one-hop pitch toward the wicket. The bowler may take a *run-up* (kind of like a running version of a baseball pitcher's windup) and must throw (*bowl*) using a straight arm action unique to the game: if the arm is bent, the *delivery* (*bowl*) is considered a *no ball* and must be bowled again. Each bowler bowls an *over* (six balls/pitches) before he's replaced by another at the opposite end of the pitch who bowls their *over* in turn. Around ninety overs are bowled in a typical day's play.

If the *bowler* knocks the *bale* off the *stumps* with the ball, the *batsman* is out (or *bowled*). The batsman must protect the wicket and try to hit the ball with the bat. He can hit the ball in any direction and if a fielder catches it, he's out (there are no fielder's gloves as in baseball, they catch barehanded). If the batsman hits the ball away from the fielders and he's not in peril of being *run out* (caught outside of the *crease* or area around the wicket when the ball is live) he can run to the opposite wicket, which is at the opposite end of the 22 yard *pitch*. There's another batsman at the opposite wicket, and he has to run to the other wicket. This gains the team one run each time the batsmen cross and reach the opposite wicket. They may run as often as is safe. If the ball reaches the *boundary* (the line around the outside of the field), four runs are scored. Clearing the boundary gains six runs. In these cases running isn't required and won't add to the score. The fielders try to hit the bale with the ball before the batsmen get to the other side. Each inning sees the entire *side* (team) get to bat, each *side* bats twice in a five-day match if time permits.

Instead of a seventh inning stretch, they stop for lunch and tea breaks. An example *test* score is 8–231 (spoken '*8 for 231*'), with a two-wicket win on the fourth day. Don't ask for an explanation, I haven't the foggiest...

I do know this, it's not as easy a game as it looks. It's hard to hit the ball coming off the ground on a bounce with the flat bat. The field of play is 360 degrees around the batsman and the fielders are bare-handed.

There's also a shorter form of the game called *One Day Cricket*. Each team is given fifty *overs* to score as many runs as possible (the side with the most runs wins), and the rules are generally the same as in a test match. Some fielding restrictions are imposed to encourage the batsmen to go for big hits, and each player may only bowl a maximum of ten overs each. The one-day form is extremely popular, crowd friendly, colourful, and exciting. A *World Cup of Cricket* is held every four years with many non-Commonwealth countries participating; the one-day form is used. The last World Cup was held in England and Wales in June and July 2019—yes, it took two months to get through all the games— 2.6 billion people around the world watched the tournament. England won. Australia is historically the most successful team.

But cricket isn't just a fancy professional game. People play weekend pick-up games in city parks, at barbecues, on the beach, out camping, in the backyard, even on boats; anywhere.

Australian Rules Football or AFL (*Footy*) is a uniquely Australian game. It was originally designed in the 1850's for cricketers to play to stay in shape during the off-season, so it pre-dates American and Canadian football. The *VFL* (Victorian Football League) was founded in 1896. In 1982 the South Melbourne club moved to Sydney. More clubs were formed in other states and it formally became the *Australian Rules League* in 1990.

Based on rugby, with similarities to basketball, soccer, and *gridiron* (American football), it's played on a cricket oval, which is a lot larger than an American football field. The field size varies, usually around 135 metres wide and 165 metres long (150 by 180 yards), with four tall posts at each end of the field.

The ball is oblong, like an American football, but the ends are less pointed and more rounded, similar to a rugby ball. The object is to kick the ball through the inner two posts (*goal posts*) for a six-point goal. It can pass though in the air or on a bounce, but must remain untouched by opponents to score a six-pointer. If it goes through the outer posts (*point* or *behind posts*), it's a one-point *behind*. Scores often go above 100

288 A Survival Guide to Australia

points and are displayed as goals and points (example: G 6 P 17—53.) In this case, there were six goals at six-points each, plus seventeen *behinds*, for a total of fifty-three points.

Footy works much like soccer, but the players can use their hands. There's a forward pass (*hand pass*), delivered with underhanded fist-hit like a volleyball serve.

The players can run the ball forward but must bounce the ball once every fifteen meters (fifty feet) as they run. This isn't as easy as dribbling a basketball, because the ball isn't round, the playing surface is grass, and they're running flat-out dodging opponents. There's a technique of throwing the ball ahead and down with a forward spin so it will bounce up to where the player will be as he/she catches while he/she runs.

Players can also do a punt-like kick (called a *foot pass*) to move the ball downfield to a team mate. An intercepted pass or a tackle is the only way to stop an advance. When a runner is tackled, the ball immediately goes back into play, without pauses between plays. The tackled player tosses the ball back to a teammate and the play resumes. It's a fast-paced game with few time-outs or stoppages in play. The game runs continuously for four twenty-minute quarters, plus time to account for play stoppage. This can seem strange to a first-time observer as the clock goes past "0" and keeps going until the horn sounds as the excess stoppage time is used up.

There are eighteen players on the field for each side, with four on the bench who can be rotated in at any time. They don't wear pads or helmets—safety gear consists of knee socks and a mouthguard. The players tend to be tall, lanky, and tremendously fit, since they must run the huge field continuously for more than an hour and twenty-minutes. Since the game is constantly running, there are no elaborate plays as in American football; it's more up to the individual player, which suits the nature of the independent Australian.

The *AFL* (*Australian Football League*) is a national league made up of sixteen teams that battle each year to a *premiership* (championship). There are also state leagues with teams from smaller cities and within urban areas, and there are suburban leagues. Like soccer and rugby, supporters can become dues-paying club members and get season tickets. Drinking beer in the stands with the members during a game is a memorable experience—and a great source of Australianisms.

Terms: The *fixture* is the league game schedule. A special game between rivals is called a *derby* (pronounced "*darby*"), such as between the two Western Australian teams the Eagles and the Dockers, which is *The Western Derby*.

One doesn't *root* for their favourite team; one *barracks* for it. To *root* means to have sex, so don't ask a girl if she *roots* for her favourite team, she's liable to slap you.

One isn't a team fan; they're a *supporter*—one *supports* their team.

A rookie is called a *debutante*. It's hard to think of a six-foot-four-inch, two-hundred-pound, sweaty, muddy Footy player as a *debutant*, but there it is.

The Most Valuable Player award in footy is the *Best and Fairest*.

Footy is played by kids and adults, in the park, backyards, the beach, and at school.

Rugby traces its roots back to *caid*, a primitive Celtic game originally played with an inflated bull's scrotum as a ball. Really.

Modern rugby began in 1823 at Rugby School in England, using a manufactured ball similar to a footy ball. Rugby is more popular than footy in the states of New South Wales and Queensland—the rugby states—with *Rugby League* (also known as *Super 14*) and *Rugby Union*. They started as one, but became two very different games.

Rugby League, as played in the Southern Hemisphere, is an international game, consisting of fourteen teams from Australia, New Zealand, and South Africa, under a consortium called SANZAR.

The game lasts eighty minutes, the playing field is 100 metres by 68 metres (110 yards by 75 yards), with thirteen players on a side. They get six tackles to run the ball downfield to *ground* the ball in the goal. When a player is tackled, his team mates drop ten metres behind him, he tosses the ball back to them, and it's back in play. The ball can only be advanced by kicking and running. To score, the ball carrier runs over the goal line and throws himself on the ground. This is a four-point *try*. Then he can kick a 2-point conversion over the crossbar, between the goal posts.

One of Rugby League's legends is John Hoppoate, a player who used to play for the Balmain (now West) Tigers. He was *turfed* (thrown) out of the league for fingering another player's *ring* (anus) during a *scrum* (pile-up). It was dubbed the "Crouching Tiger, Hidden Finger."

Rugby Union is also an international league. The Australian national team is the *Wallabies*. The New Zealand team is the *All-Blacks*.

In *Union* the field is a maximum of 144 metres by 70 metres (160 yards by 77 yards). The game lasts eighty minutes in two forty-minute halves, with fifteen players on a side. The object is to advance the ball to the opposite team's goal by running it and kicking it, and to ground it over the goal line for a *try*, which is worth five points. Then the team gets to kick the ball through the goal posts for a two-point conversion.

Both forms feature the *scrum*, which is a way of restarting the game after a stop in play because of an accidental infringement. Eight players from each side line up across from each other in three rows, with the ball on the ground in the middle. The front rows of the opposing teams interlock heads and shoulders. The whole formation pushes against each other. The object is to force the opposing team backward enough to get your front row over the ball, which is then kicked behind to the rear of the formation, to be tossed to a *back* to get the game moving again. It's a demonstration of brute force over finesse, which characterizes the game.

Being such a rough game, you don't see a lot of people playing either form of rugby in the park. Aussies call it *cross country wrestling*. Rugby is known as '*a thug's game played by gentlemen*', where soccer has been called '*a gentlemen's game played by thugs*'.

Soccer is a major sport, though not as big as footy, rugby, or cricket. The national competition is dubbed the A-League.

The Australian national team, the *Socceroos*, usually does well, the whole country stays up all night to watch the games live from wherever. It's played recreationally, with teams at all levels across the country.

Basketball   The professional league is called the *National Basketball League*, with eight teams in Australia and one in New Zealand. Several players are Americans who couldn't make it in the NBA.

The game is played recreationally, but not to the degree of cricket or footy. For a time it was Australia's third sport, which could be attributed to the worldwide appeal of Michael Jordan and his influence with the Aussie youth. Basketball's decline in OZ coincided with his retirement.

Netball is primarily a women's sport. It's a court game similar to basketball, played on a basketball court with a hoop on a 3.05 metre (ten-foot) pole at either end, *but with no backboard*. It's played recreationally in local leagues, the British Commonwealth games and the professional *Australian Netball League* (*ANL*) which has eight teams. National competitions are televised.

It's similar to basketball: the object is for the players to move the ball to the hoop and shoot goals. Unlike basketball, the only way to move the ball is by passing, no dribbling or running with the ball is allowed.   Since there's no backboard behind the hoop, players have to 'swish' the shot, but because they're not shooting on the run they have time to set for the shot. There are seven players on a side in three distinct areas on the court. Players are assigned positions and wear bibs with the initials of that position. They can't move out of their assigned area or they're *offside*.

Lawn bowling (bowls) is a very popular sport, with approximately 800,000 registered bowlers—which means one in twenty-five Australians bowl. Almost every town and suburb has a *lawn bowling club*. The clubs are well-established and are fixtures of the community. Some have *pokies* (poker or slot machines), licensed bars, and restaurants where you can eat and drink for cheap—and you can bowl, of course.

The greens are meticulously maintained by professionally trained greens keepers who go though a five-year apprenticeship. The ball is an asymmetric sphere about the size of a *rock melon* (cantaloupe). The object of the game is to get your ball closest to the *jack* (a white ball placed at the far end of the *rink*). There are usually four players on a team, the game goes twenty-one *ends* (rounds). Devotees take the game very seriously.

Note: American style bowling is called *Ten-Pin bowling*; most large cities have indoor bowling *lanes*.

Skiing/snowboarding   *Hotham*, *Thredbo*, and *Perisher* are the largest and most popular, though *Falls Creek* will give you a more intimate experience. All are located in the *Australian Alps* between Melbourne and Canberra. The slopes don't have pine trees; you ski through low eucalypts called *snow gums*. It isn't Utah, but it will get you moving down the hill on snow.

Ski areas are set up and run similar to North America. *Lifted* means a slope with chairlifts. The bunny hill is called the *learner's area* or the *nursery slope*. A *magic carpet* is a conveyor belt that skiers stand on to get to the top of the *learner's area*.

Ski New Zealand   If you're looking for something more intense, hop a flight across the Tasman Sea to Queenstown on the South Island of New Zealand. All skiing there is above the tree line, kind of like the top of Arapahoe Basin in Colorado. The slopes are steeper at the bottom than the top. There you might see a Kea, a high-altitude parrot that has the odd habit of ripping rubber off cars: wiper blades, weather stripping, etc.

Four-wheeling might not seem like a sport, but the outdoorsmanship required can involve skill, endurance, and physical ability. There are epic trips across the outback, like the *Canning Stock Route*, a three-week unsupported run down the old inland cattle trail in Western Australia.

There are also day-runs in the bush or on the beach with mates. Camping, fishing, and exploring are usually involved, often a couple of kayaks or a small *aluminium* skiff will be brought along on the roof for fun. The physical aspect involves digging your 4WD out after bogging it in the sand or mud.

Swimming   Aussie swimmers are world-class and have collected hundreds of Olympic medals. Ian Thorpe, Grant Hackett, and Libby Lenton are some recent Olympic stars. Mack Horton, Bronte Campbell, Cate Campbell, Brittany Elmslie, Emma McKeon, and Madison Wilson won Gold Medals at the 2016 Olympics. The Aussies continue to be dominant players in the worldwide sport.

The freestyle stroke was originally called the *Australian Crawl* because it was developed in Australia—a combination of an English trudgen and a South Pacific Islander flutter kick.

The beach is a sport in itself. With swimming, surfing, wind and kite sailing, snorkelling, scuba diving, jogging, beach volleyball, footy, and cricket.

Surf Life Saving clubs are government-sanctioned volunteer groups that provide safety patrols and lifeguards.

There are few paid professional beach lifeguards in Australia, so volunteer groups fill the gap. The clubs are an Australian tradition that goes back a hundred years. The safest place to go for a dip in the ocean is in front of the local *surf life saving club*. Most beach towns have one. Swim between their flags.

The *surf life saving clubs* patrol sections of beach—marked with flags—in front of their clubhouses. They're an institution similar to bowling clubs with private restaurants, bars, weight rooms, etc. You usually join as a family. There are *little nippers* (youth) programs from age seven through late-teens that train kids to be strong, safe, confident ocean swimmers. Many move on to adult programs, which are built around patrolling the beach and competing in *surf life saving carnivals*.

Throughout the summer, *surf carnivals* are held between neighbouring life saving clubs. There's a state championship and a national carnival. These are for both kids and adults and consist of beach sprints, ocean swimming and rescue surf boat races. If you can, catch a competition. If you've never seen a dozen five-man surf-rowboats shooting through the breakers, catching air off the crests, you're in for a treat.

Fishing is very popular in Australia, from snapper, herring, whiting, tailor, and mullet in the south to barramundi in the north, it's too large a subject to cover in a short section in a book like this. For more info try **www.recfishoz.com.au**.

Misc. sports Golf, tennis, swimming, surfing, fishing, motor racing, etc. are popular and work the same as in America. There are amateur baseball and American football (*gridiron*) leagues in most major capitals. Softball and T-ball are taught in the schools.

Scuba diving

If you include all the islands and inlets, Australia has a 36,700 km (22,800 mile) coastline. This provides an endless variety of dive sites. The northern half of the country has warm tropical waters with coral reefs and mangroves. The southern half has cooler waters with sponges and kelp-like algae. All abound with colourful sea life. A warm current that flows down from Indonesia and around the continent brings tropical species to the southern coast. There is coral growing off Perth and Melbourne.

Australia has good oceans, and this is one of the reasons I moved here from Southern California. American oceans are pretty picked-over. That's not to say the Australian coasts haven't been abused, they certainly have, but that's mostly around the population centres, once you get away from the cities you can find some wild ocean.

Hazards: The far north coast is dangerous because of marine crocodiles and box stinger jellyfish, especially near river mouths [see section on **wildlife**], plus tiger sharks, though I'm told they don't like the sound of bubbles (luckily I've never had first-hand experience of this). And be aware of typhoon season, December to March: these are Australian hurricanes.

The southern coasts can have *white pointers* (great white sharks), along with bronze whalers and bull sharks. *King waves* are large rogue waves that occasionally sweep people off coastal rocks. These are generated by storms off Antarctica, an uninterrupted 2,500 miles directly south.

All areas can have sharks. Every year a half-dozen swimmers are lost to sharks, and another half-dozen are lost to crocs. Tiny blue-ring octopus can paralyse you, stopping your breathing. The solution: wear a shark shield, gloves and don't go near the beach in the Kimberly, the Northern Territory or North Queensland.

Forty-years ago, when I learned to dive, I was taught that the most dangerous thing in the ocean is you. Make good choices

The **Great Barrier Reef** stretches along 2000 kilometres (1,250 miles) of North Queensland on the east coast, in the Coral Sea.

The reef is a good distance offshore, 16-to-160 kilometres (10-to-100 miles) and accessible only by boat or plane. This puts it well beyond the range of salty crocs and box stingers, which occur just off the beach near the mouths of rivers and creeks. There are nice sharks there—reef sharks—the kind that are fun to see and photograph.

Numerous day boats go out to anchored platforms on the reef, though they can be quite touristy. For the more serious diver, multi-day live-aboard dive boats go farther out to the outer reef and into the Coral Sea to volcanic coral atolls like Osprey Reef. These boats run out of Cairns, Townsville, and Port Douglas. There are island resorts scattered along the reef, like Herron, Hamilton, and Lizard Islands, that offer close-by dives on the reef, if you don't want to stay on a boat.

The smaller **Ningaloo Reef** is on the northwest coast of Western Australia, in the Indian Ocean. It's closer inshore and in some places can be dived and snorkelled from the beach,. Box stingers and crocs aren't a problem on this part of the west coast because there are no rivers. Dive boats are based out of Coral Bay and Exmouth. Do watch out for crocs in the wetter Kimberley, starting at Broome, 1,000 km. north.

In April, the whale sharks appear along the Ningaloo to feed on the coral spawn, and charter boats take divers out to swim with these gentle giants. They also offer seasonal trips to swim with manta rays and humpback whales.

Further north is pristine Rowley Shoals, reachable by long-range live-aboard charter boats out of Broome, for the few months a year it is dive-able. Further out still is Christmas Island, accessible by air.

Along the middle of the west coast is Shark Bay, a world Heritage Site, where *dugongs* (Australian manatee), dolphin, and manta rays can be found. The vast bay is quite shallow, but there are a few coral reefs if you know where to find them. Monkey Mia is famous for the wild dolphin feeding (7:30 am daily). Also in Shark Bay, at Hamelin Pool, is one of the best stands of stromatolites in the world. They're the oldest living life-form on Earth, a rock-like structure of primitive bacteria unchanged for billions of years.

Further south you come to the Houtman Abrolhos, off Geraldton (dive charters available). Then begins the shallow limestone reef structures one-to-five miles offshore, which line the coast past Perth to the southern tip of the continent, where the Indian Ocean meets the Southern Ocean at Cape Leeuwin.

Just north of Perth is the Marmion Marine Park, and just offshore is Rottnest Island, both of which have great diving in the limestone structures amidst mixed cold and warm water species of sponges, corals, and fishes. This unique ecology is attributable to the *Leeuwin Current*, which is the only warm water current in the world on a western-facing coast. Warm water from the Western Pacific pushes through the Indonesian Archipelago forming the Leeuwin, which flows down the length of the Western Australian coast, wraps around the southern coast and flows east, sometimes as far as Tasmania. Charters are available from numerous dive shops in the area.

WA has some nice diving wrecks; the *HMAS Swan* off Dunsborough, and the *HMAS Perth* off Albany, both 1960s-era destroyers sunk for dive reefs. Charters are available from shops in those towns.

Along the south coast of the Australian mainland and the island state of Tasmania, the water is cooler, with abundant sponge life, sea fans, sea dragons, thick schools of fish, etc., and yes, there are sharks.

There are great dive sites out of Adelaide, Melbourne, Sydney, and Brisbane; check out local shop websites for details.

PADI is the most popular certification, though others are recognized. As a tourist at a resort, or when you're renting gear, you'll be asked for your Certification-card (C-card), but if you're living in Australia and diving as a local, this will be a rare occurrence. When I first moved here, when I'd bring my tanks in for a fill, I'd reflexively present my C card The shop staff would look at me like I was from Mars. I don't bother anymore.

Dive gear   Tanks are also called *cylinders* or *air bottles*. Hookahs, or surface supplied compressed air systems, are used,

diving at remote areas far from dive shops. Hookahs can be on
floats or mounted on the deck of a boat. Some are battery
powered, some have small petrol motors.

Wetsuits: a full-length 2-3 mm suit is called a *steamer*, one
with short sleeves and short legs is a *springie*. 5mm one-piece
suits are common in temperate waters. A 7mm suit is
equivalent to quarter-inch.

As much as dive shop staff disregard your C-card, they'll
scrupulously check the test markings on your tank. In
Australia, tanks are hydro-tested <u>every</u> year (in the U.S., they
are visually tested yearly and hydro-tested every five years). If
you're buying a tank, check the test date stamped into the metal
and make sure it's current.

Tank valves are the same as in North America, so your
regulator will fit. Occasionally European divers bring DIN
regulators and most shops will carry adapters. But if you go
diving in remote places the yoke valve will be standard, so it
would be a good idea to swap your DIN first stage for a yoke-
type, or bring your own adapter

Air pressure is rated in *bar*, not psi. Most common
cylinders are 12 litre steel tanks (U.S. equivalent 100 cubic
foot) pumped to *240 bar* (3400 psi), and they remain at almost
the same buoyancy throughout the dive. *Aluminium cylinders*
are less common and are more buoyant at the end of the dive,
so ask for an extra 2 lbs of weight. Weights belts are often in
pounds, if not, it's 2.2 pounds to a kilo.

In Queensland, which is home to the Great Barrier Reef
and therefore gets the most tourist divers, you'll be required to
use an octopus regulator. Other states are looser. You can use
American gauges and dive computers that measure in feet and
psi, but pre-dive briefings will be in metres and *bar*.

Bar is the metric method of measuring air pressure. Depth
is measured in *metres*, temperature is in Celsius. Australian
dive computers will read in these units.

Surface pressure at sea level is one *bar* or 14.51 psi.

Divers are trained to return to the boat with *50 bar* in their
cylinder—about 725 psi.

If you're used to working in feet, be careful guessing depth
in metres. It's easy to estimate three feet to a metre, but it's

really *3.3 feet per metre*—so three metres is actually ten feet, not nine. You could easily guess your way into the next no-decompression group without knowing it and end up bent.

Sixty-feet is about eighteen metres. This is what Basic divers are limited to.

Even though I have been in Australia for 17 years and am fluent in the metric system, I still use gauges in feet and pounds of pressure. This is partly because I already own them, but mostly because I've been diving for 40+ years and in an emergency I will think in feet and pounds-of-pressure, and don't want to have to waste time converting them. On a tourist dive boat the divemaster will give you a funny look when you report depth in feet and air in pounds, but they will get used to it.

Diving for game   There are seasons for taking abalone and *crays* (spiney lobster), and most states require licenses. In some states, it's legal to spear fish on scuba, in others, it isn't. Check locally.

Australian sport fishing remains relatively unrestricted, especially when compared to many other countries. Queensland, South Australia and the Northern Territory don't even require you to hold a fishing licence. Western Australia requires licenses only when fishing off a boat or for freshwater fishing. Restrictions apply on size and number of a species taken. WA requires you bring the whole fish to shore; you can't fillet them at sea. Fillet is pronounced *"fill-et"* with a hard 't'.

In WA, you need a separate license for taking *crays* (lobster). You're allowed to use a snare, which is a loop of cable at the end of a long, spring-loaded tube: you slip the noose around the cray's tail and pull the cable through, snaring it. Night diving for crays in WA is prohibited, though divers routinely take *prawns* (shrimp) and crabs while night diving in the Swan River, which flows through the centre of Perth.

Abalone   There are three species of abalone: Roes, Green Lip, and Brown Lip.

The season for Roes Abalone Around Perth in south-central Western Australia is worth mentioning for its novel approach. The season lasts *one hour*, from 7 to 8 a.m. on four

Saturdays from mid-December thru February. The dates change every year and a license is required. Fishing for abs is done by wading out during low tide, as scuba or hookah diving isn't allowed. They're small, you're allowed twenty roes abs sized over 60 mm (2 3/8").

For *green lip* or *brown lip abs* the season is more conventional. You are allowed five, sized over 140 mm (5 1/2"). In the north (December to Feb) and south of the state (October 1 to May 15), brown lips and green lips can be taken on scuba. A license, available from a post office or online, is required for taking abs in WA.

Misc.   A *shorie* is a beach dive. The inflatable rescue tube is called a *safety sausage* (and you should <u>always</u> dive with one). An inflatable boat, like a Zodiac, is called a *rubber ducky*.

Underwater animal hazards [see the **wildlife** section] **Remember, the most dangerous thing in the ocean is you.**

Boating

There are some basic differences in boating between America and Australia.

You need a *skipper's ticket* (a boat driver's license) to operate a boat in all states. To get one, you take both a *theory* (written) test and a driving test, where you run a boat and put it through a series of *manoeuvres* Courses are privately run. Some states (like New South Wales) require you to renew the license periodically, while other states (like WA and Queensland) issue the licence for life. New South Wales also requires a separate license to operate a PWC (personal watercraft, i.e a Jet Ski). If you're visiting, you can show some sort of proficiency rating, like those required by international yacht charter services, to qualify.

Key navigational issues: In Australia, <u>the navigational buoys are reversed</u>. The old adage American boaters learned, "red right returning," is *exactly opposite in Australia*. Instead, the **green** buoy or light is on the right as you return to a harbor or channel. The navigational lights on the boats themselves are the same: port is red, starboard is green.

Even though you keep to the left when driving a car in Australia, you *keep to the right when piloting a boat*, just like driving on an American road. The 'burdened vessel' is called the *give way vessel*; you give way to the boat on your right. Sailboats have the right of way while under sail.

Tides are listed in metres. You take the number on the nautical chart and add the height of the tide to it. Tide changes can be quite extreme in the north and mild in the south.

You're required to carry: Type 1 lifejackets for everyone onboard, an anchor with line, and a bailer. Most states require children under ten to wear a life jacket at all times when underway. Some states require fire extinguishers only if you have an inboard engine, others require them on all boats. If travelling more than two nautical miles offshore you must carry an EPIRB (rescue beacon), and some states require radios.

VHF radios are used, and HF radios. In some states (Queensland, New South Wales, Western Australia, Tasmania), a glorified CB system using the 27 MHz band is also used, and is more common amongst recreational boaters, though they are being phased out in favour of VHF. On 27 MHz radios channel 88 is the hailing frequency. No radio license is required for 27 MHz radios. VHF radio is far superior, it carries further and clearer and it is what Marine Rescue monitors. For VHF, you are required to have a license, but almost no one does. The course is easy and done online, it'll cost you about A$288 to pass the licensing test.

To use an American VHF radio in Australia, you may have to put it into *International Mode*, see the radio's manual for instructions. As in the U.S., channel 16 is used for hailing.

Volunteer Marine Rescue (VMR) There is no Coast Guard in Australia. There is State Water Police for law enforcement on the water and serious rescue cases. Non-emergency rescues, safety inspections and recreational radio monitoring is done by Volunteer Marine Rescue groups, based at most harbours. VMR is whom you deal with in all cases. In an emergency they will coordinate the water police.

When you go out of the harbour on your boat you should switch onto the marine radio VMR frequency. On VHF it's

usually 77 or 82, on 27 MHz it's 88 or 91. Make contact with
the local VMR operator and *Log On* stating your vessel
registration number, number of persons on board, amount of
fuel, destination and expected time of return. When you come
back into the harbour you should contact VMR and *Log Off.*

Boat equipment   Built-in fuel tanks, especially in
fiberglass boats, tend to be about half the size of those on
American boats.

Switches on the control panels flip down for 'on, the
opposite of American switches.

Aussie trailer boaters do an interesting thing with their
dock lines. Instead of having separate bow and stern lines, they
have one long line, one end tied to the bow and the other to the
stern. That way, one person can easily control both ends of the
boat with one line. When the boat is back on the trailer, they
use the line to wrap around boat and trailer to secure the load.

Nylon anchor-line isn't commonly used on small boats
because (like so many things in Australia) it's expensive.
Instead people use *silver-line*, which is polyethylene and floats
(nylon sinks). It's cheap. As a salesman in my local chandlery
once told me, "Aussies would use shoestring to anchor if they
thought they could get away with it."

The lower unit on an outboard or out-drive is called the *leg*.
An inflatable boat, like a Zodiac or an Avon, is called a *rubber
ducky*. The tube you tow your kids around in is called a *biscuit*
or *bickie*. A slip is a *pen*. Fishermen are called *fishers*.

Water skiing: one person drives the boat, an observer at
least fourteen years of age must be watching the skier at all
times. A red flag is not raised when the skier goes down;
instead the safety person raises their hand.

Boat construction   Though fibreglass boats are
popular, aluminium boats are the most common. This isn't
surprising, since Australia has huge natural deposits of the
metal.

Here's some typical designs. *Dinghies* are boats with tiller-
operated outboards. *Centre consoles* are skiffs with a stand-up
centre control station. *Runabouts* are skiffs with forward-
steering and a windscreen. *Half-cabins* have a raised bow with
an open, covered area underneath, a wind screen and a forward

steering station. *Cabin cruisers* have a raised bow with a closable cabin. All these boats can be made of *aluminium*, fiberglass or polyethylene plastic.

Tinnies are small aluminium skiffs.

The term *yacht* in Australia refers to any sailboat, but not a motorboat, no matter how large. A twenty-foot day sailor is a *yacht*, while a sixty-foot Bertram motor cruiser isn't. A large power boat is called a *launch*.

Boat sizes are usually measured in metres. Six metres is about twenty-feet.

Aluminium boats   Aluminium pleasure craft are lighter and less expensive than fiberglass. The light weight means they can be more easily beach launched, as large stretches of the coast are without ramps. It also means a larger boat can be towed and launched. This is important since Aussies tow with smaller vehicles than in North America, and launch on rougher ramps.

The downside to *ally* boats is the rough ride. Aluminium is rigid and has no give, and the plates are harder to form into the hydro-dynamic shapes achievable in *moulded* fiberglass. Ally boats, being lighter, tend to go over the chop so you feel the bumps, instead of cutting through it as with a heavier fibreglass hull. Newer designs like Surtees (New Zealand) and Bar Crusher (Australia) have a softer ride.

Ally boats transmit engine vibration throughout the hull, which at certain RPMs can make an annoying buzz, after time it takes a toll on the welds. If buying an older *ally* boat, beware of broken welds, some of which can be hidden under the floor. Newer designs and smoother engines make newer *ally* boats more comfortable.

Other things to beware of in an aluminium boat are the use of silicone sealers: some contain acids which will eventually eat through the metal. Another danger is dissimilar metals. If a non-aluminium metal part, like a stainless-steel nut or bolt, accidentally drops under the floorboards of an ally boat and into a place where saltwater puddles, electrolysis would occur between the metals which would eat a hole in the bottom of the boat.

There are two kinds of ally boats: ones that are pressed into shape, and ones made of welded plate.

Pressed boats are mass-produced, made by pressing thin aluminium plates into the shape of half-hulls with longitudinal corrugations for strength (the corrugations allow usage of thinner, lighter materials). These are then welded together and strengthened with ribs. The bottoms are usually 3mm thick, the sides 2mm. These boats are usually smaller, lighter, cheaper, skiffs and runabouts. This type of boat is called a *tinny*, which is Aussie slang for a beer can.

Tinnies are great for close-to-shore boating/fishing/diving, and are light enough to launch off the beach (don't forget to lower the tire pressure on your 4WD before launching or you'll be making new friends). Boaters also carry them on top of their cars and 4WDs, which allows them to get onto more secluded beaches. They're a very light craft, so beware of going too far offshore in one.

The other type of ally boat is called a *plate boat*. They're made from thicker aluminium plates (usually 4mm sides with 5mm bottoms), then curved and welded together. These tend to be custom-made, larger, and heavier-duty vessels, and can range from fifteen-foot skiffs to sixty-foot commercial fishing boats.

The typical *plate boat* is about 20 feet long (6 metres), with a high, enclosed bow, a windscreen with sun canopy, high gunnels, and a swing-open gate through the transom onto a wide swim step that's actually the back two-feet of the boat. Most are powered by outboards, though inboard-outboards are also common on larger boats.

Australia leads the world in building big aluminium boats. The most notable manufacturer is Austal, based in Henderson, Western Australia, with yards in Tasmania, the Philippines and Alabama. They make 300-foot hydrofoil-catamaran ferries that go fifty knots, a 185' fast naval patrol boat, and the Independence class of Littoral Combat Ships for the U.S. Navy, that are 420 feet long and go 40 knots.

Aluminum is spelled and pronounced *aluminium* in Australia.

Fibreglass boats   Some of the better fibreglass trailer boats are: Haines Hunter, Haines Signature (two different companies), Kevalcat, Caribbean (which is Australian-built Bertram), Chivers, and Fraser. Aussie trailer boats tend to be skinnier than American ones, with the exception of the big, fast, stable twin-hull motorcats, like the Kevalcat, Noosacat, and Sharkcat.

Some American brands are imported: Boston Whaler, Sea Ray, Trophy, Bayliner, Polar, Magnum, and Mustang. Besides being quite pricey, American boats are generally larger than Australian boats and towing can be a problem.

Fiberglass is spelled fib**re**glass in Australia.

Boat trailers   The tongue wheel on a trailer is called a *jockey wheel*.

Small *tinny* trailers with a gross load under 750 kg (1800 lbs.) don't need brakes. Mid-sized trailers between 750 kg and 2000 kg (4400 lbs.), must have brakes on one axle, either hydraulic brakes or cable brakes actuated by a surge hitch. Trailers over 2000 kg require an *electric brake actuator* that works electronically off the tow vehicle's brakes to actuate an hydraulic system on the trailer. This is called an *electric-over-hydraulic* system.

If you have a non-complying system or are towing too heavy, and you are in an accident, your insurance could be negated and you could be exposed to full financial liability.

Aussie boat trailers often have sets of rollers that go the length of the boat to make launching and retrieval easier. The downside is if the winch gives way on the road, the boat can roll off. With these systems, it's important to secure the boat to the trailer with a bow-eye safety chain, stern straps and a strap around the girth. There are fines for trailering an unsecured load. It's amazing how many boats you see being towed on the highway with nothing but the winch cable securing them to the trailer.

Tinnies are so light that you hardly have to get the trailer wet to launch and retrieve. I used to back my fifteen-foot tinnie down the ramp until the bottom of the trailer license plate was just touching the water—the wheel hubs never got wet. I just pushed the boat off into the water. I did the retrieving with the trailer winch. Tinnies are great for beach launching. Don't forget to let the *tyre* pressure down to 20 psi on the tow vehicle.

Many people drive their boats onto the trailers. This works with aluminium plate boats but can be hard on fibreglass hulls, and the bottom of the outboard/leg can strike the ramp surface. With the large twin-hull power cats, the only way to get them on the trailer is to drive them on. With my current twenty-footer single-hull I back the trailer until the fenders are underwater and winch it on.

A handy trailer modification for beach launching a larger boat is to mount the spare tyre on a functional wheel hub on a swing-down bracket. In the up-position it's just a spare tyre, in the down-position it acts as a full-sized tongue wheel. You can unhitch the trailer from the boat and roll the whole thing out to deeper water to launch. To retrieve, you set the brakes on the trailer and either winch the boat on, or drive it on under its own power. Then you hook a long rope to your 4WD, pull the trailer to firmer ground above the beach and reattach it to the tow car.

American imported boats and trailers. The American maximum towable width is 2.59 meters (8'6"), which is about 3½ inches wider than the 2.5 meters Australian law allows. If you import an American boat or buy one here, beware of this.

A load wider than 2.5 metres becomes a *wide load* that needs a special yearly permit and special *wide load* signs hung on the front of the towing vehicle and the back of the boat when towed.

A boat wider than 2.7 metres (8'10") can't be towed on any freeway, or on certain highways at certain times, or at night. If you don't comply and have an accident the insurance company will refuse to pay the claim, and if there are injuries you could lose everything you own in a lawsuit.

On heavier trailers over 2000 kilos (4400 lbs.), you will need to convert to the above-mentioned *electric-over-hydraulic* system. Conventional American trailer *draw bar hitches* with surge brakes, though legal in the U.S. are illegal in Australia and will void your insurance.

Boat prices   Good quality boats can be expensive. A used fifteen-foot pressed aluminium *tinny* with a 40-

horsepower outboard on a trailer, all in good *nick* (condition), will go for A$10-15,000. A new 20-foot pressed-hull aluminium cabin cruiser with a 150-horsepower outboard on a trailer with electronics can go for A$50,000. A comparably equipped aluminium plate boat will go for A$75,000, while a fibreglass version will top A$90,000. I bought a well-used 10-year-old 23-foot Boston Whaler in Perth for what I could have bought a new one for in the U.S.

Beach launching   Just because you have a heavier trailer boat doesn't mean it can't be beach-launched. Boaters in remote areas often use old tractors, modified for beach use, to put 25' boats in the water. It's an impressive operation, especially on a day with a bit of surf.

If you do beach launch, watch the tides. You'll need at least a 4WD, and be sure to let down the air in your tires.

Sailing   There are tens of thousands of sailboats, from small harbour racers to around-the world cruisers; mono-hulls, catamarans, and trimarans.

The Aussies took the America's Cup away from the Yanks for the first time ever in 1983.

The Sydney to Hobart race is one of the top sailing races in the world, it shoves-off on *Boxing Day* (the day after Christmas).

At one time, the youngest person to sail solo nonstop around the world was David Dicks of Fremantle, Western Australia, who circumnavigated at age seventeen.

Wildlife

My basic rule is: *If it doesn't have fur or feathers, it's fatal.* This is an overstatement, but it should keep you out of trouble—the only exception is the cassowary [more below].

Only a few people out of a population of 25 million die each year from wildlife, so the odds are in your favour.

Fear not. I've been visiting Australia since 1989, been living there since 2003, and haven't been bit by anything yet other than a mosquito (though beware, *mozzies* can carry *Ross River virus*, so wear *mozzie* repellent when needed).

Snakes   Fact is, Australia has the most *venomous* snakes in the world. Not poisonous, venomous. Poisonous means if you eat it you get sick and maybe die, venomous means if it bites you, you get sick and maybe die.

Stay away from snakes. Watch where you're going in the bush or even in a backyard shed or along the edge of the beach. If you get bit, stay calm, apply a pressure bandage; don't wash the wound—and get help. Anti-venom from a local emergency room is your best course of action.

Spiders can be nasty. The *redback* is a spider similar to the black widow, except the red hourglass shape is on the back not the belly, which makes it easier to spot. Like the black widow, they hide under shelves, in old tarps, cardboard boxes, corners of sheds, etc. The bite won't kill you, but it will make you sick. It hurts instantly and intensely, and after a while you'll start to feel ill. Stay calm and get yourself to medical help, preferably a hospital emergency room. You'll be given a few injections of anti-venom and should start to feel better in a few hours.

The white-tail spider is another nasty. Its bite isn't that significant at first, but it gets much worse over time, causing tissue to die. They're about 1½" long, with a dark red or grey body and red-and-brown banded legs.

There are lots of varieties of spiders, large and small, venomous and non-venomous. If you don't know which spiders are bad, stay away from all of them.

Scorpions are in the spider family. The ones in the north tend to be larger and more venomous. Shake out your shoes before you put them on. The sting is painful, but not dangerous; it's kind of like a bee sting. If you do get stung, catch the bastard and have it identified. Treat the bite by taking an antihistamine like Benadryl; it'll control the inflammation and the itch. Stingose is a good topical for pain, available at chemists.

Insects   There are large ants that will bite hard and hang on, so watch where you step. Wasps and bees will sting. *Mozzies* (mosquitoes) can carry *Ross River Virus* and *Murray Valley Encephalitis*, so use repellent. The large March fly lands on bare skin without making so much as a tickle, then bites down and takes a piece out of you. It hurts for the moment, but the little buggers are so intent on biting that they won't fly away and can easily be smooshed.

Flies can occur in huge numbers at certain times of the year in the bush. The constant action of waving them from in front of your face is known as the *Aussie salute*. Some people wear hats with corks dangling on strings tied to the brim to repel the flies. This is effective only because the flies are too embarrassed to be seen near them. Fly nets on hats that go down to your neck are a good idea to have with you in the far north. Or break off a twig with leaves to fan them away.

Lizards are not venomous, though the bites can become infected.

There are some large lizards, like the *goanna*. Misnamed after iguanas, they're actually in the monitor family. Goannas will grow to six feet long, though most top out at about four feet, but half of that is tail. They can run fast, sometimes on their back legs. They aren't aggressive, but have a nasty, non-venomous bite. Reportedly, when frightened, they'll climb the tallest object around, and if that happens to be you, you could end up with one on your head.

Blue tongue and bobtail lizards look like the gila monsters of the American southwest, with a bobbed tail and a wide mouth. They measure about a foot long and when cornered, open their mouths and hiss, they look nasty but they're not venomous and are basically harmless. They're good to have in your garden, since they eat slugs, snails, and *slaters* (wood lice), but they'll also eat your strawberries.

Box jellyfish are a big problem along the northern tropical coasts. They occur in shallow tidal areas and near river mouths and breed in the *Wet* (rainy season), December through April. They're pale blue with a bell-shaped body about 100mm (4") long, with fifteen, three-foot tentacles in each corner that have thousands of stinging cells. They can kill a human in less than a minute.

According to medical texts, once stung you have virtually no chance of surviving. You'll experience excruciating pain and go into shock and drown before you can get to shore. If you're found, you'll be in cardiac arrest and not breathing. CPR and heart massage may keep you alive until formal medical care can be established. Vinegar can neutralize the tentacles, which can then be removed. For some reason, the texts say never use mentholated spirits. First responders should not touch the tentacles. *Heed the warning signs posted at beaches and don't swim along the shore in those months.*

The Great Barrier Reef isn't affected. The reef starts 20 miles out to sea, and box jellyfish don't go into deep water or that far offshore.

Crocodiles take several Australians each year. Again, this is in the northern tropics, near river mouths or in rivers, where you have no business being (read the signs). The *marine* (or *salty*) crocodile is the big nasty, growing to 6 metres (20 feet) and weighing 700 kilos (1,500 pounds). They can lie motionless for hours hidden in a foot of water, then spring up and grab their prey in a flash. *Stay out of their territory, away from riverbanks, and heed the signs.*

Freshwater crocs (*freshies*) are less dangerous, they live in freshwater further inland, and just in the far north. To get bit you'd just about have to step on one. Though if agitated I've seen them slap their tail so hard onto the water surface it sounded like a gunshot.

Sharks   They're out there, but you'll never see the one that gets you—or so they say—so don't sweat it. Seriously, they seem to like dawn and dusk and murky water. *White pointers* (great whites) occur along the southern coasts; tiger sharks are more tropical, but I'm told they don't like the sound of SCUBA bubbles. Bull sharks and bronze whalers can occur in temperate waters.

There are a number of shark attacks each year. Some beaches have shark nets, so if you're concerned about that, swim there. Perth has an airplane that patrols the coast during the summer and they will order the water cleared. Check with the locals before you venture out. A few people are taken every year.

The **blue-ringed octopus** is a cute little mollusc that lives all around the coasts of Australia, usually in shallow water and rocky pools. It has enough venom to kill ten people and there's no known antidote. Often you won't even know you've been bit until your vision goes blurry and you start to have trouble breathing. You can try rescue-breathing a victim and seeking immediate medical aid. Once in the hospital, breathing assistance will be applied and if the victim lives through the first twenty-four hours they'll probably make a complete recovery. When you're in the ocean, don't go poking around in holes bare-handed, wear gloves.

Stingrays Since Steve Irwin met his tragic and untimely death, people became concerned about stingrays. They're basically a harmless animal unless you're a shellfish.

You're more likely to be killed by a bolt of lighting during a blue moon in leap-year than by a stingray. The most common danger is stepping on one, and that will result in a sting that can be treated with hot water and meat tenderizer. Wear dive booties or sneakers when wading in sandy areas, and shuffle your feet. If you snorkel near one—it goes without saying— keep well out of reach of the tail.

In some beach fishing areas the rays have learned to wait for fishers to clean their catch and come right up into a few inches of water to be fed.

Cone shells Beware of these twisted, oblong-shaped, irresistibly pretty shells. Some are the size of an olive, some— like the Southern Bailer—are the size of a football. They have a stinger that can paralyse. If stung, have someone keep a close watch on your breathing and get medical aid.

Cassowaries are large flightless birds, four to six feet tall, with brilliant red-and-blue markings on their necks and a horn on their heads. They live in North Queensland and can become aggressive in self-defence. It's not the horn you have to worry about, it's the big middle toe—they try to eviscerate you. Don't run away or they'll chase you (I've done this, it is true). Stand your ground, pick up a big stick, wave it and yell at them (after running didn't work I did this, it worked). They're about as smart as a chicken.

Kangaroos and emus A herd of kangaroos is called a *mob.*

Probably the most common wildlife danger in Australia is hitting a kangaroo or *emu* (ostrich-like flightless bird) with your car. Be careful driving in bush areas around dawn or dusk when they're most active. They seem to suddenly appear alongside the road and freeze, then try to hop away across your path. Their instincts do not include anything moving as fast as a motor vehicle, especially at night when they are blinded by the headlights. That's why cars in the bush have bar-work around the front end, called *'roo bars*.

Cute & cuddlies   Enough with the scary stuff—there are lots of cute and cuddlies out there: kangaroos, wallabies, koalas, bandicoots, furry possums, and quokkas. Be careful; the koalas can bite and a big *boomer* (male) 'roo can stomp you. Anything with teeth is liable to bite if you try to pick it up.

Birds   Australia is a bird-watcher's paradise. There's everything from tiny bright-blue wrens and honeyeaters to large emus and cassowaries. There are hundreds of species of parrots, like the pink and grey galas, green and yellow twenty-eights, sulphur-crested and black cockatoos, corellas, rainbow lorikeets, Australian ringnecks, eclectus parrots and millions of *budgies* (parakeets). There are raven-like crows, magpies, giant wedgetail eagles (wingspan 2.3 metres or 7.5 feet), hawks, kites, black swans, herons, ibis, bustards, and the biggest pelicans you've ever seen.

If you love birds this is the place to be. Bring your binoculars and get a copy of *The Claremont Field Guide to the Birds of Australia*, or *The Slater Field Guide to Australian Birds*.

Ferals and exotics

Feral animals are foreign domestic animals that have gone wild. Feral cats are a problem: they kill native birds, small marsupials, and lizards. Dingos are feral: wild dogs that accompanied the Aboriginal migrations and have become wild. In some areas, packs of abandoned dogs attack sheep. Feral pigs and goats destroy flora, ripping out roots and eating native plants. Wild horses (*brumbies*) and wild camels (descended from those imported and used for desert transport in the 19th century) harm the native grasses in the inland deserts

Rabbits, which were imported as food, have taken over huge tracts of land. They destroy wheat and other crops. A series of rabbit-proof fences thousands of miles long was built in the late 19th century to keep them in the desert interior. In the late 20th century, various viruses were introduced to cull their numbers, but they've since evolved resistance to them and continue to be a pest.

Exotics are foreign wild animals that have become pests. Starlings are small swallow-like birds that were introduced to Australia, just as in North America. Huge flocks raid vineyards and orchards and can strip them bare in a few hours.

Foxes were introduced for hunting and have thrived, assuming the role coyotes play in North America, but without any natural predators except for the occasional truck on the highway. The most effective way of culling them is through poison baiting, using a formula called *1080*, which is made from native plants so native animals aren't affected. Meat is used as bait, so beware the *1080 poison* signs when walking your dog.

The cane toad was introduced to North Queensland from South America in the 1930's to control the greyback cane beetle which destroys sugar cane. Unfortunately, the beetle lives on the upper stalks of the cane and the toads can't jump that high, so it was a failure. The toads have turned into a mega-pest. Not only do they out-compete native frogs for food, they eat them, too, along with anything else they can fit in their mouths. The toads exude a slimy poison though the skin on their backs, so almost nothing will eat them, and anything that does dies. Supposedly you can get high off this poison, and it's now illegal to lick a toad in Queensland. Big cane toads can measure ten inches across and weigh ten pounds. They've spread from Queensland through the Northern Territory and are moving into Western Australia. It's predicted they could occupy almost all of coastal Australia in a few years. Professional toad trappers have been engaged to stop them. It is sport in the far north to whack them with a golf club (PETA and the RSPCA object to this). There's also a small industry making leather goods from their hides, so you can surprise the folks back home with a cane toad purse, wallet or key case. Just don't get caught licking your wallet in Queensland.

Pets

Pets in Australia are lucky beasts. In my experience, dogs seem to be better regarded and cared for than in the U.S. There are fewer problem dogs, and ones relegated to a life in the backyard are rare.

Dogs   A few peculiarities: the Rottweiler is pronounced *rot-weeler*. Dobermans rarely have their ears clipped and are much mellower as a result. Pit bulls are called *American pit bulls* and are banned from breeding due to their dangerous character.

Most of the same popular breeds are available, along with a few not widely seen in North America, such the Staffordshire terrier (or *Staffy*), which makes a great family pet (but looks like a pit bull).

Ironically, Australian Shepherds are rare in Australia, even though that breed has recently been formally recognized by the American Kennel Club. The Australian shepherd has nothing to do with Australia and was developed from working dogs in the U.S.

The Australian *Blue Heeler* breed has a similar bluish-brindle colour as an American Australian shepherd, but with a much shorter coat, wider stance, and blustery personality. *Bluies* are bred to herd cattle, they are tough as guts, and can take a stomping from a *bullock* (steer), then get up and run the bastard through a fence. As a pet they can be a bit nippy, very defensive of their owner.

Then there is the *Kelpie*, a slim, medium-sized reddish-brown dog with a tan mask. Kelpies are brilliant shepherds: one dog can gather an entire flock of sheep, drive it across meadows, through narrow gates, force them up a ramp and into a truck, often running over the backs of the sheep to urge them through bottlenecks. Try to take in a country sheepdog trial, it's amazing.

Dogs are rarely given away as puppies. Mixed-breeds, as well as purebreds, are sold, and not cheaply. A purebred Kelpie can go for several thousand dollars. If you want to get a dog but don't want to pay dearly, try an animal shelter or the *RSPCA* (*Royal Society for the Prevention of Cruelty to Animals*)

When a dog or cat is neutered or spayed, it's referred to having been *de-sexed*.

Cats can be problematic. Most are loved pets, but many go wild and prey upon the native birds and small marsupials, which have no natural defence. Politically correct cat etiquette is to keep them indoors. Feral cats are shot on sight in rural areas.

Horses are a lifestyle of their own, with breeders shows, pony clubs, rodeos, and casual riding. As with the American mustangs, some got loose and formed wild populations in the outback. They're called *brumbies*.

Birds   Parakeets are natives of the north, and are called *budgies*, short for *budgerigar*, an Aboriginal name. Cockatiels are also called *Weiros*. Budgies and Weiros are also raised in captivity in simple backyard aviaries.

Some wild parrots have been domesticated, mostly Corellas and Galahs. These are wild birds in cages, though some were injury rescues. Corellas and Major Mitchells can be good talkers, but also tend to be biters.

Many people, both in the suburbs and in rural areas, raise chickens for their eggs, and good layers are regarded as pets. Extra roosters are regarded as Sunday dinner, but they're kind of tough, so you have to cook them a while. They make a nice chicken and dumplings. It's a bit unsettling at first eating your former pets, but at least you know they aren't full of hormones and antibiotics. A tip: don't let your kids name the ones destined for the freezer.

Sheep are raised commercially by the thousands, but many people living on a few acres will have a pair to keep the grass trimmed. I named our pair Briggs and Stratton.

Alpacas   For folks with acreage who are bored with sheep, there are Alpacas, which have become a kind of Gucci sheep. They're similar to a llama, a bit smaller but with big eyes and a delicate face that makes them all look like you want to cuddle them. Beware: they can spit, and I'm told they usually aim for your eyes. The trick is to raise your hand and hold it in front of you, away from you face—they'll spit at that instead.

The males aren't afraid to fight a fox, so some *pastoralists* (shepherds) put a few out to guard the new lambs.

They were first introduced in Australia in 1989, by 2001 there were 40,000, now there may be as many as 400,000. Alpacas can go for A$400 for a pet to thousands of dollars for

---

a breeder that produces prize fleece. To help defray the costs, you can sell the fleece, because unlike other textiles, demand outweighs supply.

Migrating with a pet from North America has gotten a lot easier. The quarantine period for dogs and cats has been shortened substantially. For birds, it's another story. Some (like the African grey parrot) are banned entirely. For more info, check out the government website at **www.aqis.gov.au**.

The Motion Picture Industry

Overview There are two layers of filmmaking: Australian-financed and produced films and television drama, and American big-budget productions here for the cheap dollar.

With a small population of 25 million, an Australia film industry can't be supported on its own. Statistics show that you need a population of at least 90 million to put enough *bums* (bottoms) in seats to make it work financially, so that's where subsidies come in. With the aid of government subsidies, Australian producers manage to turn out a few-dozen small-budget features and another dozen TV series each year, along with hundreds of top-quality documentaries and *music clips* (music videos). This is important if Australia is to have a screen presence representing its culture and identity and not just disappear into the noise of American media. And, of course, there are lots of commercials.

Local production The ABC, and SBS commission and air original dramas and documentaries. The ABC also airs high-quality British drama. The three commercial networks air Australian dramatic shows, along with a lot of American shows. Australian shows, though limited budgetarily, are very well written and produced.

'Runaway' Hollywood movies There is an entirely separate, higher-budgeted layer of filmmaking: major Hollywood studio productions that take advantage of the low Aussie dollar and high Aussie production capability. *The Great Gatsby*, *Aquaman*, *San Andreas*, *Pirates of the Carribbean*, *Woolverine*, *Hotel Mumbai*, *Chronicles of Narnia*, and the *Matrix* films, were shot at world-class Australian studio complexes: *Village Roadshow* (Gold Coast Queensland), *Fox*

Studios (Sydney) and *Docklands* (Melbourne).

The Aussie dollar cycles up and down, and with it, so does American production in Australia. When the Aussie dollar is low the Yanks come, when it's high, they go elsewhere. When the Aussie dollar is sixty-five cents on the American dollar, the Hollywood producers make 35% just by bringing the money across the Pacific. In the 1990's, when the Aussie was down to about US$.54, they flocked in. From mid-2010 to mid-2013 when both currencies were trading roughly equal, production dried up and the Yanks went home. When the Aussie dollar went down in 2015 the Yanks came back. The break seems to be around US$.75. In 2020, the COVID-19 virus is presenting another positive factor to shoot in Australia: since the pandemic is more under control, Hollywood studios can get some shooting done.

American productions bring their own rules: longer hours, larger crews, more elaborate equipment and big budgets. They take advantage of cheaper crew costs and lack of actor residuals. Unless intended, American and international audiences are unaware that the film they're watching was shot in Australia. *Ghost Rider Vengeance* (2012) takes place in Texas but was shot in Melbourne; the producers imported dozens of American left-hand drive cars, faked signs and cheated the 'look'. *Winchester* (2018) takes place in Northern California where some of the exteriors were shot, but most of the production was done in Melbourne's Dockland Studios.

Australian film history   Cinema in Australia grew on its own, in isolation from the rest of the world, as an expression of its own distinctive culture. It had a significant impact in the early years of cinema on par with the U.S. and Europe.

The first feature film produced anywhere in the world was Australian: *The Story of the Ned Kelly Gang* (1906). The artform developed quickly and produced many narrative films.

By 1912, in a country with a population of only 4½ million, 51 feature films were made. That year, the many producers and exhibitors merged to form *Australasian Films and Union Theatres*. But film production dwindled in 1914 when Australia joined Europe fighting WWI. Production also dwindled in Europe, but not in America which didn't get into the war until 1917. In those three years, the Americans refined film into a popular art form, developing a large commercial industry with studios and stars and dazzling new techniques, plus a sophisticated distribution system. When the war ended in 1918, the American film industry was far ahead of the rest of the world. In Australia, as in Europe, people wanted to see American films.

In the 1920's a distribution deal between *Australasian Films* and various American distributors made it cheaper to import films from the U.S. than produce them in Australia. By 1923, American films made up 94% of the movies shown in Australian theatres. The Australian industry didn't come back in force until the 1970's.

The remaining small industry turned out uniquely Australian dramas like *Far Paradise* (1928), *The Sentimental Bloke* (1932), *The Flying Doctor* (1936), *The 40,000 Horsemen* (1940), comedies like the *Dad and Dave* series, inspirational WWII films like *The Rats of Tobruk* (1944), and films showing Aboriginal issues like *Jedda* (1955). But Australian cinema was overshadowed by imported British and American productions. The ABC consistently produced Australian films.

Things started to change in the 1960's when *The Australian Film Producers Association* got the government to rule that all TV commercials had to be produced in Australia. The Melbourne and Sydney film festivals inspired young filmmakers who responded to the French 'New Wave'. In 1971 *The Australian Film Development Corporation* began funding films and the industry was reborn. A new generation of Australian filmmakers, using lighter, cheaper cameras, began innovating and experimenting with low-budget movies on uniquely Australian themes.

The 1970's saw a new kind of innovative Australian film that involved personal stories in iconic Australian settings, both historical and contemporary. *Picnic at Hanging Rock* (1975), directed by Peter Weir, was the true story of the mysterious unsolved disappearance of several schoolgirls and their teacher during a picnic at Hanging Rock, Victoria, on Valentine's Day 1900, and the subsequent effect on the local community. *Muriel's Wedding* (1994), directed by PJ Hogan and starring

A Survival Guide to Australia

Toni Collette, is a coming-of-age movie about a socially awkward young woman whose ambition is to have a glamorous wedding and improve herself by moving from her dead-end home town to Sydney. *Gallipoli* (1981), directed by Peter Weir and starring Mel Gibson, was about two young Australian men who go from naïve innocence to resolute veterans during the disastrous WW1 Gallipoli campaign. *Breaker Morant* (1980), Directed by Bruce Beresford and starring Edward Woodward, Jack Thompson and Bryan Brown, and *The Lighthorsemen* (1987), directed by Simon Wincer, featured recurring themes of loss of innocence in war, establishing *mateship* and *larrikinism* (a *larrikin* is a rowdy, unsophisticated, good-hearted person) as foundations of the Australian identity. *Shine* (1996), directed by Robert Scott Hicks, was the true story of a brilliant concert pianist (David Helfgott) who suffers a mental breakdown and struggles through his own recovery (Geoffrey Rush won the Oscar for best actor). *Kenny* (2006), directed by Clayton Jacobson and starring his brother Shane, is a comedy mockumentary that follows the day-to-day life of a very likeable *bloke* who supplies *dunnies* (portable toilets) to concert venues and fairs, speaking directly to the camera about what his trade has taught him about the human condition.

Australian films, though comparatively small, deal brilliantly with ordinary people in ordinary lives by making their stories interesting, identifiable and emotional. Domestic Australian productions are generally quality films on relatively small budgets.

On Aussie sets you won't see twenty big trucks and fifty people standing around waiting. Things are on a smaller scale, half the size of an American set. A grip drives the grip truck, the electrics best boy drives the lighting truck, etc. The *DOP* (director of photography) operates the camera, the make-up person often also does hair, there are no stand-ins, you grab anyone around when lighting the set. The soundman helps load the grip truck, usually just to get to the pub sooner.

Dramas like *Lantana, Jindabyne, Samson and Delilah*, and *Rabbit Proof Fence* deal with contemporary and historic Australian issues. Comedies like *Strictly Ballroom, Priscilla,*

Queen of the Desert, and *The Castle* offer the unique Aussie melding of pathos and humour.

TV dramas come and go seasonally: medical, cops, sci-fi, produced at studio facilities in Sydney, Melbourne, and on the Gold Coast south of Brisbane.

The perennial hit TV series *'Home and Away'* is a nighttime soap set in a beachside town. It has been shooting for 26 seasons. It airs Monday through Thursday at 7 pm on the *Nine Network*. It's filmed in-studio and on the beaches of northern Sydney.

'Neighbours' is another long running nightly soap, airing at 6:30 on *Ten* or *Peach*. In its 28th season, it focusses on realistic stories and portrays adults and teenagers who talk openly and solve their problems together. It is syndicated all over the world.

Children's TV production is helped by a government mandate that requires locally produced and themed kids shows each year. According to *Screen Australia*:

> *A broadcaster must screen a combined total of at least 260 hours of C programs (for children other than preschoolers) and at least 130 hours of P programs (for preschool children) per year from any source, with a combined total of at least 390 hours. Children's programs must be broadcast within specific children's time periods and must meet other content and advertising requirements to meet the quotas.*

Production offsets of 40% assist production. Australian-produced series air in New Zealand, South Africa, the UK, and Europe.

Filmmaking Talent Exports. Many great Australian filmmakers go to the U.S. and Europe to work on a scale unavailable in Australia. Some prominent directors are: Peter Weir (*Witness, Dead Poets Society, Master and Commander*), Phillip Noyce (*Patriot Games, Clear and Present Danger*), Mel Gibson (*Braveheart, Apocalypto*), Bruce Beresford (*Driving Miss Daisy, The Black Robe, Mao's Last Dancer*),

George Miller (*Mad Max Fury Road, Happy Feet*), and Baz Luhrmann (*Moulin Rouge, The Great Gatsby*.)

Some great Australian cameramen are: John Seale (*The American President, Cold Mountain, The Perfect Storm*), Dean Semler (*Dances with Wolves, We Were Soldiers, Bruce Almighty*), Russell Boyd (*Master and Commander, Tin Cup*), and Don McAlpine (*Mrs. Doubtfire, Chronicles of Narnia*).

Ratings Australian films have a rating system similar to the one in the U.S.: G, PG, M, MA15+, R18+, X18+ and CTC (not yet classified). X18+ is only available in the Northern Territory and the ACT. Ratings and censorship is the responsibility of the Australian Classification Board.

Funded films are small films funded by state film boards, which are of social or cultural relevance.

If Australia, with its small population, wants to have a screen identity to represent its culture domestically as well as internationally, it has to subsidize films. Each state has a film board that provides seed money to help productions get started. There's a long process to get funding, with many steps of script approval and budget review along the way, but it's a way of nurturing an otherwise neglected part of the industry and of providing a springboard for new directors, writers, and cinematographers.

The federal government has had numerous film boards to promote production. The *Australian Film Commission* (*AFC*) stimulated production and the *Film Finance Commission* provided financial assistance. In 2008, they merged to form *Screen Australia* which provides one-stop shopping for production and funding assistance.

In their words:

Screen Australia supports the development, production, promotion and distribution of Australian narrative (drama) and documentary screen content. The agency invests directly in Australian television, film and digital original titles, and administers the Producer Offset tax incentive for Australian screen stories. The Producer Offset is a refundable tax rebate for producers of Australian feature films, television and other projects. Because it's underpinned by income tax legislation, it represents a source of funds for producers of eligible Australian projects

.

Producers apply for the rebate after they've secured guaranteed financing but before production commences. They're then eligible for a *refundable tax rebate* of 40 percent of a feature film budget and 20 percent of a TV production.

Most Australian films are subsidized. By American standards they are low budget, but what makes them stand apart is they have a lot of *Heart*. Film lovers coming to Australia owe it to themselves to watch *Bran Nue Dae* (brand new day), *The Dish, Strictly Ballroom, The Castle, Ten Canoes, Samson and Delilah* and *Rabbit-Proof Fence*.

The Great Australian Film Tax Rort: In the 1980s the Labor government established *double tax credits* for film production, and the number of movies being produced increased significantly. But, typically Australian, many *rorts* (frauds) occurred. Producers made films just to get the tax credit; it didn't matter if the films were good or bad or even made a profit. A businessman would put the money up for a film and write off double the expenses against his taxes.

Besides producing some bad films, the policy also produced many good ones. *The Man from Snowy River, My Brilliant Career, Mad Max, Crocodile Dundee, Breaker Morant* and *The Year of Living Dangerously* are a few. It stimulated the industry, creating jobs and establishing an international reputation for Australian films and filmmakers that lasts to this day.

In 1999, because of the *rorts*, the government tax commissioner announced that he was disallowing $800 million in film investment tax credits, and that scared off investors. Ironically, a few days later he rescinded that ruling, but investors never returned. Double tax credits were discontinued. Motion picture production has fallen off since then, leaving only low-budget semi-subsidized films, foreign productions using Australian locations, and runaway American films.

Film festivals and awards   There are numerous film festivals. Some are big, like the Melbourne International

Festival and the Brisbane International Festival. Some are small and off-beat, like the Adelaide Fringe Festival and the Eye Scream Festival. Tropfest, held each February, began small but is now huge: a nationwide short film competition culminating with the sixteen winning films screening simultaneously in outdoor theatres in all the capital cities. It draws large crowds.

The Australian equivalent of the Emmys is the *Logies*.

The Australian equivalent of the Oscars is the *Australian Academy of Cinema and Television Arts Awards*. Unlike everything else in the country they have no nickname, just the AACTA Awards.

Movie industry technical information

Production   The basic shooting day is ten hours long. If overtime is required, the assistant director will go around to the crew and ask if anybody objects. Overtime is usually less than half an hour. Lunch break is forty-five minutes and usually six hours into the day. Crafts services are limited: hot water for tea or instant coffee, and a few *biscuits* (cookies). There will usually be a tea break for snacks around 4:00 p.m. If the day is behind schedule, this might be at wrap.

Crew   Despite different terms and more humane hours, movies are shot pretty much the same as in North America. The crews are competent and professional, but not as well paid. Crews are much smaller; there are fewer trucks and crew double-up duties. There are no drivers per se; departments handle their own trucks.

Australian productions work on the English system. Crewing is slightly different and some jobs have different names:

The Director of Photography is called the *DOP*. He/she usually operates the camera. If a second camera is used, a camera operator will run it; otherwise, no camera operator is employed.

The first assistant cameraman is called the *focus puller* (**Important Note:** lens focus marks are in feet, not metres).

The second assistant cameraman is called the *clapper loader*.

The sound mixer is sometimes called the *soundo*.

The microphone boom person is called the *boom swinger*.

A trainee is called an *attachment*.

An insert car is called a *tracking vehicle*.

Grips work with the camera, they don't do anything that has to do with lighting, including cutters, bounce reflectors and silks. All C-stands, cutters, nets, and diffusion in front of the lights, silks, and *fleckies* (reflectors) are handled by the gaffer and his electricians (sometimes called *sparkies*).

Hair and makeup are often done by the same person.

Lighting stand-ins are rarely used. Often the clapper loader or an AD will stand on the actor's mark if needed. If asked, the actors themselves will oblige.

There is a *safety officer* on each show who is responsible for safety on the set. They supervise work from a safety standpoint and coordinate traffic control when shooting on the street. Quite often they are ex-stuntmen.

Police aren't normally present when shooting on the street. If necessary, an independent traffic management company will be hired to provide warning signs, *witches' hats* (safety cones) and *lollipop men* (flag men holding stop signs).

There are no teamsters; someone from each department will drive that department's truck(s).

Different terms

Music videos are called *video clips*.

TV commercials are called *TVCs*.

A TV season is called a *series*, as in 'the second *series* of *Friends*', meaning all the shows in the second season.

The slate is called the *clapper board*.

Video assist is called *video split*, or just the *split*.

A tree branch used to create a dappled shadow effect is called a *dingle*.

An umbrella is a *brolly*.

A *grovel mat* (or *grovelly*) is a furniture pad or anything you throw on the ground for an actor or camera operator to sit, kneel, or lie down on to shoot a scene.

A *lazy leg* is an extendable leg on a light stand (*rocky mountain leg* in the U.S.).

Oysters means to shoot with available or natural light,

(from *oysters natural*).

A bit on the piss means a Dutch angle (tilted framing).

A *KD* is a pop-up canopy to provide shade and rain protection.

If you leave your mobile phone on and it rings during a take (or do anything equally stupid on a set), you'll be *slabbed*. This means you'll have to buy a *slab* (case) of beer to share with the crew after wrap the next day.

Slates and scene numbers   The numbers on the slate (*clapper board*) and the camera report, are done English-style, which is different than in North America. It's not based on the scene number in the script, but on the *shot number*.

The slate will have a box for Scene number, Shot number and Take number.

In America a letter is added to the Scene number to show a different angle of coverage of the same scene as the previous set up. In the Australian system the Scene number doesn't change with each new set-up. Instead the shots are differentiated by *shot number*: shot numbers go up sequentially from the first shot of the movie. So a pick-up shot for a scene filmed days earlier would have the same Scene number, but a totally different Shot number on the slate. Good camera reports are critical.

Shot number conventions: at shot 100, the director buys the beers; shot 111, the producer; shot 123, the sound crew; shot 216, electrical; shot 246, the grips.

Unions   There's no strong motion picture union. The *MEAA (Media Entertainment and Arts Alliance)*, was formerly known as *ATAEA*, and traces its history back to the early 1900's. It has about 14,000 members. The members are not just film crew, but actors, journalists, musicians, potentially anyone working in media.

Unlike the IATSE in North America, it has little clout. The contract and working conditions can been seen at: meaa.org/download/mppa-summary-2020/

A lot of work is done outside the Alliance, but the *award rates* (scale) that are set by it are used as a starting point for negotiations when one is hired.

Residuals are sometimes paid to actors, directors, or

writers, though often there are buy-outs. There is no strong Directors, Writers or Screen Actors Guild deals.

Booking agents Each capital city has booking agents. Call them to hire crew or to seek representation. Check online, or with the government film board in that state.

Conclusions?

Generalizations are generally too general, but if any can be drawn from my years of living here, it's simply that Australia is probably what the U.S. would be like if there had been no American Revolution.

If you remember your history, after the Revolutionary War the U.S. intentionally distanced itself from Great Britain. The U.S. developed on its own, and by the turn of the 20th century had a well-established identity, along with a substantial population, and had become industrialized.

Australia, on the other hand, was a decentralized group of British colonies until 1901, and like Canada, had a small population and was dependant on the motherland for both manufactured imports and export markets. Australia bought many household items and machinery from the UK, and sold the UK wool, grain and gold.

But Australia lacked the lush interior of the North American continent, so development was limited to the southern coasts which could only support a limited population.

Unlike Canada, which is next door to the U.S. and shares a long border, the Australian identity evolved in near isolation on the far side of the world. Australia developed its own cultural peculiarities and idiosyncrasies—in a delightful kind of way.

Australia is gradually changing from a sunny version of provincial England to a British-influenced version of America. The internet has allowed it to virtually participate in the life of the rest of the world, but remain safely in protective isolation.

My personal conclusion is to take a lesson from the Aussies, don't take anything too seriously, and learn to say: *"No worries, mate...she'll be right."*

Australian-American Dictionary

Just because Americans and Australians use a language based on English doesn't mean they speak the <u>same</u> language. They are *"...two peoples separated by a common language."* The big stuff is obvious; it's the subtle differences that get you. An American living in Australia finds him or herself having to repeat things and having to ask for things to be repeated. It's partly the accent and partly the terminology. The accent you'll have to pick up on; it's like learning to play music by ear. The terminology is absorbed over time. The next section is your cheat sheet.

The following contains about 1800 Australian words and phrases, their meanings and usages, which will be handy when travelling, doing business, or settling in Australia. Some words and terms are hard to evaluate grammatically, so the categorization is loose. My apologies to Merriam-Webster, Thorndike-Barnhart, and Funk & Wagnall's for having the audacity to call it a 'dictionary'. I kept the definitions and examples as brief and specific as possible.

I hope you have as much fun using it as I had in putting it together.

Australian	American	Details—Usage
a bit rough (adj)	something sub-standard	"Your work is *a bit rough.*"
A4 (n)	standard business-size letter (8.25" x 11.75")	
abattoir (n)	slaughterhouse	
ABN (n)	Australian Business Number	A tax number that qualifies you as a business.
a bit on the piss (adj)	tilted camera angle in the movies	same as "Dutch angle" in U.S.
Abo (n)	derogatory term for Aboriginal	It's like the 'N' word, don't use it.
Aborigine (n)	indigenous Australians	Latin: 'from the beginning'

abseil (v)	to rappel (rock climbing)	
ace (adj)	great	"That's *ace!*" Used in Melbourne.
ACT (n)	Australian Capital Territory	Australian equivalent of the District of Columbia
ADF (n)	Australian Defence Forces	Army, Navy, Air Force, SAS
adjustable spanner (n)	crescent wrench, monkey wrench	
aerial ping pong (n)	Australian Rules Football (Footy)	
aggro (adj)	Aggravated, aggressive	"He's acting kind of *aggro.*"
agistment (v) (adj)	horse boarding	
air bottles (n)	Scuba tanks	also 'air cylinder'
airy fairy (adj)	wishful thinking, unrealistic	
alcopop	flavoured alcoholic mixed-drinks in a bottle or can.	
all the fruit (adj)	all the accessories or goodies	"I ordered the new Ford with *all the fruit.*"
all the go (adj)	the latest thing, very popular	"The new Mazda is *all the go.*"
ally (n)	aluminium	
aluminium (n) (note second letter "i" in the last syllable)	British/Australian pronunciation and spelling of aluminum	(see text section on **pronunciation differences**)
always in the shit (adj)	always in trouble	
amber fluid (n)	beer	
ambo (n)	ambulance driver	
anti-clockwise (adj)	Counter-clockwise	

anti-social behaviour (adj)	Hooliganism, disruptive actions (also known as *"hooning"*)	anything from hot-rodding to being drunk in public, painting graffiti, harassing oldies, etc.
ant's pants (adj)	real good, the best	
"Any joy there?"	Had any success?	
Apple Mac (n)	name for any Apple or Macintosh computer	
apples, she'll be apples (adj)	alright, it'll be OK	also *apps*
arc up (v)	to get mad	"Look out, or I'm going to *arc up*."
argy-bargy (adj)	argument	
arse (n) (pronounced *ass*)	ass	
arsey (adj)	lucky	
arvo (n) - pronounced *ah-vo*	afternoon	
as cross as a frog in a sock (adj)	angry	
as full as a goog (adj)	drunk	From English slang for egg: *googy*.
ashveldt	asphalt	
a sparrow's fart (n)	dawn	"I'll wake you at *a sparrow's fart*."
at the end of the day	when all is said and done	
at the mo (adj)	at the moment	
ATO (n)	Australian Tax Office	equivalent to the IRS
AUD, AUD$, A$ (n)	Australian dollar	
Aunty (n)	The ABC (Australian Broadcasting Corporation)	Australia's government-owned public broadcasting networks
AUSFTA (n)	Australia-United States Free Trade Agreement	
Aussie (n)	Australian	

Aussie salute (v) (n)	waving flies from in front of your face	
Autogas (n)	LPG, liquid propane gas	Used as a fuel in cars.
auto trimmer (n)	auto upholsterer	
autumn (n)	fall (The word "fall" is not used.)	Leaves don't seasonally fall off eucalyptus trees.
average (adj)	mediocre	"The meal was pretty *average.*"
avos (n)	avocados	
awning over the toy shop (adj)	a man's beer belly	
award rates (n)	minimum standard pay and conditions (pay scale)	
B & S (n)	Bachelor and Spinsters Ball	A drinking and dancing party for single people, usually in rural areas.
BAC (n)	blood alcohol concentration	used to determine drink driving
back bencher (n)	Member of Parliament not holding a ministerial position	
on the back foot (adj)	being defensive, under attack	"The accused politician was *on the back foot.*"
back block	remote piece of land	
back chat (v)	To talk back to someone insolently	
back hander (n)	a bribe	
back of Bourke (adj)	far away	From the remote town of Bourke in western New South Wales.
back-to-front (adj)	opposite	
backy (n)	tobacco	"Got any *backy*?"
backyard job (n)	improper or illegal job	

bad trot (adj)	a period of bad luck	"I've had a *bad trot* this week."
bagging (v)	giving someone a hard time	
bags (v)	claim (kid's term)	"I *bags* the front seat."
bail up (v)	a hold up, to corner someone	
bailiff (n)	private process server, marshal of the court	
bale (n)	The top piece on a cricket wicket.	
ball and chain (n)	wife	
ball huggers (n)	Speedos (also see budgie smugglers)	
Bali belly (adj)	diarrhea	Bali is a popular vacation spot in nearby Indonesia.
balls-up (adj)	screw-up, mistake	
ball-tearer (adj)	something really special	
balustrade (n) (pronounced *bah-liz-trahd*)	Railing, hand rail, banister	
banana bender (n)	person from Queensland	
bandicoot (n)	a small marsupial about the size of a rabbit	
bangle (n)	bracelet	
Banksia (n)	a flowering tree indigenous to Australia	
barbed wire (n)	Four X beer	XXXX looks like barbed wire
barbie (n)	barbecue	
barbie pack (n)	sausages, steak, and chops to cook on a barbecue	"I went to the shops and bought a *barbie pack*."
bar heater (n)	electric heater, radiator	
Barmy army (n)	English cricket fans	

barney (n)	a fight	
barrack (v)	to cheer for	
barramundi, barra (n)	a tasty, brackish water fish from the northern coast of Australia, often served in restaurants or as fish and chips	pron: 'bear-a'
barrister (n)	lawyer who appears in court	usually suggested by your solicitor
BAS (n) (pronounced *baaz*)	Business Activity Statement	Tax form for figuring your GST payment.
bash (v)	to try something	"I'll give it a *bash*."
bashed (v)	hit, battered, assaulted	"The man was *bashed* in the robbery."
bathers (n)	swimsuit	"He put on his *bathers*."
battle axe, battle axe block (adj)	(real estate) rear lot, flag lot	A land-locked lot that has a narrow section to connect with a road.
battler (n)	someone working hard but barely making it	
Beak (n)	Magistrate, a person's nose	
bean curd (n)	tofu	
beanie (n)	knit cap	
beaut, beauty (adj)	great, real good	"That car's a real *beaut*!" "You little *beauty*!"
beavering (v)	working hard	
bed-sit (n)	an efficiency or studio apartment	
beer buddy (adj)	drinking buddy	
bee's dick, a (adj)	a small amount	"Move it a *bee's dick* to the left"
beet root (n)	beets	
behind (n)	a one-point score in footy	
bell (v)	to call someone	"I'll give you a *bell* later."
bench top (n)	kitchen counter	

bend the elbow (v)	drink too much	"He's been known to *bend the elbow.*"
berko (adj)	angry, beserk	
berley (n)	chum, bait (fishing)	"*Berley* is spread behind the boat to lure in the fish."
bespoke (adj)	custom made	
bevvies (n)	alcoholic drink	
beyond the black stump (adj)	far away, referring to giving bad directions.	"We live just *beyond the black stump.*" (The outback is littered with burned-black stumps.)
bickie (n) also spelled: bikkie	cookie (from *biscuit*)	"We baked *bickies.*"
bickie (n)	dollar	
biffo, biff (v) (adj)	a fight	"I gave him the *biff.*" "We had a bit of a *biffo.*"
'bigger than Ben Hur' (adj)	Describing something elaborate of over-built	
big note, to (v)	to boast or brag	"Sean was *big noting* himself again."
bikies (n)	motorcyclists	Usually referring to members of bad-guy motorcycle gangs.
bickie or bicky (n)	cookie	
bicky barrel	cookie jar	
billabong (n)	pool in a streambed or waterhole.	
billy (n)	A pot used on an open fire to boil water for tea or cooking.	
billy cart (n)	homemade wooden cart, soapbox racer	
biltong (n)	jerky	South African term
bin (n)	trash can (green top for rubbish, yellow top for recyclables)	"Put out the rubbish *bin.*"
bin (v)	To throw something away.	'bin that rubbish.'

bindies (n)	little stickers that grow on grass	
bingle (n)	minor car accident	"He was in a *bingle*."
bird (n)	girl, gal	From British slang.
biro (n) (pronounced *bye-ro*)	ballpoint pen	Laszlo Biro invented the ballpoint pen. Biro is a brand name, and *biro* is used generically for any ballpoint pen.
biscuit (n)	cookie	
bit of a train smash (adj)	a disaster, something that doesn't work well, a mistake	"The job was a *bit of a train smash*."
bities (n)	biting bugs	"The *bities* are out tonight."
bits (n) (adj)	pieces	"Pick up all the *bits*."
bits and bobs (adj)	miscellaneous things	
bitumen (n)	asphalt, pavement	
bitzer (n)	mongrel dog, something pieced together from various parts	bits of this and that
bizzo (n)	business	"Mind your own *bizzo*."
black spot (n)	trouble spot in a roadway targeted for improvement or policing	
block, block of land (n)	lot (real estate)	"We bought a *block* in Subiaco."
bloke (n)	man, guy, fellow	"He's a good bloke."
bloodnut (adj)(n)	person with red hair	
bloody (adj)	very, also an expletive	"That *bloody* fool!"
"Bloody oath!"	"Very true!"	
bloomers (n)	shorts worn over undies and under a skirt	
blower (n)	telephone	"Get on the *blower* and call him."

blowie (v) (n)	windy weather, a blowfly, blowfish	
blow-in (adj)	someone unexpected and uninvited	
blow in the bag (v)	taking a breathalyser test	
bludge, bludger (n)	person who dodges work	
blue (n)	a fight	
blue heeler (n)	a cop	
blue metal (n)	granite gravel	
blue tongue (n)	a bobtailed lizard, common in WA	
blue, make a (adj)	make a mistake	
bluestone (n)	granite	"They walked over a *bluestone* bridge.
bluey (n)	multiple meanings: traffic ticket, a type of cattle dog, $10 bill, bluebottle jellyfish, a person with red hair, a fight	
Blundies (n)	Blundstone work boots	
Blu-Tack (n)	an adhesive putty that is used to hang posters on walls, etc.	
board shorts, boardies (n)	surfer's baggie swim trunks, knee-length or longer	
bob-a-job (n)	An odd-job performed by a kid for a neighbor, usually for a small amount.	A *bob* is slang for a pound, the Aussie denomination of money before switching to the dollar in 1966.
Bob's your uncle	and there you have it, a done deal	
bodgy (adj)	bad quality, worthless	
boffin (n)	expert	
bog-in (v)	to start eating	

bog standard (adj)	ordinary, basic, unadorned	"His Holden was *bog standard.*"
bog (n)	toilet	"I gotta go to the *bog.*"
bogan (n)	a low-life person	
bogey (n)	fifth wheel-hitch on a semi-truck (also called a booger)	
bogged (adj)	stuck, vehicle stuck in sand or mud	"We got *bogged* on the beach."
boilermaker, boilie (n)	person qualified to cut and fabricate metal, a welder	
bolshie (n) (adj)	revolutionary, agitator, rebel	From *Bolshevik.*
bonk (v)	to have sex	
bonnet (n)	car hood	
bonzer (adj) (pronounced *bon-za*)	great	
boofhead (n) (adj)	idiot	
boofy (adj)	fluffy, usually referring to hair	
booking (v)	reservation for a restaurant, hotel, hire car	"I made a *booking* for dinner."
booking out, booked out (adj)	booked up, no vacancy	
boom swinger (n)	person who holds the mike boom on a movie crew	
boomer (n)	large male kangaroo	
boomerang (adj)	loaned item that hasn't been returned	
boondy (n)	(Western Australian term) dirt clod	"I chucked a *boondy* and hit him in the eye."
boot (n)	car trunk	
booze bus (n)	police van used in road blocks to catch drink drivers	

boozer (n)	pub or tavern, a drinker	
booze-up (n)	drinking spree	
bore (n)	well (water)	
bossy boots (adj)	pushy person	
bottle shop, bottle-o (n)	liquor store	
bottler (adj)	something excellent	
bounce (adj)	bully	
bourse (n)	stock exchange	
bowled me over (adj)	surprised	"You could have *bowled me over.*"
bowler (n)	the pitcher in cricket	
bowser (n)	gas pump	"He got petrol from the *bowser.*"
box (n)	jock strap cup	
box and dice (adj)	everything	From "the whole box of dice."
box of beer (n)	case of beer	also *slab* or *carton*
Boxing Day (n)	the day after Christmas	
brackets (n)	parenthesis (punctuation)	
brass, brass razoo (adj)	money	"He hasn't got a *brass razoo.*"
brassiere (n)	bar, inexpensive restaurant and bar	
breaker (n)	person who breaks horses for riding	
brekky, brekkie (n)	breakfast	
brickie (n)	brick-layer	
brickie's cleavage (adj)	crack of a man's ass, visible when his pants slide too low	
bring a plate (v)	pot luck, bring something to share	
Brizzie (n)	Brisbane	
brolly (n)	umbrella	
brown-eyed mullet (n)	turd	

Brownie Guides (n)	Brownies (first level of Girl Guides)	
brumby (n)	mustang, wild horse	
bub (n)	baby	
Buckley's, Buckley's chance (adj)	no chance at all	"He hasn't got *Buckley's* chance of winning the Lotto."
bucks night (adj)	bachelor party	
budgie smugglers (n)	Speedos (tight swimsuit, like competitive swimmers wear)	
budgie, budgerigar (n)	parakeet	Aboriginal word
bug (n)	delicious crab-like crustacean (Queensland)	
bugger (v) (adj)	unpleasant person, affectionate term for someone, an exclamation of amazement	"*Bugger* them all!" "He's a *bugger*." "I'll be *buggered*."
"Bugger off!" (v)	"Go away!"	
bugle (adj)	smelly, gone bad, dishonest, or a spokesman	
bulk billing (n) (v)	Medical billing where physician directly bills the government and accepts whatever the government pays as full payment.	
bull bars (n)	Big brush bar on the front of a vehicle for protection from hitting kangaroos or emus in outback and shopping trolleys in supermarket car parks.	also *'roo bars*
bull dust (n)	deep dust on a dirt road	

bull twang (adj)	lies	
bum (n)	butt, ass, derrière	
bum bag (n)	waist pack	*"Fanny"* is a word not used in polite company.
bumf, bumph (adj)	official documents, forms, toilet paper	
Bundy (n)	Bundaberg rum, made in Bundaberg, Queensland	
bunfight (n)	argument, dispute, brouhaha	
bunger (n)	firecracker (usually large and illegal), cigarette	
bunged (adj)	broken	"Bring that *bunky* regulator over here."
bung hole (n)	anus	"Put that in your *bunghole!*"
bung (v)	to put an object on something	"*Bung* that tyre on my ute."
bunky (adj)	busted, broken	
bunny (adj)	victim	
Bunyip (n)	legendary swamp monster, Aussie bogeyman	
burl (v)	to try	"Give it a *burl.*"
bush (n)	anyplace outside a town	
bush bash	a race through the bush	
bush oyster (n)	spit-out nasal mucus, a "loogy"	
bush pig (adj)	objectionable person	
bush ranger (n)	outlaw	
bush telegraph (n)	spreading rumors or gossip, the grapevine	
bush tellie (n)	campfire	A *tellie* is a television.
bush tucker (n)	native food foraged or hunted	
bushfire	brushfire	

bushie (n) (adj)	person who lives in the bush	"He's a bit *bushie*."
busker (n)	street performer, usually paid by tips	
bust-up	fight, brawl	
busy as a cat burying shit (adj)	being busy	
busy bee (n)	volunteer work party	
butcher (n)	half-pint glass of beer (South Australia)	
butter up (v)	To fix a mistake you've made.	
BYO (adj)	restaurant where you can bring your own alcohol	
cack (v)	to laugh	
cack-a-dacks (v)	to drop trousers, to moon someone.	
cactus (adj)	dead	"That car is *cactus*."
caesars (n)	Caesarean section	"Too posh to push."
cake hole (n)	mouth	
Call diverting	Call forwarding	(on a telephone)
call Ralph (v)	to vomit	
CALM (n)	Western Australian Department of Conservation and Land Management	In 2007, changed to DEC, Department of Environment and Conservation.
camp (adj)	one who acts very gay	"…camper than a row of tents."
Canadian canoe (n)	canoe	Differentiates from simply *canoe*, which can also mean a kayak.
cane it (v)	drive fast	
cane toad (n) (adj)	Amphibian originally imported to control beetles that has become an exotic pest. Also a nickname for a person from Queensland.	
canteen (n)	school cafeteria	

capsicum (n)	bell pepper	
capsule	infant car seat	
Captain Cook (v)	a look (rhyming slang)	"Go take a *Captain Cook.*"
car bays (n)	parking places	
car park (n)	parking lot	
caravan (n)	travel trailer	
carer (n)	caregiver	
cark, carked, carked it (v)	to die	"He *carked* it."
carn (v)	short for "come on"	used as encouragement
carriageway (n)	roadway	
carry on like a cat burying shit (adj)	very busy	
carry on like a pork chop (v) (adj)	throw a fit about nothing	
carton (n)	case of beer, also *box* or *slab* of beer	
cashie (adj)	J=job paid off the books	
caster sugar (n)	fine grain sugar used for icing	
cat flap (n)	doggie door	
cat's piss, mean as (adj)	cheap, stingy	
cattle duffer (n)	rustler	
CBD (n)	Central Business District, downtown area of a city	"I've got to go into the *CBD.*"
celebrant (n)	A person who performs a non-religious wedding or funeral.	
cellar door (n)	wine tasting room	
chalk and cheese (adj)	no comparison	"The difference between Budweiser and Crown Lager is *chalk and cheese.*"
chalkie (n)	teacher	
champers	champagne	

chase him up (v)	look for him	"I'll *chase him up*."
chasie (n)	tag (game of)	
chat (n)	shit	
chat show (n)	talk show	
chat up (n)	flirting talk	"He was *chatting* her *up*."
Chateau Cardboard (adj)	cheap wine that comes in a cardboard box	
cheek, cheeky (adj)	impudence, to show gall	"The *cheeky* bastard stole my girl!"
cheerio	goodbye	
cheers	thanks, good bye, also a drinking salute.	
chemist (n)	pharmacy, pharmacist	"I'll drop by the *chemist's* and have a chat with the *chemist*.
chewie (n)	chewing gum	
chicken salt (n)	Chicken flavoured salt, used as a condiment	
Chiko Roll (n)	vegetable-filled deep-fried spring roll (fast food)	
China (n)	old friend	rhyming slang: China plate = mate
Chinese whispers (v)	Rumours. A story that changes each time it's told.	Racist stereotyping?
chin wag (n) (v)	a chat	
chippy (n)	carpenter	
chips (n)	French fries	
chock a spaz (v)	throw a fit	
chock-a-block (adj)	full	"The theatre was *chock-a-block*."
chockers (adj) (pronounced *chokkas*)	full (from *chock full*)	"After that meal, I'm *chockers*!"
chocolate sauce (n)	chocolate syrup	
choke a darkie (v)	defecate	
choccy (n)	chocolate	

choof-off (v)	go away quickly	
chook (n)	chicken	
chookas (v)	used in the theatre to wish people luck,	much like "break a leg"
chook raffle (n)	money raiser selling chicken	Can also be used generically for any raffle.
Chrissy (n)	Christmas	
Christmas on a stick (adj)	Sarcastic comment about someone who thinks he or she is special.	"What do you think you are, *Christmas on a stick?*"
Christmas tree (n)	Western Australian native tree (nuytsia floribunda) that blooms orange around Christmastime.	A member of the mistletoe family, Aboriginal people peeled and ate the suckers, which are sweet and taste like candy.
chuck a brown eye (v)	to hang a BA, to "moon" someone	
chuck a sad (adj)	to be depressed	
chuck a sickie (v)	To take a sick day from work, often when you're not sick.	
chuck a wobbly (v)	throw a tantrum	
chuffed (adj)	pleased and excited	"He was *chuffed* about his promotion."
chukas	good luck	
chunder (v)	throw up (from "watch under")	"He got seasick and *chundered.*"
CJs (cock jocks) (n)	Speedos (also *budgie smugglers*, *ball huggers*)	
clacker (n)	anus	From "cloaca;", platypus or bird anal pore.
cladding (n)	siding (building materials)	"The house has aluminium *cladding.*"

clanger (n)	a lie, accidental insult, faux pas, embarrassing mistake	
clawback (v) (adj)	the recovery of funds already disbursed	"The plan would *clawback* benefits."
Clayton's (adj)	fake, substitute	Comes from a non-alcohol whiskey-like beverage called *Clayton's*.
cleanskin (n)	bottle of wine with no label; something that hasn't been used; an unbranded cow	cleanskin wines can be bought cheap, or custom-relabelled
clobber (n)	clothes, belongings	
clothes peg (n)	clothespin	
cloud cuckoo land (adj)	fantasy	
clucky (adj)	feeling motherly	A hen goes *clucky* when she begins to sit on her eggs.
coach (n)	tour bus	
Coat Hanger, the (n)	Sydney Harbour Bridge	
cobber (n)	friend, mate	old term, rarely used
cockatoo (n)	type of Australian parrot	
cockie (n)	a cockatoo, a farmer, a cockroach	
cockie gate (n)	a homemade farm gate	
cockroach (n)	person from New South Wales	
codswallop	load of shit	"Sounds like *codswallop* to me."
compere	master of ceremonies	
cohort (adj)	a group at the same level	commonly used for students
coldie (n)	a cold beer	
collected	died	
college (n)	a high school	

collywobbles (n)	butterflies	She had the collywobbles before her speech.
come a cropper (v)	to fall off (a horse)	
come a gutser (adj)	made a bad mistake, had an accident	
come on like a raw prawn (adj)	being disagreeable	
compo (n)	worker's compensation	
concession, concessionaire (n)	student or senior (for discounts)	"Entrance is $5; *concessionaires* $3."
conchy (adj)	From "conscientious;", person who would rather study or work than play.	
"Cooee!" (exclamation)	"Hey, where are you? I'm over here!"	A way of calling out to someone in the bush.
cooee (adj)	nearby, within ear shot	"It's not within *cooee* of here."
cooker (n)	oven	
cool drinks (n)	sodas	
Coolgardie safe (n)	a cabinet for storing perishable foods, used before refrigeration	Named after the town of Coolgardie, where it was invented. It was a box covered in wet hessian (burlap) that kept the contents cool through evaporation.
cordial (n)	flavoured sweet drink like Kool-Aid	comes in liquid concentrate, you add a little to a glass of water
corflute (n)	waxed cardboard used in making signs	
corker (adj)	really good	"This band is a *corker*!"

coronial (n)	having to do with a coroner	"The *coronial* inquest proved he was murdered."
corroboree (n)	Aboriginal traditional celebration with song and dance	"We danced and sang at the *corroboree*."
cos (n) (pronounced *koss*)	romaine lettuce	
cot (n)	baby crib	
cotton (n)	generic term for any type of thread	
cotton wool (n)	cotton balls	
counter meal (n)	A meal served by ordering at a counter.	Counter meals are common, from fast food to mid-priced restaurants and pubs
country cousin (adj)	a dozen (rhyming slang)	
course (n)	a series of doses (prescription drugs)	"I took a *course* of Imodium to get rid of traveller's tummy."
cozzie, cossie (n)	swimsuit	From *swimming costume.*
crack a fat (v)	to get an erection	
crack onto (v)	hit on someone romantically	
cracked a spack (v)	throw a fit, go crazy, get very angry	
cray (n)	lobster	From *crayfish*
crash hot (adj)	very good	
crazier than a cut snake (adj)	crazy, in a friendly sort of way	
creche (n) (pronounced "*kresh*"	day care centre, baby's room	
"Crikey!"	"Wow!"	
crim (adj)	criminal	
crisps (n)	potato chips	Not to be confused with *chips*, which are French fries.
crook (adj)	sick or ill, can also mean "thief"	"I feel *crook*. I think I'll take a sickie."

cross country wrestling (adj)	The game of rugby.	
crotchet (n) (pronounced "crotch-et")	quarter note (music)	
crow eater	person from South Australia	
crust (adj)	wage money	
CSIRO (n)	Commonwealth Scientific and Industrial Research Organisation	Official scientific arm of the government.
CUB (adj)	acronym for *Cashed-Up Bogan*	A *bogan* (low-life) who's come into money and is indulging questionable tastes.
cubby (n)	kids playhouse, tree house	
cuppa (n)	cup of tea or coffee	"Hey mate, ya wanna *cuppa?*"
Curly (n)	nickname for a bald man	
curly (adj)	something difficult	'that job was a bit curly'
cut lunch (n)	sandwiches	
cylinder (n)	Scuba tank	also *air bottle*
dab hand at (adj)	one who's good at something	
Dad & Dave (v)	to shave	rhyming slang
dag (n)	a funny character; a nerd; a goof-off; a bit of dung stuck to a sheep's behind	
daggy (adj)	outdated	"His clothes were *daggy*."
daks, dacks (n)	trousers	Also *strides*
damper (n)	simple unleavened scone-like bread	A traditional campfire bread cooked in the outback, now available in supermarkets.

date (n)	Ass, buttocks	"Get off your *date!*"
date roll (n)	roll of toilet paper	
dead horse (n)	tomato sauce	rhyming slang
deadly treadly (n)	bicycle	
dear, dearer (adj)	expensive	"That BMW is a bit *dear.*"
deed poll (n)	power of attorney	
debutante (adj)	anyone making their debut (pronounced *de-boo*), most commonly used in sports	
deep sewerage (n)	Sewer service piped to a treatment plant.	As opposed to septic systems
dekko (v)	to look	"Have a *dekko* at this."
demersal (adj)	various bottom fish species	
demister (n)	car windshield defogger	
demob (v)	leave the armed forces	From *demobilize.*
demountable (n)	modular or temporary building, as at a school, mine site, etc.	
deputy principal (n)	vice principal	
der (adj)	phoney look of stupidity	
dero (n)	derelict, homeless person, vagrant	
de-sexed (adv)	neutered or spayed (dogs and cats)	
despo (adj)	desperate	
details (n)	personal information, (name, address, phone number, ID numbers, etc.)	"Write down your *details*, mate."
devon (n)	bologna (baloney), regional term used in Melbourne	

Devonshire tea (n)	A small meal of scones, whipped cream, and tea	Served in better tea rooms.
diary (n)	appointment book or calendar, Day Runner	
dicky (adj)	defective	"His heart was *dicky* since birth."
did a runner (v)	to leave unexpectedly, to abscond	"He owed me money and *did a runner*."
diddled (v)	to trick someone out of something	
didgeridoo, didge (n)	Indigenous Australian wind instrument made from a tree branch hollowed by termites.	Makes a droning sound; native name *yirdaki*.
dieback (n)	scientific name: *phytophera cinnomomii*, a disease that attacks the roots of some native trees. Imported in fruit trees, it's a fungus that spreads through wet soil.	Predominantly in WA, it's killing off the native jarrah, banksia, and grass tree forests. Can be treated short-term with sprays or injections of weak solution of phosphorus acid. (Outlook: grim.)
digger (n)	Australian soldier	
dill (n)	an idiot	"He's a *dill*."
dim sums (n)	testicles	
dinger (n)	condom	
dingle (n) (v)	cucoloris or go-bo (movie industry)	A device hung in front of a light source to create a shadow effect.
dingo (n)	indigenous, coyote-like wild dog introduced by Aboriginal migrants 10,000 years ago.; a small stand-up earth-moving tractor	

dingo's breakfast (adj)	"A yawn, a piss and a look around."	What you do in the bush after getting out of your *swag*.
dinkum (adj)	real, true	
dinky, dink (v)	giving someone a ride on your bicycle, usually on the handlebars	"Give us a *dink*."
dinky di (adj) (pronounced *dinky-die*)	real, genuine.	"He's a *dinki-di* Aussie."
dipstick (adj)	an idiot, loser	
display home (n)	model home (real estate)	
display village (n)	model homes (real estate)	
disposal (v)	a pass in footy	
divvy van (n)	police paddy wagon	From *division van*.
DIY (adj)	do-it-yourself	Part of the Aussie tradition of self-reliance.
doddle, it's a (adj)	it's easy	
do not take (v)	do not take internally (prescription)	From warning label on pharmaceutical crèmes, ointments, etc.
do up (v)	to fasten	"*Do up* your seat belt."
do your nut (v)	throw a tantrum	
dob (v)	to tell on someone	"He *dobbed* on me."
docket (n)	receipt, ticket	
doco (n)	documentary (film, video, or radio)	
dodgy (adj)	not good, suspicious	"His work is a bit *dodgy*."
dogsbody (n)	worker doing tedious, menial tasks	
dog's breakfast (adj)	a mess	"You look like a *dog's breakfast*."
dog's eye (n)	meat pie	rhyming slang

dog whistle (adj)	political term, statements that appear innocent but convey coded messages to a specific group.	
dole (n)	welfare	"He's on the *dole*."
dole bludger (adj)	welfare cheat	
don't come the raw prawn (v)	"Don't try to play me for a fool."	
done my dash (v)	"I'm finished; I already did it."	"I've *done my dash* with marriage."
donga (n)	pre-fabricated cabin with few creature comforts	Common accommodation on mine sites and trailer parks
donger (n)	penis	
donk (n)	engine	
donkey vote (adj)	In preferential voting, just going down the list and numbering in order, not really voting.	
donkey's years (adj)	a long time	
donnybrook (n)	a fight	
doodle, it's a (adv)	it's a cinch	
doodle (n)	penis	kids' speak
doona (n)	comforter, quilted bed cover	
Dorothy Dixer (adj)	an obvious or easily answered question	Named after Dorothy Dix, an early 20th century American advice columnist.
dosh (n)	money	"Bring the *dosh*."
doss (v)	to sleep	
doss house (n)	boarding house	
double G (n)	a very nasty type of thorn	
down the gurgler (adj)	failure, down the tubes	

down the track (adj)	somewhere far from here	
Down Under (n)	Australia and New Zealand	
draught (n)	Aussie spelling for "draft", wind or beer.	"I feel a *draught*." "I'll take a *draught* beer."
dreaded lurgy (n)	infectious cold or flu	
dreamtime (n)	Aboriginal mythology	
drink driver (n)	drunk driver	
drink with the flies (v) (adj)	drink alone	
drive-away (adj)	out-the-door price (car dealership)	Price of the car, GST, stamp duty, license, and third party insurance included.
drongo (adj)	idiot, dimwit	
drop (n)	wine, drink	"The Cab-Merlot is a good *drop*."
drop off the perch (v)	to die	"Old Bob *dropped off the perch* last week."
drop your guts, drop lunch (v)	to fart	
dropkick (n)	an idiot, someone no-one wants to hang around with	
drug driver (n)	driver under the influence of drugs	
drum (n) (v)	a tip-off, inside information	"Give me the *drum*."
dry as a dead dingo's donger (adj)	dry, thirsty	
dry as a nun's nasty (adj)	very dry	
dry as a pommy's towel (adj)	very dry	From the old myth that the English rarely bathe.
dry hire (adj)	equipment rented without the operator	

dual carriageway (n)	road with two lanes in each direction and a centre divider down the middle	
duchess (n)	sideboard (furniture)	
duck's dinner (adj)	drinking on an empty stomach	
duco (n)	car paint	
duff, up the (adj)	pregnant	
duffing (v)	cattle rustling	
dummy (n)	baby pacifier	
dunny (n)	toilet usually, but not always, outdoor	
dunny roll (n)	toilet paper	
durry (n)	cigarette, tobacco	
Dutch oven (v)	To fart under the blankets.	
dux (adj)	top in the class, valedictorian (school)	"He's the *dux*."
earbash (v)	too much talk, non-stop chatter, nagging	"She was *earbashing* me."
ears flapping (adj)	to listen intensely	
earth (n)	electrical ground	"The negative wire was connected to *earth*."
earth closet (n)	19th century self-composting dry toilet	
earth leak circuit breaker (ELCB) (n)	ground fault interrupter	Automatically shuts off the current if there's a short.
easy on (v)	calm down	
easy peasy (adj)	easy job or task	
EFTPOS (n)	debit card, *Electronic Funds Transfer At Point Of Sale*	Can access check or savings accounts by credit or bank card through a terminal in a shop or bank.
egg soldier (n)	strip of toast dipped in egg yolk	

Ekka (n)	the annual Brisbane Exhibition	First held in 1876, now the Royal Queensland Exposition.
elastic bands (n)	rubber bands	Also called *lackies*.
ensuite (adj)	toilet/bathroom attached to room	in hotel room or accommodation
entree (n)	on a menu, appetiser, salad, soup course	
equal-first	tied for first place	
esky (n)	ice chest	From *Eskimo cooler*.
euro (n)	a small type of kangaroo, wallaby	
evo (n)	evening	
excess (n)	deductible (insurance)	"My car insurance has a $200 *excess* on theft."
excursion (n)	a school field trip	
expression of interest (n)	a real estate term meaning one is asked to bid on a property	
exy (adj)	expensive	
face fungus (n)	a beard	
fag (n)	cigarette	
fair dinkum (adj)	the truth, genuine in an Aussie sense	
fair go (adj)	to give a good chance	"Give it a *fair go*."
"Fair suck of the sav!"	"Give me a chance!"	
fairy bread (n)	triangles of white **bread** covered with butter and topped with multi-coloured "hundreds and thousands (sprinkles).	
fairy floss (n)	cotton candy	
fairy lights (n)	small white Christmas lights	

fancy dress (n) (adj)	costumes: <u>not</u> a formal dress or tuxedo (you rent a tux at a *suit hire*)	"They went to a *fancy dress* ball."
fang it (v) (adj)	to drive fast	"The hoons were *fanging it* on the road."
fanny (n)	slang for vagina, not used in nice company	Call a fanny pack a *bum bag.*
fault (n)	problem	"We found the *fault* in the motor."
fell off the back of the truck (adj)	something stolen	
feral (n)	hippie; wild person; a wild-looking loud car with lights, bars, and stickers; wild kids	
fete (n)	small event	
fibro (n)	asbestos board used in construction of old houses	
figs (n)	balls, male genitalia	
figjam (adj)	acronym for: *F**k, I'm Good, Just Ask Me*, an egotist	
file (n)	binder, notebook for punched paper	
filter lane (n)	the transition road on the left or right side of the roadway	
filter light (n)	turn arrow	
fine (adj)	(weather) clear and sunny, used instead of "fair"	"Tomorrow's weather will be *fine*."
fining (v)	clearing weather	"It's *fining* up for the weekend."
FIRB (n)	Federal Investment Review Board	
fire brigade (n)	fire department	
firies (n)	firemen	"Quick, call the *firies*."

first in, best dressed (adj)	first come, first served	
first past the post (adj)	The one with the most votes wins, majority not needed.	election term
fisher (n)	fisherman	
fisho (n)	fish seller, fisherman	
fitted (v)	installed, mounted, put on	"We had new tyres *fitted* to the ute."
fitter (n)	one who assembles mechanical equipment, mechanic	
fixings (n)	screws, nuts & bolts, nails	
fixture (n)	game schedule (sport)	
fizzy drinks (n)	sodas	
FJ (n)	The most famous model of Holden automobile.	"My favourite car is a 1953 *FJ* Holden."
flake (n)	fillet of shark (in fish & chips)	
flannel (n)	a washcloth or hand towel	
flare (n)	a tiki torch, a boat signalling device	
flash (adj)	fancy, stylish	"His new clothes were *flash*."
flash as a rat with a gold tooth (adj)	a sleazy charmer	
flash for cash (n)	traffic or speed camera	
flat (n)	apartment	
flat chat (v)	very busy, very fast	
flat out like a lizard drinking (adj)	very busy	
flat spot (adj)	an opening in the schedule	"Do you have a *flat spot* tomorrow?"
flat stick (adj)	full speed	
flatmate (n)	roommate	

fleckie (n)	reflector used to bounce light onto the subject in camera work.	
flick (v)	to get rid of someone, usually a date	"She gave me the *flick*."
flick it on (v)	quick resale	
float (n)	a horse trailer	
flog (v)	to sell something	"I'm going to *flog* off my old Ford Falcon."
fluoro (n)	fluorescent light	
flutter (n)	a bet	
Flying Doctor Service (n)	Air rescue service for remote areas	
flywire, flyscreen (n)	window screen	
flywire door (n)	screen door	
fob off (v)	to treat someone rudely	
follow on customer (adj)	repeat customer	
football (n)	soccer (Europe)	
footpath (n)	sidewalk	
Footy (n)	Australian Rules Football	
forkie (n)	forklift driver	
form, form room (n)	high school home room	
fossick (v)	to search, prospect	"I was *fossicking* in the op shops."
four-be-two (n)	Jew	Rhyming slang. A two-by-four piece of wood is what Australians call a four-by two, which rhymes with Jew.
fraka (v) (adj)	fracas	
franger (n)	condom	

franking credits (n)	Tax credits for investors on dividends from company profits that have already had taxes paid on them.	Eliminates double taxation: first on company's profits, second on dividends from those profits. A standard stock benefit.
freckle (n)	anus	
Fremantle Doctor (n)	afternoon sea breeze off Perth	
Freo	Fremantle, the port of Perth	
freshie (adj)	freshwater crocodile, fresh cow pile	"Don't step in that *freshie*, mate."
fried eggs (adj)	flat breasts	
fringe (n)	bangs (hair)	"She trimmed her *fringe*."
from go to whoa (adj)	from start to finish	
fronted	to tell someone off to his/her face	He fronted me full on!
front bencher (n) (adj)	member of Parliament who holds a ministerial position	"He's a *front bencher*."
front foot, on the (adj)	on the offensive, pushing ahead	"The new manager is *on the front foot*."
Frosties (n)	Name used for Frosted Flakes cereal.	
fruit machine (n)	slot machine	
full, full as a boot (adj)	drunk	"He's a bit *full*."
full bottle (n) (adj)	Completely, expert, the whole thing	
full milk, full crème milk (n)	regular milk	
full stop (n)	a period (.) (punctuation)	
function (n)	banquet	
function centre (n)	banquet hall	
funfair (n)	a small carnival	
funny bunny (n)	a gay man	

furphy (n)	unreliable rumor, tall tale, scuttlebutt	Named after the Furphy water cart used in WWI; soldiers got the gossip while filling their water jugs.
G-clamp	c-clamp	
Gabba, the (n)	Woolloongabba, the Brisbane cricket ground	
galah (adj)	noisy idiot, also a pink-and-grey parrot	named after the noisy parrot
gannet (adj)	someone who is always hungry, or will eat anything	
gaol (n)	jail	(pronounced the same)
gap year (n) (adj)	A period of time taken off school, usually between high school and university, to travel and work.	
gap (n)	The difference in what Medicare pays for a medical service and what the healthcare provider charges.	The patient has to make up the difference.
garbo (n)	garbage truck driver	
gas (n)	propane, LPG	
gas bagging (v) gas bagger (n)	referring to one who talks too much	
gasper (n)	cigarette	
gazetted (v)	to be made official in government publications	"The company was *gazetted* last week."
gazumped (v)	outbid	"He was *gazumped* on that property."
gee gee (n)	a race horse, first horse out of the starting gate	
g'day (v)	good day	standard Australian greeting
get nicked (v)	go away	

get the arse (adj)	to get fired	
getting up, getting the shits up (v)	to verbally abuse someone	"I'm *getting up* him for the rent."
gin (n)	offensive name for an Aboriginal woman	
ging (n)	slingshot	
Ginger (n)	nickname for a person with red hair	
ginger group (n)	group within a political party with differing views	
Girl Guides (n)	similar to Girl Scouts	
give a gobful (v)	to verbally abuse	
give 'em some stick (v)	verbally abusing someone	
give it a burl (v)	try it out	
give it a miss (v)	to avoid something	
give them curry (v)	give them trouble	
give up (n) (v)	the equivalent of a punt in Australian Rules Football (Footy)	
give you a hoy (v)	to get in touch.	
glandular fever (n)	mononucleosis	
globe (n)	lightbulb	
go for a burn (v)	to test drive a car, to drive fast	
go like clappers, go like a shower of shit (v)	to go very fast	
goanna (n)	monitor lizard	Early arrivals mistook them for iguanas, hence the name.
gob-smacked (adj)	very surprised, "mouth agape"	"He was *gob-smacked* when he saw the bill."
"God bless his cotton socks."	He's completely wrong, but we still love him.	

gold coin (n)	$1 or $2 Australian coins (gold-coloured)	"Admission to the charity fete by *gold coin* donation."
"Going around the twist"	Gone crazy	
gone troppo (adj)	tropical madness, having too a good time	
gong (n)	medal	'she picked up a gong for the 100 meter dash'
good nick (adj)	good condition	"The old ute's in *good nick*."
good oil (adj)	good information, useful idea	
good on ya	well done, good job	Often just *onya* is used.
Good Sammy's (n)	the Good Samaritan charity	sometimes just "Sammy's"
googie (n)	egg	"I'll have a *googie sanger*."
good value (adj)	worthwhile	"That ute is *good value*."
goonbag (n)	plastic bladder from inside a cardboard wine box	
goss (n) (v)	gossip	"What's the *goss*?"
grey nomads (adj)	retired who live in caravans travelling.	(a caravan is a travel trailer)
grazier (n)	large scale sheep or cattle farmer	
greenie (n)	environmentalist, member of the Greens Party	
gridiron (n)	American football	Football is soccer, Footy is Australian Rules Football, *gridiron* is American football.
grinning like a shot fox (adj)	happy, smug	If you ever shot a fox, you'd know why.
grizzle (v)	to complain	

grog (n)	beer, liquor	
grommet (n)	young surfer	
grouse (adj)	good, cool	
grundies (n)	underwear	
GST	Goods and Services Tax	ten percent nationwide
guernsey (adv)	To be given praise.	The coach gave him a guernsey after the game.
guernsey (n)	jersey, shirt	
gum sucker (n)	resident of Victoria	
gum, gum tree (n)	eucalyptus tree	
gunya (n)	temporary shelter	Aboriginal: *ganya*
gurgler (n)	the drain	"When the wife and kiddies left, my life went down the *gurgler*."
gutful of piss (adj)	drunk	
gutzer, come a (v)	to have an accident; something that didn't work out	
gyno (n)	gynecologist	
gypboard (n)	sheetrock, gyprock	wallboard made of gypsum
hail damage	cellulite	
hair lackies (n)	elastic hair bands	
handle (n)	glass of beer (Northern Territory), pitcher of beer (Western Australia)	
Hansard (n)	Printed transcript of State and Federal Parliament sessions, with minor corrections and explanations added.	Like the U.S. Congressional record
happy as Larry (adj)	very happy	
happy little vegemite (adj)	cheerful person	From a 1950's advert.

hard word (adj)	a stern talking to	"I gave him the *hard word* about that mistake."
hard yakka (n)	hard work	
Hardie Board	asbestos board used in construction of old homes	
Hardie Fence (n)	corrugated pressed fibre and cement boards used for fencing	
hash key (n)	The pound sign on a telephone.	"Dial the number then press the *hash key*."
hasn't got a brass razzoo (adj)	one who has nothing. one who is broke.	"I haven't got a *brass razzoo*."
have a burl (v)	give it a try	
have a fang (v)	to eat	
have a go (v)	to try	
have a lend of (v)	take advantage of someone's gullibility	
have a naughty (v)	to have sex	
have themselves on	to kid one's self	"He is having himself on."
heaps (adj)	many, lots of	"I have *heaps* of good ideas."
heat beads (n)	charcoal briquets for the BBQ	
HECS (n)	Higher Education Contribution Scheme	a university loan
hens night (n)	bachelorette party	
he's past it (adj)	over the hill	
High Court (n)	Equivalent of the U.S. Supreme Court	
high dependency unit (n)	intensive care ward in a hospital	
Hills Hoist (n)	Australian designed variable height rotary clothes line	
hire (n) (v)	rental, to rent	"I dropped off the *hire* car."

his blood's worth bottling (adj)	a great guy	
hissy fit (v)	to lose one's temper	"He's just having a *hissy fit.*
hit and giggle (v)	women's tennis game	
hob (n)	stovetop, gas or electric	
Holden (n)	General Motors Australia auto manufacturing subsidiary	See section on **Australian cars.**
holiday (n)	vacation	"She's on *holiday.*"
holus-bolus (v)	everything, all at once	
home and hosed (adj)	finished, fixed, all done in a positive way	
home open (n) (adj)	open house (real estate)	Very short, less than an hour long.
hook turn (v)	Method of turning right in traffic around trams in Melbourne.	See section on **driving**
"Hooly-dooly!"	"My goodness!"	
hoon (n)	hooligan	Usually a 16–35-year-old male displaying anti-social behavior, often in an automobile.
hooroo	goodbye	
hoover (v)	to vacuum	From the Hoover vacuum cleaner.
horses for courses (adj)	A way of pointing out obvious differences.	From "different horses for different courses."
hotchpotch (adj)	Aussie for "hodge podge", an odd collection	
hotel (n)	a pub with a bottle shop, can also be a place that rents rooms	
hottie (n)	hot water bottle	"On cold nights, I sleep with a *hottie.*"

hotting up (adj)	heating up	"The real estate market is *hotting up.*
"How'd ya pull up?"	"How did you do?"	
"How ya goin?"	standard greeting, American equivalent: "How ya doing?"	
how's your father (adj)	to have sex (British slang)	"We were indulging in a spot of *how's your father.*"
humpy (n)	temporary shelter	Aboriginal: *yumpi*
hundreds and thousands (n)	coloured candy sprinkles	
hungi (n)	a charcoal-filled hole in the ground you cook in	
hurl (v)	to vomit	
I'll pay that (v)	I admit, you outsmarted me.	
ice block (n)	Popsicle, sometimes used for ice cube.	
ice cream spider (n)	soda float	Usually coke with ice cream on top, since root beer isn't generally available.
icy pole (n)	Popsicle	
identity (adj)	person of note, celebrity	"Prominent Perth *identity* Joe Blow was arrested."
"I'll be stuffed!"	expression of surprise	
impact sprinkler (n)	rainbird sprinkler	
impost (n)	customs duty; tax penalty; race horse handicap weight	
imputation (adj)	way of avoiding double taxation on dividends	See section on *franking credits.*
I'm stuffed (adj)	I'm tired.	
incursion (n)	An exhibition that travels to a school	

interval (n)	intermission, as in a play or concert	"The band will return after the *interval*."
inverted commas (n)	quotation marks	
invigilator	proctor	one who oversees a formal test
irrits (v)	to irritate someone	
iso (adj)	isolation	
it's a goer (adj)	it will work	
it's a take (adj)	it's a fraud	
it's gone missing (adj)	it's disappeared	
I-tie (n)	Italian	
it's gone walkabout (adj)	it's missing	
it's yum (adj)	it's yummy	
jab (n)	an injection by hypodermic needle	
Jack Dancer	cancer	rhyming slang
jackeroo (n)	cowboy	
jacket potato (n)	baked potato with the skin on	
jacking-up (v)	hassling someone	
jaffle (n)	toasted sandwich	
jam (n)	jelly	
jamball donut (n)	jelly donut	
jarrah (n)	A type of eucalyptus tree found in SW Western Australia, it produces a very hard, heavy wood used in furniture	Also known as *Swan River Mahogany*, it was heavily logged and exported. At one point, the streets of London were paved with it.
jelly (n)	Jell-O	
jillaroo (n)	cowgirl	
jimjams (n)	pajamas (spelled *pyjamas*)	
Joe Blake (n)	snake	rhyming slang
joey (n)	baby kangaroo	

joule (n)	metric measurement of energy equivalent to the calorie, short hand: *J*	approx. 4.2 Joules per calorie
journo (n)	journalist	
jug (n)	kettle, pitcher of beer	
jumbuck (n)	sheep	
jumped-up (adj)	one full of self-importance, arrogant	
jumper (n)	sweatshirt, sweater, jersey	"It's cold today, wear a *jumper*."
jumper punch (n) (v)	A technique in footy where one player grabs another's jumper (jersey) and punches him in the chest, making it look like they're grappling.	Illegal, but hard to enforce.
just across the road (adj)	someplace nearby	
k's (n)	kilometres	"It's a hundred *k's* from here."
kangaroos loose in the top paddock (adj)	describing a crazy person	
kebab (n) (pronounced *kee-bab*)	wrap with meat, cheese, salad, sauce	not on a skewer, not a shish-kebab
keen (adj)	eager	"He's *keen* about that property."
keen as mustard (adj)	enthusiastic	
Kelpie (n)	a breed of Aussie sheepdog	
kerb (n)	Aussie spelling of *curb*	
kero (n)	kerosene	
kettle of fish (adj)	problem	"That's a different *kettle of fish*"
Khyber Pass (n)	ass	rhyming slang

kindy (n) (pronounced *kin-dee*)	kindergarten	U.S. equivalent to preschool. *Pre-primary* is the U.S. equivalent of kindergarten.
king hit (v)	sucker punch, to "cold cock" someone	"The hoon *king hit* him."
kiosk (n)	snack bar at a theatre	
kip (n)	flat piece of wood used to toss the pennies in the game of Two Up	
kip (v)	to nap	
kit (n) (adj)	equipment	"I bought all the latest *kit*."
kit, (as in: get your kit off) (adj)	get naked	
kitchen bench (n)	kitchen countertop	
Kiwi (n)	New Zealander	From the kiwi fruit that grows there.
knackered (adj.)	exhausted	
knickers in a knot, don't get your (v)	to get upset	
knickies (n)	underwear	
knob head (adj)	dick head	
knobble (v)	interference causing someone to fail, also to stop a horse from whinnying	
knock (v)	to criticise	
knock back (v)	rejected, turned down	"The proposal was *knocked back*."
knock shop (n)	brothel	
knuckle duster (n)	brass knuckles	
Kombi (n)	VW bus	
kW	kilowatt	Measurement of electricity (1,000 watts); also the power of an engine, 1 kW= .746 horsepower
lackies (n)	rubber bands	From "elastic bands".

Lady Muck (adj)	arrogant woman who puts on airs	
lair, lairy (adj)	flashily dressed, brash, vulgar man, to dress someone or something in bad taste	
lair it up (adj)	act brashly or vulgarly	
Lamington (n)	sponge cake covered in chocolate and coconut	
land bank (adj)	to hold onto land for later release	
laneway (n)	alley	"Put the rubbish bin in the *laneway*."
larking around (v)	goofing off	
larrikin (n)	harmless prankster, loud goof-off	
lash (v)	to leave	
laughin', we're (adj)	we got it made	"We sell that house and *we're laughin'*."
launch (n)	large power boat	
laundrobar (n)	No-frills laundromat	
lay by (adj)	lay away, to put a deposit on something and gradually pay it off	
leadlight (n)	stained glass windows	
leave it with me (v)	I'll do it.	
leavers (n)	recent school graduate	"The school *leavers* gave the cops strife."
lecturer (n)	instructor at a university or TAFE	
leg (boating) (n)	outboard motor or out-drive lower unit	"The *leg* broke and stranded them on the reef."

leg spin bowler, spin bowler (adj)	Bowler in cricket who flips the ball off his wrist as he releases it.	"Shane Warne was the best *leg spin bowler*."
lemonade (n)	Seven-Up, Sprite, or any clear lemon soda	<u>not</u> fresh-squeezed American style lemonade.
let off (v)	to be laid off from a job	
letter box (n)	mailbox (home)	You <u>put</u> your mail into a *post box* and <u>receive</u> it in your *letter box*.
letter drop (n) (v)	bulk mail	
let your hair open (v)	let your hair down, relax	
licensed restaurant (n)	restaurant that can serve liquor	
lifestyle (adj)	leisure, quality of life, enjoying oneself	
lift (n)	elevator	"Take the *lift* to the top floor."
lift your game (adj)	improve	
like a shag on a rock (adj)	something that sticks out like a sore thumb.	
like a two-bob watch (adj)	something unreliable	
like buggery (adj)	with lots of energy	"Run *like buggery*!"
like the clappers (adj)	fast	
lippy (n)	lipstick	
liquid laugh (v)	vomit	
little boy (n)	small red sausage	
littlies (v)	small children	
little vegemites (adj)	children	
lob, lob in (v)	drop in for a visit, often unannounced	
locums, locums tenens (n)	temporary worker, especially a doctor	
loggerwood (n)	a person going nowhere, deadwood	

lollies (n)	candy	
lollypop man (n)	Person with the "stop" and "slow" signs, directing traffic at a road construction site.	The signs are round and on a stick, like a large lollypop.
London to a brick (adj)	absolute certainty	
long paddock (n)	side of the road where livestock graze during droughts	When the fields are bare, farmers let the cattle graze the grass alongside the road.
long service leave (n)	a sabbatical	
long weekend (n)	a three-day holiday weekend	
longneck (n)	large bottle of beer in South Australia	
loo (n)	toilet	
loo tickets (n)	toilet paper	
lorry (n)	truck	
lost the plot (adj)	went crazy	"He *lost the plot* and trashed the office."
lot (adj)	a daily dosage of medicine (pharmaceuticals)	
lot, the (adj)	everything	"I'll have a hamburger with *the lot*."
lounge, lounge room (n)	living room	
lubra (n)	Aboriginal woman (from *lubara*, Aboriginal word from Tasmania)	Not a popular word to use; American equivalent would be squaw.
lunch bar (n)	independent fast food shop serving sandwiches, rolls, pies, etc.	
lurk (adj)	illegal activity or endeavour	

lurks (adj)	benefits of a situation outside legal or ethical guidelines.	
lurks and perks (adj)	benefits: illegal (lurks) and legal (perks)	"They're the *lurks and perks* of elected office."
Macca's (n) (pronounced *Macker's*)	McDonald's	
mad as a cut snake (adj)	very angry	
maggoted (adj)	very drunk	
mail (n)	gossip	"I've got the latest *mail* on her."
main, mains (n) (adj)	main course in a restaurant	
make a good fist, to (adv)	to do a good job	
make a quid (v)	earn a living	A *quid* is slang for a pound (unit of money in Aus. until 1966).
mall (n)	street with shops closed to car traffic	A large enclosed building full of shops is called a shopping centre.
mallee bull, as fit as a (adj)	strong and fit	The Mallee is tough cattle country in the dry southeast.
malley root (n)	prostitute	rhyming slang
manchester (n)	household linen, sheets, etc.	
mandarin (n)	tangerine	
mappa Tassie (adj)	woman's pubic area	From *map of Tasmania,* which is triangular-shaped.
Margherita pizza (n)	Cheese and tomato pizza with spices	
mark (n)	clean catch in footy (Aussie rules football)	sets up a free kick

marri (n)	a type of eucalyptus tree in Western Australia (also known as *red gum*)	
marriage celebrant (n)	non-religious person licensed to conduct weddings and funerals	
marron (n)	large freshwater crawfish	a delicacy, farm raised in WA
mate (n)	friend, buddy	
mates rates (n)	special deal for friends	
maths (n)	math, mathematics	For some reason, the "s" is left on.
matilda (n)	mattress, sleeping roll	Story goes, the lonely sheepmen danced with their mattresses, hence *Waltzing Matilda.*
MCG	Melbourne Cricket Ground	The cricket stadium in Melbourne.
mean (adj)	stingy	
mean as cat's piss (adj)	mean, stingy, tight-fisted	
meat pie (n)	A round of pastry rolled over a meat or vegetable filling.	Individual serving size, can be eaten like a sandwich.
Medicare (n)	Universal healthcare for all Australian residents and citizens.	It's pretty good, it isn't ideal, but at least everybody's covered.
Melbourne Cup (n)	most famous horse race in Australia, held in Melbourne the first Tuesday in November	The whole country celebrates, goes to parties; women wear fancy hats.
Merc (n) (pronounced *Merk*)	Short for Mercedes Benz	Not a Mercury; Mercury's aren't sold in Australia.
methylated spirits, metho (n)	methylated spirits, used as a solvent and cleaner	They add the methylated part so people won't be tempted to drink it.

Mexican (n)	person from the south of Queensland along the New South Wales border; also *snowbirds* who travel to Queensland from southeast Australia to avoid the cold winter	
mickey mouse (adj)	really good, but can have the opposite meaning in some regions	
middy (n)	half-pint glass of beer	
milk bar (n)	corner shop that sells take-away food	
milk shake (n)	flavoured milk, usually not thick like in the U.S.	
milko (n)	milkman	
mince (n)	ground meat: beef, lamb, chicken, turkey	Aussies don't call hamburger ground meat; hamburger is pre-formed patties of ground meat.
minim (n)	half note (music)	
misso (n)	girlfriend	
mixed grill (n)	sausages, steak, and chops, cooked on a BBQ	
mo (n)	moustache	
mob (n)	any group of people (not necessarily harmful); a herd of kangaroos	
mobile (n) (pronounced *moe-byle*)	cellular phone	
mod cons	modern conveniences	"My new apartment has all the *mod cons*."
moggie (n)	house cat of indeterminate breed	

moke (adj)	bad horse	originally meant *donkey*
Molly Dooker (n)	left-handed person	
money for jam (adj)	easy money, money for doing nothing	
money for old rope (adj)	an unexpected gift	
mongrel (adj)	bad person or thing	
moot (n)	jamboree for older Boy Scouts (Rovers)	
mooted (v)	suggested	
motza (n) (alternate spelling: *motser*)	large amount of money, usually a gambling win	From Yiddish
move on order (v)	police order to disperse	
mozzie (n)	mosquito	
much of a muchness (adj)	much the same	
mud map (n)	map or diagram drawn in the dirt, any hand drawn map	"I'll draw you a *mud map* of how to get there."
muddy (n)	mud crab	
muesli (n)	rolled oats and grain cold cereal	
mug (adj)	friendly insult	
mug punter (adj)	lousy gambler	
mulga (n)	a type of tree, also name for the *bush* (rough country)	
mulies (n)	sardines (baitfish)	same as pilchards
mull (n)	marijuana	
mull up (v)	roll a joint and smoke it	
mullet (n)	haircut favoured by *bogans*: short on the top and the sides, long in the back	
Multanova (n)	portable speeding camera	Brand name of the Swiss-made device.
munted (adj)	messed up	

mushy peas (n)	over cooked peas served mushy	
muso (n) (pronounced *muse-oh*)	musician	
mystery bag (n)	sausage	
naff (adj)	something trendy, but can have opposite meaning.	
nappies (n)	diapers	
narked, narky (adj)	annoyed, short-tempered	
narniebar (n)	banana	
narrowcast (n) (v)	limited radio station	
Nasho (n)	National Service (the draft)	
Nashos (n)	Soldier's association for those who were drafted under the National Service Act 1951-1972	
naught (n)	zero	
naughts and crosses (n)	tic tac toe	
neck yourself (v)	to commit suicide	
neddies (n)	race horses	
needle (n)	hypodermic injection, shot	also *jab*
Never-Never, the (n)	the interior desert of Australia	
new chum (adj)	immigrant, new arrival	
New Holland	original name for Australia	
newsreader (n)	anchor person on TV or radio	
nibblies (n)	finger foods, hors d'oeuvres	"You bring the wine, I'll bring the *nibblies*."
nick (v)	to steal	"He *nicked* those sunnies at Woolie's."
nick off	go away, get lost	used as an order or request

nick over (v)	go there	"I'll *nick over* to the bottle shop for a slab of stubbies."
niggle, niggling (adj)	minor complaint, pain, inconvenience	
nil (n)	zero	also *naught*
nipper (n)	young surf lifesaver, little kid	
Nm	Newton Meter	Measurement of torque, U.S. equivalent of foot-pounds (1Nm=.738 ft/lbs.)
nobble (v)	to tamper with or damage	
no drama (adj)	one level up from *no worries*	
no great shakes (adj)	not outstanding	
no-hoper (n)	a loser	
nong (adj)	slow-witted person	
no object (adj)	no problem	
no room to swing a cat (adj)	a small or cramped place	
no shortage of oscar (adj)	having lots of money	
no standing (n)	a no parking zone	"No parking" signs say this.
not a patch on (adj)	not as good as	
not fussed (adj)	not worried	
not in a pink fit (adv)	not until hell freezes over	
not much chop (adj)	not very good	
not on (adj)	not right, not happening, won't work	
not on your nellie (adj)	no way	
not the full quid (adj)	a way of describing an imbecile	

not to be taken (adj)	do not take internally	Directions printed on poisons, ointments, etc.
not within cooee (adj)	beyond hearing distance	An Aussie might yell "*cooee*" to locate someone in the bush.
no worries (adj)	OK, no problem	
NSW (n)	New South Wales	
NT (n)	Northern Territory	
nuddy, in the (adj)	naked	
nudge the bottle (v)	to drink too much alcohol	
nuff nuff (adj)	a person who was poorly educated or not terribly bright.	
Nullarbor Plain (n)	The treeless desert between South Australia and Western Australia	Nullarbor is Latin for "no trees."
nursery slope (n)	bunny hill (skiing)	
NZ (pronounced: "en-zed") (n)	abbreviation for New Zealand	"We're going to *en-zed* on holiday."
ocker (n)	an unsophisticated person, a laid-back character, uncouth Aussie male	
ockie strap (n)	bungee cord	From "octopus."
off one's face (adj)	describing one who is drunk	
off with the fairies (adj)	describing one who is a bit loony	
offsider (n)	sidekick, assistant, helper	
"Oi!"	"Hey!"	
oil (adj)	information	"Give the *oil* on that project."
old fella (n)	penis	
oldies, olds (n)	adults, parents, seniors	"Let's ask the *oldies* if they know."

omelette (n) (Chinese restaurant)	egg foo yung	
on a good lurk (adj)	on a good job	
ono (adj)	abbreviation in classified ad for *or near offer*	Used the same as "obo" ("or best offer") in U.S.
on the back foot (adj)	on the defensive	
on the boil	going well	
on the bones of his bum (adj)	destitute, broke	
on the mend (adj)	getting better	
on the nose (adj)	bad-smelling, stinky, anything bad	
on the turps (adj)	drunk	
on your bike (v) (pronounced *onyerbike*)	get out of here, go away, get going	
onya	short for "*good on you*," i.e., "well done"	commonly used as a congratulation
op shop (n)	thrift store	opportunity shop
open slather (adj)	A situation where there are no limits or constraints on behaviour.	"Liberalizing liquor store hours would give *open slather* to public drunkenness."
oregon, oregon pine (n)	light American pine wood used in furniture, panelling	technically referring to Douglas Fir, grown as a crop in Australia
O.S. (adj)	overseas	"Les is *O.S.*"
outback (n)	distant Australian bushland	
outcome (n) (adj)	results	
outgoings (adj)	expenditures	
oval (n)	athletic field or stadium	
over east (adj)	the east coast of Australia	
overtime loadings (n)	overtime pay	

oysters (motion pictures)	to shoot in available (or natural) light	From "oysters natural"
Oz (n)	Australia	
packing polenta (adj)	scared	
paddlepop (n)	Popsicle	*Paddlepop* is a brand name, but it's used generically for any Popsicle.
paddock (n)	fenced pasture	
panel beater (n)	auto body repairman	
pando (n)	pandemic	
para, paralytic (adj)	very drunk	
paroo uppercut (adj)	to hit someone in the jaw with a 2 x 4	
partner (n)	spouse, married or not, of either sex	
pash, pashing (n) (v)	making out, a long, passionate kiss	
pasty (n)	A round of pastry rolled over a meat or vegetable filling, a meat pie.	
pastoralist (adj)	large scale cattle or sheep farmer	
Pat Malone (adj)	on my own, alone (rhyming slang)	"I went with *Pat Malone*."
Pat the Rat (adj)	meddling neighbour	from a character in Aussie TV show "Sons and Daughters"
patch (n)	area, business	"Tend your own *patch*." (Mind your own business.)
pavement pizza (n)	vomit	
pavers (n)	exterior brick flooring	

Pavlova, Pav (n)	a light and dreamy meringue dessert	Whipped egg whites, vanilla, and sugar, created in Perth in 1935 for the visiting Russian ballerina, Anna Pavlova.
pawpaw (n)	papaya	
paying out	to insult	I just got a paying out by that bloke
pay rise (n)	pay raise	
PAYG (n)	payroll withholding tax	*Pay As You Go*
PBS (n)	Prescription Benefit Scheme	Medicare's subsidized drug system
PCYC (n)	Police & Citizens Youth Club	like the YMCA
peak hour (adj)	rush hour (traffic)	
peanut paste (n)	peanut butter	
pearler (adj)	of excellence	"The batsman hit a *pearler.*"
pear-shaped (adj)	a situation that's gone bad	"When things go bad, they go *pear-shaped.*"
peckish (adj)	hunger-induced crabbiness	"I'm feeling *peckish.*"
pelican crossing (n)	crosswalk where pedestrians activate red crossing lights.	short for **PE**destrian **LI**ght **CON**trolled crossing: *PELICON*
pelmet (n)	valance	"The curtains hung behind the *pelmet.*"
pen (n)	slip (boating)	"Tie up the boat in the *pen.*"
penalty rates (n)	rates of pay higher than normal rates, for work performed outside normal working hours	
penciller	bookie's clerk	
pension day (n)	the day government pension *cheques* arrive	
pensioner (adj)	retiree	

pergola (n)	A covered area, patio, walkway, etc.	
periodical tenancy (adj)	month-to-month rental (real estate)	
person of interest (n)	suspect (police work)	"He was declared a *person of interest* by the police."
Perspex (n)	clear plastic panel: Lucite, acrylic, Plexiglas	actual chemical name: polymethyl methacrylate
perve (n) (v)	a pervert, to lust	
petrol (n)	gasoline	
physio (n)	physical therapist	
pickled (adj)	drunk	
pie (n)	an individual sized meat pie, with meat and/or vegetable filling, can be eaten like a burger	
piece of piss (adj)	something easy	"That job's a *piece of piss*."
pig's arse (adj) (pronounced *ass*)	I disagree	"In a *pig's arse!*"
pig's bum (adj)	something that's not true	
pikelet (n)	small pancake served cold	
piker (adj)	willing outcast	
pilchards (n)	sardines (bait fish)	same as mulies
pinch (v)	to steal	"You *pinched* the last bickie."
pineapple (n)	$50 note	Because it's yellow.
pint (n)	large glass of beer	
pipped (adj)	marginally beaten for price, stolen, taken illegally	
pipped at the post (adj)	beaten by a hair	
pips (n)	seeds in fruit or vegetables	
piss (n)	beer	

piss off (v)	go away	
pissed (adj)	drunk	'he was pissed as a newt.'
piss tank (adj)	big drinker	
pitch (n)	cricket field	
plagon (adj)	gallon bottle of cheap wine	
plant the foot (v)	to drive fast	
play funny buggers (adj)	to cheat, act stupidly	
play over (n)	play date (kids)	
plonk (n)	cheap wine	
P & C (n)	Parents and Citizens Association	equivalent to U.S. PTA
pokies (n)	slot machines, poker machines, gambling machines	
polenta (n)	corn meal	
pollie, pols (n)	politician	
polony (n)	bologna, baloney (lunch meat)	
poly, poly pipe (n)	polyethylene pipe used in irrigation	
Pom, Pommy, Pommy bastard (n)	Anyone from England. There are numerous explanations.	"Prisoner of His Majesty," "Port of Melbourne," "Permit of Migration," also rhyming slang: pomegranate (immigrant)
pommy shower (adj)	to use deodorant instead of bathing	
pong (adj)	bad smell	
poo (n) (v)	feces, from any species	
poo tickets (n)	toilet paper	
poof, poofter (n) (pronounced *poof-tah*)	gay man	(impolite word term)
poor fist (adj)	a bad effort	
pop (v)	to go	"I'm going to *pop* over to the shops."

porky (adj)	a lie (rhyming slang: pork pie)	"He told another *porky.*"
porridge (n)	any hot cereal	
port (n)	suitcase	From *portmanteau.*
posh (adj)	fancy, elegant	
post (n)(v)	mail	
post box (n)	mailbox (corner)	"You send your mail in a *post box;* you receive your mail in a letter box."
postie (n)	postman	
pot (beer) (n)	half pint glass of beer (Queensland, Victoria)	
pot plants (n)	potted plants (not marijuana)	
power point (n)	plug outlet	usually individually switched at outlet, 240 volt
poxy (adj)	bad	
pozzy, possie (adj)	position	"What's your *pozzy* on that issue?"
P-parking	on a sign indicating a paid parking zone	The maximum time allowed follows the "P." A ticket can be purchased at a nearby *kerb*-side vending machine.
PPS (n)	Prescribed Payments System	Tax collection system for business with a high cash income.
pracs, practicals (n)	science experiment	
prairie dog (n)	gay man	
pram (n)	stroller, baby buggy	
prang (n) (v)	car accident	
prawn (n)	shrimp	
preference shares (n)	preferred stocks	
preggers (adj)	pregnant	
Premier (n)	elected head of an Australian state	equivalent to U.S. state governor

premiership (n)	championship	"The Eagles won the footy *premiership* in 2006."
pre-primary (n)	Equivalent to U.S. kindergarten	Kindergarten, or *kindy,* is preschool.
preselect (v)	nominations in the Australian political process	Done by a closed party committee, not by popular vote.
presenter (n)	announcer, DJ **(radio, TV)**	
prezzy (n)	gift, present	
primary school (n)	elementary school	
prime mover (n)	tractor-truck that pulls a semi-trailer	
prolly (adv)	probably	
pub-crawl (n) (v)	drinking tour of the local taverns	
puffed (adj)	tired	"I was *puffed* after work."
puffer (n)	inhaler (pharmaceutical)	
pull your head in (v)	get real,	
pull your socks up	get it together, improve	
puncy (adj)	effeminate, weak	
punnet (n) (adj)	basket of berries, about 250 grams	"I bought a *punnet* of strawberries."
punt (v)	to gamble	In Australian Rules Football, a *punt* is a kick at the goal.
punter (n)	paying customer, tourist, also a gambler	"The *punters* rode the coach to the museum."
purler (adj)	something great	
purple patch (adj)	things are going well, in a good place	"I'm in a *purple patch*."
push bike, pushie (n)	bicycle	"I'll ride my *pushie* to school."
pushchair (n)	wheelchair	
pusher (n)	child's stroller	

put on the wobbly boot (v)	to get drunk	
put the wind up (v)	to urge someone on	"I *put the wind up* him."
put some ginger into it	try harder	
p/w	per week, referring to rentals	Apartments, furniture and appliances are rented by the week.
Qantas (n)	Australian airline	"Queensland and Northern Territories Aerial Service"
Queenslander	house on stilts	popular style in Queensland
Qnsld. (n)	abbreviation for Queensland	
quango (n)	Quasi Autonomous Non-Governmental Organization	A semi-official regulatory board with actual power.
quantity surveyor (n)	construction cost manager	
quaver (n)	eighth note (music)	
Queens Council, Q.C. (n)	senior barrister (courtroom lawyer)	
Question Time (n)	public session in Parliament where members question each other	This is where it all comes out in government: the good, the bad, and the ugly.
queue (n) (v)	the line to enter something, to line up	"We got in the *queue* for the movie."
queue-jumping (v)	butting in line	
quid (n)	slang for a pound (Aussie currency up to the 1960s)	"I made a good *quid* off that game."
quids	something you feel strongly about	"I wouldn't move for *quids*!"
quango	quasi non-governmental organisation	

quokka (n)	small marsupial the size of a soccer ball, indigenous to an island off Perth	
rack off (v)	go away, get lost	
radiogram (n)	older multi-band radio set	
Rafferty's Rules (adj)	no rules	
rage (n) (v)	a party, to party	
raisins (n)	large dried grapes, larger than American raisins	American-type raisins are called *sultanas*.
ranga (n) (adj)	red-haired person (derogatory)	From "orangutan" (an ape with reddish hair).
rapt (adj)	overjoyed	"I'm *rapt* about it."
ratbag (adj)	mild insult, untrustworthy person	"You old *ratbag!*"
ratepayer (n)	taxpayer, landowner	
rates (n)	property taxes	
rationalisation (v)	To eliminate equipment or staff to make a business more efficient.	
rattle your dags (v)	to ride your bike	
raw prawn (v)	To bullshit someone, to be disagreeable, to act ignorant	"Don't come the *raw prawn* with me!"
ready as a drover's dog (adj)	horny	
reception (n)	registration desk in a hotel, front counter in a restaurant	"I'll pay the bill at *reception*."
red ned (adj)	cheap red wine	
redundant (v) (adj)	laid off from work	"I was made *redundant*."
referee (n)	a reference (job seeking)	
reffo (n)	refugee	
Reg Grundies (n)	Underwear, undies	Rhyming slang

registrar (n)	doctor who is a specialist	
rego (n)	car registration	
relief teacher (n)	substitute teacher	
rellie, rellies, relo (n)	relative(s)	
removals, removalists (n)	movers, moving company	"When they shifted to Cairns, they called the *removalists*."
rendered (adj)	plastered wall finishes	plaster that covers brick.
renos (v)	renovations	
repayments (v)	mortgage payments	
ressies (n)	reservations, a booking	
results (adj)	final outcome	
resume (v)	how the government takes back land for public use	"The state *resumed* our paddock to build the highway."
reticulation (n)	sprinklers, irrigation	
retrenched (adj)	laid-off, fired	
retrospective (adj)	retroactive	"The law takes effect *retrospectively*."
return (adj)	round trip	"The flight is $750 *return*."
revise	review	in school studies
rev up (v)	to get mad	
Rice Bubbles (n)	Rice Krispies	
Richard Cranium (adj)	dickhead	
ridgy-didge (adj)	something that's true, genuine	
ring (n)	asshole	
ring (v)	to call on a telephone	"I'll *ring* you later."
ripper (adj)	something outstanding	
risen (v)	adjourned	"The jury has risen."
road train (n)	truck pulling two or three trailers	
Rock Eisteddfod (n)	dance competition between schools	
rock melon (n)	cantaloupe	

rocket (n)	arugula lettuce	
rock-up (v)	to arrive	
roll (n)	type of sandwich served on a roll, also a sausage wrapped in dough	
rollback (v)	backwash	"You can have a sip of my Coke, but don't *rollback.*"
rolled oats (n)	oatmeal	
rollie (n)	a "roll your own" cigarette	
rona (n)	Corona virus	
roo (n)	kangaroo	
roo bar (n)	Brush bar on the front of a vehicle for protection when colliding with a kangaroo.	Also good for protecting your paint from shopping trolleys at the mall.
roofie (n)	roofer	
root (n) (v)	crude slang for having sex	
root rat (adj)	one who only thinks about sex	
rooted (adj)	exhausted, ruined	"I'm *rooted.*"
rooting around (adj)	screwing around	
ropable (adj)	very angry	
rort (v)	to steal, illegally taking advantage of the system (an Aussie tradition)	"The *pollies* travelling first class on the *ratepayers* is a *rort.*"
rotten (adj)	drunk	
rough as guts (adj)	bad, poorly made	"That truck rides *rough as guts.*"
roundy	roundabout	Circular traffic intersection
rounds of the kitchen (v)	to tell someone off	
rouse (v)	to upbraid someone	
Rovers (n)	designation for older Boy Scouts	

RSL (n)	Returned Service League	Australia's primary veteran's association
rubber (n)	eraser	
rubbery (adj)	unprovable, non-rigorous	
rubbish, to (v)	to criticise	
rug up (v)	to cover up for the cold	
Rugby League (n)	Gentlemen's game played by thugs.	
Rugby Union (n)	Thug's game played by gentlemen.	
running around like a blue ass fly (adj)	running around like a chicken without a head	
run out (n)	Sale featuring the last units.	"Come to the Ford run out sale!"
SA (n)	abbreviation for South Australia	
sack, to (v)	to fire someone	"The boss *sacked* him for taking too many *sickies*."
salad (n)	sandwich topping: lettuce, tomato, shredded carrot, etc.	
saltie (n)	saltwater crocodile	
Salvos, Sally Ann (n)	Salvation Army	
sandgroper (n)	Western Australian	
Sandman (n)	Holden panel van, a favourite car of surfers in the 1980s	
sandwich (n)	small finger sandwiches, big ones are called *rolls*	
sanga, sanger, sarnie, sammos (n)	sandwich	
sanny (n)	hand sanitizer	
sarvo (n)	this afternoon	contraction of *this arvo*

sausage sizzle (n)	weenie roast, cooking hot dogs on a BBQ	
scab duty (n)	picking up rubbish at school for punishment	
scheme (n)	plan (no negative connotation)	"We're on *scheme* water."
schmick (adj)	something that's real good	"Your shoes are *schmick!*"
schnitzel (n)	breaded fried meat	
school leaver (n)	high school graduate	
schoolie (n)	high school student in final month of final year	
schoolies week (n)	spring break for *school leavers*	
schooner (n)	pint of beer (Queensland, Victoria), half-pint (South Australia)	
scoob (n)	marijuana cigarette	
scorching (adj)	fast	
Scotty (adj)	's got no friends and never will	
Scouts (n)	co-ed scouting in Australia, no Boy Scouts or Girl Scouts	
scratchies (n)	instant lottery ticket	
screamer (n)	party lover, easy drunk	
sealed road (adj)	paved road	
SEATS (n)	Stock Exchange Automated Trading System	replaced the "cry-out" trading on the *share* (stock) exchange floor.
see your last gum tree (v)	to die	
secateurs (n)	garden clippers	
semibrieve (n)	whole note (music)	
semiquaver (n)	sixteenth note (music)	

sending to Coventry	a racehorse that is not being run to win, a non-starter, no chance of success	
seppo (n)	an American (rhyming slang)	*Yank* rhymes with septic tank, *seppo* is short for septic, hence *seppo*.
series (n)	Used to describe each season of a TV show.	"The second *series* of "Friends" start tonight."
serve (adj)	a serving	"I'd like a *serve* of rice."
serve (v)	to tell one off	"I *served* them up."
serviette (n)	napkin	
servo (n)	service station	
set down (v)	to seat	"The jury was *set down* last week."
settlement (n)	escrow (real estate)	"The property is in *settlement*."
sex-worker (n)	prostitute	
shadow government (n)	the minority party *shadow ministers* in Parliament	a *shadow minister* is appointed for every actual minister
shag (v)	to have sex	
shaggin' wagon (adj)	panel van	
shaping up a beaut (adj)	turning out nicely	
shambolic (adj)	shameful	
shares (n)	stocks (stock market)	also known as: *share market*
shark biscuit (n)	novice surfer	
sheety (n)	sheet metal worker	
sheila (n)	young woman	From Gaelic: *shaler*.
she'll be right (adj)	it'll be OK	
shickered (adj)	drunk	From Yiddish.
shift (v)	to move something, also to move house	"They *shifted* from Perth to Sydney."
shifter (n)	wrench (tool)	

shift worker (adj)	one who works the night shift.	
shiraz (n) pronounced: *sheer-ahz*	sirah (wine)	
shirt lifter (n)	gay man	
shirty (v)	to get upset	"Don't get *shirty*."
shit house (n) (adj)	poor quality, toilet	
shocker (adj)	a surprise	"His appearance was a bit of a *shocker*."
shockies (n)	shock absorbers	
shonky (adj)	dodgy, cheap, not right, unreliable	
shot though (v)	to leave quickly	"He was late for the plane, so he *shot through* the meeting."
shopping centre (n)	equivalent of an American mall	In Australia, a mall is a shopping street, closed to car traffic.
shopping town (n)	shopping centre	
shops (n)	stores	"I'm going to the *shops*."
shorie (adj)	shore or beach dive (Scuba diving)	
short and curlies (adj)	pubic hairs	"She got him by the *short and curlies*."
short listed (adj)	finalist	"She was *short listed* for the Booker Prize."
short of numbers in the Upper House (adj)	stupid, low I.Q.	
short soup (n)	wonton soup (Chinese restaurant)	
shout (v)	to buy a round of drinks, to pick up the tab	"It's my *shout*."
show pony (n)	show-off	"He's a *show pony*."
shrapnel (n)	coins	Australian coins are big
shtum (verb)	quiet, silent	From Yiddish. 'They kept it *shtum*'.

sick (adj)	good	"Hey, mate, that's *sick!*"
sickie (n)	sick day	"He's taking a *sickie* to go surfing."
side (n)	team (sport)	"The Australian *side* won the game."
sighted	Viewed, read, seen	"He sighted the document."
Silk (n)	court lawyer, Queens Council or Q.C. (from the silk robes worn in court)	"He and his fellow *Silks* attended court"
silly season (adj)	The time from just before Christmas through Australia Day (Jan. 26), when everyone is on holiday and little gets done business-wise.	
silverbeet (n)	swiss chard	
silverside (n)	corned beef	"We're having *silverside* for tea."
silvertail (n)	rich person	
sin bin (n)	penalty box in Rugby League	
singlet (n)	tank top (clothing)	"He wore a *singlet* to the beach."
sink a few (v)	to drink a few beers	
sister (n)	nurse (not necessarily of a religious order)	
sit (v)	to take an exam	"I'm to *sit* the exam."
sixty-sixes and ninety-nines (n)	quotation marks	also called *inverted commas*
skerrick (adj)	a small amount	
skim the discs (v)	to turn the brake rotors (automotive)	
skint (adj)	broke, out of money	
skite (v)	to brag	
skittled (v)	physically knocked over	"He got *skittled* by the car."
skiver (n)	person who dodges work	

skivvy (n)	long sleeve crew neck shirt	
skoll (v)	to chug a beer	
sky show (n)	fireworks show	
slab (n)	case of beer	also *carton, box*
slabbed (v)	Being penalized for a mistake by having to buy beer for everyone (a *slab* is a case of beer).	"The director *slabbed* the cameraman when his mobile rang in the middle of a take."
slag (adj)	promiscuous person	
slash (v)	to urinate	"Hold my beer while I take a *slash*."
slate (v)	to criticize	"She *slated* me for being late."
slater (n)	sow bug, wood lice	
sledge (v)	to make a derogatory remark, often amongst sports competitors, heckling	
sleep out (n)	sleeping porch	
sleeps (adj)	a way of counting days	"It's only 5 sleeps until Chrissie"
slip lane (n)	merging lane	
slip, slap, slop	*slip* on a shirt, *slap* on some sunscreen, *slop* on a hat.	Slogan from advertising campaign to counter the intense effects of the Southern Hemisphere sun. Australia is the skin cancer capital of the world.
sloppy joe (n)	sweatshirt	
SLSC (n)	Surf Life Saving Club	local volunteer beach lifesaving service
smack (v)	to spank someone	
smash (n)	car accident	
smash repairs (n)	auto body repair shop	also *panel beaters*
smokey	bangstick (diving)	anti-shark weapon, stick with a shotgun shell on the end

smoko (n)	a work-break: cigarette, coffee, tea, etc.	"I'm going for a *smoko.*"
snag, snagga (n)	sausage	The Aussie hot dog: grilled, not boiled.
snedging (v) **snedger (n)**	re: bicycle seat sniffing	
snog (v)	to kiss	
soapies (n)	soap operas on TV	
Socceroos (n)	Australia's national soccer team.	
soft-roader (n) **(adj)**	light duty 4WD	"The RAV4 is comfy, but it's really just a *soft-roader.*"
softy (n)	non-alcohol drink, software expert, soft-hearted person	
soft toy (n)	stuffed toy	
solicitor (n)	a lower-level lawyer who specializes in contract law and may appear in lower courts	gives legal advice and draws up legal papers, appoints a barrister for court cases
sook (n) (adj)	wimp	
sorted (v)	to arrange, fix, or solve something	"Did you get your taxes *sorted?*"
spag bol, **spaghetti** **bolognaise, (n)**	spaghetti in meat sauce	
spanner (n)	wrench (tool)	
spares (n)	parts (machinery)	
sparky (n)	electrician	
spat it (v)	was very surprised	From *spat the dummy.* A *dummy* is a baby pacifier.
speckie, speccy (n)	spectacular	"The sky show was *speckie!*"
speech marks (n)	quotation marks, also *inverted commas*	
spew (v)	to throw up	
spewing (adj)	very angry	

spider (n)	soda with ice cream on top, like a float	originally brandy and lemonade
spill vote	When a ruling political party votes out its leader between elections, causing a change in government leadership.	
spinner (n)	the pitcher in the game of cricket	
S-pipe (n)	elbow pipe (plumbing)	
spirit of salts (n)	hydrochloric acid	
spit the dummy	to get upset	A *dummy* is a baby pacifier.
spivs (adj)	assholes	
splash the boots (v)	urinate	
splashed out on (adj)	overspent	"I really *splashed out* on her present."
spoof (adj)	semen stains	
sport	sports	no "s," one of those Aussie plural things
spotties (n)	driving lights, spotlights	
spotto (adj)	spotless	"I want the house *spotto* by the time I get back."
spray	spirited speech, getting yelled at	'we copped a spray when the team lost.'
spread (n)	plasterer	
spring onion (n)	scallion, green onion	
springy (n)	short wetsuit (shortie)	
sprog (n)	child	
spruik, spruiker (n)	to promote; a huckster, pitchman, super salesman	
sprung (v)	caught doing something wrong	
squatter (adj)	large landowner from early times	government tenant

squirrel grip	To grab a man by the testicles	an illegal move in sports
squirt, on the	drinking heavily	
squiz (v)	to look	"Take a *squizz* at that *hoon*."
stall (n)	row of seats in a theatre	
standover man (n)	thug, strong-arm man, enforcer	
stands out like a shag on a rock (adj)	it's obvious	
stands out like dogs' balls (adj)	it's obvious	
starkers (adj)	naked	
station (n)	large grazing property	Bigger than a ranch; we're talking tens of thousands of acres.
steady on	get real	
Steak and Kidney (n)	Sydney (rhyming slang)	
steamer (n)	full-length one-piece wetsuit	"The water is cold; I'm going to wear my *steamer*."
stickybeak (n) (v)	nosey person, busy body, looky-loo	"He's a *stickybeak*." "I'll have a *stickybeak* at that display home."
stock take (n) (v)	inventory	"Myer are having a huge end of year *stock take* sale."
stockman (adj)	station hand, cattle herder	
Stolen Generation (n)	Referring to the generation of Aboriginal children of mixed-blood who were forcibly taken from their families and raised as domestic servants.	Most never saw their families again. This is blamed for the breakdown of the Aboriginal family. It is considered by most Australians as a national tragedy and disgrace.

"Stone the crows!"	"I'll be darned!" "Wow!"	
stonkered (adj)	drunk	"I'm *stonkered.*"
stood down (v)	laid off, forced to resign	"They were *stood down* without pay."
stores (n)	supplies	"The *stores* were delivered to the clinic."
stoush (n)	a fight	
strap on the nosebag (v)	to eat (a nosebag is used to feed a horse when it's hooked to a wagon)	"The executives had a long meeting, then proceeded to *strap on the nosebag.*"
strata, strata-titled (n)	condominium style ownership	"He sold his *strata* home at the beach development."
stretcher (n)	cot	"The toddler slept well on the *stretcher.*"
"Strewth!"	it's the truth, from "God's truth!"	"*Strewth*, I'm dry!"
strides (n)	trousers	
strife (adj)	trouble	"That old car gave him *strife.*"
"Strike a light!"	expression of amazement	
Strine (n)	The word *Australian*, spoken with a thick accent.	"That bloke speaks fair dinkum *Strine.*"
stripy (adj)	striped	"He wore *stripy* trousers."
stroppy (adj)	in a bad mood	
stubby, stubbies (n)	bottle of beer, also short-short pants	
stubby holder (n)	can cooler	
stuffed (adj)	tired, also something that's broken	"I'm *stuffed.*" "That car is *stuffed.*"
stuffed up, I'll be (adj)	expression of surprise	
stumps, at (adv)	To quit for the day, finished, from cricket.	
suit hire (n)	tuxedo rental	

sultanas (n)	seedless raisins	In Australia, raisins are larger dried grapes with seeds.
summonsed (v)	to receive a legal summons	strange suffix
sundowner	early evening drinks	
sunnies (n)	sunglasses	
superannuation, super (n)	retirement fund	
supply bill (adj)	budget or appropriation bill in Parliament	
Supreme Court (n)	state superior court	where serious crimes are tried
surety (n)	bail bond	
surfies (n)	surfers	
surf lifesaver (n)	beach lifeguard (see SLSC)	
surf ski (n)	small, sit-on-top ocean kayak	
sugar soap (n)	caustic soda for cleaning before painting	
supergrass (adj)	informant	
surgery (n)	doctor's clinic/office	
suss (v)	suspicious	
suss out (v)	find out information	
swag (adj)	a lot of something, plenty	"The new Ford has a *swag* of extras."
swag (n)	traditional Aussie sleeping roll used in the bush; a Matilda, as in "Waltzing..."	bedding and padding inside a heavy canvas sack
swagman, swaggie (n)	tramp, hobo	
Sweet Fanny Adams	nothing, (actually *f**k all*, *FA*, or *Fanny Adams*)	
sweets (n)	dessert	
swimming costume, swimmers (n)	bathing suit	"She put on her *swimmers*."

swings and roundabouts (adj)	checks and balances	
swish (adj)	good, in fashion (no gay connotation)	"You look *swish.*"
switched on (adj)	tuned in	"He was *switched on* about the issues."
swotting, to swot-up (v)	to study	
ta (interjection)	thank you	imitation of baby talk
ta ta arms	flabby arms	
TAB (n)	Totalizator Agency Board,	neighbourhood legal betting shop
tailor made (adj)	ready made cigarette	not hand-rolled
take away (n) (v)	take-out (food)	
taken the mick out of (v)	to make fun of someone	
taking the piss (out of) (v)	to mock someone, to bring someone back to level	
tall poppies (adj)	successful people	
tall poppy syndrome (n)	Aussie habit of resenting and putting down successful people	
tallie (n)	big bottle of beer	
TAS	abbreviation for Tasmania	
Tassie (n)	Tasmania	
Taswegian (n)	person from Tasmania (derogatory)	
tat (n)	tattoo	
tea (n)	dinner, evening meal	
tea towel (n)	dish towel	
Technicolor yawn (v)	to vomit	
teddy (n)	any stuffed toy	not exclusively a teddy bear

TEE (n)	Tertiary Entrance Exams (Western Australia)	Extensive testing on high school *leavers*. The primary criteria for admittance to university.
tee-up (v)	to set up an appointment	We'll *tee-up* a meeting
telly (n)	television	
Telstra (n)	the partly-government owned phone monopoly	It was once wholly government-owned and is currently being privatized.
tenement	mining claim	
ten-pin bowling (n)	American style bowling, as opposed to lawn bowling.	
test (n)	a cricket game	
texta (n)	felt-tip marking pen	Texta is a brand, but is used generically for any felt-tip coloured pen.
TFN (n)	Tax File Number	equivalent to Social Security Number
"Thank your mother for the lunch money."	"You've been taken advantage of."	
the lot (n)	everything	"In the divorce, she took *the lot*."
the lot (n) (as on a hamburger)	everything on it	Usually lettuce, tomato, shredded carrots, a slice of beet, a slab of bacon, and a fried egg; for some reason, cheese isn't included.
the order of the boot (adj)	to get fired	
the whole box of dice (adj)	everything	
thingo, thingy (n)	a thing, gizmo, watchamacallit	

thisiv (n)	this afternoon	For those too lazy to say *sarvo*.
tight arse (adj)	stingy person	
throw a tanty (v)	throw a tantrum	
throw a wobbly (v)	throw a tantrum	
throw-down (n)	small bottle of beer	
tickets (v)	bragging	"You've got *tickets* on yourself."
tickety-boo (adj)	good, OK	
timber (n)	wood for construction	"The house was built of *timber* and iron."
timber getter (n)	logger	
tin-arsed (adj) (pronounced *assed*)	lucky	
tinkle (v)	to call someone on the telephone	"Give me a *tinkle* tomorrow."
tinny (adj)	lucky	"You *tinny* bastard!"
tinny (n)	aluminum can of beer	
tinny (n)	aluminium skiff.	
tip (n)	garbage dump	"I took that load of rubbish to the *tip*."
tip truck (n)	garbage truck	
tipping (v)	sports betting, predicting the winner of a game or series	Tipping competitions are common and legal.
tired and emotional (adj)	drunk	
toast soldier (n)	strip of toast dipped in egg yolk	
toey (adj)	edgy, horny, nervous	
toff (n)	upper class or richly-dressed person	British slang
togs (n)	sports clothes, swim suit	
toilet (n)	restroom, bathroom	
tomato sauce (n)	ketchup	
tonne (adj)	metric ton, 1,000 kilos, 2,200 lbs.	
toolies (n)	older male sexual predator	

Top End (n)	far north of Australia	
top-dress (n) (v)	to surface a playing field	
top of the wazza (adj)	being in a number one position	
torch (n)	flashlight	
towing A-frame (n)	tow bar for pulling one car with another	
tosser (adj)	a show-off, a braggart	
town bike (adj)	slut	
track (n)	trail	"They hiked along the *track*."
trackies, tracky-dacks (n)	track suit, sweatpants	
tracking vehicle (n)	insert car (movie production)	
tradie (n)	tradesman (carpenter, bricklayer, etc.)	
tranche	portion of money	legal term
trannie (n)	transistor radio	
trapezium (n)	trapezoid (geometric shape)	
trolley (n)	shopping cart, hand truck	
trouble and strife (n)	wife	rhyming slang
truckie (n)	truck driver	
true blue (adj)	patriotic Aussie	
tuck shop (n)	school cafeteria	
tucker (n)	food	
turfed (v)	thrown out	"He got *turfed* out of the pub."
turnover (v)	Order used instead of "roll camera" on an Aussie movie set.	
turps (n)	turpentine, also any hard liquor	"He's on the *turps*."
twenty-eight bird (n)	Australian ringneck parrot	Their cry sounds like, "Twenty-eight!"
twenty to the dozen (adj)	to do something very fast	

Twigged, to twig (v)	To understand	"I couldn't quite twig it."
Two Up (n)	gambling game, tossing two coins into the air to see how they land	Played in the bush and casinos.
two-pot screamer (adj)	one who gets drunk easily, often sloppily	
typhoon (n)	Southern Hemisphere hurricane	
tyre (n)	tire	
Ugg boots (n) (also spelled *Ugh*)	slip-on casual boot made of fleecy sheepskin	
ULP (n)	Unleaded petrol (gasoline)	
Uluru (n)	Ayers Rock	Aboriginal name for the huge red rock in the centre of the country.
Uncle Chester (adj)	child molester	
unco (adj)	uncoordinated	
undercroft (n) (adj)	split-level home: garage below, living areas above	area under main floor of a building, with it's own entrance
undercroft parking (adj)	parking on ground level with living, working areas above	
underdaks (n)	underwear	
uni (n)	university	
unpick (v)	opposite of 'to pick'	
up himself (adj)	inflated ego, also "head up his ass"	"He's *up himself.*"
up the duff (adj)	pregnant	
ute (n)	flatbed pickup truck	Short for *utility*.
vague out (v)	not paying attention	
van (n)	enclosed truck, ute, also short for *caravan* (travel trailer)	
VB (n)	Victoria Bitter beer	

veg, veggies (n)	vegetables	"I bought fruit and *veg* today."
Vegemite (n)	a salty black yeast spread eaten on toast	
veggo, vejjo (n)	vegetarian	
verandah (n)	balcony, patio, etc.	
verge (n)	roadside parkway between sidewalk and street	"He parked on the *verge*."
VET (n)	Vocation Education Training	
VIC (n)	abbreviation for the state of Victoria	
video library (n)	video rental store	
vigneron (n)	winemaker	From the French.
village bike (adj)	promiscuous woman	
Vinnie's (n)	St. Vincent De Paul's charity	
voucher (n)	coupon, certificate, receipt	
vox pops (n)	man-on-the-street interview	
WA (n)	Western Australia	
WACA (n) (pronounced *wack-a*)	West Australian Cricket Association, the Perth Cricket Oval	
wack (v)	a try at something	"I'll take a *wack* at it."
WAFL (n) (pronounced *waffle*)	West Australian Football League	
wag (adj)	amusing person	
wag, wagging school (v)	playing hooky, ditching school	
WAGS	Wives And Girlfriends	Female spouses of sports stars
waist pack (n)	fanny pack ("fanny" in Australia means female genitalia, so it isn't normally used)	also *bum bag*

walkabout (n)	Aboriginal walk in the Outback, of indeterminate length, a rite of passage. Can refer to anybody who's left unexpectedly.	"He's gone *walkabout*."
Wallabies (n)	name of Australia's National Rugby team	
wallaby (n)	small kangaroo-type marsupial	
wanker (adj)	common usage: arrogant, stupid person who thinks he's great	actual meaning: one who masturbates
war paint (n)	woman's makeup	
warrigal (n)	dingo (wild dog)	
watch house (n)	police station	
way gone (adj)	very drunk	
weatherboard (n)	a sheet or board made of fibre and cement or wood, used in home construction	
weepie (n) (adj)	sad story, movie, or TV show	
wedding tackle (n)	penis	
weir (n)	dam	"The Mundaring *Weir* created the C.Y. O'Connor Reservoir."
weiro (n)	cockatiel	a small parrot
well turned out (adj)	well dressed	
we're laughing (adj)	something that turns out well	"Fix this car and *we're laughing*."
wet (adj)	the rainy season in the tropics	
wettie (n)	wetsuit	
whacker (n)	an idiot you have no patience for	
wharfie (n)	dock worker	

What's the John Dory?	What's the story?	rhyming slang
wheelie bin (n)	the main trash can for the house, with wheels on the bottom.	"Take the *wheelie bin* out to the street so the garbos can empty it."
whilst (adj)	while	
winding up (v)	to pull someone's leg	"You're *winding* me *up*."
whinge (v)	to complain	
whip hand (adj)	top position, really good at something	"He's the *whip hand* on the farm."
whipper-snipper (n)	motor-powered weed-wacker or brush cutter	
white ant (v)	to undermine, sabotage	
white ants (n)	termites	
white pointers (n)	great white sharks; topless sunbathers	
"Who opened their lunch?" (v)	"Who farted?"	
"Who's your daddy?"	an insult	
whole meal (adj)	whole wheat bread	
woof pigeon (adj)	kookaburra	
whoop-whoop (n)	the boondocks, someplace far away, a small unimportant town	"He lives way out *whoop-whoop*."
whopped (v)	to play hooky from school	
wicket (n)	The three posts and top piece (bale) in the game of cricket.	
willy willy (n)	mini-tornado, dust devil	
willy woofter (adj) (pronounced *woof-tah*)	gay man	
wind cheater (n)	windbreaker, light jacket	
windy (v)	to fart	

witch's hat (n)	orange plastic safety cone used on roadways	
witchetty grub (n)	a large insect larvae eaten as bush tucker; it's tasty (?)	
wobbly (n) (v)	to lose one's temper	"He threw a *wobbly*."
wog (n)	immigrants from Southern Europe; flu or cold; insects.	not considered a racist term as in the UK
wombat (adj)	Play on words: describing one who eats, roots (has sex), and leaves.	Wombats are animals that eat vegetative material such as roots and leaves.
won't be a minute	please wait	
won't be a moment	please wait	
won't be a sec	please wait	
won't be a tick	please wait	
wooden spoon (n)	sports award for last place	
woofy (adj)	something that isn't good	
Woolie's (n)	short for Woolworth's, half the Aussie grocery store duopoly, Coles being the other half.	
working bee (adj)	volunteer work party	
wowser	spoil sport, people who don't drink	old post-colonial term
wring its neck (adj)	to drive a vehicle hard	
wurst (n)	baloney or bologna, regional term used in South Australia	
wuss (adj)	coward	
Y-fronts	men's briefs	From the y-shaped flap in front
yabber (adj)	lots of talk	
yabby (n)	freshwater crawdad	
yakka (adj)	work	"It's hard *yakka*."

Yank (n)	an American,	from anywhere in the U.S., not just the north
yankee shout (adj)	round of drinks where everyone pays for themselves	
yardie (n)		Former Prime Minister Bob Hawke once held the world speed record for drinking one.
yips, the (adv)	An athlete's stress under pressure	He got the yips and missed the putt.
yobbo, yob (n)	uncouth male	
yodel (v)	vomit	
yonnie (n)	stone of useable size for building	
yonks (adj)	a long time	"It's been *yonks* since I've seen you."
"You der!"	"You idiot!"	
you got told (v)	you got in trouble	school kid talk
"You little ripper!"	exclamation upon hearing good news	
youse	plural of "you"	
Yowie (n)	mythical Australian monster, like Bigfoot	
zack (n)	sixpence (five cents)	"He isn't worth a *zack*."
zed (n)	pronunciation of the letter "z"	
Zimmer frame (n)	walker (medical equipment)	device used by people for whom a cane isn't enough
zine (n)	small magazine	

INDEX

About the Author

Rusty Geller was born and raised in suburban Los Angeles. After graduating from the University of Southern California, he spent several years travelling and trying to write the Great American Novel. He eventually ended up in film school and embarked on a twenty-five-year career as a cameraman in the motion picture industry, specializing in Steadicam. His movie credits are at **www.rustygeller.com.**

In his spare time, he writes and photographs travel-adventure stories, which have appeared in magazines like *Skin Diver, Aloha, Treasure Diver, Mountain Biking,* and *American Cinematographer.*

In 2003—in what would either be the smartest or dumbest move in his life—he stepped out of the rat race and migrated with his family to Western Australia, hoping to find something that was no longer available in Southern California: a wide-open, uncrowded land with a warm ocean and slower-paced lifestyle. He now lives on the water with dolphins and seabirds in the backyard. It could be worse.

Notes

417

Notes

Notes

Notes

Notes

Notes

Notes

Notes